HANDBOOK FOR TRAVELLERS

IN

CONSTANTINOPLE,

BRÛSA, AND THE TROAD.

HANDBOOK FOR TRAVELLERS

IN

CONSTANTINOPLE,

BRÛSA, AND THE TROAD.

WITH MAPS AND PLANS.

LONDON:

JOHN MURRAY, ALBEMARLE STREET.

1893.

PREFACE.

THE great changes that have taken place in TURKEY within the last few years have rendered necessary a new Edition of the Handbook.

Owing to the labour of revision it has been found impossible to complete the portion of the Handbook for Turkey in Asia relating to Anatolia and Mesopotamia so soon as was anticipated, and therefore the descriptions of Constantinople, Brûsa, and Troy are now published in a separate volume for the convenience of a largely increasing number of travellers. The text has been rearranged and to a large extent rewritten. The map of modern Constantinople has been revised; new maps of Ancient Constantinople, the Bosporus, the Dardanelles, and the Plain of Troy have been prepared, and plans of some of the more interesting churches and mosques at Constantinople have been added. Special attention has been paid to the antiquities of Constantinople; Brûsa and Nicæa are described fully for the first time; and a description is given of the Anatolian Railway as far as it has been opened for traffic. In the Introduction will be found a short sketch of the Osmanli Empire, which it is hoped will enable the traveller to understand some of the peculiarities connected with its organisation and administrative system. A new feature in the Handbook is the Index and Directory, which contains lists of hotels and tradespeople, sailings of steamers, tariffs of prices, and other necessary details.

Although the Editor has gone over the greater part of the ground in person, he has taken great care to secure accuracy and practical utility by obtaining the assistance of friends who are either resident in the country, or have visited it during recent years. He is deeply indebted to his comrades, colleagues, and friends for the valuable aid they have afforded him, and he feels that without their assistance the work would have been impossible.

The map of Ancient Constantinople has been prepared by Professor A. van Millingen, of Robert College, who has also contributed the description of the antiquities of the city, and revised all that relates to it and to the Bosporus. Troy has been revised by Mr. Frank Calvert, United States Consul at the Dardanelles, and Brûsa by Mr. A. Scholer, British Vice-Consul at that place.

C. W. WILSON.

December 2nd, 1892.

CONTENTS OF PART I.

INTRODUCTION.

SECTION I.

CONSTANTINOPLE, THE BOSPORUS, BRÛSA, THE HELLESPONT.

EXCURSIONS FROM CONSTANTINOPLE.

MAPS AND PLANS.

INTRODUCTION.

a. INTRODUCTORY REMARKS.

THOSE parts of Turkey now most commonly visited by English and American travellers are Constantinople, the Bosporus and Brûsa, the Dardanelles and the Troad, Smyrna and Ephesus, Rhodes and Cyprus. They are all on or near the routes regularly followed by the great lines of French, Austrian, Russian, Italian, and English steamers, in their courses to and from Syria and Egypt.

Every object of interest in and around Constantinople may be reached in carriages, tramways, or *kaïks*. Small and well-appointed passenger steamers run many times daily from Constantinople up the Bosporus, calling at the picturesque villages on both the European and Asiatic shores.

The principal coast towns of Asia Minor are in direct communication with the capital by steamer, and most of them are connected with the more important towns in the interior by roads which are passable for the two-horsed *arabahs* of the country.

Smyrna has a good supply of carriages, and most of the streets may be traversed in them, though some of the bazârs can only be examined on foot. The Smyrna Railways take the traveller to Sardis, Thyatira and Philadelphia in the Valley of the Hermus, and to stations within easy reach of the numerous sites of biblical and classic interest in the Valleys of the Lycus and Maeander. Ephesus can be reached by rail from Smyrna in about two hours, so that a single day's excursion, if well planned, will enable the traveller to see the site and ruins.

The more remote districts, and all parts of the interior of Asia Minor, can be traversed on horseback. The roads are indifferent, hotels almost unknown, and accommodation for travellers, where it exists at all, wretched. Those who propose to explore the country thoroughly must be prepared to rough it, and to encounter at the same time some discomfort and occasionally a little risk. Great care must be taken to

Turkey.   *b*

choose the proper season for travelling, as many districts are subject to malaria during the summer and autumn.

Yet still for those who are vigorous and accustomed to the saddle, an exploring tour through Asia Minor during summer or autumn will be found safe and pleasant, if the needful precautions be taken to provide suitable equipage, servants, guides, and guards. The fresh air, the constant exercise, the ever-changing scenes, the interest attached to historic ruins, and the excitement springing from intercourse with strange, and often wild and primitive races, all tend to keep mind and body in full vigour.

Ladies can visit Constantinople and the Bosporus, Smyrna and parts of the country near it, the Danube, Brûsa, the Dardanelles, and Salonika; and if accustomed to the saddle they may prolong their excursions into Asia Minor, Syria, and Mesopotamia.

The precautions necessary to avoid danger from brigands and amateur robbers, and from the much more formidable malaria of such regions as the plains of Ephesus, Tarsus, and the Troad, will be given in connection with each place. The modes of travel and requisites for the road will also be stated below.

b. ROUTES FROM ENGLAND TO TURKEY.

The extension of railways has made Turkey much more accessible than it used to be, and there is now an extensive choice of routes from England to Constantinople and Asiatic Turkey.

The point which embraces most objects of interest is Constantinople; but the centre best adapted for the traveller in Asia Minor is Smyrna. Trebizond is the best starting-point for a tour in Armenia; Samsûn for Pontus and N. Cappadocia; Smyrna for the Seven Churches, Phrygia, and Central Asia Minor; Adalia for Pamphylia; Mersina for Cilicia and S. Cappadocia; and Alexandretta for N. Syria and Mesopotamia.

Constant alteration of routes and time-tables make it impossible to give minute information as to railways and steamers. This must be sought in the usual quarters; we shall confine ourselves here to general information.

I. THROUGH AUSTRIA AND THE DANUBIAN PRINCIPALITIES.

(1.) From *London* to *Vienna*, by Paris; by Queenboro', Flushing, and Dresden; by Calais, Cologne, and Nürnberg; by Ostende, Cologne, and Nürnberg; or by Harwich and Rotterdam.

From *Vienna* to *Constantinople*, by Budapest, Belgrâd, Sofia, Philippopoli, and Adrianople.

From London to Constantinople by the *Orient Express*, which leaves Paris twice a week, takes 3½ days' continuous travelling. 1st class only, *wagon-lit*, and dining-saloon. An ordinary *express train*, with through carriage, 1st and 2nd class, leaves Vienna every morning for Constantinople. *Time* 48 hours. *Return tickets* issued. The *fares* by Orient Express are about 20 per cent. higher than those by ordinary express.

Passports and *luggage* are examined beyond Vienna :—On the *outward* journey, at Belgrâd, Czaribrod, and Mustafa Pasha; on the *homeward* journey, at Hermanli, Pirot, and Semlin.

(2.) From London to Vienna and Belgrâd as in (1). From Belgrâd by rail to Nisch, Vranja, Uskub, and Salonika. From Salonika by steamer (Index) to Constantinople, Smyrna, &c.

(3.) From London to Vienna as in (1). From Vienna by rail to Budapest, Orsova, Bucharest, Giurgevo, and Smarda; steam ferry across the Danube from Smarda to Rustchuk; from Rustchuk by rail to Shumla and Varna; and thence by steamer to Constantinople.

This route may be varied by taking the train from Temesvar to Baziasch, and the steamer thence, through the *Iron Gates*, to Orsova or Turn Severin.

The *Orient Express*, the only train which connects with the special trains from Rustchuk to Varna, and with the steamers from Varna to Constantinople, leaves Paris twice a week. *Time* from London to Constantinople about 4½ days. At *Varna* the train runs on to a railway pier, whence the boats of the Railway Company embark passengers. In bad weather embarkation or disembarkation is very unpleasant. During the *winter months*, December to February, this route is often *closed*, as the ice in the Danube stops traffic.

Passports and *luggage* are examined, beyond Vienna, on the *outward* journey, at Verciorova (Roumania), Rustchuk (Bulgaria), and Constantinople; on the *homeward* journey at Varna (Bulgaria), Smarda (Roumania), and Orsova (Austria-Hungary). Baggage registered through to Constantinople is examined at the end of the journey.

(4.) From London to Vienna as in (1). From Vienna by *Danube steamer* to Rustchuk, and thence to Varna and Constantinople as in (3); or, by Danube steamer to Braila and Galatz, and thence by steamer through the Black Sea to Constantinople.

The Danube is chiefly a *summer route*, as the river navigation is often closed by fog or ice from December to March. It is most pleasant in June. Mosquitoes are at times very troublesome, and intermittent fevers are prevalent in August and September. This route allows the traveller to see much in a short time; it takes him to Vienna, Hungary, Budapest, Transylvania, Servia, and Bulgaria; the main course of the Danube, the Dobruja, and the Black Sea are seen; and the approach to Constantinople is by the Bosporus. The Danube is quicker as an *outward* route, down stream, than as a *homeward* route, up stream.

II. BY TRIESTE.

From London to Vienna and Trieste by rail; 1st or 2nd class. From Trieste by the steamers of the *Austro-Hungarian Lloyd Company* to Constantinople once a week, by Corfu and the Piræus, and once a fortnight by the Thessalian Coast; and to Smyrna once a week. The *Navigazione Generale Italiana* to Constantinople once a week, by Venice, Brindisi, Corfu, and Piræus. The *Mahsûse Company* to Constantinople once a fortnight. See *Trieste* (Index).

The Trieste route may be varied by returning *viâ* Venice, Milan, Turin, and across the Alps.

Return tickets, available for four months, are issued by the A.-H.

Lloyd Company, and a reduction is made for a family ticket of three or more. The voyage may be broken at any port. The steamers are good, and each carries a doctor and stewardess.

III. By Brindisi.

From London to Brindisi by rail. From Brindisi by the steamers of the *Austro-Hungarian Lloyd Co.*, once a week to Corfu, Piræus, and Constantinople. *Navigazione Gen. It.*, once a week to Corfu, Piræus, and Constantinople; and by transhipment at Piræus to Smyrna. See *Brindisi* (Index).

IV. By Marseilles.

From London to Marseilles by through or stopping trains. From Marseilles by the steamers of the *Messageries Maritimes*, once a week to Constantinople, alternately by Smyrna and Syra; once a fortnight to Piræus, Salonika, Smyrna, Mersina, Alexandretta, and Syrian coast. *Fraissinet et Cie.*, once a week to Salonika and Constantinople, and once a week to Smyrna, Mytilene, and Constantinople. *Navigazione Gen. It.*, once a fortnight to Chio, Smyrna, and Constantinople. See *Marseilles* (Index).

The steamers of the *Messagerie Maritime* are good and comfortable, and carry stewardesses. A reduction of 10 per cent. on *return tickets* from Marseilles available for four months; and on *family tickets* for three and over. Luggage can be shipped from London.

V. Through Voyage by Steamer and Return Ticket.

There are several first-class Liverpool steamers belonging to the Cunard Company; Messrs. Leyland; Moss; and Papyanni, which grant a first-class ticket in and out for £30 to £35. A gentleman and his wife can obtain a reduction.

This affords a most agreeable trip, particularly for an invalid, and occupies about six weeks or two months. The route generally is Gibraltar, Malta, Syra, Constantinople (a week or ten days), Smyrna (a week), perhaps Alexandria, Malta, and sometimes Lisbon, and so home. Some of these are splendid vessels, and in the autumn there is often pleasant society.

VI. Cross Communications.

Constantinople and Smyrna are great steam centres, each of them having lines to London, Liverpool, Marseilles, Italy, Messina, Corfu, Trieste, Alexandria, the Syrian coast, Cyprus, Crete, Rhodes, Mytilene, Chio, Syra, Lemnos, Piræus, Salonika, Dardanelles, and Gallipoli.

Constantinople has besides steamers to the Danube, and every part of the Black Sea.

Between Constantinople and Smyrna there is communication several times a week. Steamers leave in the afternoon, and land their passengers at their destination the next morning but one. Most of them touch at Gallipoli, the Dardanelles, and Mytilene.

There are also steamers running between the Piræus, Constantinople, and Smyrna.

As Constantinople and Smyrna communicate with the same places, it is easy to visit both, and accomplish all the other purposes of the journey.

The chief lines in the Levant are—

AUSTRIAN.—A line from Trieste to Constantinople, Smyrna, and the whole coast to Alexandria.

The Danubian line, running down the Danube, and serving Kustenjeh, Varna, and the Black Sea ports of Anatolia.

EGYPTIAN.—The Khedivieh Company, running steamers from Constantinople to Smyrna and Alexandria. These and the Turkish steamers afford but indifferent accommodation to Europeans, and are sometimes filthy and crowded with third-class passengers.

ENGLISH.—The London Company; four Liverpool Companies.

FRENCH.—A mail line from Marseilles to Constantinople and Smyrna, connecting with the Black Sea and the coast of Syria. Two trading lines (Fraissinet and Co., and Paquet and Co.).

GREEK.—A line from Trieste to the Piræus, Constantinople, and the Black Sea ports.

ITALIAN.—A line from Trieste, Venice, and Brindisi to Smyrna, Constantinople, and Black Sea ports, and a line from Marseilles to Italian ports and Constantinople.

RUSSIAN.—A line runs from Odessa to Constantinople and the Black Sea ports; and a line from Odessa to Constantinople, the Syrian coast, and Egypt.

TURKISH.—The Mahsûse, running steamers from Constantinople to Smyrna, Makaroneia, Salonika, Varna, and Trebizond. Courtji and Co. run steamers to Crete, Volo, the Danube, and Trebizond.

In the Levant, all these steamers carry deck passengers, the Turkish women being commonly on the left hand side of the quarter-deck. The worst accommodation is on board the Greek and Turkish steamers.

The Austrian and French carry stewardesses.

The coasting steamers are generally of a smaller class than the through mail steamers.

Heavy baggage can be sent through, by the Messageries Maritimes, to Constantinople and Smyrna, from their agency, 51, Pall Mall, but the expense is high, and the packages must be strong, and even then are not well treated, although the Messageries profess to carry luggage.

c. RAILWAYS.

The Railways of Turkey are :—

I. The Railway from Constantinople to Adrianople, Philippopoli, Bellova, Sofia, Czaribrod, and the Servian frontier, where it connects with the Pirot-Nisch-Belgråd line. The portion of the line between Bellova and Czaribrod belongs to Bulgaria; that from Constantinople to Bellova to the *Cie. d'Exploitation des Chemins de fer Orientaux*, of which Baron Hirsch is President.

II. Adrianople to Kuleli Burgas, and Dedeagatch on the Ægean.

III. Adrianople to Tirnova Semenli, Yeni Zaghra, and Jamboli.

This line has been extended by the Bulgarian Government to Burgas on the Black Sea.

IV. From Varna to Rustchuk, 140 m. long, commenced in 1863, and opened in 1866.

V. From Salonika to Uskub and Mitrovitza; with a branch from Uskub to the Servian frontier, where it connects with the Vranja, Nisch, Belgråd line.

VI. From Haidar Pasha to Ismid, Adabazar, Bilejik, Eski-shehr, and Sari-keui. This line has passed from the hands of an English to those of a German Company, and is now being extended towards Angora.

VII. From Smyrna to Manissa, and up the valley of the Hermus to Kassaba, and Alashehr, the ancient Philadelphia; with a branch to Ak Hissar (Thyatira) and Soma. There is a branch line from Smyrna to the suburban town of Burnabat.

VIII. From Smyrna to Ayasoluk (Ephesus), Aidin (Tralles), and Dineir (Apamea).

IX. From Mersina to Tarsus and Adana.

d. PASSPORT, FIRMANS, TEZKEREHS, &c.

A *Foreign Office passport* must be taken by British subjects. The traveller who crosses the Continent, *en route* for Turkey, should have his passport *visé* in London by the Turkish Ambassador. When a journey in the interior is contemplated, a passport is indispensable, for it constitutes the title which gives the traveller a right to a **Yol Tezkereh**, or *travelling passport*, which is now obligatory. This document is an acknowledgment on the part of the Ottoman authorities of the claim to aid and protection which the passport establishes, and it is given because the police agents in the interior cannot read a foreign passport, and are incompetent to pronounce on its validity. It is obtained by payment of a small fee on application through the Consulate (Index), and a *visa* is required for every fresh journey, and in each Vilayet. **Firmans** are now never issued to ordinary travellers. A **buyuruldu**, or order to the police to provide horses is rarely given, except by a provincial Governor. It is always useful in case the traveller should want horses, or send a messenger, as he then only pays the postmaster at the rate fixed by law.

The right of search of travellers' baggage at the **Custom House** exists, but, as a rule, is not offensively exercised; under ordinary circumstances a franc bestowed on the *Kolji*, or inspector, will pass the personal belongings of a traveller without inconvenient overhauling. But it must be remembered that this inspector cannot pass books or sealed parcels, and that these must be submitted to superior authority. If books taken by the inspector are not returned the next day, application should be made for them through the Consulate. Foreign cigars and tobacco, ammunition, rifles, and revolvers are prohibited. Fowling-pieces are admitted without difficulty.

e. POSTAL AND TELEGRAPH SERVICES.

Post.—The postal service of Turkey consists of an *International* and of an *Inland* service. The *former* is conducted by Turkey and by five

European Powers that maintain P. Offices at Constantinople, Smyrna, and other coast towns; the *latter* is conducted solely by the *Imperial Ottoman Post.* Letters may be sent by international post from all towns in the interior at which there is an international telegraph station; and by internal post from any post town. The mail lines to the interior are numerous, and the mail is carried with regularity and despatch, but the charges are high. The principal lines are to Baghdad by Sivas, Diarbekir, and Mosûl; and to Aleppo by Afiûm Kara-hissar, and Konieh. There are few cases of letters being lost in transit, and the P. O. officials in the interior are always ready to make arrangements for forwarding letters to places where there is no P. O. All charges must be paid at P. 19 to the Mejidîeh.

Telegraphs.—The *internal* telegraph service of Turkey is conducted by the *Direction Générale des Postes et Télégraphes,* and the *external* either by that Company or by the *Eastern Telegraph Company,* which owns all the submarine cables running into Constantinople. Telegrams *in Turkish* may be sent from any telegraph station in the Empire; and in *Latin characters* from the following stations in A. Minor and the Islands :—

Adalia.	Candia.	Kerassund.	Rethymo.
Adana.	Canea.	Konieh.	Rhodes.
Aintab.	Cheshmeh.	Kyrenia (Cyp.)	Sabanja.
Aivali.	Chio.	Larnaca.	Samos.
Aleppo.	Dardanelles.	Lattakia.	Samsûn.
Alexandretta.	Diarbekír.	Lefkeh.	Scala Nova.
Amara.	Dikeli.	Lemnos.	Sivas.
Angora.	Erzerûm.	Limasol.	Skutari.
Antioch.	Eski-shehr.	Mersina.	Smyrna.
Ayithodori (Cyp.)	Famagusta.	Mitylene.	Tarsus.
Baghdad.	Fao.	Mosul.	Trebizond.
Bapho (Cyp.)	Gallipoli.	Nasriyeh.	Tripoli.
Bashkaleh.	Geiveh.	Nicosia.	Troodos.
Bassora.	Gümush-khâneh.	Ordu.	Van.
Bilejik.	Ismid.	Pandorma.	Vurla.
Brûsa.	Kastambul.	Pergamos.	Yuzgat.

One of the clerks at these stations generally speaks French. The rates per word are :—(1) From station to station in a Vilâyet, P. ½. (2) From a station in one Vilâyet to a station in another, or to Cyprus, P. 1. (3) From any station to Crete, Chios, Tenedos, and Lemnos, P. 1½. A supplementary tax, equal to the charge of five words, is levied on each telegram. The rates per word, in francs, to the following States are :— Austria, 0·34; Egypt, 1·25; England, 0·76; France, 0·56; Germany, 0·55; Greece, 0·28; India, 3·48; Malta, 0·69; New York, 1·25; Western States of America, 1·90. For rates to other States, see *Levant Herald Almanac* or *Annuaire Oriental.* Local rates at Constantinople, see Index.

N.B.—The Mejidîeh is only counted as worth P. 19 in paying for telegrams.

t. MUHAMMADAN YEAR AND TIME.

The Muhammadan *year* consists of 12 lunar months, named, Muharrem, Sefer, Rebi ul-evvel, Rebi ul-akhir, Jemazi ul-evvel, Jemazi ul-akhir, Rejeb, Shaban, Ramazân, Shevval, Zilkadeh, and Zilhijeh. These months have alternately 30 and 29 days, and the year having thus only 354 days, it results that the 1st Muharrem is each year 11 days earlier than the preceding, and makes the round of the seasons every 33 years. As the lunar year actually contains 354 days, 8 hrs., 48' 34·4", and it was desirable that a year should contain an integral number of days, it was arranged that there should be 19 years of 354 days, and 11 years of 355 days in a cycle of 30 years, thus making each year an integral number.

Mussulmans reckon from the day of Muhammad's flight (*hejret*) from Mecca to Medina, which fell on Friday, the 16th July, A.D. 622; and their era is called the *Hejra*. As the 538th year of the Hejra commenced Friday, July 16th, A.D. 1143, it follows that 521 of our years are equal to 537 Moslem years. To convert a Moslem date, roughly, to a Christian one, add 622 years, 197 days, to the Moslem date, and from the total deduct so many times 11 days, or for leap years 12 days, as the Moslem date has years. The 1st Muharrem A.H. 1310 fell on the 26th July, 1892.

The Moslem *day* is reckoned from sunset to sunset, and is divided, like our day, into 24 hours, which are counted as twice 12. Sunset is always twelve o'clock, and as the length of the day varies throughout the year, Turkish watches have to be altered at least every 5 days. *Time at Constantinople* is set by the clock of the Yeni Valideh Jami', in Stambûl.

The following table gives the time of sunrise and sunset for the latitude of Constantinople for every 5 days of the month throughout the year. In Asia Minor, south of Constantinople, the sun rises a few minutes later and sets a few minutes earlier in summer, and rises earlier and sets later in winter than the times given in the table. The greatest difference at midsummer and at midwinter, in the latitude of Cape Anamûr is about 15 min.

DAYS.	JANUARY. Sunrise.	JANUARY. Sunset.	FEBRUARY. Sunrise.	FEBRUARY. Sunset.	MARCH. Sunrise.	MARCH. Sunset.	APRIL. Sunrise.	APRIL. Sunset.	MAY. Sunrise.	MAY. Sunset.	JUNE. Sunrise.	JUNE. Sunset.
	H. M.	H. M.	H. M.	H. M.	H. M.	H. M.	H. M.	H. M.	H. M.	H. M.	H. M.	H. M.
5	7 27	4 41	7 13	5 15	6 37	5 49	5 47	6 22	5 1	6 54	4 32	7 23
10	7 27	4 45	7 9	5 20	6 30	5 54	5 40	6 26	4 56	6 58	4 30	7 26
15	7 26	4 50	7 4	5 26	6 23	5 59	5 32	6 32	4 51	7 2	4 29	7 30
20	7 25	4 55	6 59	5 32	6 14	6 5	5 24	6 38	4 46	7 7	4 28	7 33
25	7 23	5 0	6 50	5 39	6 ··	6 9	5 16	6 42	4 42	7 12	4 29	7 35
30	7 20	5 6	6 43	5 45	5 58	6 15	5 9	6 47	4 37	7 16	4 30	7 36

DAYS.	JULY.		AUGUST.		SEPTEMBER.		OCTOBER.		NOVEMBER.		DECEMBER.	
	Sunrise.	Sunset.	Sunrise.	Sunset.	Sunrise.	Sunset.	Sunrise.	Sunset.	Sunrise.	Sunset.	Sunrise.	Sunset.
	H. M.	H. M.	H. M.	H. M.	H. M.	H. M.	H. M.	H. M.	H. M.	H. M.	H. M.	H. M.
5	4 32	7 35	4 57	7 14	5 28	6 31	5 57	5 42	6 32	4 55	7 7	4 32
10	4 35	7 33	5 2	7 10	5 31	6 26	6 1	5 35	6 37	4 49	7 11	4 31
15	4 38	7 32	5 7	7 3	5 36	6 17	6 6	5 28	6 44	4 44	7 15	4 30
20	4 42	7 29	5 11	6 57	5 41	6 9	2 12	5 19	6 49	4 40	7 19	4 32
25	4 46	7 25	5 16	6 49	5 46	6 0	6 18	5 11	6 55	4 36	7 22	4 33
30	4 52	7 22	5 20	6 42	5 51	5 51	6 24	5 4	7 0	4 33	7 25	4 36

Thus on the 20th June, 12 o'clock, Turkish is 7.33 P.M., and our midnight is 4.27 Turkish; on the 20th December, 12 o'clock, Turkish is 4.32 P.M., and our midnight 7.28 Turkish.

g. MONEY, WEIGHTS, MEASURES.

The *circular notes* of the London bankers, the best and most convenient mode of taking money abroad, can easily be negotiated at Smyrna, Constantinople, and other large cities. The *Imperial Ottoman Bank* at Constantinople gives *letters of credit* payable in the principal towns; and issues *bank notes* for T£5, and T£2, which have gold values. *Letters of credit* can also be obtained from the Constantinople agents of merchants residing in the interior. *Cheques* or *bills of exchange* upon London bankers can be cashed at the agencies or sub-agencies of the Imperial Ottoman Bank, viz. :—Adalia, Adana, Aidin, Denizli, Konieh, Manissa, Mughla, Nazli, Sivas, and Smyrna; and, if the drawer be known, by native merchants. Bills on London and Constantinople are sometimes at a *premium.* Money can be remitted by the I. O. Post in *gold* coin. *Small change* is very scarce in the interior; in many places it is impossible to change a lira, and difficult to change a mejidîeh. *Travellers* in A. Minor are recommended to obtain a letter of credit from the I. O. Bank; to carry gold for large payments, such as hire of transport, &c.; and to purchase silver and small change at every large town for minor expenses on the road. All silver coin, especially mejidîeh, should be carefully tested before accepted, as much *false coin* is in circulation.

The coinage consists of gold, silver, and metallic pieces. The *money unit* is the gold *gurúsh*, called by Europeans *piastre*, and of these 100 go to the Osmanli *lira*, or Turkish pound, which constitutes the *monetary standard.* The piastre is divided into 40 *paras.* The *gold piastre* is a nominal coin, and must be distinguished from the *silver piastre*, which is of less value, as gold is at a premium of 7 to 8 per cent. Thus in changing a lira P. 108 is received less P. ½, which the money-changer keeps as his charge. The silver P. is used in all the transactions of daily life, and small retail accounts are kept in it. The *gold coins* are the 5, 2½, 1, ½, and ¼ lira pieces; the *silver coins*, called mejidîeh, from Sultan Abdul Mejid who first coined them, are the mejidîeh (P. 20), and the 10, 5, 2, and 1 piastre pieces. The *metallic coins* are of three kinds:— the *altilik*, which pass at about five-sixths of their nominal value, and bear on one face the Sultan's cypher, and four small sprays surrounded by an ornamental border; the *beshlik*, which pass at half their nominal value, and bear the cypher and one spray within a plain border; and the *metallik*, which bear the cypher within a crescent surrounded by a border of rosettes, and also pass at half their nominal value. The altilik and beshlik coins are being gradually withdrawn from circulation, but there are still large numbers of them in the country. *Copper coins* are not current at Constantinople, but they circulate at Smyrna and other large towns in A. Minor. The *kâ'ime*, or paper money, issued during the Turco-Russian War, has disappeared. The most useful *foreign gold coins* are the 20-franc piece, and the sovereign, *Inglíz lira.* The money unit and the value of the coins have been frequently changed during the present century, and the result is a currency chaos bewildering to strangers.

TURKISH CURRENCY.

	Nominal Gold Piastres.	Approximate Silver Piastres.	Approximate value in Sterling.
GOLD COINAGE.			
			£ *s. d.*
Piece of 5 liras . . .	500	540	4.10.10
Piece of 2½ liras . .	250	270	2 . 5 . 5
Lira	100	108	18 . 2
Half lira	50	54	9 . 1
Quarter lira	25	27	4 . 6½
SILVER COINAGE.			
Mejidîeh		20	3 . 4
Half mejidîeh		10	1 . 8
Quarter mejidîeh (*cheyrek* or *beshlik*) . .		5	10
Piece of 2 piastres		2	4
Piastre		1	2

	Nominal value, Silver Piastres.		
METALLIC COINAGE.			
Altilik	6	5	10
Beshlik.	5	2½	5
Yuzlik (100 *paras*) ⎫		1¼	2½
Yirmilik (20 *paras*) ⎬ metallik	2½	½	1
Onlik (10 *paras*) ⎭		¼	½
Piece of 5 paras . . .		⅛	¼

1. The mejidîeh is only counted as worth 19 silver piastres in paying bridge tolls, tram, boat and railway fares, and all Government dues, &c.

2. There are ½ and ¼ altiliks and beshliks in circulation at, respectively, five-sixths and half their nominal value. A *purse* is P. 500.

The pound sterling equals about 110 gold, or 118 silver piastres.

The 20-franc piece equals about 88 gold, or 95 silver piastres.

The Austrian ducat equals about 52 gold, or 56 silver piastres.

The *rates of exchange*, which are constantly fluctuating, are given in the daily papers.

In many localities the difficulties of the Turkish coinage are further complicated by the mejidîeh possessing a *conventional value* for ordinary transactions. Thus in Smyrna it is worth P. 32; and if a traveller be told that an article costs P. 20 and he tenders a mejidîeh, he will receive P. 12 change, whereas in Constantinople nothing would be returned. The value also varies according to the commodity purchased; in buying coffee, for instance, it is P. 25, in buying opium, P. 20, &c.

The *Cyprus currency* consists of pounds sterling, shillings, and copper piastres, nine of which go to a shilling.

The figures which are useful for understanding coins, numbers in tezkerehs, accounts, numbers of houses (as houses are now numbered in many of the large cities), and dates on coins and Mussulman monuments, are:—

1	ı	4	≤	8	٨
2	٢	5	◇ or O	9	٩
3	٣	6	Ч	0	•
		7	V		

Small change is at a premium, owing to the insufficient amount of it in circulation, and this has led to the profitable business of money-changing which is carried on by *Sarrâfs*, who are principally Jews. The Government, instead of increasing the quantity of small change, allows the insufficient supply to be made a source of profit. The public offices, local steamers, tramways, &c., give no change, and make money by selling the metallic coins they collect to the Sarrâfs who, in turn, derive an advantage from putting the coins again in circulation. No one can therefore live in Turkey without having recourse to the money-changers.

The word *bakhshish* is one that will soon become familiar to the traveller in the East; it means a gratuitous gift of money, which an Oriental will often expect in return for any service however trifling; but nevertheless care must be taken not to mistake an act of hospitality or kindness for a priced service. Should the traveller, on arriving at a town or khân, find the gates closed, this magic word will cause them to fly open; in short, there are few difficulties it will not remove; it has the same power all the world over, though called by different names.

As a general principle among Moslems, payment for service is considered to depend on the rank of the individual served. The rich man is expected to give according to his rank.

WEIGHTS AND MEASURES.

Since 1881 the use of the French decimal system has, according to law, been obligatory in all parts of the Empire; but, except in the Government offices, the law has never been enforced and the old weights and measures are still in general use. They are:—

WEIGHTS—

1 kerat = 3·093 grains.
16 kerats make 1 dram.
1½ drams „ 1 miskal = 74·245 grains (used for *drugs, attar of roses, pearls, &c.*).
400 drams „ 1 oke = 2·828 lbs.
44 okes „ 1 kantar.
4 kantars „ 1 cheki.
18 kantars „ 1 tonnellata = 1 ton.

Silk is sold in tefehs of 210 drams each; *liquids* are sold by weight.

MEASURES—

Grain is sold by the kileh (1·018 bushels) of 8 kûtis, at Constantinople. In the provinces the capacity of the kileh varies largely.

Cotton stuffs, carpets, etc., are sold by the endazeh = 25·91 inches; 2 jeras = 1 rûp, 8 rûps = 1 endazeh.

Silks and *woollen stuffs* are sold by the arshin (pîk) = 26·772 inches, which is also divided into 8 rûps and 16 jeras.

Land is measured by the donum = 1099·37 square yards; 24 parmaks = 1 zîra or arshin (29·84 inches); 1,600 square zîras = 1 donum. An English acre = 4·4 donums.

In 1889 the metric system of weights was made obligatory for cereals; and in 1892 it became universally obligatory. The old names are used under the new system, causing much confusion; thus the oke = 1 kilogramme, the batman = 10 kilos, the kantar = 100 kilos, and the cheki = 1000 kilos; the kileh = hectolitre, the arshin = mêtre, the farsang = 10 kilometres.

h. THE TURKISH EMPIRE.

(1.) **History.**—Early in the 13th century a small tribe of *Oghuz Turks*, flying before the Mongols from its original home in Central Asia, passed through Persia and entered Armenia under the leadership of its hereditary chief **Suleiman Shah.** His son and successor **Et-Toghrul** (*Ertoghrul*), whilst on his way to seek a home under the Seljûk Sultan at Iconium, came suddenly upon two contending armies. He at once rode to the assistance of the weaker party, and by a vigorous charge decided the fortunes of the day. The army he had saved was commanded by the Seljûk Sultan Ala-ed-din, who, in gratitude, bestowed upon Et-Toghrul lands on the Byzantine frontier which included the towns of Dorylaeum, now *Eski-shehr*, and *Sugut*, ' willow,' on the military road from Dorylaeum to Nicæa, *Isnik*. At Sugut, in A.D. 1258, was born **Osman** (*Othman*), son of Et-Toghrul, the prince from whom the race derives its name of *Osmanli*, corrupted by the Greeks into *Ottoman*. Osman distinguished himself whilst still young, and received from the Seljûk Sultan the emblems of princely rank. He rapidly extended his principality, and on the 27th July, 1299, first invaded the Byzantine territory. His advance was along the road from Sugut to Prusa, *Brúsa.* The castle of *Keupri-hissar* was stormed, *Yeni-shehr* was occupied, and in 1301 the Byzantine army was completely defeated at *Koyun-hissar.* About this time the Seljûk Empire having fallen to pieces, ten separate Turkish dynasties arose from its ruins. Osman established himself in Phrygia Epictetus; caused the *Khutbe,* or public prayer, to be said in his name; took the title of Emîr, and coined money. The assumption of these marks of sovereignty may be regarded as the birth of the Ottoman Empire. In 1326 *Brûsa* was taken by Osman's son, Orkhan, and the same year Osman died.

Orkhan made Brûsa the capital of his Empire and continued the war against the Byzantines, taking Nicomedia, *Ismid,* in 1326, and Nicæa, *Isnik,* in 1330. In 1336 Pergamos, *Bergamo,* the capital of the neighbouring Turkish state of *Karasi,* was conquered and annexed; and by 1346 Orkhan had become so powerful that John Cantacuzene, hoping to secure his alliance, gave him his daughter in marriage. Ten years later, however, Suleiman Pasha, Orkhan's eldest son, crossed the Hellespont (1356) and seized the castle of *Tzympe* on the opposite coast. *Gallipoli* was occupied shortly afterwards, and the Crescent firmly planted on the continent of Europe. During Orkhan's reign the most important civil and military institutions of the nation were founded. His brother, Ala-ed-din, who acted as Vizier, created a standing army of cavalry and infantry, organised the famous corps of Janissaries, regulated the finances, consolidated the new conquests, and introduced laws respecting the dress of the various subjects of the Empire that lasted for centuries.

Murad I. (*Amurath*) extended the European conquests of his father; made *Adrianople* the capital of the Ottoman Empire (1361); defeated the Hungarians and Servians on the banks of the *Maritza* (1363); captured *Nissa,* now *Nisch* (1376), and, on the 27th August, 1389, fell in the moment of victory, by the hand of an assassin, on the memorable field of *Kossova.* At his death the Ottoman dominions in Europe comprised nearly the whole of ancient Thrace, Rumelia, and Bulgaria. His son, **Bayezid I.** (*Bajazet*), surnamed *Yilderim,* 'thunderbolt,' added Servia, Wallachia, and Greece, in Europe; and Pontus, Paphlagonia, and Karamania, in Asia, to the Empire. In 1396, Bayezid defeated Sigismund, King of Hungary, and he was preparing to lay siege to Constantinople, when the advance of the Mongols under Timûr-lenk (Tamerlane) compelled him to cross to Asia. The decisive battle took place on the plain of *Chibukabad,* near *Angora,* and ended in the defeat and capture of Bayezid, who, after having been carried about for eight months in the train of his conqueror, died of a broken heart. Bayezid was the first of the Osmanlis to adopt the title of Sultan, and the first to infringe the law of the Prophet that forbids the use of wine. After eleven years' interregnum and civil war the Empire was reunited, 1413, under **Muhammad I.** *Pehlevan,* 'champion,' whose successful reign is noted as the period when a taste for literature, and a fondness for poetry, first prevailed amongst the Osmanlis. **Murad II.** (*Amurath*) had to contend during the greater part of his reign against the Hungarians, Servians, Bosnians, and Wallachs, under the renowned general Hunyades, and against the Albanians under the equally celebrated Scanderbeg. The war was carried on with varying success, but the advantages finally rested with the Sultan, who thoroughly reconquered Servia and Bosnia, and inflicted two crushing defeats on the Hungarians, at Varna (November, 1444) and Kossova (October, 1448). Murad II. is the only sovereign who has twice abdicated, and his life in his Epicurean retreat at Magnesia, *Manisa*, is one of the most romantic incidents in Turkish history.

Muhammad II., 'the Conqueror,' took Constantinople by storm on the 29th May, 1453, conquered the Peloponnesus (1454), Trebizond (1455), the Crimea (1475), and Otranto (1480), and, though he met with severe reverses at Belgrâd (1456) and Rhodes (1480), he largely extended the Ottoman Empire. As a soldier, a legislator, and far-sighted statesman, he ranks amongst the highest of the Osmanli Sultans, and many of his political institutions have lasted to the present day. In the reign of his successor, **Bayezid II.**, the *Sufi*, 'mystic,' the Ottoman navy first distinguished itself. **Selim I.** captured Tabrîz (1514); conquered Syria (1516), and Egypt (1517); and nearly doubled the extent of the Ottoman Empire. The reign of **Suleiman I.**, 'the Magnificent,' is one of the most important in Ottoman history. It is the period during which the power of the Osmanlis was at its height, and it has not inaptly been called the 'Augustan age' of Turkey. Suleiman took Belgrâd (1521), and Rhodes (1522), and he conquered Hungary (1526); but the checks that he received before the walls of Vienna (1529) and at Malta (1565) mark the limits of Turkish conquest. The only important additions to the Empire of a later date were Cyprus (1571), and Crete (1669). The Ottoman navy was greatly developed, and under Khaireddin Pasha, known to Franks as Barbarossa, Torghut, (*Dragut*), and Piale, held complete command of the Mediterranean. Suleiman, '*Kanûni*,' was not only a great conqueror but an enlightened ruler. Every branch of the administration was improved; the earliest of the capitulations was granted to France (1535); the law was codified by the celebrated Ibrahim of Aleppo; and the right of the *Rayah* to property in the land he tilled, subject to the payment of certain rents and dues, and to the performance of certain services for his feudal superior, was acknowledged. So much better, indeed, was, at this time, the condition of the Turkish Rayah than that of the Christian serf, that peasants flocked across the border from the neighbouring states to live under the milder sway of the Osmanli Sultan. New buildings rose rapidly in the principal towns; Constantinople was adorned with the splendid edifices that still attest the genius of the architect, *Sinan*; and the capital was thronged with poets, historians, and legal and scientific writers, who were honoured with the protection and patronage of the Sultan.

During the reign of **Selim II.**, 'the Sot,' Cyprus was conquered (1570–71); but the battle of *Lepanto*, illuminated though it was by the splendid valour of *Kilij Ali*, who afterwards rebuilt the fleet, proved that the Turks were not invincible at sea. **Murad III.** (*Amurath*) conquered Georgia and Azerbijan, but his reign is marked by the prevalence of venality and corruption; and by the outbreak of insubordination amongst the *Janissaries*, who attacked the Serai, and more than once forced the Sultan to comply with their demands. It was during this reign that the first English Ambassador was accredited to the Porte. Under **Muhammad III.**, and his successors, the Empire showed increasing signs of weakness; the Ottoman princes were no longer trusted with liberty and employed in the service of the State, but were brought up in a part of the seraglio called the *Kafess*, or ' cage' ; the Cossacks ravaged the south coast of the Black Sea: the Persian conquests were surrendered ; and the feud between the Throne and the Janissaries was the cause of frequent anarchy and much misery at Constantinople.

Murad IV., the last Sultan to take the field at the head of his army, re-conquered Baghdad ; and, during the reign of **Muhammad IV.**, the genius of *Muhammad Kiuprili,* the Grand Vizier, raised Turkey for a few brief years to comparative power.   But the splendid victory of Montecuculi at *S. Gothard* (1st August, 1664) showed that the superiority in arms had passed from the Turks to the Christians, and formed a turning-point in the military history of Turkey.   Nineteen years later, on the memorable 11th September, 1683, the Turks were defeated by Sobieski before the walls of Vienna; and disaster followed disaster until **Mustafa II.** was com-pelled to sign the *Treaty of Carlowitz* (26th January, 1699), and surrender some of the fairest provinces of his Empire.   From that date the military power of Turkey ceased to overshadow Europe ; and her history has since been that of one long, unending struggle to maintain her position in the face of the open, or scarcely concealed, hostility of Russia.   The struggle has been on the whole unfavourable to Turkey; but it has been marked by partial gleams of success such as the *campaign on the Pruth,* in 1711, when Peter the Great was surrounded, and only saved from destruction by the wit of Catherine; as well as by the undying heroism of her soldiers. Some of the principal land-marks are : the *Treaty of Passarowitz* (21st July, 1718), which gave Belgrâd and Hungary to Austria; the *Treaty of Belgrâd* (1st September, 1739), which restored Belgrâd, Bosnia, and Servia to Turkey; the defeat and destruction of the Turkish fleet by the Russian fleet under Elphinstone at *Cheshmeh* (7th, 8th July, 1770); the fatal *Treaty of Kainarji,* signed by **Abdul Hamid I.** on the anniversary (21st July, 1774) of the Treaty of the Pruth, which completely altered the relative positions of the two Empires and contained the clause on which Prince Menschikoff, in 1853, founded the claim of Russia to the general protection of the Christian subjects of Turkey; the annexation of the Crimea by Russia (1783); the capture of *Ismail* by Suwarrow (1790); and the *Treaty of Jassy* (9th January, 1792), which extended the Russian dominions to the Dniester.

A new era seemed to open with the commencement of the reforms o **Selim III.**, who projected changes in nearly all the departments of the State; but the attempt of the Sultan to form a standing army drilled on the model of the armies of Western Europe, and the outbreak of war with England and Russia, led to a revolt of the Janissaries, who deposed Selim and placed **Mustafa IV.** on the throne.   An attempt to restore Selim, in 1808, resulted in the murder of the dethroned Sultan, the deposition of Mustafa, and the elevation of **Mahmûd II.**, ' the Reformer,' to the throne.   Mahmûd grappled with the evils around him in the true heroic spirit ; and amidst the disappointments and disasters of his chequered reign he never ceased to reorganise the, troops, the fleets, and the finances of his empire; to encourage education; to promote commerce; to give security for person and property ; and to remove by degrees the most galling of the burdens that pressed upon his Christian subjects.   The principal events are :—the

Treaty of Bucharest (1812), which made the Pruth the Russian boundary; the outbreak of the Greek *War of Independence*, and the massacres of Turks at Jassy, and of Greeks at Constantinople (1821); the destruction of the Janissaries (1826); the humiliating *Treaty of Akkerman* imposed by Russia upon Turkey (7th October, 1826); the *battle of Navarino* (1827); the war of 1827–29, closed by the *Treaty of Adrianople*, which advanced the frontier of Russia to the Lower Danube, gave her Georgia, Mingrelia, &c., and made Greece an independent kingdom; the occupation of *Algiers* by France (1830); the seizure of *Syria* by Muhammad Ali (1832); the *Treaty of Hunkiar Iskelesi* (8th July, 1833), by which Turkey was bound to an offensive and defensive alliance with Russia, and engaged, when required by Russia, to close the Dardanelles against the armed vessels of other Powers; the renewal of the war with Egypt; the defection of the Turkish fleet, and the disastrous battle of *Nezib* (25th June, 1839).

Abdul Mejid, a few months after his accession, issued the *Hatti Sherif of Gül-khâneh,* which guaranteed to all Ottoman subjects, irrespective of religion, security for their lives, their honour, and their property. In 1840 the operations of the British fleet on the coast of Syria compelled Muhammad Ali to come to terms with the Sultan; and in 1841 the *Convention of London* recognised the Bosporus and Dardanelles as Turkish waters, and not highways for the fleets of all nations. The remaining events of importance are:—the *Crimean War* (1853–55), and the *Treaty of Paris* (30th March, 1856); the promulgation of the *Hatti Humayûn,* which maintained and extended the provisions of the Hatti Sherif of Gül-khâneh in favour of the Christians; the disturbances in the *Lebanon* (1860); the repudiation by Russia of the article in the Treaty of Paris neutralising the Black Sea (1870); the deposition and death of **Abdul Aziz,** the deposition of **Murad V.,** and the accession of **Abdul Hamid II.** (1876); the grant of a *Constitution* (1876); the opening of the first *Turkish Parliament* (12th March, 1877); the war with Russia, ending in the advance of the Russians to San Stefano, within a few miles of Constantinople, and signature of the *Treaty of San Stefano* (3rd March, 1878); the *Cyprus Convention* (1878); the *Treaty of Berlin* (13th July, 1878); the occupation of *Tunis* by France (1881); and the occupation of Egypt by England (1882). The last disastrous war with Russia resulted in the loss of Thessaly, and the strip of Eastern Anatolia containing Batûm and Kars; the complete independence of Roumania, Servia, and Montenegro; the grant of autonomy to Bulgaria and Eastern Rumelia; and the administration of Bosnia and Herzegovina by Austria.

(2.) **House of Osman.**—The following is a list of the sovereigns who have ruled Turkey since the foundation of the Empire, with the dates of accession.

	A.D.		A.D.
Osman (son of Et-Toghrul) .	1299	Murad II. (his son) . . .	1421
Orkhan (his son). . . .	1326	Muhammad II. 'The Con-	
Murad I. (his son) . . .	1360	queror' (his son) . . .	1451
Bayezid I. 'Thunderbolt' (his		Bayezid II. 'The Mystic'	
son)	1389	(his son)	1481
Interregnum	1402	Selim I. 'The Great' (his son)	1512
Muhammad I. 'The Champion'		Suleiman I. 'The Magnifi-	
(his son)	1413	cent' (his son). . . .	1520

	A.D.		A.D.
Selim II. 'The Sot' (his son)	1566	Osman III. (son of Mustafa	
Murad III. (his son). . .	1574	II.).	1754
Muhammad III. (his son) .	1595	Mustafa III. (son of Ahmed	
Ahmed I. (his son) . . .	1603	III.)	1757
Mustafa I. (brother of Ahmed I.)	1617–1618	Abdul Hamid I. (son of Ahmed III.)	1774
Osman II. (son of Ahmed I.)		Selim III. (son of Mustafa	
Murad IV. (son of Ahmed I.)	1623	III.)	1788
Ibrahim (son of Ahmed I.) .	1640	Mustafa IV. (son of Abdul	
Muhammad IV. (son of Ibrahim).	1649	Hamid I.)	1807
Suleiman II. (son of Ibrahim)	1687	Mahmûd II. 'The Reformer' (son of Abdul Hamid I.) .	1808
Ahmed II. (son of Ibrahim).	1691	Abdul Mejid (his son) . .	1839
Mustafa II. (son of Muhammad IV.)	1695	Abdul Aziz (son of Mahmûd II.)	1861
Ahmed III. (son of Muhammad IV.)	1703	Murad V. (son of Abdul Mejid)	1876
Mahmûd I. (son of Mustafa II.)	1730	Abdul Hamid II. (son of Abdul Mejid)	1876

Many of the above names have been corrupted by foreign pronunciation; thus Osman has become Othman; Murad, Amurath; Bayezid, Bajazet; Ahmed, Achmet; and Suleiman, Solyman.

(3.) **Area; Population; Territorial Divisions; and Geography.**—The Ottoman Empire, *Osmanli Vilayeti*, lies partly in Europe, partly in Asia, and partly in Africa. Including the tributary provinces, its area is estimated to be about 1,670,000 square miles, and its population 33,151,848.

	Area. Square miles.	Population.
Europe.		
Immediate provinces	63,850	4,500,000
Bulgaria and Rumelia	37,869	3,154,375
Bosnia and Herzegovina . .	23,570	1,504,091
	125,289	9,158,466
Asia.		
Immediate provinces	751,388	16,133,000
Samos	210	43,117
	751,598	16,176,117
Africa.		
Tripoli	398,873	1,000,000
Egypt	394,240	6,817,265
	793,113	7,817,265
Total	1,670,000	33,151,848

Turkey. c

The territories under the direct control of the Sultan are divided for administrative purposes into *Vilâyets*, or provinces, and independent *Sanjaks*, or districts. The territorial divisions are: in *Europe*, 1, Constantinople; 2, Chatalja; 3, Adrianople; 4, Salonika; 5, Kossova; 6, Janina; 7, Monastir; 8, Skutari of Albania: in the *Islands* and *Asia*, 9, Archipelago; 10, Samos; 11, Crete; 12, Ismid; 13, Khudavendghiar (Brûsa); 14, Karasi; 15, Aidin (Smyrna); 16, Kastambûl (Kastamûni); 17, Angora; 18, Konieh; 19, Trebizond; 20, Sivas; 21, Adana; 22, Memûret ul-Aziz (Kharpût); 23, Dersim; 24, Erzerûm; 25, Van; 26, Bitlis; 27, Hekkiâri; 28, Diarbekr; 29, Mosul; 30, Baghdad; 31, Basrah; 32, Zor; 33, Aleppo; 34, Syria; 35, Lebanon; 36, Jerusalem; 37, Yemen; 38, Hejaz: in *Africa*, 39, Tripoli; 40, Benghazi. Of these Nos. 10, 11, and 35 have special governments; Nos. 2, 12, 32, and 36 are Sanjaks; and the remainder are Vilâyets.

European Turkey, which includes parts of ancient Thrace, Macedonia, and Epirus, is in great part mountainous. In the eastern half are the Balkan and Rhodope mountains, enclosing the rich plain of Eastern Rumelia, and culminating in the *Rilo-Dagh*, over 8000 feet high; in the western are the lofty ranges of Albania, including the *Shar-Dagh*, Mons Scardus, which rises to a height of 9000 ft. The rivers are the *Maritza*, Hebrus, *Kara-su*, Nestus, *Struma*, Strymon, *Vardar*, Axius, *Drin*, Drilo, and the *Usumi*, Apsus. In the northern districts there is a hot summer and a cold winter; in the southern, which are sheltered by the Rhodope mountains, a Mediterranean climate. It is a fruitful country with an intelligent and industrious population of Turks, Greeks, Bulgars, Albanians, Serbs, and Wallachs.

Asiatic Turkey is divided by the Turks into Anatolia, Mesopotamia, Syria, and Arabia; and the first may conveniently be subdivided into Western and Eastern Anatolia. *Western Anatolia* is a fertile plateau, from 3000 to 4500 feet above the sea, which extends from the Aegean to the Anti-Taurus mountains, and is buttressed north and south by the Pontic and Taurus range, from 7000 to 10,000 feet high. Mount Argæus, the centre of a volcanic district near the eastern end of the plateau, is over 12,000 feet. The climate is extremely diversified, ranging from the intense summer heat of the southern coast districts to the severe winter cold of the plateau. The products are equally varied; from the northern mountains come walnut and boxwood, and from the south and west figs and grapes. It supports a hardy population of Turks, Greeks, Armenians, Circassians, Turkomans, and Yuruks. *Eastern Anatolia*, which is separated from the lower ground on the west by the Anti-Taurus, is a rugged plateau, above which rise many peaks culminating in Mount Ararat, 17,000 feet high. In the north the summers are short and very hot, and the winters long and extremely cold. In the southern districts the climate is far more temperate. Much of the country is of an inaccessible nature, and here roads are few and the people lawless. In the heart of the highlands are Lake Van and the headwaters of the Euphrates and Tigris. The inhabitants are Turks, Armenians, Kurds, Greeks, and Nestorians. *Mesopotamia* is the great plain, broken only by the Sinjar Hills, through which the Euphrates and Tigris find their way from the mountains of Kurdistan to the Persian Gulf. It was formerly, under a well-devised system of irrigation, one of the most fertile regions of the earth, and might become so again if the irrigation works, now gone to decay, were restored. At present it is largely peopled by nomad Arabs, and irrigated only in a few isolated districts. *Syria*, the long strip of mountain and hill country which borders the Mediterranean from Mount Taurus to the Sinaitic Peninsula, is separated from Mesopotamia by the Syrian desert. The Syrian mountains culminate in Lebanon and Anti-Lebanon, from 10,000 to 11,000 feet, and sink as they run southwards through the hills of Galilee and Judaea to the desert of the Tih. The rivers are the Orontes, Leontes, and the Jordan, which discharges its waters into the Dead Sea. The people are Ansarieh, Maronites, Druses, Arabs, Syrians, and Jews. The *Arabian territory* consists of the provinces of Yemen and Hejaz on the Red Sea; the latter including the sacred towns of Mecca and Medina.

African Turkey comprises the tributary province of *Egypt*; and *Tripoli*, which includes the territories of Barca and Fezzan.

(4.) **Reigning Family; Constitution;** and **Government.**—The *present Sultan* is Abdul Hamid Khân II., who succeeded to the throne in 1876. He was born in 1842, and is the 34th sovereign of the House of Osman, and the 28th since the conquest of Constantinople. According to law, the succession is vested in the eldest male of the royal family. Formerly, as a matter of policy, all males of the House of Osman, other than the sons of the reigning Sultan, were put to death. This cruel practice has been abolished since the accession of Mahmûd II.; but the males of the royal house are not allowed to take part in the government of the country or to hold active commands in the army and navy.

The *princes* are called simply *Effendi*, a title formerly lordly, but now of little more significance than ' Esquire' at home. The *princesses* are called by Europeans Sultana, but by Turks Sultan, the word sultan being put after the name of the woman. Thus the Turks say ' Adileh Sultan,' and not ' the Sultana Adileh.' The princesses have the right of speaking to any man to whom they may give permission to enter their presence. On the other hand, every woman is obliged to unveil her face in the presence of the Sultan; and he can enter the harem of a private house without infringement of etiquette on the part of the ladies. The princesses are generally given in marriage, by the Sultan, to favourite pashas; and they often possess great political influence. The chief female personage of the Empire, however, greater than any wife, is the mother of the Sultan, the *Valideh Sultan*. The Valideh Sultan of the day has frequently exercised a direct and important influence on home and foreign politics, and assiduous court was paid to her by ministers of state and political intriguers.

The Sultans have long ceased to contract regular marriages, and the *Harem* has become a state institution. All children born in the Harem, whether of free women or slaves, are legitimate, and of equal lineage. The inmates come by purchase, by gift, and by free will; and a large proportion of them are Circassians. A certain number, designated by the Sultan, have the title *Kadyn*, or ' Ladies of the Harem;' the rest, called *Odalik*, remaining under them as servants. The superintendent of the Harem, who bears the title *Khasnadâr Kadyn*, and is usually an elderly lady, keeps up communication with the outer world through the eunuchs, whose head is the *Kizlar-aghasi*, or ' chief eunuch—an important personage holding rank next to the Grand Vizier, and the Sheikh-ul-Islâm.

Constitution.—Turkey is 'a theocratic absolute monarchy, in principle subject to the direct personal control of the Sultan, who is at once a temporal autocrat and recognised khalif, or successor of the Prophet, and consequently spiritual head of the Moslem world. This theocratical absolutism is tempered not only by traditional usage, local privilege, the juridical and spiritual precepts of the Kurân and its Ulema interpreters, and the Privy Council, but also by the growing force of public opinion, and by the direct and indirect pressure of European Powers.'

Turkish, like all *Moslem law*, has its source in the Kurân; but the short Sûras of the Kurân not being sufficient to satisfy the requirements of a powerful Empire, the *existing law* grew up by gradual accretions. Next to the Kurân, the sources of Moslem law are :—the 'six revered books'—traditions derived from the first four khalifs and chief disciples of Islâm; decisions made by celebrated Imâms in the first centuries; the *fetvas*, or formal decisions on questions proposed to the Sheikh-ul-Islâm ; and *adet*, or custom, which is equal in authority to positive law. After the conquest of Constantinople this mass of law was codified by Khosrev Mollah in a work called 'The Pearl,' which is much esteemed. Under Suleiman the Magnificent, the law was again codified by Ibrahim Haleby in his great work *Multeka-ul-ubhur*, the 'Confluence of the Seas,' which became the law of the Empire. The most recent codification is the *Mejelleh*, made within the last twenty years. These codes embody the *Sheriat*, divine or canon law. A new period opened in 1839 with the promulgation of the *Hatti Sherîf of Gül-khâneh*, which was followed in 1856 by the *Hatti Humayûn*. These Hatts promised to all the inhabitants of the Empire, without distinction of faith, equal civil, political, and religious rights. Their publication was followed by the issue of a Penal Code, a Commercial Code, a Vilâyet law, and several firmâns and Vizierial orders, which are collected together in the *Dustûr*, and known as the *Nizâm* or Common Law. The Nizâm, construed when obscure by the Sheriat, is the law generally administered, but many questions are still reserved for trial in the Sheri Courts, in accordance with the Sheriat. Turkish law recognises, amongst Ottoman subjects, the broad distinction of Moslem and non-Moslem; and as every man has to belong to some organization, all non-Moslems must be members of one of the *Millets*, or religious communities recognised by the Government. All subjects, however humble their origin, are eligible to, and may fill the highest offices in the State.

Government.—The Sultan, as Padishah, concentrates all powers within his person; and the legislative and executive authority is exercised under his supreme direction by the *Grand Vizier*, who is at the head of the administration, and the *Sheikh-ul-Islâm*, who superintends public worship and the administration of justice according to the Sheriat. The Grand Vizier, *Sadr Azam*, who is appointed by the Sultan, is assisted by ten Ministers; and they, with the Sheikh-ul-Islâm, form the Privy Council, *Mejlis-i-Khass*, which corresponds to our Cabinet. The Ministers are :— the President of the Council of State; Minister of War and Grand Master of Artillery; Minister of Marine; Minister of Interior; Minister for Foreign Affairs; Minister of Justice; Minister of Finance, Mines, and Forests, and Civil List; Minister of Evkaf (charitable bequests); Minister of Public Works, Commerce, and Agriculture; Minister of Public Instruction. The work of the Ministries is carried on by councils, as the councils of state, finance, war, &c., and these constitute the *Divân*. Each of the 'Millets' has two representatives, elected by the Grand Vizier, on the Council of State.

The *Sheikh-ul-Islâm*, or 'Grand Mufti,' is appointed by the Sultan with the nominal concurrence of the Ulema; and he is at once head of that body and Vicar of the Sultan in religious affairs. Next in rank to the Sheikh-ul-Islâm are the *Kazasskers* (Chief Justices) of Rumili (Europe) and Anadoli (Asia), and the Kâdi of Stambûl. The *Ulema* is a body comprising all the great judges, theologians, jurists, and teachers of Moslem law; and it is recruited from the Softas or students at the Medressehs. They are divided into three classes. 1. The *Imâms*, who are charged with the conduct of public worship; they include the *sheikhs*, preachers; the *khatibs*, who recite the Khutbe, or official Friday prayer; the *imâms* proper, who celebrate marriages and conduct burials; the *muezzins*, who call to prayer; and the *kaïms*, who have the charge of the mosques. 2. The *Kâdis*, judges of all kinds, who are divided into *mollahs*, *kâdis*, and *nâibs*. 3. The *Muftis* of the Provinces, doctors of law and exponents of law, who give decisions on all legal questions submitted to them.

(5.) **Religious Communities** (*Millets*). **Foreigners.**—The Sultans, since the conquest of Constantinople, have always recognised the division of their non-Moslem subjects into *Millets* or religious communities; and to these communities they have granted important privileges and immunities. They are permitted the free exercise of their religion; the management of their own monasteries, schools, hospitals, and charitable bequests; and in certain cases to exercise judicial power. Until 1839 there were four such *Millets*: the Roman Catholic, Greek, Armenian, and Jewish communities; but since that date the Roman Catholic Armenians, the Protestants, the Bulgarians, the Maronites, and the Nestorians have been recognised as separate 'millets.'

Muhammad, 'the Conqueror,' and his successors made the Patriarchs of the Christian communities high officers of the Empire, with great civil and religious power over the laity. A note with the Patriarch's seal would send any one to exile or prison without inquiry. The Patriarchs had access to members of the Divân at any time, and their views were received as authoritative with respect to their own people. The Hatti Sherif of Gül-khâneh (1839) had an unexpected effect on this Patriarchal system of government. It introduced the novel idea that men were equal before the law; gave the râyahs courage to contend for their rights; and diminished the civil power of the clergy. The Armenian laity were the first to come forward and demand a share in the administration of the affairs of their 'millet.' After a very long struggle with the Patriarch and clergy, who had acquired complete spiritual and temporal control over them, they obtained (1847) a Vizierial Order establishing two councils, under the presidency of the Patriarch, one of priests for ecclesiastical affairs, and one of laymen for civil affairs. This was followed by the elaboration of rules, for the better government of the Armenians by Patriarchal authority, which having been approved by the Turkish Government were issued in 1860 and may be called the *Armenian Charter*. Under this charter Armenian affairs are managed by spiritual and temporal councils, which are elected by the Armenian General

Assembly and presided over by the Patriarch, who is himself elected by the Assembly. The Patriarch thus remains the official representative of the Armenian millet, and the medium through whom the orders of the Turkish Government are carried out, but all real power has passed into the hands of the councils. The success of the Armenian laity deeply affected the other communities, and their affairs are now managed in a similar way by Councils elected by the members. In each of the vilâyets there are *Provincial Councils* for the management of local affairs, under the presidency of the official representatives of their respective millets.

Foreigners, residing in Turkey, are, in virtue of the capitulations, under the laws of their respective countries ; and are amenable to tribunals presided over by their Consuls. Cases between two foreign subjects are tried in the Consular Court of the defendant. Foreigners are amenable to the Ottoman tribunals in all cases, civil and criminal, in which an Ottoman subject is concerned. In civil cases the tribunal is the Commercial Court, which is a ' mixed ' tribunal,—i.e. two of the assessors are foreigners. In all cases a dragoman of the Consulate is present to see that the trial is conducted according to law. Foreigners owning real property are amenable to the Ottoman Courts in questions relating to their landed property. Writs issued by an Ottoman tribunal against a foreign subject must be served through the Consulate of the party to whom they are addressed. Domiciliary visits on the part of the Ottoman authorities are not legal unless a consular officer is present.

(6.) **Provincial Administration. Justice.**—For purposes of **Administration** the Turkish Empire is divided into Vilâyets, Sanjaks, Kazas, Nahiehs, and Kariehs or Mahallehs. At the head of the *Vilâyet* ' Province ' is the *Vâli*, or Governor-General, who is appointed by the Sultan, and is responsible for public safety and the general government of his province. In important vilâyets the vâli has an assistant (*muavin*). The chief administrative officers are : the *Defterdar* (Director of Finance), the *Mektûbji* (General Secretary), the Directors of Public Works, Mines and Forests, Public Instruction, Cadastre, &c., and the Chief of Police (*Alai Bey*). In some vilâyets there is also a Foreign Secretary. The Vâli is assisted by an Administrative Council (*Idâreh Mejlis*), which consists of the Kadi, Defterdar, Mektûbji, the spiritual chiefs of the non-Moslem communities (*Millets*), and four elected members, two Moslem and two non-Moslem. Each vilâyet has also a *General Council*, which should be convoked once a year, but is rarely called together.

The *Sanjak* (District), of which there are two or three in a vilâyet, is governed under the vâli, by a *Mutessarif* (Lieut.-Governor) appointed by Imperial order. There are a finance officer (*Muhassabaji*), a secretary (*Tahrirat Mudiri*), representatives of the various Ministries, and an *Idâreh Mejlis*, as in a vilâyet. The *Kazas* (sub-districts), of which there are three to six in a sanjak, are governed under the Mutessarifs, by *Kaimakams* (Governors) appointed by the Government. Each has a secretary (*malmudir*), and is assisted by an Idâreh Mejlis, similar to that of the sanjak. The *Nahiehs* (Communal Circles), of which there are three or four in a kaza, are governed by Mudîrs (Administrators), each of whom has his staff and administrative council. The *Karieh* (Commune), corresponding to the quarter (*mahalleh*) in a town, is a group of forty to fifty houses. Each commune has two *Mukhtars* (Head-men or Mayors), elected by the villagers, and in mixed villages each community elects two mukhtars. The mukhtars are assisted by a Council of Elders (*Ikhtiar Mejlis*), and have charge of the *bekjis* (field-guards) and the *korujis* (foresters).

The **administration of justice** is an independent service. In each karieh the Council of Elders acts as a Court of compromise; in each nahieh there is a similar but larger Court; in each kaza a Court of First Instance (*Bedayet Mahkameh*), consisting of a President and two Assessors, one Moslem, one non-Moslem; in each sanjak a *Bedayet Mahkameh*, divided into two sections, Civil (*Hukuk*) and Criminal (*Jeza*), and a Commercial Court (*Tejaret Mahkameh*); and in each vilâyet there is a Court of Appeal (*Istinaf Mahkameh*) in two sections, Civil and Criminal, and a Commercial Court. There is a right of appeal from each Court to the one above it, and from the Vilâyet Court of Appeal to the High Court of Justice at Constantinople. In each vilâyet there is a Public Prosecutor (*Mudaiumûm*), and in each sanjak an assistant Public Prosecutor, who represent the Ministry of Justice, and are appointed to see that the laws are properly carried out. In each vilâyet there is also an Inspector (*Mufettish*), who reports to the Ministry of Justice on the state of the courts and prisons, the conduct of the Judges, and the general adminis-tration of justice.

In addition to the above Courts, which administer justice according to the *Nizâm*, or Common Law, there is in each administrative division a *Sheri Court* that takes cognizance of disputes between Moslems coming under the *sheriat*, or Canon Law. In the Sheri Courts the Kadi is sole judge and interpreter of the law.

(7.) **Army. Navy. Mercantile Marine.**—The Turkish army consists of the *Nizâm* (Regular Army), *Redifs* (Reserves), and *Mustahfiz* (Land-sturm). Military service is compulsory on all Moslems excepting the inhabitants of Constantinople. Non-Moslems pay an exemption tax (*Bedel Askerieh*) of six shillings per head on all males. Every soldier serves six years in the Nizâm, eight in the Redif, and six in the Mustahfiz. The Empire is divided into seven *military districts*, the head-quarters of which are at Constantinople, Adrianople, Monastir, Erzinjan, Damascus, Baghdad, and Sanaa (Yemen). There are local troops in Crete, Tripoli, and the Hejaz, recruited, however, in Asiatic Turkey. The *peace strength* of the army is about 10,000 officers and 150,000 men; but, in time of war, by calling out the Redifs and Mustahfiz, it would be possible to place 800,000 men under arms. The artillery is armed with Krupp guns of late pattern; the Nizâm, at present armed with the Martini-Peabody rifle, is to be supplied with the Mauser Magazine rifle.

The Turkish **Navy** possesses six so-called sea-going ironclads, and eight smaller ones for coast defence; besides a large number of gunboats, and other steamers, including twenty torpedo-boats, and two Nordenfeldt submarine boats. The armament of the ironclads is out of date, the boilers are old, and the ships themselves are rarely taken out of the Golden Horn. The torpedo boats are well looked after, and the crews constantly exercised. The crews are raised by conscription; the length of service is eight years in the active service (including three on leave), and four years in the Redifs. The peace strength is about 15,000 men, a number that is doubled in time of war.

Turkey has no **Mercantile Marine.** The *Mahsûse* line of steamers is owned by the Admiralty. The *Shirket-i-Hairieh* is a privileged company, with a monopoly of the Bosporus passenger trade. *L'Egée* (Courtji & Co.) carries the Ottoman flag, but the capital is Greek. There are numerous small craft owned and manned by Ottoman subjects, Moslem and non-Moslem, but they are not built or equipped for long sea voyages, and do not ply beyond the waters of the Black Sea and the Levant.

(8.) **Rank. Decorations.**—Great importance is, and always has been, attached to **rank** in Turkey. The strict rules of etiquette demand that every man should be paid the honour due to his *rutbe,* or grade in the official hierarchy. A Turk, when paying a visit, knows the exact spot at which his host should meet him, the words with which he should be greeted, and the particular part of the dîvân upon which he should be invited to seat himself. The host often releases the rules of etiquette, to show honour to a guest; the guest never attempts to break them. A breach of etiquette on the part of host or guest, when intentional, is regarded as an insult.

All civil rank is classed according to relative military rank, and at a very early date the military and civil services were divided into *Viziers, Mirimirans,* or Pashas of the second class, *Mirlivas,* or Brigadiers, *Mirakhirs,* or Masters of the Horse, and *Kapuji-bashis,* or Chamberlains. This lasted until the suppression of the Janissaries, when Mahmûd II. established the four classes of *Ula, Sanieh, Salisseh,* and *Rabea,* for the civil service. The order of precedence was finally settled in 1861. According to this after the Grand Vizier, the Sheikh-ul-Islâm, and the Kizlar-aghasi, come the *Mushîrs,* Field Marshals and Ministers; and then follow persons having the rank of Vizier, Kazasker, Bala, and Kadi of Stambûl. After these high dignitaries come officials holding the rank of *Ûla-senf-evel,* equivalent to *Ferik* (Lieutenant-General); *Ûla-senf-sani,* equivalent to *Mirliva* (Brigadier-General); *Sanieh-senf-evel,* equivalent to *Mir-alai* (Colonel); *Sanieh-senf-sani,* equivalent to Kaimakâm (Lieutenant-Colonel); *Salisseh,* equivalent to *Binbashi* (Major); and *Rabea,* in degrees corresponding to *Yuzbashi* (Captain), *Mulâzim* (Lieutenant).

The **Turkish Orders** are the Mejidîeh, in seven classes, founded by Abdul Mejid in 1851; the Osmanieh, in four classes, founded by Abdul Aziz, in 1860; and the *Nishân-i-skefket,* founded in 1878 by the present Sultan, for ladies who had rendered services during the war with Russia.

Mushîrs and Viziers are addressed as *devletli,* or 'excellency'; Kazaskers and Balas, as *atufetli.* The title *hazretleri* is used as a mark of respect when addressing a number of the official hierarchy.

(9.) **Trade. Commerce. Manufactures. Agriculture.**—In 1889–90, the *exports* paying duty were valued at £13,782,000, and the *imports* at £19,113,000; but a stricter custom-house supervision would largely increase these figures. The principal *commercial ports* are Constantinople, Dedeagatch, and Salonika in Europe, and Trebizond, Samsûn, Smyrna, Mersina, Alexandretta, and Beirût in Asia. The largest exports are to Great Britain, France, Austria, and Italy, and the largest imports from Great Britain, Austria, France, and Russia. The chief *exports* are raisins, wheat, raw silk, olive oil, mohair, coffee, opium, wool, cocoons, &c.; and the *imports* sugar, cotton thread, cotton prints, sheeting, calico, petroleum, coal, &c.

In the interior there is little *commercial activity*, owing to the want of good roads, and agents of British houses are rarely seen at any distance from the coast towns. The extension of the railway to Angora will probably lead to a large increase in the fruit, honey, and wax trade, and a line from Samsûn to Amâsia and Sivas would open up one of the best grain-producing districts in Asiatic Turkey.

Silk, carpets, soap, attar of roses, and tobacco are *manufactured*, and there are a few steam flour-mills, and steam cotton and silk spinning-machines; and glass, porcelain, fez, and paper manufactories. Some of the Turkish jewelry, leather work, and embroidery is very good; and in some places good strong cloth is made.

Agriculture is everywhere in a very backward state, excepting in some of the coast districts, where great improvements have been made in recent years in the culture of the vine.

(10.) **Finance. Taxation. Land Tenure.**—Until 1881 the financial affairs of the Ottoman Empire were in a state of complete disorganisation; but since that year, they have steadily improved, owing to the reduction and consolidation of the Foreign Debt, consequent upon the decree of the 20th December, 1881, and to the regulation of the Internal Debt. Between 1854–74 several loans were contracted, making a nominal debt of £223,196,740, of which £13,700,000 was guaranteed by England and France, and secured on the Egyptian Tribute. The annual payment on the debt, interest, and sinking fund was about £14,000,000, whilst the revenue of the Empire was not more than £20,000,000. The loans were spent on unproductive works, palace necessities, arms, ammunition, &c., and the natural result was national bankruptcy. The troubles in Bosnia and Herzegovina led to a partial suspension of payment in October, 1875, and on the 9th of July, 1876, a Government decree announced that no further payments of interest would be made until the internal affairs of the Empire had become more settled. After October, 1875, the Government was obliged to obtain advances from banking-houses in Galata at high rates of interest. In 1881, an arrangement, afterwards embodied in a decree, was come to between the Turkish Government and the delegates of the bondholders of England, France, Austria, Germany, and Italy, under which the debt was reduced to £106,437,234—that is, the creditors gave up about 50 per cent. of their claims. The Government on its part agreed to hand over certain items of revenue to a Commission consisting of delegates appointed by the bondholders of the different countries of Europe. The Galata bankers acquiescing in this arrangement became first mortgagees, and the nominal amount of their loans was consolidated into a Privileged Debt of £8,170,000. The Commission, or *Conseil d'administration de la dette publique Ottomane*, sits at Constantinople and administers the 'ceded revenues,' which are the stamp, salt, silk, spirit, fish, and part of the tobacco duties, besides the contributions from Cyprus and Eastern Rumelia, and the Bulgarian Tribute. The decree of the 20th December, 1881, provides for the application of the 'ceded revenues' to the payment of interest and amortisation of the debt, subject to the preferential deduction for 22 years of £T.590,000 for the interest and redemption of the debt to the Galata Bankers (Priority Bonds).

In 1883, the Tobacco Régie (monopoly) was instituted and granted for thirty years to a financial group consisting of the Vienna Kreditanstalt,

Herr Bleichröder, and the Imperial Ottoman Bank. In 1884, a Licence Tax was established, and the pernicious system under which the various Departments paid their debts in orders (*havalehs*) on the Provincial Governments was abolished. In 1884-85, the unification and conversion of the debt was carried out; in 1886, the Government regulated its current debt to the Ottoman Bank by transferring to the Bank stock worth £T.4,500,000, and setting apart the customs dues of certain ports for the interest and sinking fund; and in 1890 the conversion of the Priority Bonds, and the unification and conversion of the internal bonds were successfully carried out. The agents of 'the debt,' and of the Tobacco Régie, are found in all the large towns throughout the country.

Amongst the Turkish debts is also the Russian War Indemnity of £32,000,000, payable in annual instalments of £320,000, and a floating debt.

The *revenue* is between sixteen and seventeen million pounds, and the *expenditure* between nineteen and twenty. The annual deficit is met by various expedients, which need not be mentioned here.

The **taxes** are not oppressively heavy, but the mode of collection gives rise to great abuses. The towns and villages are exploited to such an extent by the tax collectors that the people have in every case to pay, in money or kind, half as much again as the tax itself. The principal taxes are: the *Ushr*, 'tenth,' or Tithe, which is levied on all agricultural produce, cereals, vegetables, cotton, opium, fruit, oil, honey, wood, charcoal, &c., is collected sometimes in kind, and sometimes in money. The arrangements for the collection of the tithe are made by the Administrative Councils of the Vilâyets. The crops are valued in spring, and, after the valuation has been reported to the Treasury, the Councils decide whether the tithe is to be sold or collected by the Government. The actual quantity of produce taken from the peasant or cultivator is about 15½ per cent. The *emlâk verghisi*, or Property Tax, of 4 per 1000 on the value of all property occupied by the owner, and 4 per cent. on all houses and land leased to others; and the *temettu verghi*, or Income Tax, of 3 per cent. on profits and income of all kinds. Serious abuses exist in the assessment and collection of the verghi taxes. Crown lands pay no taxes. The *bedel askerieh*, or Military Exemption Tax, levied on all non-Moslems, through the heads of their 'millets,' at the rate of P.5000 for every 180 adult males. The *sheep and goat tax*, which varies from P.1½ to P.4 per head. The *Tapu*, or Land Tax, including succession and mortgage duties, and 5 per cent. on every sale of land. The stamp, salt, silk, spirits, and tobacco duties, the judicial receipts, &c. The *custom duties* are 8 per cent. on all imports, and 1 per cent. on all exports. There are also *Municipal taxes*, which vary in the different towns.

Land is divided into five categories: *Mulk*, or freehold, which can be disposed of by the owner at his pleasure, but reverts to the State if he dies without heirs. *Mirieh*, or Government lands, which were originally granted to soldiers as military fiefs, but are now bought and sold through the agents of the *Beit-ul-Mal*, a branch of the Finance Department. If a holder of Mirieh land leaves it fallow for three years, or dies without heirs, his property reverts to the State. The *Vakûf*, or endowed lands, are either lands granted by the Sultan, or freehold land dedicated by the owner, to some religious or charitable foundation. Most of the Vakûf lands are in the hands of officials and notables, who hold at very low rentals, and resist investigation. The administration of these lands by the Evkaf Department is said to be very corrupt. *Metrûk*, or public lands, are given over by the Government to communes for specified purposes. *Salieh*, or waste lands, are unoccupied lands, ½ hr. from a house; they are sometimes sold by auction, and under certain conditions become the property of the person who cultivates them.

(11.) **The Press.**—Few changes are more remarkable than those which have followed the publication of the first newspaper in Turkey, during the Crimean War. The Press, notwithstanding the strict censorship to which it is subjected, exercises a wide-spread influence. In the large towns in the interior the newspaper reader has almost entirely supplanted the story-teller; and the events and politics of the day are discussed, throughout the country, in a manner that was quite unknown twenty years ago. Each Vilâyet has its *official journal*, and the principal Constantinople papers have a large circulation in the provinces. The newspapers are political, religious, scientific, literary, and commercial; and the languages in which they are published offer an interesting study. There are papers in Arabic, Armenian, Bulgarian, English, French, Greek, Hebrew, Italian, Persian, Spanish, Turkish, Turkish written in Armenian character, and Turkish written in Greek character.

The first *press law*, under which newspapers were free within certain prescribed limits, was promulgated in 1861. In case of transgression, the responsible editor of the offending paper was summoned before a tribunal *ad hoc*, and if convicted was punishable by fine, imprisonment, or suspension of his newspaper. In 1866 this law was suspended, and in lieu of it the Press was placed under the *Régime Administratif* of the Foreign Office. By this the Porte assumed arbitrary authority over the Press, and when an article appeared that caused displeasure at the Porte, the paper publishing it was forthwith suspended or suppressed. After the death of Sultan Abdul Aziz the authority of the Porte was exercised in an increasingly arbitrary manner until 1886, when a *preventive censure* was introduced. One member, or two, of the staff of the *Press Bureau* is told off to each newspaper office, and revises all the matter before it goes to press. These censors are incapable of forming an opinion as to the merits or demerits of a political or economic article; but they have a quick eye for prohibited subjects and words. The only effect of the system is to paralyse the Press and to deprive it of all authority, as well on matters of fact as of opinion. All papers are watched by the Press section of the *Cabinet Particulier* of H.I.M. the Sultan.

i. TURKISH LANGUAGE.

It has been thought useful to supply the traveller with a brief sketch of the mechanism of the Turkish language, such as may assist him in understanding what he hears, and in applying any words which he may pick up; although in the limited space at our disposal it is impossible to do more than supply some elementary notions to such as do not care to study the subject thoroughly.

The Turkish is, like the English, a mixed language. With a Turkish construction it works up Arabic and Persian words. Common Turkish is almost pure Turkish, but owing to its poverty the literary language introduces Persian and Arabic copiously. It is expressive, soft, and musical, not difficult to speak, but very difficult to write. The Turkish characters are, with some slight difference, the same as the Arabic and Persian. They are written from the right to the left. The chief books of the Turks are those on poetry, law, and theology. Printing was introduced at Constantinople in the sixteenth century; but the copies of the Koran are still multiplied in manuscript.

There is, practically speaking, no definite article in Turkish, though *o* or *ol* is sometimes used as such, and inflection will often supply its place. The indefinite *a* or *an* is expressed, as in some other languages, by *bir* (one).

The various relations of nouns expressed in most modern languages by prepositions are, in Turkish, represented by affixes.

The following is the declension of the word *ev*, house:—*ev*, the house; *evin*, of the house; *eve*, to the house; *evi* (acc.), the house; *evden*, from the house; *evler*, the houses; *evlerin*, of the houses; *evlere*, to the houses; *evleri* (acc.), the houses; *evlerden*, from the houses.

If the last vowel of the word declined is *e* (as in the above example), or if it is *i* or *ü*, the declension is similar to that of *ev*. These vowels sounds are said to be 'soft.' If, on the other hand, the last vowel in the word is a 'hard' vowel, such as *a*, *o* or *u*, those in the terminations or affixes must also be hard. Thus *dost*, friend, makes *dostun*, *dosta*, *dostu*, *dostdan*; plural, *dostlar*, *dosilarun*, *dostlari*, *dostlardan*.

For similar euphonic reasons a *k* when it occurs between two vowels is often changed into *gh* or *y*; and a *y* or an *n* is often introduced to prevent the juxtaposition of two vowel sounds. The ear is the ultimate guide in these cases, and it will not be found that they present great difficulty in ordinary conversation.

Adjectives are indeclinable, and precede the noun; *Beuyük adamlardan*, from great men.

The numerals leave the noun in the singular; *Bin at*, not *bin atlar*, a thousand horses.

The possessive case requires the addition of an *i* to the name of the thing possessed. Thus *Pâsha* is a Pasha, *ev*, a house; the Pasha's house is not *Pashanin ev*, but *Pashanin evi*, lit. of the Pasha his house.

The possessive affixes for nouns which end in a vowel are :—*m*, my ; *n*, thy; *si*, his or her ; *miz*, our ; *niz*, your ; *lari*, their. Thus *torba*, a bag, becomes *torbam*, my bag; *torban*, thy bag ; *torbasi*, his or her bag; *torbamiz*, our bag ; *torbaniz*, your bag; *torbalari*, their bag.

For nouns which end in a consonant, it is necessary to insert a vowel between the noun and the affixes of the 1st and 2nd person, while the affix for the 3rd person singular is changed from *si* to *i*. Thus *at* a horse makes *atim*, *atin*, *ati*, *atimiz*, *atiniz*, *atlari*, my horse, thy horse, &c.

It is to be noted that nouns with the possessive affix are declinable. Thus *atim*, my horse; *atimin*, of my horse; *atima*, to my horse; *atimi* (acc.), my horse; *atimdan*, from my horse; *atlarim*, my horses; *atlarimin*, of my horses; *atlarima*, to my horses ; *atlarimi* (acc.), my horses; *atlarimdan*, from my horses. It will be seen that the sign of the plural *lar* comes between the noun and the possessive affix.

In all the above cases the vowel sounds are varied according to the euphonic rules alluded to before; which rules, in fact, are of universal application throughout the language.

Verbs are conjugated by means of affixes only, and without pronouns. The principle tenses of *gitmek*, to go, are the following:—

Gidyôrim, I am going.	*Gidyôridim*, I was going.
Giderim, I go.	*Gideridim*, I used to go.
Gitdim, I went.	*Gitdidim*, I had gone.
Gidejeyim, I am about to go.	*Gidejekdim*, I was about to go.
Gitmaliyim, I ought to go.	*Gitsem*, If I go.

The conjugation of *gidyôrim*, I am going, is given below. The other tenses are conjugated in the same or in a somewhat similar manner.

Gidyôrim, I am going.	*Gidyôriz*, we are going.
Gidyôrsin, thou art ,,	*Gidyôrsiniz*, you ,, ,,
Gidyôr, he (she) is ,,	*Gidyôrler*, they ,, ,,

The imperative is formed by cutting off the termination *mek* of the infinitive; thus *git*, go.

If the vowels in the infinitive are hard (*e.g. bakmak*, to look; and *vurmak*, to strike) the usual substitution of hard vowels for soft takes place throughout the conjugation.

Various derivatives, each of which is conjugated as above, can be made by introducing syllables between the root and the affixes: thus—

Gieurmek, to see.	*Gieurülmek*, to be seen.
Gieurüshmek, to see one another.	*Gieurdürmek*, to cause to see.
Gieurünmek, to cause oneself to be seen.	

The negative is formed by introducing *m* and a vowel just before the affix, thus—

Gieurmemek not to see. *Gieurüshmemek*, not to see one another, &c.

There is also a derivative which indicates inability to perform the action referred to, thus—

Gidememek, not to be able to go.
Bakamamak, not to be able to look.

The interrogation is made by introducing *m* with the proper vowels *Gider-mi-sin?* Art thou going? *Vurajak mi?* Will he strike? *Sen mi geldin?* Was it you who came?

Turkish being a non-Aryan language, its grammar and syntax differ greatly from those of English, Latin, and other Aryan languages. In translating from Turkish into English, one has usually to begin at the end of the sentence; sometimes it is necessary to go forward a whole page, and work one's way backward to the beginning. This is one of the great difficulties of literary Turkish.

The traveller who wishes to obtain any further insight into the language on the spot is especially recommended to learn what he can colloquially, rather than by taking lessons from a professional master, who will prove completely wedded to a defective routine system of teaching. Let him avoid encumbering and embarrassing his brain by any attempt at formally studying the literary Turkish, which will only create confusion, and, even if learnt, would be useless for conversational purposes, a great proportion of the words used in the written language being unknown to the middle and lower classes.

The best book for the tourist who only wishes to obtain a slight knowledge of the language is :—

Redhouse's *Turkish Vade Mecum*, Trübner & Co., 6s. It is a small book, easily carried in the pocket, and contains a very good vocabulary and an epitome of the grammar. All the words are printed in English characters.

For those who wish to study the language further, the following dictionaries and grammars are recommended :—

Redhouse's *Eng.-Turk. Lexicon.* Quaritch. One vol. 18s.—Samy Bey Fraschery's *Dictionnaire Turc-Français.* Constantinople. One vol. 30s.—Wells' *Practical Grammar of the Turkish Language.* Quaritch. One vol. 15s.—Redhouse's *Grammaire Raisonnée de la Langue Ottomane.* Paris. Gide et Cie. One vol. 16s.—Wahrmund's *Praktische Grammatik der osmanisch-türkischen Sprache.* Giessen. J. Ricker. One vol. 16s.— A useful key or appendix to the last-named work (price 2s.) has also been published.

VOCABULARY.

In this vocabulary, in Turkish words, the letters should be pronounced somewhat as follows :—

a, as in 'father,' but shorter; or like the u in 'under.'
â, as in 'father.'
e, as in 'met.'
i, as in 'sit.'
ï, like ee in 'meet.'
o, as in go, pronounced short.
ô, as in go, pronounced long.
.., like oo in 'foot.'
û, like oo in 'boot.'
ü, as the French u in 'tu.'
ai, like i in 'fight.'
ey, as ey in 'they.'
eu, as the French eu in 'meute.'
ch, as in 'church.'   (N.B. *c* has not been used except in the combination *ch*.)
g is always pronounced hard as in 'go,' even when it precedes an *e* or an *i*.
gh indicates a very soft guttural *g*.
h, as the English aspirate *h*, except at the end of words terminating in *ah* or *eh*, when it is usually dropped, and only the vowel pronounced.
kh, as the English aspirate *h*, but in a more guttural manner.
s is always pronounced soft as in 'send' or 'invest'; never as in 'music.'
sh, as in 'bush.'
y is always used as a consonant.

The other consonants are pronounced the same or nearly the same as in English.

The apostrophe ' indicates a slight hiatus such as exists in English in the pronunciation of two such words as ' the act.'

The ordinary rules for the accent are as follows:—

(1.) If there is a long vowel, it carries the accent. Thus the first syllable is accentuated in *Pâsha*, and the second in *mushir*.

(2.) If two consecutive consonants occur, the syllable preceding them is accentuated; as for instance the first syllable in *mevlevi* and in *sakka*.

(3.) In other cases the syllables are equally accentuated.

The transliteration has been so arranged as to show as far as possible the colloquial pronunciation of the words. It is very important to observe the various rules given above, and not merely to pronounce the letters in the way one naturally would if the words were English.

Selâm, peace or welfare.—*Selâm aleykum*, peace be unto you, or prosperity and welfare attend you. The reply is *Aleykum selâm.*— The Turks only give this salutation between Mussulmans, and it should not be addressed to them, although the Persians and Indian Mussulmans give it to Englishmen. It is safe to say, *Sabâh sherifiniz hair ola*, good morning, or *Ahsham sherifiniz hair ola*, good evening. Then follow—

Hosh geldin—Sefa geldin, Welcome. (Said by the master of the house.) The reply is *Hosh bulduk.*

Eyí mi siniz effendim? *Keyfiniz eyi mi?* Are you well, Sir?

Mashallah! What God wills! Used as an expression of surprise, praise, or pleasure.

Inshallah! Please God! This is used as an affirmative expression, and also in reference to all future proceedings.

Let us see, By and by, *Bakalum.*	Fish, *Baluk.*
Look, *Bak.*	Wood, *Odun.*
Stop, *Dur.*	Fire, *Atesh.*
Come in, welcome, *Buyurun.* A word of invitation—At your service.	Tobacco, *Tütün.* Pipe, *Chibûk.*
	Great coat, *Yaghmurluk.*
	Umbrella, *Shemsïeh.*
Come, *Gel.*	Where is ——? —— *nerede?*
How many? *Kach?*	Stable, *Ahir.*
Give me ——, —— *Bana ver.*	Horse, *At, Haivan, Begir.*
Bring me ——. —— *Bana getir.*	Mule, *Katir.*
Evet, Yes. — *Yôk*, No. — *Hair*, a polite no.	Ass, *Eshek.* Camel, *Deve.*
	My horse, *Atim.* Your horse, *Atin.*
Tea, *Chai.*	Where is my horse? *Atim nerede?*
Lemonade, *Ilimonâta.*	Saddle, *Eyer.* Girth, *Kolan.*
Sherbet, *Sherbet.*	Rein, *Dizgin.*
Wine, *Sharâb.*	Whip, *Kamchi.*
Sugar, *Sheker.*	Stick, switch, *Chibûk.*
Water, River, Brook, *Sû.*	Quick, *Chapuk.* Slow, *Yavâsh.*
Hot water, *Sijâk sû.*	How far is it —— ? —— *ne kadar uzak?*
Cold water, *So'ûk sû.*	
Fresh water, *Taze sû.*	How many hours is it to ——? —— *kach sa'at?*
Bread, *Ekmék.* Meat, *Et.*	
Cheese, *Peynir.*	What's o'clock? *Sa'at kach?*
Salt, *Tuz.*	Is there a khan here? *Burada khân varme?*
Milk, *Süt.* Eggs, *Yimurta.*	
Fowl, *Tawuk.*	Horse-shoe, *Nal.*

Shoeing-smith, *Nalband.*
What is the nearest road to —— ?
—— *en yakin yol hangise.*
Ford, *Gechid.*
Fountain, *Cheshmeh.*
Spring, *Bunar.*
What ruins (inscriptions, &c.) are there near here? *Buralarda ne kharâb var dir?*
Have you any coins or curiosities? *Eski paralar yakhod tuhaf var mi?* or, *Eski sikkeler ya assare attika var mi?*
Mosque, *Jâmi'.*
Cemetery, *Mezâr, Mezârlik.*
What do you want? *Ne istersin?*
What is the name of this? *Bunun adi ne dir?*
What is your name? *Adin ne?*
Let us go, get on, *Gidelim.*

'Make way!' a call when on horseback in the streets of Stambûl, *Destûr!* or *Vardah!*
Is, *Dir.* Good, *Eyi.* Bad, *Fena.*
I want, *Istiyôrim.*
I want a newspaper, *Bir gazetta istiyôrim.*
There is no water, *Sû yôk.*
Is not, *Deyil.*
The town is not far, *Kasaba uzak deyil.*
Very, *Pek.*
The house is very near, *Ev pek yakin dir.*
A thing, *Shey.*
Thank you, *Teshekkür ederim.*
I do not want anything, *Hich bir shey istemeyôrim.*
Good-bye, *Allaha ismarladik.*

After eating or drinking, the bystanders salute you with—

Âfiet-olsun, May it do you good!
Allah-râzi-olsun, May God favour you!
The constant recognition of the Deity among Orientals is exemplified by the frequently-recurring expressions of
Shükür Allah, May God reward you; *Allah râzi ola*—Praise be to God; *Allaha emânet ola*—*Allah bereket versin*—May God receive you, &c.; terms by which they express their gratitude for favours conferred on them.

Haide, Chabuk—the usual expression used to hasten anyone, your *surûji* (postilion), for instance, signifying 'quick,' 'make haste.'
Kach Ghrûsh—How many piastres? or—What is the price?
Peki for *pek eyi,* Very well!
Bâshka—Other, different.
—— *var*—There is (some)——
—— *yók*—There is no——
—— *var mi*—Is there any—— ?
Chôk—Very, exceedingly, much, too much!
Haide git!—Be off with you! ⎫ Are useful phrases for getting rid
Istemem—I don't want (it.) ⎭ of beggars, touts, &c.

Numbers.			
1, *Bir*	9, *Dokuz*	60, *Altmish*
2, *Iki*	10, *On*	70, *Yetmish*
3, *Üch*	11, = 10-1, *On-bir*	80, *Seksen*
4, *Deurt*	12, = 10-2, *on-iki,* &c.	90, *Doksan*
5, *Besh*	20, *Yirmi*	100, *Yüz*
6, *Alti*	30, *Otuz*	1,000, *Bin*
7, *Yedi*	40, *Kirk*	First, *Birinji, ilk*
8, *Sekiz*	50, *Elli*	Second, *Ikinji.*

Turkish Words used Geographically.

Ak, beyâz, white.
Kara, siâh, black.
Sû, water, river.
Dâgh, mountain.
Geul, lake.
Irmak, river.
Keui, village.

Shehir, town, city.
Maden, mine.
Tepeh, hill.
Dereh, valley.
Yol, road.
Kaya, rock.

Tash, stone.
Kapu, gate.
Serai, palace.
Keupri, bridge.
Aghach, tree.
Kasaba, town.

For a very useful vocabulary of Turkish and English, in a portable form, the traveller is referred to Redhouse's *Vade Mecum.*

TURKISH TITLES OF HONOUR AND NAMES.

The titles and functions of the dignitaries of the Ottoman empire differ from those of Western Europe, so that an enumeration of them may be useful to the traveller.†

Pâdishâh is the chief and popular title of the Sultan; it is said to signify Father of all the Sovereigns of the Earth. The Turks seldom say Sultan. He is also styled Vicar of God; Successor of the Prophet; *Imâm-ul-Muslemin,* or Pontiff of Mussulmans; *Âlem Penah,* refuge of the world; *Zil-ullah,* shadow of God; and *Hunkiâr,* or manslayer. He is the head of the Sunnite sect, and is recognised as such by Mussulmans of that sect in our empire of India. He is regarded as Khalîf, successor of the Prophet, and many Mussulman pilgrims visit Constantinople to see him and the great metropolis of Islâm.

The *Sheikh-ul-Islâm,* or grand mufti, is chief of the Ulema, a class at once judicial and religious, and combines in his person the highest power of each kind. His peculiar office is that of supreme interpreter of the law. He is consulted by the Sultan on doubtful points, and his sanction is always desired to any new laws or reforms.

The *Serasker* is the minister of war and commander-in-chief of the army.

The *Top-khâneh-mushîri,* commander-in-chief of the artillery, and governor-general of all the fortresses of the empire.

The *Kaptân Pâsha,* supreme commander of the navy, or Lord High Admiral of the Turkish empire. His power is absolute in everything relating to the marine, and he controls the management of the arsenals and the ships of war.

The *Umûri-kharjîeh-nâziri,* or minister for foreign affairs, formerly called *Reyis Effendi.*

The following are some of the principal aghas or officers of the imperial household. They live in the palace. Their power has much declined:—

The *Kizlar-aghasi,* chief of the black eunuchs, holds an important office, and formerly ranked next to the Grand Vizier and the Sheikh-ul-Islâm. He has the title of *Mushîr,* or first-class pasha. He has the control of everything relating to the imperial harem and apartments, and the government of all the eunuchs.

† For the proper pronunciation of Turkish names and words, see p. [30].

The *Khazineh-humayûn-vekîli,* or keeper of the Sultan's privy purse, is one of the chief officers of the black eunuchs, and is himself a eunuch, and is classed among the functionaries of the first rank.

The *Kapu-aghasi,* or chief of the white eunuchs, is the first officer of the imperial chamber, and ranks after the kizlar-aghasi, of whom he formerly had precedence.

The *Hekîm-bâshi,* the chief physician of the palace, is the head of the medical profession throughout the empire. He has under him the imperial physicians in ordinary, about twelve in number, of whom two are in attendance every twenty-four hours. Several of them are European physicians settled at Pera. His office is one of great influence and power, more political than medical, as he has ready access to the palace. There are besides many other officers of the Palace, too numerous to mention.

The following are some of the principal names, words, &c., with which the traveller in Turkey will find it useful to be acquainted :—

Agha is the title 'gentleman,' applied *par excellence* to eunuchs, and given in the army to officers below the rank of major. It is usually given as a title of respect to inferiors in the employ of government, and is borne by gentlemen of the old Turkish stock in the provinces.

Almeh, female singers and dancers, who perform at private houses for hire.

Altilik, a debased silver coin, equal to 6 *ghrush* or piastres.

Anadoli, Anatolia, Asia Minor.

Arnaût, a name by which the Turks designate an Albanian.

Baba, father ; also a term of endearment, and used to an old man.

Bairâm, a festival of three days, which succeeds the Ramazân, when all the mosques are illuminated. It is the Moslem Easter.

Bakkâl, a grocer, or chandlershop-keeper.

Bakshish, a gratuity, fee.

Bash, head, chief.

Bashi-bozuk, modern irregular cavalry. Lit. 'crack-brained.'

Bazâr, a market for the sale of provisions. This term is used mostly by Europeans; what we understand as a bazâr is called *bezesten* and *charshi.* The natives call a fair, *bazâr.*

Beshlik, a silver coin, equal to 5 piastres.

Bey, a title formerly of the holder of an imperial fief (*bey-lik*); now given to lieutenant-colonels in the army and to the superior officers of the navy, and their descendants, so that it is a common title of the Turks in Stambûl, and sometimes is found in the lower classes in towns. In speaking to a bey or gentleman the phrase is *Bey effendi.*

Beyler-bey, bey of beys, a rank equal to the ancient one of pasha of two or three tails.

Bezesten, a bazâr or building for the sale of valuables, silks, jewellery, &c.

Bin-bashi, a colonel in the army.

Charshi, a bazâr composed of covered streets of shops for the sale of valuables.

Chelebi, a gentleman.

Chibûk, a pipe ; *chibûkji,* a pipe-seller ; also the servant who lights them.

Chiftlik, a farm, an estate in the country.

Chingeni, gipsy.

Chojuk, boy.

Defterdar, a receiver of government dues; the chief finance official in a viláyet.

Demir yolu, railway.

Dervish, a sort of Turkish monk. There are numerous orders of them which are distinguished by their dress. They bear the name of their founder, and some of them claim to practise the greatest austerities and privations.

Divân, a term used for the great assembly of dignitaries of state.

Dragoman (by the Turks called *Terjumân*—whence the French *Truchement*), an interpreter, ranging from the Dragoman of an embassy down to a laquais-de-place or street touter.

Effendi, a title applicable especially to the civil servants of the State. It is also given to gentlemen generally, and, when used in addressing a person, is equivalent to 'Sir' from the Greek αὐθέντης, *master*). It is then *Effendim,* my lord, or monsieur.

Emir, prince; *Emir-ul-muminin,* Prince of the faithful; a title of the Sultan.

Euren, ruins.

Ferejeh, a cloak worn by ladies out of doors, entirely concealing the person.

Ferik, a general (of division) in the army, or lieutenant-general, who is a pasha.

Fetvah, a judicial decision either of the Sheikh-ul-Islâm, or of a Mufti, as interpreter of the law.

Firenk, European, Frank—adjective and noun.

Firmân, an imperial edict or order, headed by the Sultan's *tûrah* or sign-manual.

Giawur, Ang. *Giaour* (from *Gueber,* a fire-worshipper), a word of contempt, and when pronounced alone, and while a Christian is passing, means an infidel. In conversation it is employed to designate Christians in general.

Gumruk, customs' duties, custom-house.

Gumrukji, customs' officer.

Hajji, a pilgrim; one who has made the pilgrimage to Mecca.

Hammâl, a porter.

Hammallik, porterage.

Hanum, wife or lady; *Beuyük-hanum,* first wife or head of the family; married woman.

Harim—literally, sanctuary; the apartments of the women, as opposed to the *salâmlik,* those of the men; the female family; the courtyard of a mosque.

Hatti-Sherif, an imperial ordinance.

Hejra, Ang. *Hegira,* flight. The Moslem era dates from the year of the Hegira or flight of the Prophet from Mecca, A.D. 622.

Hekim, a physician; *Hekim-bashi,* the chief physician.

Helva, a sweetmeat of which the Turks are very fond, made of almonds, honey, and perfumes, and sold in the streets by men, thence called *helvajis.*

Imâm, Turkish priest, or leader in public worship; literally, he who leads or is at the head. Thus, Imâm, *par excellence*, or *Imâm-ul-Muslemîn*, the chief of the faithful, one of the Sultan's titles.

Imâret, a hospital or soup kitchen for the relief of the poor, travellers, students, &c.

Ingilíz, English, Englishman.

Islâm, the Muhammadan faith.

Jâmi', a mosque of the higher class, in which the Friday prayer is read. The imperial mosques have generally attached to each a *sheikh*, a *khatîb*, from 2 to 4 *imâms*, 12 *muezzins*, and 20 *kayims*, who are supported out of its revenues.

Juma, Friday, the Moslem Sunday.

Kâdi, a judge.

Kahveji, a coffee-bearer; the keeper of a coffee-house.

Kaïk, a light shallow boat used on the Bosphorus.

Kaïkji, a boatman.

Kaimakâm, the governor of a sub-district (*kaza*); a lieutenant-colonel in the army.

Kaptân, the commander of a ship; term applied to a European.

Kapu, a gate; *Pâsha-kapusi*, the gate of the pasha, *i.e.* the Sublime Porte, the government offices (the word used for Sublime Porte is *Bâb Âli*).

Kapuji, a chamberlain, an officer of the seraglio, a doorkeeper.

Kavâs, a private armed attendant.

Kaza, an administrative sub-district, a subdivision of a *sanjak*.

Khalíf, a title of the Sultan, meaning vicar or successor of the Prophet.

Khân, a title of the Sultan; an inn or house for travellers; sometimes a passage, court, or alley.

Khânji, the keeper of a khân.

Kharâb, ruins.

Khatîb, the person who conducts the Friday service in the mosques.

Khoja, a teacher: a common title for schoolmasters, inferior members of the Ulemas, public writers and copyists, and scholars.

Kiâtib, a writer, copyist, or secretary, particularly at the Porte; *Bash-kiâtib*, chief registrar of a court of law.

Kiâya, master, steward, lieutenant; head of a corporation of artisans. *Kiâya bey*, formerly the title of the minister of the interior, now that of the personal representative of a governor; *Kapu-kiâya*, the representative at court of each governor of a province.

Kibleh, the point to which a Moslem turns when at prayer.

Kiervan, a caravan; *Kiervan-bashi*, leader of a caravan; *Kiervan-serai* (caravanserai), an inn or khân.

Kismet, predestination, fate.

Kitâb, a book.

Kiz, girl.

Kôja, an elder; *Kôja-bashi*, the delegates of municipalities, municipal magistrates; head of a village.

Konak, a town-house, as opposed to *yali*, a country house; the house of the governor; a halt, station, or post.

Kuleh, a tower, villa.

Kurban-bairâm, the feast of sacrifices, celebrated by rejoicings, processions, and illuminations.

Kur'ân, knowledge, commonly written Koran: a book written by Muhammad, which his followers claim to contain a Divine Revelation.

Líra, a Turkish pound.

Mangal, a copper brazier or charcoal pan.

Medreseh, a college, attached chiefly to the great mosques.

Meidan, an open square or piece of ground; *At-meidan,* the ancient hippodrome, now the horse-market; *Et-meidan,* the provision-market; *Ok-meidan,* the archery ground.

Mejidieh, a silver coin, 20 piastres; or gold, 100 piastres; an order or decoration; so named after the late Sultan.

Mejlis, a council; *Mejlis-i-khass,* the privy council; *Mejlis-i-valai,* the council of state.

Mekteb, school in general; a primary or elementary public school.

Mesjid, a small mosque or oratory. These have neither a *sheikh* nor a *khatib* attached to them.

Mevlevi, a dancing dervish.

Mir-alai, colonel of a regiment.

Mollah, a member of that division of the Ulema whose function is the administration of justice; a judge of one of the superior courts.

Mudaiumûm, the public prosecutor in a *vilâyet.*

Mudir, the administrator of a *nâhiyeh;* a director or manager employed by a company.

Muezzin, an inferior officer of a mosque, who calls to prayer from the minaret.

Mufti, an interpreter of the law; a member of the Ulema.

Mukhtar, the head-man of a village or Quarter of a town.

Mushir, a field-marshal in the army; a privy councillor, always styled pasha.

Mussellim, a governor of a city.

Mutesarrif, the governor of a *sanjak.*

Nâhieh, a sub-division of a *kaza.*

Namaz, the Moslem prayer recited five times a day.

Nefer, a soldier.

Nishân, a decoration, medal, the *Mejidieh.*

Nizâm, the regular troops.

Oda, chamber, room, court, office, box at a theatre.

Oyhlu, son.

Osmanli, the name by which the Turks designate themselves.

Panâyir, a fair.

Pâsha (from the Persian word 'Pa-sha'—viceroy), a title of dignity, military and civil, which always follows the name; the viceroy or governor of a province.

Posta, letter post-office.

Râki, an ardent spirit; a liqueur.

Ramazân, the ninth month of the Turkish year, in which falls the fast of 28 days of that name.

Râyah, a non-Mussulman subject of the Sultan.

Bedif, the reserve, into which Turkish soldiers are enrolled aft--
Turkey.

five years' active service.   It forms a second army when called out occasionally, and corresponds to the *Landwehr* of Germany.

Reis, president ; chief; captain of a ship.

Rûm, a Greek.

Rumili, Rumelia, the name by which the Turks designate their European territories, as distinguished from their Asiatic.

Sakka, a water-carrier.

Sanjak (lit. flag), an administrative district, a subdivision of a *vilâyet ; Sanjak-i-sherîf,* the imperial standard.

Sarrâf, a money-changer ; a banker.

Selâm, health ; a salutation; compliments.

Selamlik, a saloon ; the apartments of the men, as distinguished from the *harîm.*

Shekerji, a seller of sweetmeats.

Stambûl or *Istambol,* Constantinople; *Stambûl-Kâdisi,* the chief judge, and *Stambûl-effendi,* the chief of the police at Constantinople.

Sunneh, tradition, the highest religious authority after the Koran ; *Sunnis* or *Sunnites,* the orthodox, as distinguished from the sectarian (*Shias, Shiites*) followers of Ali.

Tandûr, the Turkish and Levantine substitute for a fireplace, consisting of a wooden frame in which is a copper vessel full of charcoal.

Tanzimât, the reformed system of government introduced by Sultan Mahmûd.

Tatar, a courier.

Tekkeh, a Muhammadan monastery.

Tezkereh, a passport, note.

Türbeh, a tomb, mausoleum.

Türk, a rustic or clown; hence the Turks never use this word to designate themselves, but apply it to the Turkomans and other tribes of Central Asia. (*See* Osmanli.)

Ulema, a hierarchical body, at the head of which is the Sheikh-ul-Islâm.   It comprises within it all the judges (*mollahs, kâdis, nâyibs*), the interpreters of the law (*muftis*), and some functionaries of public worship (*sheikhs* and *khatîbs*).

Vakuf, property consecrated to the mosques, or to institutions of piety and benevolence.

Vapor, steamboat ; *Kara vapor,* locomotive engine.

Vilâyet, a province of the empire governed by a *Vâli.*   Each is divided for administrative and fiscal purposes into *livas* or *sanjaks,* which are again subdivided into *kazas.*

Virane, ruins.

Yali, a summer residence or camping-ground, a country house.

Yashmak, a veil of white muslin worn by Turkish ladies which fastens under the chin.   It entirely conceals the features, and leaves an opening for the eyes.

Yuruk, a nomad of Asia Minor.

Yüz-bashi, a captain in the army.

Zabtieh, policeman.

Zâdeh, son.

SECTION I.

CONSTANTINOPLE, THE BOSPORUS, BRUSA, THE HELLESPONT.

CONSTANTINOPLE.

HISTORICAL SKETCH.

In the year B.C. 658 a band of Greeks from Megara settled on the promontory over which are now spread the buildings and gardens of the *Seraglio*, and called their new home BYZANTIUM. According to tradition the site was indicated to the colonists by the oracle of Apollo at Delphi, which bid them establish themselves opposite to " the land of the blind "—in allusion to the blindness of the Megarians who, a few years previously, had settled at Chalcedon, *Kadi Keui*, when they might have occupied the superior position on the European shore of the Thracian Bosporus.

Byzantium grew and throve and soon became a considerable place, whose possession or alliance was very valuable to contending Powers. Having submitted to the Persians, it recovered its independence after the defeat of Xerxes, and became a member of the Athenian confederacy, till the Athenian power was in its turn overthrown. It was the first and most important city to join the second Athenian league, B.C. 378. In B.C. 340 it was besieged by Philip of Macedon, and was only saved by the timely arrival of reinforcements which Demosthenes urged the Athenians to send to the assistance of their ally. During this memorable siege a bright light in the form of a crescent was, it is said, seen in the sky, and regarded by the Byzantines as a sign of deliverance. The *Crescent* which is found on Byzantine coins, and which was adopted by the Osmanlis as their device after the capture of Constantinople, is supposed to commemorate this portent. There is, however, some evidence that the Seljûk Turks had used the crescent long before the rise of the Osmanlis.

For the aid which the Byzantines gave Rome during the war with Antiochus and Mithridates, Byzantium was granted the rank of a free and confederate city, and the right to levy tolls on ships coming out of the Black Sea,—a right it had long exercised on its own account. In A.D. 196 it was taken by Severus after a three years' siege, and completely destroyed as a punishment for having taken the side of his rival Pescennius Niger. Severus afterwards relented, and rebuilt the city under the name of Antonina; but it never fully recovered until Constantine determined to make it the capital of the Roman Empire. The only remaining monuments earlier than the foundation of " New Rome "are the *Column of Claudius Gothicus* in the gardens of the Serai (p. 42); and, possibly, some portions of the Hippodrome.

Constantine (A.D. 306–337) surrounded his new capital, which was twice

Turkey.

the size of Byzantium, with walls; divided it into 14 Regions or Quarters; and adorned it with palaces, churches, baths, forums, statues, &c. He brought distinguished families from Rome, and allured settlers by the grant of privileges and immunities, so that the city rose at once to greatness. On the 11th May, 330, New Rome was dedicated with 40 days' festivity; and of this period there remain the Hippodrome (p. 39); the "Burnt Column" (p. 42), which marks the site of the Forum; the "Serpent Column" (p. 41) brought from Delphi; the cisterns *Yeribatan Serai* and *Bin bir derek* (p. 72); and perhaps the aqueduct (p. 71) and the baths discovered by M. Texier (p. 83).

In the following slight sketch it is only possible to notice the more important events connected with the history of the city, and the periods during which the principal buildings were erected. The city was completed by Constantius (337–361); and Valens (364–378) constructed, or repaired, the aqueduct (p. 71) which bears his name. Theodosius I., 'the Great' (378–395), erected the Obelisk (p. 41) in the Hippodrome; and his son, Arcadius (395–408), who became first Emperor of the East, laid out the Forum, in which there was a column with his statue (p. 43). Theodosius II. (408–450) built the land walls (pp. 32–36), and rebuilt or repaired the sea and harbour walls (pp. 25–32); his successor Marcian (450–457) erected the column known as the *Kiz Tash* (p. 43); and to Anastasius (491–518) are ascribed the palace of Blachernæ (p. 37), the cistern of S. Mocius (p. 72), and the great defensive wall which ran from *Silivri*, on the Sea of Marmara, to Lake Derkos on the Black Sea. After the bloody suppression (532) of the Nika rising, during which many of the finest buildings were destroyed, Justinian (527–565) adorned the city with magnificent churches and public edifices, of which there remain only the churches of S. Sophia (pp. 44–50) and SS. Sergius and Bacchus (p. 50). The aqueduct, *Muallak Kemer*, is attributed to Justinian, during whose long reign silk was introduced from China (553), and the "civil jurisprudence was digested in the immortal works of the *Code*, the *Pandects*, and the *Institutes*." Heraclius (610–641) surrounded the Blachernæ Quarter by a wall (p. 38); and this quarter of the city was further protected by the walls (pp. 37, 38) built by Leo the Armenian (813–820) and Manuel I., Comnenus (1143–80), who also enlarged the Blachernæ Palace. The land, sea, and harbour walls were thoroughly restored by Theophilus (829–842), and further repairs were executed by Michael III. (842–867), Basil I. (867–886), Basil II. (976–1025), and other Emperors. The Hebdomon Palace (p. 36) was built by Constantine VII., Perphyrogenitus (913–949), during whose reign the column in the Hippodrome, known as 'the Colossus,' was restored. During the time of the Comneni, 11th and 12th centuries, numerous churches were built; and the water supply was greatly improved by Andronicus I., Comnenus (1183–1185), who constructed the large reservoirs in the forest of Belgråd (p. 98).

The history of Constantinople is almost a record of its sieges; it was threatened by the Huns in the reign of Theodosius II., and by the Huns and Sclavs in that of Justinian. For ten years, 616–626, a Persian camp was maintained at Skutari in face of the capital; and in 626 an unsuccessful attack was made on it by the Persians and Avars. In 668 the Arabs first appeared before its walls and attacked it seven times, once every year (668–674); a second invasion, under Moslemah in 717, was defeated largely through the use of *Greek fire;* and a third was led by Harûn er Rashíd, who made peace (782) with Constantine and Irene. In 813 the city was besieged by Krum, prince of the Bulgarians, and on four occasions, 865, 904, 941 and 1043, it had to withstand the attacks of the Russians. During the winter of 1096–97, the Crusaders, under Godfrey de Bouillon, halted several months at Constantinople; in 1147, Conrad III., Emperor of Germany, and Louis VII. of France, passed through the city on the occasion of the second Crusade.

At the end of the 12th century the Byzantine Empire was hurrying rapidly to its end; the Seljûk power was rapidly rising in Asia Minor; the islands and coasts of the Ægean were harried by Norman and Saracenic corsairs; and the European provinces were the scene of constant disorder. The Byzantine armies were composed of foreign mercenaries, the military nobles of the West were encouraged to take service at the Byzantine Court; the merchants from Amalfi, Pisa, Genoa, and Venice were granted various privileges and immunities; and the Empire was covered by a network of Italian factories. The Frank population of Galata alone is said to have been more than 60,000. In 1203, the fourth Crusade, at the instance of the Venetians, turned aside from its object to replace Isaac II. on the throne; and on the 17th July of that year the Crusaders, led by the blind Doge, Dandolo, took Constantinople by assault. Shortly afterwards, a terrible fire, originating in a drinking bout of some Flemish soldiers, destroyed the richest quarter of the city, and many priceless works of art and ancient manuscripts perished in the flames. In 1204, the Latins drove out the Byzantine Emperor, and set up a Frank in his place. They sacked the city, and wrought more ruin in a few days than all previous enemies had done in as many centuries. The Imperial palaces were robbed of their treasures, the churches and tombs of the Emperors were plundered and destroyed, the bronze statues that adorned the Hippodrome and public places were melted down and coined into money, and the celebrated bronze horses of Lysippus were carried off as a trophy to Venice.

The Latin Empire lasted until 1261, when Constantinople was taken by the general of Michael Palæologus, who was then reigning over the Greek Empire of Nicæa. The Byzantine Empire was re-established, but it was too weak to resist the rising power of the Turks, who besieged the city in 1398 and 1422, and finally stormed the walls on the 29th May, 1453, when Constantine XI., the last of the Emperors of the East, perished on the breach.

Constantinople now became the capital of the Osmanli Empire, and, from having been for centuries the object, became the starting-point of invasion. The conqueror, Muhammad II., re-peopled the city by gathering immigrants from all quarters, put an end to the independence of the Genoese in Galata, proclaimed himself Protector of the Greek Church, nominated a new Patriarch, and granted a Charter which secured to the Greeks freedom in the exercise of their religion, Patriarchal jurisdiction in ecclesiastical affairs, and many privileges which they still enjoy. The embellishment of his new capital also occupied his attention; the most skilful artists and workmen were collected from all parts of the empire, and mosques, minarets, fountains, and tombs arose in every quarter of the city. S. Sophia and other churches were turned into mosques, and amongst the buildings erected were the Mosque of Muhammad II., on the site of the

Church of the Holy Apostles, afterwards rebuilt by Mustafa III. (p. 62), the Chinili Kiosk (p. 69), part of the Serai, the " Seven Towers " (p. 39), and the Mosque of Êyûb (p. 21). Bayezid II. (1481–1512) built the beautiful mosque (p. 63) that bears his name, but the best building period of the Ottoman Turks was the reign of Suleiman I., the Magnificent (1520–1566). The Mosques Suleimaniyeh, Selimiyeh, Shah-zadeh, Rustem Pasha, Mihri-mah, Piâle Pasha, Atik Ali Pasha, &c., and the throne room in the Serai, attest the skill of Sinan and the other architects employed. Suleiman also repaired the water conduits, and improved the water supply. During the reign of Ahmed I. (1603–1617), the Mosques Ahmediyeh and Yeni Valideh Sultan (pp. 61, 64), were built, and Murad IV. (1622–1640) built the charming Baghdad Kiosk in the gardens of the Serai. With the defeat of Kara Mustafa before the walls of Vienna (1683), a new era commenced. Constantinople again became the special mark for ambition or revenge, the power of the Ottoman Empire rapidly declined, and, with the exception of the fountains of Ahmed III., and the great reservoirs and aqueducts of Mahmûd I., no important works or buildings were erected until the re-naissance under Sultàn Abdul Mejid in the present century.

In 1770 Constantinople was menaced by a Russian fleet in the Medi-terranean; and in 1774 Sultan Abdul Hamid I. set his seal to the disastrous Treaty of Kainarji in the palace of Ainali Kavak, which was demolished by Mahmûd II. An English fleet, under Admiral Duckworth, appeared before the city in 1807 and threatened bombardment, but was eventually obliged to withdraw. The same year Selim III. was dethroned by the Janissaries; and in 1808 the Serai was attacked and taken by Mustafa Bairakdar, Selim III. was murdered, Mustafa IV. was deposed and put to death, and Mahmûd II., "the Reformer," was seated upon the throne. Other events connected with the capital are: The massacre of the Greek residents during the Greek insurrection (1821); the destruction of the Janissaries in the Et Meidan (1826); the landing of Russian troops at the mouth of the Bosporus to protect the city against Muhammad Ali, and the signature of the Treaty of Hunkiar Iskelesi (p. 103) in 1833; the signature of the Hatti Sherif of Gûl-Khâneh (p. 66) on the accession of Abdul Mejid (1839); the arrival of the British and French armies during the Crimean War (1854); the construction of the outer bridge, and the building of the Dolmabaghcheh Palace by Abdul Mejid (1839–1861); the building of the palace of Cheragan and of the Mosques Yeni Valideh Sultan at Stambûl and Orta-keui during the reign of Abdul Aziz (1861–76); the great fires at Stambûl (1865) and Pera (1870); the opening of the railway to Adrianople (1873); the series of events that led to the deposition and death of Abdul Aziz, the deposition of Murad V., and the accession of Sultan Abdul Hamid II. in 1876; the opening of the first Turkish Parliament at Dolmabaghcheh (1877); the advance of the Russians to San Stefano and signature of the treaty (1878); the unsuccessful attempt of Ali Suavi to replace Murad V. on the throne (1878); and the opening of direct railway communication with Western Europe (1888).

Under the Emperors of the East, Constantinople preserved the treasures of ancient thought and learning whilst the rest of Europe was plunged in barbarism, and became the greatest commercial city in the world. She sent out missionaries who gave to the Sclavs their alphabets, and imparted to them some rudiments of civilisation, and most of the Greek manuscripts

we possess were at one time stored in her libraries. The causes
the theological and political stagnation of her people whilst a spirit
was awakening in the West cannot be considered here. During
of the city by the Latins all commerce was transferred to th
Italy; and the establishment of Greek artists in Italy led to t
development of the formative arts in the 13th century. The capt
Turks scattered Greek learning among the Latin and Teutonic r
Greek manuscripts of the Bible conveyed to Western Europe
of the principal causes of the revival of learning. (Canon
Encyc. Brit.)

CONSTANTINOPLE.

§ 1.—SITUATION AND LOCAL GOVERNMENT.

Constantinople, the capital of Turkey, is situated at the jui
the Bosporus and the Sea of Marmara, in 41° 0' 16" N. :
28° 59' 14" E. Long. It stands upon two continents, and is ma
three towns, which are separated from each other by arms of the
Europe are Stambûl and Pera-Galata, divided by the inlet of th
Horn; and in *Asia* is Skutari clinging to the slopes of Bulgurlu.
conquest by the Turks it has been the residence of the Sultan
seat of Government, religious and secular; the home of the £
Islâm, of the Greek and Armenian Patriarchs, and of the Chief
the Jews who respectively represent the communities of which
the spiritual chiefs.

The capital, with its environs, constitutes a *Vilâyet*, which i
into 10 *Cercles Municipaux* and 6 *Kazas*. The affairs of the vi
administered by a *Préfet*, who is assisted by a Council (*Mejli*
large clerical and official staff. Each Cercle Municipal is div

several Quarters (*Mahalleh*), and has at its head a *Director.* The Kazas are administered by *Kaimakams,* and each is subdivided into two or more *Nahiehs,* which are governed by *Mudirs.*

The *Cercles Municipaux* are :—1. Sultan Bayezid; 2. Sultan Muhammad; 3. Jerah Pasha (Psamatia), in Stambûl; 4. Beshiktash; 5. Yenikeui; 6. Pera; 7. Buyukdereh, on the European side of the Bosporus; and, 8. Anadoli Hissar; 9. Skutari; 10. Kadi Keui, on the Asiatic side. The *Kazas* are :—Princes' Islands, and districts near the city in Asia and Europe.

§ 2.—POPULATION.

Constantinople is " a city not of one nation but of many, and hardly more of one than of another. You cannot talk of Constantinopolitans as you talk of Londoners or Parisians, for there are none—that is to say, there is no people who can be described as being *par excellence* the people of the city, with a common character or habits or language" (*Bryce*). Nobody knows exactly the number of the population or the proportion which its various elements bear to one another; but it has been estimated that the inhabitants of the city are not less than 873,565, and that amongst them are representatives of nearly every nation of the globe. Except the Pashas and the various officials and hangers on upon the government, the Moslems are mostly poor people, and many of them are very lazy. "Plenty of them are ecclesiastics of some kind or other, and get their lodging and a little food at the mosques; plenty are mere beggars. The great bulk are ignorant and fanatical, dangerous when roused by their priests, though honest enough fellows when left alone, and in some ways more likeable than the Christians." The richer folk, for the most part, wear cloth coats and trousers, and the red fez; the poorer Turks retain the native dress and are remarkable for their sobriety. In the khâns and bazârs of Stambûl may be found men from nearly every part of Asia, who offer a most interesting ethnographical study. The Stambûli Turks have little, if any, Turkoman blood in them; they are "a mixture of all sorts of European and Asiatic peoples who have been converted to Islâm, and recruited (down till recent times) by the constant kidnapping of Christian children and the import of slaves from all quarters."

The Turkish Christians, Greeks, Armenians, and Bulgarians have little in common, for each cherishes its own form of faith, and they hate one another nearly as cordially as they all hate the Turks. Many members of each community are wealthy, highly educated, and admirable men of business; but a large proportion are as poor as their Moslem neighbours. Besides these natives there is a motley crowd of strangers from the rest of Europe. Eight or nine languages are constantly spoken in the streets, and five or six appear on the shop-fronts. The best place to realise this strange mixture of nationalities is on the outer bridge (p. 14), over which passes an endless crowd of every dress, tongue, and religion. These races have nothing to unite them; no relations, except those of trade, with one another; everybody lives in a perpetual vague dread of everybody else;

there is no common civic feeling and no common patriotism. The numbers according to religious beliefs are said to be :—

Moslems	384,910
Greeks	152,741
Greek Latins	1,082
Armenians	149,590
Roman Catholics (native) . . .	6,442
Protestants (native)	819
Bulgars	4,377
Jews	44,361
Foreigners	129,243
Total . .	873,565

§ 3.—CLIMATE.

The **climate** of Constantinople is healthy, owing to the fine position of the city, its natural drainage, and the currents of the Bosporus; but it is subject, in winter, to great changes. During the most severe winters there are many warm sunny days, and the changes from blighting cold to almost summer heat are often sudden and unexpected. This renders the climate for six months in the year very trying to delicate constitutions, and especially to persons suffering from pulmonary affections. Travellers in search of a mild climate should avoid Constantinople in winter, late autumn, and early spring. The fine weather period, from 1st May to 30th September, is generally dry and healthy, and the temperature more equitable. The climate is greatly affected by the vicinity of the Black Sea and the Sea of Marmara; the winds from the former are cold and charged with moisture, while those from the latter diffuse a soft and genial atmosphere. The difference of temperature between Constantinople and the upper Bosporus is sometimes very great, especially in spring; and the variable weather renders precaution necessary on the part of strangers. The temperature is low in December, January, February, March, and April, and high in July and August. Heavy snow sometimes falls in the winter; and occasionally the frosts are severe and prolonged. In the winter of 1879–80 there were 63 nights with frost. Observations at Constantinople and Skutari for a period of 20 years give the following results :—

	Constantinople.	Skutari.
Mean temperature . .	57° 7′	58° 4′
Maximum temperature .	99° 1′	103° 6′
Minimum temperature .	17° 2′	13° 0′
Rain	28·3 in.	29·29 in.
Number of rainy days .	112	128·6

Most of the rain falls between the 1st November and 31st March. Travellers should lead a regular life, wear warm clothing in winter, and take ordinary precautions against a chill, especially after over-heating themselves.

§ 4.—GENERAL DESCRIPTION.

There is no lovelier scene on earth than that which opens up before the traveller as he approaches Constantinople from the Sea of Marmara. Nowhere else is there a picture so bright, so varied in outline, so rich in colour, so gorgeous in architecture. On the left, washed by the waves, the quaint old battlements extend from Seraglio point to the Seven Towers, a distance of nearly five miles; and over them rise in picturesque confusion the terraced roofs, domes, and minarets of Stambûl. To the right the white mansions, cemeteries, and cypress groves of Skutari run away along the Asiatic shore eastward far as the eye can see. In the centre is the opening of the Bosporus, revealing a vista of matchless beauty, like one of the gorgeous pictures of Turner. The steamer glides on, sweeps rapidly round the Seraglio point, and drops anchor in the Golden Horn. The view here is grander still, and more intensely interesting. On the S. rise in succession from the still waters of the inlet, the seven low hills of the ancient city, crowned with domes and tapering minarets, and buttresses, with fantastic houses, and shattered walls—walls all broken now, but which in the age of archers and Greek fire so often baffled those who ventured to attack them.

On the northern bank of the long "Horn," above the crowded buildings and Genoese tower of Old Galata, appear the heights of Pera, gay and fresh with the residences of European ambassadors. Facing the city and the mouth of the Golden Horn, on the Asiatic shore, lies Skutari, with its bright houses and monuments, and clusters of dark cypresses; and near it Kadi Keui, once known to fame as Chalcedon. Looking northwards past the splendid portals of Dolmabâgh-cheh, and the graceful minarets of its adjoining mosques, one sees a long reach of the Bosporus, all aglow with Imperial palaces and kiosks, and villas, and terraced gardens.

Nor is the scene less gay and animated on water than on land. Huge ironclads, flying the red flag and crescent, lie at anchor within a cable-length of the shore; passenger steamers from every country in Europe are ranged in double rows opposite the quays of Top-khâ-neh, the chief artillery store of Turkey; corn-ships from Odessa or the Danube lie side by side with graceful Greek feluccas and Turkish coasters; while hundreds of kaïks, gay and swift as dragon-flies, flit hither and thither over rippling waters of the deepest blue. There is no scene in the world like that around one in the Golden Horn.

Constantinople is made up of three cities, each of which is in many respects entirely distinct from the others. Stambûl, the old city, occupies the site of the capital of the Greek Empire, on a tongue of land having the Sea of Marmara on the south, the Bosporus on its eastern apex, and the Golden Horn on the north. It is about 13 miles in circuit, triangular in form, and the wall on the land side is 4 miles long. The Golden Horn is a deep inlet, half-a-mile wide where it joins the Bosporus, and gradually narrowing as it curves up towards the Sweet Waters some 6 miles distant. On its northern side, along the steep slopes, and over the summits of low rounded hills, are spread the suburbs of Galata, Pera, and Top-khâneh. On the eastern side of the Bosporus, one mile from Stambûl and the same from Top-khâneh, is the Asiatic quarter of Constantinople— Skutari.

Galata is the business quarter for European merchants. It lies close along the harbour at the foot of a steep hill. It has one long winding street running parallel to the Golden Horn, and off it open innumerable alleys, passages, and lanes, which in dirt and wretchedness surpass the vorst parts of Stambûl. **Top-khâneh** is a continuation of Galata, extending along the shore to the Bosporus, and away beyond toward the magnificent palace of Dolmabâghcheh. It takes its name from the *Top-khâneh* or "cannon-foundry" established here. The landing-place for travellers passing the custom-house is in this quarter.

On the summit of the ridge above Galata and Top-khâneh is the suburb of **Pera**, which is studded all over with the splendid mansions of European ambassadors, intermixed with new gardens, old cemeteries, and sombre cypress groves. Several spacious barracks and a number of large private mansions have been built on the sides and summit of the ridge farther north, commanding magnificent views of the Bosporus and Sea of Marmara. This, in fact, is the aristocratic part of Constantinople, and by far the most beautiful. The palaces and gardens of the Sultan, with the adjoining mosques, line the shore, and the heights behind them are finely wooded. New roads have been made in several directions, so that one can visit the chief points of interest in a carriage. There is also a carriage-road from the palace of Dolmabâghcheh over the hills to the Sweet Waters.

The principal *hotels*—indeed all the hotels frequented by European travellers—are in Pera, and most of them in the Grande Rue. The situation is high and good; but the approach to them on foot from the Golden Horn is disagreeable, being through narrow, steep, dirty lanes. Of late great improvements have been effected, so that the hotels are rendered easy of access even for ladies. A carriage-road, somewhat steep, has been made from the main street of Galata to the Grande Rue of Pera, so that one can drive from the hotels to all parts of the city, including the principal mosques and places of interest in Stambûl. There is also a short funicular railway from Galata to Pera; the station in Galata is near the end of the outer bridge, and that in Pera is close to the Grande Rue. Trains run every few minutes; the carriages are drawn up the steep incline by a steel cable. The tramway from Chichli to Galata passes through Pera.

Fires in Constantinople are of frequent occurrence and often very destructive, desolating whole quarters of the city. Great precautions are now taken both to prevent them, and to check their progress. Arrangements are made to give the earliest possible notice to all parts of the city when and where a fire has broken out. For this purpose watchmen are stationed day and night on three commanding spots—the Galata tower, in Galata; the Serasker tower, in Stambûl; and the high hill below Kandili, on the Asiatic side of the Bosporus. Cannon are fired from the last-mentioned place to announce that a fire has broken out. A red balloon, lighted within, is raised at the same time to the top of a mast; at the Serasker Tower, balls, and at Galata Tower flags are hoisted, showing by their number in what quarter the fire is. At these two posts there are firemen waiting, fast runners, who, the moment the fire is discovered, run to their different quarters to inform the regular watch, setting up the cry of fire, and the quarter where it has occurred. The fire-engines are in the hands of firemen who are paid by enjoying some special privileges; but the engines are small boxes, which are carried on the shoulders of four men; these run headlong, crying, *Yangin Var,* "fire!" at the top of their voices. Having reached the place of conflagration, they wait to be hired by people whose houses are in danger. There is another set of firemen who prove eminently useful on such occasions. They are soldiers armed with axes and long poles, with iron hooks at the end. These tear down the wooden houses, and so isolate the fire, as effectually to put an end to its ravages. Still, a fire in Constantinople is an awful scene; 2000 houses and shops have been known to burn in the space of a few hours. It is indeed impossible to describe the confusion and horror of the sight. Men, women, and children escaping from their abandoned homes, each dragging or carrying upon his shoulder whatever he happened to catch at the moment. The police are powerless for good. Evil-intentioned men rush into the houses and rob them, under the pretence of being friends of the family. They have often been known to spread the conflagration by carrying burning coals into dwellings yet unreached by the flames. There is no doubt, however, that the narrowness of the streets, and the light inflammable materials of the houses, are the chief causes of these calamities; and it is a source of satisfaction to find that the streets are now widened after every fire, and that many stone houses are erected in the place of the former wooden buildings. There is now a fire brigade, *itfai alai*, organised on a European model by Count Szecheny. It consists of 3 battalions of firemen, 2 at the Taksim Barracks, and 1 at the Seraskerat. It is well managed and has done good service during the last 10 or 12 years.

In the month of *Ramazân* (the Muhammadan Lent) the daily round of Turkish life is reversed. Between dawn and dusk eating, drinking, and smoking are strictly prohibited. Everyone eats, drinks, and pays visits by night; and those who can afford to do so spend half the day in bed. When the fast occurs in summer the labouring classes, who have to work during the daytime, suffer extremely from exhaustion and thirst. The moment of sunset—the signal for the *iftár*, or breaking of the fast—is eagerly looked for by everyone; it is announced by the firing of cannon. It might be imagined that the first act of the hungry and thirsty would be to eat and to drink; but numbers of Turks may be seen, cigarette in hand, or their pipes filled, and the fire to light them, ready, awaiting the welcome signal, every other gratification being postponed for that of inhaling the fragrant weed. The night is passed

in devotional forms and revelry. All the mosques are open, and all the coffee-houses and shows—*Kara-ghioz* and others; the two last are crowded with Turks, smoking, drinking coffee, and listening to singers and storytellers. The minarets are illuminated, and the streets are crowded with the faithful. The 27th night of this month is celebrated with peculiar pomp by the officials of the capital, and large sums of money are spent by the Government every year to render the occasion one of peculiar interest. It is called *Leilet-el-Kadr*, the "night of power," *Kadr geyjesi*, because on this night, as Moslems believe, the Divine Decrees for the ensuing year are annually settled and fixed, and taken from the *preserved table* by God's throne, and given to the angels to be executed. On this night Muhammad received his first revelations; when the Kurân, say the commentators, was sent down from the aforesaid table, entire and in one volume, to the lowest heaven, from whence Gabriel revealed it to Muhammad by parcels, as occasion required. The celebration chiefly consists in magnificent illuminations, whose focus is on the great wharf of Top-khâneh; they, however, extend over the whole city, and on both banks of the Bosporus and the Golden Horn; and many war vessels are brought out of the Arsenal, and rafts are anchored in the stream, whence fireworks are displayed. After a reception at the palace, the Sultan formerly went in his state barge to the Mosque of S. Sophia, afterwards to Top-khâneh, whence he viewed the great display of pyrotechnic art. The best view is obtained from the water, but the traveller should by no means occupy a kaïk, which runs great risk of foundering among the large boats that are rapidly moving to and fro in the dark; a strong boat is alone safe, such as lie between the Top-khâneh landing and the new bridge.

The *Bairâm*, which succeeds the *Ramazân*, presents three days of unmixed festivity. Every Turk who can afford it appears in a new dress;

visits are exchanged, and parties are made up to the favourite spots in the vicinity. On the first day at sunrise the Sultan receives all the ministers of state, the principal civil and military officers of the Empire, the Sheikh-ul-Islâm, the Kazi-askers, and the members of the Magistrature. The ceremony, which is conducted with great pomp, is highly picturesque, and is a sight to be seen. A similar ceremony takes place, seventy days afterwards, on the first day of *Kurban Bairâm* (feast of sacrifice). This festival lasts four days, during which sheep and oxen are sacrificed, and there is general festivity. The two Bairams are kept as a universal holiday, the shops are shut, and business is everywhere abandoned for pleasure.

§ 5.—How to see Constantinople.

Constantinople has three great attractions—historic interest, beauty of position, and diversity of population. A thorough examination of the **Old Walls**, the **Byzantine Churches**, the **Seraglio**, the **Hippodrome**, the **Cisterns**, the **Mosques**, the **Bazârs**, the **Tombs**, and the **Cemeteries**, including the English cemetery at Skutari, where so many British soldiers lie buried, would occupy from 2 to 3 weeks. But for travellers who are pressed for time the following programmes are recommended.

Three days.—*First day.* Galata Tower, **Seraglio** Grounds, Museum of Antiquities, S. Sophia, Yeri Batan Serai, Hippodrome, Mosque of Sultan Ahmed, Cistern of 1001 Columns, Tomb of Sultan Mahmûd II., the Column of Constantine, the Mosque of Sultan Bayezid, the Seraskerat Square, and the Mosque of Sultan Suleiman. *2nd day.* Bazârs in morning; Bosporus in afternoon. *3rd day.* The old Walls, Eyûb, and the Sweet Waters. If one of the days be Friday, time should be found to see the

Sultan going to mosque, and the whirling dervîshes.

Six days.—*Monday.* Galata Tower, Seraglio Grounds, Museum of Antiquities, S. Irene, Fountain of Sultan Ahmed, S. Sophia, Yeri Batan Serai, Tomb of Sultan Mahmûd II., Column of Constantine, Cistern of 1001 Columns, Hippodrome, Mosque of Sultan Ahmed, Museum of Ancient Costumes, Palace of Justinian, SS. Sergius and Bacchus, Armenian Patriarchate and Church. Return from Kûm Kapu, or Yeni Kapu, by rail, or by water along the foot of the sea-walls. *Tuesday.* In the morning the Bazârs; in the afternoon the Bosporus and Robert College. *Wednesday.* The Walls, visiting *en route* Vlanga Bostan, Mir-Akhor Jamisi, Yedi Kuleh, Golden Gate, Balukli, Kahriyeh Jami', Hebdomon Palace, Eyûb. Return by steamer or kaïk to Galata. *Thursday.* English Cemetery, *viâ* Kadi Keui, or Haidar Pasha, Howling Dervîshes, Bûlgurlû, American College for girls. Return from Skutari steamer landing-stage. *Friday.* Selamlik (Sultan's visit to mosque), Whirling Dervîshes, Large Cemetery Pera, Sweet Waters (in spring). *Saturday.* American Bible House, Mosque of Sultan Bayezid, Tower of Seraskerat, Mosque of Sultan Suleiman, Aqueduct of Valens, Mosque of Sultan Muhammad II., Column of Marcian, open cistern near the Mosque of Sultan Selim, Phanar, Eski Imâret Mesjidi, Zeirek Kilisse Jami'. Return by inner bridge.

§ 6.—General Hints to Visitors.

Everyone should ascend the **Genoese Tower** at **Galata** for the sake of the view. The panorama from the **Seraskerat Tower** in **Stambûl** is more extended, but the ascent is fatiguing.

Every *Friday* the Sultan goes to one of the mosques in state, attended by dignitaries and a body of troops. This ceremony is called the **Selamlik**. The mosque selected is known about

10 A.M., and His Majesty usually sets out about 12. The square in front of the mosque is lined with troops, and a brilliant effect is produced by the great variety of the uniforms and costumes worn by the naval and military officers, and by the higher court, civil, and religious officials. The mosque usually selected is the *Mejidieh Jami'*, to the l. of the road from Beshiktash to Orta-keui, and near the Palace of Cheragan; or the *Hamidieh*, near Yildiz Kiosk. There is always a large crowd, but visitors, accompanied by a kavâs from the Embassy or Consulate, can generally obtain a good position for seeing the pageant at the Guard House (*Kullûk*). Formerly, when the procession went by water, it was a beautiful sight. The Sultan's kaïk, 100 ft. long, white and gold, of elegant form, at the stern of which he sat under a canopy, flew through the water manned by twenty-six rowers, picked men. His suite and pashas followed in other kaïks. Salutes were fired from ships and batteries as soon as the procession started.

The devotional exercises of the **Dancing Dervîshes** are held on *Tuesday* and on *Friday*, after the Sultan returns from the mosque. Those of the **Howling Dervîshes** may be witnessed at Skutari every *Thursday*, and at Kassim Pasha every *Sunday*, between 1 and 2 P.M.

In the *spring* the **Sweet Waters of Europe** is a favourite resort of the Moslem upper classes on a *Friday* afternoon. The shortest way to this valley is by road; the pleasantest is by kaïk from the Inner Bridge, up the Golden Horn. In the *summer* months the Moslem ladies make the **Sweet Waters of Asia** their *Friday* afternoon resort. The spot where they gather is within a few minutes' walk of Kandili, where the Bosporus steamers call. It may also be reached by kaïk.

The **bazârs** (p. 74) ought to be visited on the earlier days of the week,

since on Friday the Turks close, on Saturday the Jews, and on Sunday the Christians.

The **ceremonies** of the **Greek Church** at *Easter* are worth seeing, especially the midnight service on Easter-eve, in the Patriarchal Church at Phanar.

The **festival** of **Our Lady** at Balukli on *Friday* in *Easter week* (old style) is of special interest.

The **Seraglio**, the **Treasury**, and the **Imperial Palaces** can only be visited by an order obtained through an Embassy. *Admission* to the principal **mosques**, P. 10 each person. *Overshoes* should be worn, and taken off at the doors; or large *slippers*, sometimes kept at the mosques, should be put over the boots on entering. Mosques should not be visited on Fridays or during the hours of prayer.

Passports should always be carried on the person, as they are sometimes demanded by the police. *Strangers* should not go out at night unattended; and in any difficulty with the police reference should at once be made to the Consulate.

Tourists on arriving in the East sometimes wear a **fez**. This is a very unwise thing to do, as by donning the native head-gear the traveller, *ipso facto* loses his foreign prestige.

Turkish Festivals. The **Bairam receptions** of the Sultan take place at sunrise in the great hall of the *Palace* of *Dolmabâghcheh*. Strangers are admitted to the gallery by card, obtained through the Embassy from the Grand Master of the Ceremonies. During the month of **Ramazân** the *evening prayer* in the Mosque of S. Sophia, especially on a *Friday*, is an imposing sight. The galleries of the mosque are accessible to strangers on payment of a small fee. On leaving the mosque the tourist will find a stroll through the adjacent quarters interesting; the Turks are enjoying themselves after their day of fasting; they have taken their evening meal at sundown, have attended mosque, and are now thronging the coffee-houses and the shows—*Kara-ghioz* and others—which are open all night.

The procession of the **Sureh-Emineh** —the despatch of the Sultan's gifts to the Grand Sherîf of Mecca—takes place early in the month of *Shaban*, which precedes that of Ramazân. It has lost much of its former Oriental stateliness, but is still worth a drive to the heights of Yildiz. The *Hirka-i-Sherîf*, the *Kadr Geyjesi*, the *Mevlûd*, the *Mirâj Geyjesi*, and the *Leilet-ul-Regel*, give occasion for illuminating the mosques, and the spectacle of the towering minarets with their garlands of lamps is singularly beautiful.

The **birthday** and anniversary of the **accession of the Sultan** are both celebrated by general illumination and by exhibitions of fireworks, furnished by the Ordnance Department, which are fired from rafts at different points on the Bosporus. On these occasions the greatest display is at the *Palace* of *Yildiz*, but in the summer, when the upper classes are *en villégiature*, the best effects are to be seen on the Bosporus, which is illuminated almost without a break from *Dolmabâghcheh* to *Yeni Mahalle*, the illuminations extending from the water's edge far up to the wooded slopes on either side.

On the 10th **Muharrem** the Persians at Constantinople commemorate the *martyrdom of Hussein*, the son of Ali. The ceremony takes place in the court of the *Valideh Khân*, and commences soon after sunset. In the lurid glare of numberless torches pass by the mourners beating their breasts, or chaunting Persian dirges; the white-robed martyrs; the white horse of Hussein with its blood-spattered saddle, to which is attached a white dove, emblematic of the martyr's pure soul; and the fanatics who, after the manner of the priests of Baal, shout and cut themselves until the blood runs down and stains their white shirts a crimson hue. It is a strange,

weird spectacle, not to be witnessed by those who have weak nerves, o dread heat and a crush. A specia enclosure is reserved for the Persiar Ambassador, who represents the Shah. Visitors are admitted anc treated with courtesy; they should gc before sunset to secure good places and avoid the crowd.

When visiting *Stambûl*, expense may be saved by taking the train (tunnel) from Pera to Galata, walking across the bridge, and hiring a carriage at the Stambûl end.

§ 7.—Police Regulations.

Police regulations in Constantinople do not differ much from those in other European cities. But the police, *zabtieh*, who are all Moslems, are wanting in knowledge and tact, and they are not always to be relied on in case of a difficulty. It is, however, easy to keep out of trouble. In the frequented parts of the city a foreigner runs no risk whatever of molestation, if his own conduct is discreet. If, however, he penetrates into the quarters inhabited exclusively by Mussulmans, he should be always accompanied by a dragoman. The children in these quarters are prone to hooting and throwing stones, and any resentment of these offences is certain to lead to difficulty. If a traveller strays into one of these quarters, the best thing to do is to make his way out of it as soon as possible. Should a traveller get into trouble, the only course to follow is to exercise the utmost patience, and on arriving at any police station, to send a note to the Consulate. But, as a rule, it may be said that travellers who abstain from eccentricities of conduct run no risk of coming into collision either with the population or the police.

§ 8.—Golden Horn and Bridges.

The promontories on which Constantinople lies are separated by the last and largest of those inlets which cut the western shore of the Bosporus. This inlet is a large and important harbour, running from E. to N.W., which has always, by reason of its form and its fulness, been called the **Golden Horn** (Gr. *Chrysokeras,* Tk. *Stambûl Limani*). It is "like a stag's horn," Strabo says, "for it is broken into wavy creeks, like so many branches, into which the fish *pelamys* (πηλαμύς) running is easily snared." In former times this fish was a source of rich revenue—ever, from time immemorial, rushing down from the Sea of Azov and the Black Sea, and, when it approaches the white rock on which stands the *Maiden's* (miscalled *Leander's*) *Tower,* glancing off it, and shooting straight into the Horn, but never enriching the rival city on the coast of Asia—Chalcedon, "the City of the Blind." (*Encyc. Brit.*) Procopius describes the inlet as being "always calm, and never crested into waves, as though a barrier were placed there to the billows, and all storms were shut out from thence, through reverence for the city," and, he adds, "the whole of it is a harbour, so that when a ship is moored there the stern rests on the sea and the bows on the land, as though the two elements contended with one another to see which of them could be of the greatest service to the city."

The *width* from Seraglio Point, the ancient *Keras,* to Top-khâneh, the ancient *Metopon,* is about 1000 yds., and thence the Golden Horn curls up in a course of little more than 4 m. to the foot of the hills, where it receives the waters of two streams, the *Cydaris* and *Barbysus* of the ancients—the two whelps of the oracle. The first stream, *Ali Bey Su,* has its source near the vill. of Pyrgos; the second, *Kiat Khâneh Su,* rises to the N. of the vill. of Belgrad, and passes out to the Horn through the *Valley of the Sweet Waters of Europe*—the favourite resort of Turkish ladies on Friday afternoons in spring. On the *S. shore of the Horn,* which has its regular outline slightly broken by

the projecting points of Phanar, Balat, Aivan Serai, and Eyûb, lie *Stambûl, Ortajilar,* and *Eyûb;* on the *N. shore,* which is indented by the spacious bay of Kassim Pasha, are *Galata, Kassim Pasha, Ainali Kavak, Haskeui, Piri Pasha, Kaliji Oghlu, Sudluje,* and *Kara Agatch.*

The harbour is capable of floating 1200 ships, and the water is so deep that men-of-war of the largest size can moor close to the shore. The only inconvenience experienced by the shipping arises from the powerful currents that flow from the W. or descend from the N. Two *iron pontoon bridges* divide the harbour into three sections:—The **Outer Port of Commerce,** in which merchantmen and steamers lie; the **Inner Port of Commerce,** between the bridges; and the **Port of War,** in which the Turkish men-of-war are moored, and on the shores of which are the **Naval Arsenal,** *Tersâne,* and the **Admiralty,** *Divân Khâneh.*

The **Inner Bridge,** *Mahmûd Keuprisi,* or *Azab Kapu K.,* occupies the position of a bridge of boats thrown across the Golden Horn, from Un Kapan to Azab Kapu, by Sultan Mahmûd II., in 1837, to facilitate communication between Stambûl and Galata and Pera. Before that date the only bridge was one on piles which, even before the Turkish conquest, connected Aivan Serai with Piri Pasha. The **Outer,** or **New Bridge,** *Valideh Sultan Keuprisi,* or *Kara-keui K.,* between the E. part of Galata and Stambûl, was constructed to take the place of a bridge of boats thrown across the Horn in 1845, by the Valideh Sultan, mother of Sultan Abd-ul-Mejid, who derived a large income from the tolls. It is situated almost in the centre of Constantinople, at the point where the traffic is largest; and the view from it, which embraces Stambûl with its lofty minarets, the Golden Horn with the heights of Eyûb beyond, Galata, Pera, the Bosporus and outer port covered with countless ships and boats, Skutari, and the Asiatic shore, is most beautiful and interesting. Even of greater interest is the scene on the bridge itself, where a motley crowd, representing nearly every nation of the East and West, is constantly passing; and soldiers, kavasses, dervîshes, water-carriers, cake-sellers, and veiled women may be seen struggling forward amidst horses, carriages, and laden animals in picturesque disarray.

On the l. of the bridge, going from Galata to Stambûl, lie portions of the old bridge of boats, which are reached by steps, and serve as *Landing Stages* for the boats plying to the Bosporus, Skutari, Kadi Keui, and Princes' Islands (*see* Index). The stages are covered with cafés, barbers', and bakers' shops, fruitsellers, &c., and on them also are the *booking offices* of the steamboat companies. The steamers that ply on the Golden Horn start from the rt. side of the bridge near Galata. A small *toll*, collected in a primitive way by men in white smocks, is levied on all foot passengers, animals, and wheeled vehicles. The annual revenue is over £T40,000.

§ 9. — GALATA—PERA—TOP-KHÂNEH —KASSIM PASHA—HASKEUI—EYÛB.

Galata, where strangers arriving by sea usually land, lies along the N. shore of the Golden Horn, and rising up to the crest of the hill includes the great tower that crowns it. It is separated from *Kassim Pasha* on the W. by a cemetery, known as the *Petits Champs des Morts,* and adjoins *Top-khâneh* on the E.; whilst to the N. and above it *Pera* stretches forward along the ridge that runs parallel to the Bosporus.

Galata—originally known as **Sykai,** *the fig-trees*—was protected in early Byzantine times by a wall, and formed the 13th ward of the city. Justinian the Great rebuilt its walls, gave it the privileges of a city, and named it **Justinianopolis.** The name **Galata,** of which the derivation is uncertain, appears in the 9th century. The suburb was also called **Pera,** from its position on the opposite side of the harbour to Constantinople. A tower, called the **Tower of Galata,** to which the northern end of the chain closing the harbour in time of war was attached, stood on the site of the *Offices of the Board of Health.* The capture of this tower, in 1203, enabled the Latin Crusaders to lower the chain and break into the harbour with their fleet. In 1267, after the restoration of the Greek Empire, the Emperor Michael Palaeologus, in return for services rendered to his cause, finally settled the Genoese, who had previously occupied a quarter in Constantinople, in Galata. The colony held of him by feudal tenure, and was practically independent, having its own laws and Government administered by a Podesta. In 1348 the question of rebuilding the walls gave rise to disputes between the colony and the metropolis, that ended in war. The Genoese were successful, and erected a double line of walls and towers that had a common point in the present **Galata Tower.** During the last siege of Constantinople the Galata Genoese assisted Muhammad II., in the hope of obtaining favourable terms and a renewal of their charter. But their hopes were disappointed; their land walls were dismantled, and, like other Christian subjects of the Sultan, they were compelled to pay the *Kharâj,* poll-tax, and appear unarmed.

Galata, though many European merchants have latterly established themselves in Stambûl, is still the principal seat of European commerce. The Head Offices of the *banks* and *steamboat agencies* are situated in it; and at the foot of the Galata Tower is gathered a cluster of *English Institutions,* **Consulate, Consular Court, Prison, Seamen's Hospital, Literary and Mechanics' Institute, Post Office,** and **Sailors' Home.** A long, narrow, dirty street, which broadens into the **Grande Rue of Galata,** and is followed by the tramway to Orta-keui, runs parallel to the sea from *Azab Kapu* to *Top-khâneh*. Here, and in the adjoining side - streets, are warehouses, small shops, cafés, and filthy lodging-houses, in which one of the most depraved populations of Europe finds a home. A steep street, **Yuksek Kaldirim**, *high pavement*, or **Step Street**, which has more than 100 steps, leads directly from Galata to Pera. The **carriage-road** between the two suburbs, with its tramway, winds up from the outer bridge and passes by the *Petits Champs* and the *Municipality House*. The **Funicular Railway** (*see* Index), which is much used, takes passengers direct to the square near the Tekkeh of the Dancing Dervîshes in Pera.

The old **city gates** of Galata have disappeared, but a few fragments of the **walls** may be seen near the *Galata Tower;* and the memory of the **ditches** is preserved in the two streets, **Hendek**, "*the ditch*," and **Lule Hendek**, N.W. and E. of the Galata Tower. Most of the solidly-built **warehouses** are of Genoese construction, and, below the Imperial Ottoman Bank, in the narrow street **Pershenbe Bazâr**, is the old **Palazzo del Podestà**, with round arches and a few remains of Byzantine ornament. The ancient churches have almost entirely disappeared. **S. Peter's**, *San Petro*, in the Pershenbe Bazâr, was founded in the 13th century, and rebuilt in 1731; it contains a *picture* of the *Virgin*, said to have been painted by St. Luke, and *relics* of *S. Catherine*. **S. George's**, *San Giorgio a Monte*, near the I. Ottoman Bank, was rebuilt on old foundations in 1677. **S. Benoit**, in the *Monastery of the Lazarists*, dates from Genoese times; it has a hospital, schools, and a printing press attached to it. The *Imperial Ottoman Bank*, formerly occupied as an old **Franciscan Monastery**, used at one time, as the *fleurs de lys* upon it indicate, as the residence of the French Embassy. The Bank has now built new premises in Tramway Street. The Greek Church of S. Nicholas was built by Greeks from the Crimea in 1475. **Yeni**, or **Sultan Valideh Jami'**, was built on the foundations, and

with the material of the **Church of San Francesco** by the mothers of Sultans Mustafa II. and Ahmed III. in 1679. **Arab Jami'** is a rectangular building, ornamented externally by pilasters, with Ionic capitals. According to some it is a Byzantine ch., but it is more probably a Genoese ch. on Byzantine foundations. It was turned into a mosque in the 17th century, and is easily recognised by its *minaret*, a square tower and spire. There is a tradition that a *mosque* was built on this site, in 717, by the Arabs when besieging Constantinople.

The **Galata Tower**, called in the Middle Ages the **Tower of Christ**, or **of the Cross**, was built in 1348, probably on the foundations of an earlier Byzantine tower ascribed to the Emp. Anastasius Dicorus; and in the present century it was repaired by Mahmûd II. The tower, which is one of the most striking features in Galata, is now used as a **fire-station**, whence the quarters of the city in which fires break out are signalled with flags by day and with lanterns by night. It is round, massively built, and about 150 ft. high. The basement is unoccupied, and the first storey, in which the watchmen live, is reached by 141 steps; here there is a large circular chamber with 14 windows, and a raised platform in front of them, on which the watchmen place seats for visitors. Forty additional steps lead to a second storey, which has a smaller circular chamber, equally pierced by 14 windows, and an external gallery, whence there is a magnificent *panorama*. On this storey there is a curious *old clock*, said to have been taken from S. Sophia. The *lantern*, which is hexagonal in form and in two sections, completes the structure.

From the Galata Tower travellers obtain the best *general view* of the city, and it should be one of the first places visited. The *panorama* may best be described by following the windows in the watch-chamber from l. to rt., commencing with that next the entrance from the steps.

1st Window.—Direction N.W. Foreground, the houses of Galata; beyond them, on the shore of the Golden Horn, the fine buildings of the **Admiralty**, *Divân Khâneh;* then, l., the **Marine Arsenal**, *Tersâne,* with the Turkish fleet anchored in front, and rt. the **Marine Hospital**, *Khasta Khâneh,* with its two-storeyed tower. The Golden Horn is partially concealed by a wooded hill, but on the further shore, at the point where it disappears, are the cypresses of the Cemetery of Eyûb, and, at the foot of the hill, the two minarets of the Mosque of Eyûb. To the l., along the shore of the Golden Horn, are the suburbs of Eyûb and Ortajilar, with the *Mosque of Sali Mahmûd Pasha;* and on the projecting spit in front of them the quarter of Aivan Serai, the *Blachernæ Quarter* of the Byzantine city. In the far distance, on the horizon, are the **Barracks** of Ramiz Chiftlik.

2nd Window.—Direction N.N.W. In the foreground the wide Rue Hendek, leading to the *Place Karakol,* behind which are the cypresses of the Petits Champs des Morts, *Kuchuk Mezâristan.* In the background is the *Valley of Kassim Pasha,* whence the white dome and tapering minarets of a mosque rise above the trees. Beyond the valley are the suburbs of *Kassim Pasha,* and the dark cypresses of a *Turkish Cemetery,* in the midst of which is the white minaret of a *tekkeh.* Further away is the bare plateau of Ok Meidan, *place of arrows,* on whose W. slope is the vill. of **Haskeui**; and then, on a higher hill, the villages of Kaliji Oghlu and Sudluje, the *Jewish Cemetery,* and, in the distance, the barren hills beyond the Valley of the Sweet Waters of Europe.

3rd Window.—Direction N. In the foreground the high chimney of the Funicular Railway, and the western portion of Pera. In the background the Quarter S. Dimitri, with the ch. of the same name, and amidst trees, in the distance to the l., the Mosque of Piâle Pasha.

4th Window.—Direction N.N.E. In the foreground the Grande Rue of Pera; to its rt. the *Tekkeh,* and gardens of the Dancing Dervishes; and, further to the rt., the Swedish Legation and Russian Embassy. Beyond and to the rt. of the Embassies the Lyceum of Galata Serai, with its courts and gardens, and in the distance the suburbs of Pankaldi and Chichli. To the l. of the Grande Rue, the flagstaff of the British Embassy, and in the distance the suburb of Feri-keui.

5th Window.—Direction N.E. In foreground the English Memorial Church, and to its rt. the Italian Hospital and Mosque of Jehanjir. In the background to the l. the Jesuit's School, the Greek Church of the Holy Trinity, with its domes and towers, and the buildings at Taksim. To the rt. of the Greek Church, the German Hospital, and beyond it the German Embassy, with the cypresses of the Grands Champs des Morts.

Turkey.

Beuyuk Mezâristan, to the l., and, in the distance, to the rt., the heights of Orta-keui.

6th Window.—Direction E.N.E. The Quarters of Yeni Charshi, Top-khâneh, and Fundukli, with the Bosporus beyond. In the foreground the Barracks of Top-khâneh, with their mosque and lead-covered cupolas; to their rt. the upper storey of the Top-khâneh, or *Ordnance House;* the *Mosque of Top-khâneh,* or Mahmûdiyeh; the Arsenal, and *Gun Factory,* with its *Esplanade,* partly covered with guns, and its *Clock Tower;* the Fountain of Top-khâneh; and the old Mosque of Kiliji Ali Pasha. Beyond the Bosporus, the Asiatic coast from Vaai-keui, with its large yellow cavalry barrack on the l., to the marble Palace of Beylerbey and Skutari on the rt.

7th Window.—Direction E.S.E. Foreground, Galata and the Bosporus. On the Asiatic side Skutari, with Mount Bûlgurlû on the l. On the shore to the l., Beuyuk Jami'; to its rt., Yeni Valdideh Jami', and further to the rt. the small white Mosque Ayazma. Half-way up the hill to the rt., in the midst of trees, Eski Valideh Jami', with two large minarets; and in front of it, in the sea, the Maiden's, or Leander's Tower. Further to the rt. the cypresses of the great Turkish Cemetery, and beyond, in the distance, the mountains that border the Gulf of Ismid.

8th Window.—Direction S.E. Foreground, Galata, with the Monastery of S. Benoit, and the square tower of the Greek Church of S. Nicholas. The outer *port of commerce* covered with ships. On the Asiatic side to the l. the large Mosque Selimiyeh, with the yellow Selimiyeh Barracks immediately to its rt., and then the Military Hospital, the pyramid in the British Cemetery, the Haidar Pasha Railway Station, and Kadi Keui, the ancient Chalcedon.

9th Window.—Direction S.S.E. On the Galata shore, the small Mosque Kermankish, with the Custom House to its l., and the Board of Health to the rt. The entrance to the Golden Horn, and on the further side Seraglio Point, on which stands a large store-house. To the rt. follow remains of the Old Wall; Odun Kapusi; the lofty Sebet-jilar Kiosk, with the yellow buildings of the Medical School behind it; and the *workshops* of the Railway Company. On the hill, above the shore-line, the Seraglio, *Serai,* and its square tower picturesquely situated amongst the trees, with the Baghdad Kiosk and Column of Claudius to the l.; and the Chinili Kiosk, *Museum of Antiquities,* and the Serai Walls running from Yali Kiosk Kapusi to the Marmara. Beyond Seraglio hill are the Sea of Marmara; Kadi Keui and Phanar Baghoheh point on the Asiatic side; Princes' Islands; and, in the distance, the lofty range of the Bithynian Olpmpus.

10th Window.—Direction S. In the foreground, two or three square towers, which formed part of the walls of Galata, and the outer bridge crossing the Golden Horn from *Kara-keui* to *Stambûl.* On the hill above the Horn the great Mosque of S. Sophia, with its four minarets; to the l. the Treasury and the small dome of the Church of S. Irene; to the rt. the Mosque of Sultan Ahmed, with six minarets; the Burned Column; Vizîr Khân; the small Mosque of Atik Alî Pasha, and the larger Mosque of Nûri Osmaniyeh. Below the Mosque of Sultan Ahmed is the Sublime Porte, a large building with a central colonnade; and near the shore. from l. to rt., are the Railway Station, the Stambûl Custom House; Baluk Bazâr; and the Yeni Valideh Jami', a pyramid of domes and semi-domes, with two minarets. In the distance are the Marmara, with the islands of Plate and Oxia; and the mountains of Bithynia.

11th Window.—Direction S.S.W. In the foreground the British Consulate General, with Yeni Jami' to the rt., and the *inner port of commerce* between the two bridges. On the Stambûl side, to the rt. of Yeni Valideh Jami', the Drug Bazâr, *Misr Charshi*, covered by small domes, and, higher up, the large Valideh Khân, with a forest of chimney-pots. To the rt. of the Khân are the Grand Bazâr, *Bezesten*; the Mosque of Sultan Bayezid; the Serasker's Tower, below which is the Mosque of Rustem Pasha; and the Seraskerat.

12th Window.—Direction S.W. In the foreground Galata, with the narrow street, Pershenbe Bazâr, running down to the harbour. On the Stambûl side, to rt. of the Seraskerat, the Mosque of Sultan Suleiman, *Suleimaniyeh*, with its four minarets, on the 3rd hill of the city; the house of the Sheikh-ul-Islâm; the Shah-zadeh Mosque; and then, in the far distance, Yedi Kuleh, *Seven Towers*, and Daûd Pasha Jamisi. Further to the rt., but more advanced, is the Aqueduct of Valens, *Bosdogan Kemeri*, crossing the valley between the Mosques of Sultan Suleiman and Sultan Muhammad II.

13th Window.—Direction W.S.W. In the foreground Arab Jami', with its church-like spire; fragments of the Old Walls of Galata; and the Inner Bridge, which separates the Ports of War and Commerce. On the hill beyond the Horn, the Mosque of Sultan Muhammad II., "the Conqueror," surrounded by Türbehs.

14th Window.—Direction W.N.W. In the foreground Galata, the Mosque of Azab Kapu, at the head of the Inner Bridge, and the Port of War. On the Stambûl side, the Military School; the Mosque of Sultan Selim, with two minarets; Gûl Jami' near the shore; the high-lying Mihrimah Jami'; the Greek School; the Greek Quarter of Phanar; the Jewish Quarter of Balat; and the Quarter of Aivan Serai. Tekfûr Serai and large portions of the Land Walls are visible; and on the horizon, beyond Mihrimah Jami', are the Daûd Pasha Barracks.

Pera or **Bey Oghlu** crowns the summit of the hill on which Galata and Top-khâneh are situated. It is the seat of the diplomatic bodies, and is inhabited by Christians, native and foreign. Its appearance is that of an Italian town, and in its streets may be heard every language of Europe. The town has repeatedly suffered from disastrous fires, especially in 1831, in 1850, and in 1870, when more than 3000 houses, including the British Embassy and the United States Consulate General, were burned down. Pera is traversed from end to end by the **Grande Rue**, which follows the water-parting between the Bosporus and the Golden Horn for about ¾ m., from *Step Street* in Galata to *Place Taksim*, so called from the **Taksim**, or water-station, shaded by trees, where the water brought from the *forest of Belgrâd* is distributed to Galata and Pera. From the *Place du Tunnel* to *Galata Serai*, where it is cut in two by the wide macadamised street, **Yeni-Charshi**, leading to *Top-khâneh*, the Grande Rue runs from S. to N., and is narrow and badly paved. But from *Galata Serai* onward to *Taksim*, where the fire of 1870 destroyed everything, it runs from S.W. to N.E., and is wide enough to take a tramway. Between the *H. d'Angleterre* and the *Russian Embassy* it is crossed by the street **Kumbaraji Yokusu**, *bomb-shell ascent;* this street, rising above Top-khâneh, is said to have been formed by the track of Muhammad's fleet of boats, which were rolled up to the crest of the hill and then down to the inlet below Kassim Pasha. In the *Grande Rue* and adjoining streets are the residences of the ambassadors and ministers accredited to the Porte, the hotels, restaurants, theatres, cafés chantants, and good shops, in which all the necessaries of life can be obtained at high prices.

The principal buildings are the **British Embassy**, rebuilt after the fire of 1870; the **Austrian, French,** and **Russian Embassies**; the **Municipal buildings**; the **Tekkeh** of the *Dancing Dervishes* (p. 79); the **Russian Consulate General**; the **Lyceum**, formerly the **Galata Serai** (p. 77); **Abraham Pasha's House;** the Greek **Church of the Holy Trinity;** the Greek **Girls' School**, built by M. Zappa, and called *Zappion;* and the

English Memorial Church, *Christ Church,* erected to commemorate our countrymen who fell in the Crimea. The ch. was originally intended to be erected from the designs of Mr. Wm. Burges, who gained the first prize in the general competition; but subsequently it was decided that Mr. Street's design should be executed. The plan of the building is that of a simple parallelogram, with chancel, low side passages, and a schoolroom under the eastern end. The style chosen is the first pointed Gothic. The nave is 52 ft. high, the chancel 38 ft., and has a groined roof. It is ornamented with marbles from Panderma (Sea of Marmara) and Iles d'Hyères. Externally it is plain and has a somewhat heavy effect, on account of the colour of the stone employed.

Towards the W., immediately above the cemetery, *Petits Champs des Morts,* is a public garden, the **Municipal Garden of Pera,** or **of the Petits Champs,** which is well laid out and commands a fine *view* of the Golden Horn and Stambûl. A band plays in summer, and there is a café-restaurant, and a large room in which theatrical and other performances are held. To the N., beyond *Place Taksim,* are the **Drill-ground** (l.), the **Artillery Barracks** (rt.), and the **Taksim Gardens** (rt.), from which there is a magnificent *view* of the Bosporus, Skutari, and the Asiatic shore. A band plays at stated times, and there is a café and open-air theatre. Behind the Artillery Barrack is the large cemetery, **les Grands Champs des Morts,** which is a favourite resort of the inhabitants of the suburbs; here the Armenians hold their great *festival of the dead,* when booths are erected, and dancing, singing, and story-telling take place among the tombs. Beyond the Taksim Gardens is the **old Armenian Cemetery,** which contains some curious monuments. The tombstones are covered with inscriptions in Armenian, and on most of them are carved devices, which either mark the trade or occupation of the deceased; or

denote the manner of his death. There are several representations of decapitated bodies, with the heads between the hands; and some of the deceased suspended from a gibbet. To the N. of the cemetery, in the suburb of **Pankaldi,** is the Turkish Military School, *mekteb-i-harb;* and between these two places and the Bosporus are the **Mejidîeh Barracks** for Infantry, the **Gümush-su Cavalry Barracks,** and the **Machka Barracks.**

Top-khâneh, *Gun House,* so called from the gun foundry established in it, is a continuation of Galata. The **Grand Rue** of Top-khâneh, a section of the wide street which connects Galata and Dolmabâghcheh, and is followed by the tramway to Ortakeui, passes through its centre; and the broad macadamised street, **Yeni Charshi,** runs up the hill to join the Grande Rue of Pera at Galata Serai. The **Arsenal** occupies a wide terrace on the shore of the Bosporus, and comprises a gun foundry, and workshops in which the heavy guns are finished, and gun-carriages and small arms are made and repaired. There is a large *esplanade,* on which hundreds of guns are packed, and in its centre stands a pretty *clock-tower.* On the opposite side of the street are the **Artillery Barracks,** with their mosque, and the house of the Grand Master of Artillery. The **landing-place,** *Top-khâneh Iskelesi,* is one of the most frequented in Constantinople, and there are always large numbers of *kaïks* waiting for hire Near it *kaïk-building* may be seen in all its branches; the peculiar oars are manufactured with the most primitive tools. In the **market-place** close by horses stand for hire; and a motley crowd, which is worthy of study, assembles on market days. Here is the **Fountain of Top-khâneh,** a fine specimen of Turkish art, erected by Ahmed III. It is a square edifice of white marble, highly decorated with well-sculpured arabesques and verses from the Kurân, which were once painted and gilt. Near the market-place are the shops in which the red

Turkish *pipe-bowls* are made, and chibûk stems of jasmine, cherry, and other woods, as well as mouth-pieces, cigar-holders, &c., are sold. Many Circassians live in the vicinity, who are said to carry on slave dealings in an unostentatious manner, so as not to attract the attention of foreign Governments; and to supply the harems of the Pashas and wealthy Turks.

Near the fountain is the **Kilij Ali Pasha Jami'**, erected in 1580 by the celebrated Kaptân Pasha, who broke through the Christian fleet at the battle of Lepanto, and afterwards reconstructed the Turkish navy. In a small cemetery behind the mosque is the *Türbeh* of Kilij Ali decorated, internally, with Persian tiles; and the tomb of a Turkish admiral, who died during the Crimean War. Close to the gun-foundry is the **Mahmûdiyeh Jami'**, built in 1830 by Mahmûd II.; and on the hill-side to the N.E., whence there is a fine view, the **Jehanjir Jami'**, built in 1886 on the site of a mosque erected by Suleiman I., in honour of his son Jehanjir. N. of Top-khâneh is the purely Turkish Quarter of **Fundukli**, the ancient *Aianteion*, and later *Argyropolis*, which extends as far as Dolmabâgh-cheh, and stretches up the hill to the imposing edifice built, in 1875–7, for the **German Embassy**, beside the Grands Champs des Morts. The altar of Ajax, and the Temple of Ptolemy Philadelphus were on the seashore. According to Greek tradition the Apostle Andrew planted Christianity here.

Kassim Pasha, a large suburb W. of Pera and Galata, stretches along the shore of the Golden Horn, and extends inland, on both sides of a filthy stream, to the Greek suburb of **S. Dimitri**. The streets are dirty and narrow, and the only attractions to a stranger are **Kassim Pasha Jami'**; the mosque and **Tomb of Sururi**, grammarian, jurist, and tutor to the sons of Suleiman I.; the **Tekkeh** of the **Rufâî**, *Howling*, **Dervishes**, who go through their religious services every Sunday afternoon; and the **Tekkeh** of the **Mevlevi**, *Dancing*, **Dervishes**.

The **Dockyard** and **Naval Arsenal** extend along the shore of the Horn from Azab Kapu to Haskeui, and occupy the site, probably that of an old Byzantine arsenal, selected by Muhammad II. for the construction of the first Turkish fleet. Within the enclosure are the **Admiralty**, *Divân Khâneh*, a handsome building on a projecting point; dry docks, capable of receiving the largest men-of-war; barracks; naval hospital and school; convict prison; workshops fitted with modern appliances for building and fitting out ships of war; and depôts for naval stores. In one spot are shown the state barges of the Sultans who have occupied the throne for nearly a century past. Here lies at anchor, during most of the year, the greater part of the Turkish navy. The old hulls of several ships of war, lying along the shore and preserved as store-ships, deserve attention. A line of rafts, each bearing a guard-house, is anchored at a little distance from the shore, and boats are not allowed to pass inside.

The establishment of the **Arsenal**, *Ter-âne*, from the Italian *darsena* (or perhaps from the Turkish *Tersa-khâneh*, a prison for prisoners of war), arose from the natural instinct of national pride prompting the Turks to be independent of other nations for the construction of their navy. So about 30 years ago, English shipwrights, mechanics, and engineers were invited to settle beside the dockyard of Haskeui, and form a naval school. The success has not been great, for though one ironclad has been built and launched, "she is the dearest ship ever built." Imported skilled labour, imported iron, imported coal, and above all imported money, make a long bill. The English, or rather Scotch, colony of engineers did much to educate the Turks, and whatever success has been attained is owing to them. A lecture-room serves as a chapel on

Sunday, and a clergyman of the Church of Scotland acts as chaplain. *Admission* by order of the Minister of Marine, or Director of the Arsenal.

In the valley N. of Kassim Pasha is **Piâle Pasha Jami'**, picturesquely situated amidst trees. It was built by the Kaptân Pasha who defeated the Christian fleet under Doria in 1560, and is probably the work of the celebrated architect *Sinan*. It differs from other mosques in the unusual position of the minaret, which is said to be due to the wish of the admiral that it should represent the mast of a ship. The interior is decorated with verses from the Kurân, written by the noted caligraphist *Cherkess Hassan Effendi*; the *minber*, pulpit, is a fine piece of wood-carving; and the *mihrab* is covered with beautiful tiles. Attached to the mosque are a *medresseh*, college; a *tekkeh*, monastery; a *hammam*, bath; and a *sebil*, well.

On the heights to the W. of Piâle Pasha is the **Ok-meidan**, *place of arrows*, where in former days the Sultans practised shooting with bow and arrow, and throwing the *jerid*, spear. A number of small stone pillars and obelisks, with Turkish inscriptions, mark the longest bow-shots and casts with the spear. There is a fine *view* of the Golden Horn and Stambûl from the hill, which can be reached direct from Pera by way of S. Dimitri or Pankaldi.

Adjoining the Ok-meidan is the **Cemetery of the Jews**, of desolate and dreary aspect, and entirely denuded of trees. The countless marble tombstones in this wide-spreading Golgotha appear like the relics of some great city. Both this and the Ok-meidan are prominent objects in passing up and down the Golden Horn.

Haskeui is a large village, the E. portion of which is occupied by Jews, and the W. by Armenians. Formerly, the wealthy Armenian bankers resided in large houses on the heights, where they could live unmolested; but the security they now enjoy has led them to forsake their retreat and take up their residence in Pera, leaving their Haskeui houses to go to ruin or pass into the hands of the Jews. There is a large Armenian church here, and a small chapel of the Protestant Armenians crowns the hill.

Near Haskeui, and now covered by the workshops of the Arsenal, was the site of the *Palace of Ainali Kavak*, built by Ahmed I., in which the disastrous *treaty of Kainarji* was signed. Further up the Horn are the suburbs of **Piri Pasha**; **Kaliji Oghlu**, with its *Engineer School* and *Bombardier Barracks*; and **Sudluje**, with its *Artillery Depôt*.

The village of **Eyûb**, a beautiful and picturesque suburb, the Byzantine *Kosmidion*, is situated beyond the walls of Stambûl, at the extremity of the Golden Horn, and on the side opposite to Haskeui; it is surrounded by gardens and Turkish cemeteries, thickly planted with the dark cypress. It takes its name from *Eyûb Ansari*, the standard-bearer and companion in arms of the prophet Muhammad, who was killed at the first siege of Constantinople by the Arabs, A.D. 668. His tomb was revealed in a dream to the celebrated Mollah Akshemsedîn, during a critical period of the last siege, and its discovery raised the drooping spirits and inflamed the fanaticism of the Turkish soldiers. After the capture of the city, Muhammad II. built the **Mosque of Eyûb**, which is held so sacred that no Christian is allowed to cross its threshold or live in the suburb. In it the Osmanli Sultans, after their accession, are girded with the sword of Osman, the founder of the dynasty. The ceremony, which corresponds to the crowning of a Christian sovereign, is always performed by the chief of the Mevlevi Dervîshes, who bears the title *Chelebi Effendi*, and resides at Konieh. The **Mosque** is an elegant building of white marble, with a large dome, several small, and semi-domes, and two graceful minarets. In the court is a large plane-tree, and on the W. side, in a court planted with trees, is the *tomb of Abu*

Eyûb, with many costly lamps hanging round it.

As a place of burial, *Eyûb* is held in high veneration, and its **cemeteries**, with their mausoleums and richly decorated tombs, surrounded by trees and flowers, are well worth a visit. Some of the tombs are enclosed by gilt railings, and others are resplendent with coloured and gilt arabesques and verses from the Kurân. In the vicinity are the tombs of Sheikhs-ul-Islâm, Grand Viziers, and chief eunuchs; and in their midst lies one of the greatest of Viziers, *Sokolli*, who, after the death of Suleiman I., victoriously concluded the campaign of Szigeth.

From the hill above Eyûb one of the *finest views* of the Golden Horn is obtained. *Fezes* for the army are made at Eyûb, in a manufactory established by Sultan Abdul Mejid in the Palace of the Valideh Sultan, mother of Selim III. They are also imported from Tunis and France.

Among the *türbehs* are those of the Valideh Sultan, mother of Selim III., and her two daughters, all three biers being enclosed within rich mother-of-pearl railings; to this mausoleum is attached a *medresseh*, college, a *mekteb*, school, an *imâret*, kitchen for the poor, and a *sebil*, well. Here are tombs of two children of Sultan Abdul Mejid, a son and daughter, the bier of the former decorated with a fez and golden tassel; and of the two children of Adileh Sultan, sister of Sultan Abdul Aziz. Their biers are covered with richly embroidered velvet and shawls, and beneath the fez are their respective epitaphs; one is as follows: "A flower that had scarcely bloomed was prematurely torn from its stem. It has been removed to those bowers where roses never languish. Its parents' tears will supply refreshing moisture. Say a *fâtiha* for its beatitude, 1259" (1843). It may be added that the heart-broken mother survived her last child but a few weeks.

§ 10.—ANCIENT CONSTANTINOPLE.

Constantine the Great, having determined to remove the capital of the Roman Empire from the banks of the Tiber, selected, A.D. 328, as a site for his new seat of Government, the Thracian promontory, upon which a colony from Megara had founded, B.C. 658, the town of Byzantium. No other position could have offered him to an equal extent the security, wealth of resource, and beauty, suitable to the first city of a great dominion.

The **Byzantium** of that day was the one rebuilt by the Emperor Severus, when he recognised the folly of having destroyed the older town, A.D. 196, for its obstinate devotion to the lost cause of his rival, Pescennius Niger. The strategical importance of a city commanding the water-way between the Euxine and the Mediterranean was too great to be lightly abandoned. The elevated ground within the Seraglio enclosure was the site of the Acropolis, and, without doubt, the primitive town was gathered round it. But the *Byzantium of Xenophon* and that of Severus was a much larger city. Its *walls* extended as far west along the Golden Horn as the point now occupied by the Stambûl Custom House. There they turned to cross the promontory, and, climbing its northern slope, reached the summit of the ridge, above the Grand Bazâr. At that point stood the *principal gate* of the city. Then, instead of proceeding, as is often supposed, in a direct line down the promontory's southern slope to the Marmara, the walls followed, according to Zosimus, a somewhat circuitous course, and struck the sea at a point opposite Skutari, probably in the vicinity of the Seraglio new lighthouse. At the same time a *fortified outpost* or suburb seems to have occupied the territory, marked now by the Shah-Zadeh Mosque.

The *fortifications* erected by Constantine stood nearly 2 m. (15 stadia) W. from the walls of Byzantium. Constantinople was consequently at first smaller than it ultimately became, and has remained to the present time. Until the ancient city can be thoroughly explored by means of excavations, only the general course of *Constantine's walls* can be indicated. Along the Horn, they went as far W. as Un Kapan Kapusi, at the Stambûl end of the Inner Bridge. Leaving the shore, they took an oblique direction up the flank of the 4th hill, until they reached the ridge between the Mosque of Sultan Muhammad II. (the Conqueror), and the Mosque of Sultan Selim, at a point not far from the large cistern behind the latter edifice. In their onward course they kept well within their limits the Church of the Holy Apostles, on whose site the Mosque of Sultan Muhammad II. stands, and then made across the valley of the Lycus for the 7th hill. That hill they traversed to the E. of the quarter now known as Alti-Mermer, and then descended to the Marmara between Vlanga Bostan and Psamatia. The portion of this course that can be most accurately determined is on the 7th hill. For Alti-Mermer is the Turkish translation of the Greek 'Εξακιόνιον, the alias of 'Εξωκιόνιον—the *district of the Outer Column* — the name given to the ground immediately outside the walls of Constantine, on account of the presence there of a column surmounted by his statue. Furthermore, on the verge of the Alti-Mermer Quarter, beside an old Christian church, now styled Îsa-Kapu-Mesjidi, is a point known as Îsa-Kapusi—the Gate of Jesus. The neighbourhood of the church accounts for the use of the Saviour's name; while the allusion to a gate is explained by the existence of an ancient gate here as late as 1507, which was none other than the Παλαιά Πόρτα, placed by Byzantine writers in this part of the city. The gate was a portal of magnificent proportions in Constantine's walls, and formed, in fact, the first triumphal entrance into the city. It survived the gradual effacement of the city's earliest limits, as Temple Bar outlived the walls of London.

Constantinople was inaugurated as New Rome 11th May, 330. Its fitness to be a great capital appeared, in the fact that it was soon found too small for the population that crowded within the walls. Accordingly in 413, under Theodosius II., the boundaries of the city were enlarged and carried forward to the picturesque line of towers and walls, which still enclose Constantinople on the west. Later changes in the line added little to the city's area; they rather gave additional strength to the fortifications. In laying out Constantinople, Rome served as a model. But the form of the ground on which the two cities respectively stood was, notwithstanding the 7 hills in each, too dissimilar to permit anything like slavish imitation; and the *genius loci*, beside the Bosporus, was far too strong to be resisted.

During its long history of over 1100 years, the city naturally passed through many vicissitudes, and changed its aspect from time to time. The most remarkable changes were associated with Constantine the Great, Theodosius II., Justinian the Great, Basil I., the Comneni, the Fourth Crusade, and the Palaeologi. Here we can indicate in the briefest manner only some of the more striking or permanent features of the city. The 7 hills are now marked thus:—The 1*st* by S. Sophia; the 2*nd* by the Burnt Column; the 3*rd* by the War Office; the 4*th* by the Mosque of Sultan Muhammad II.; the 5*th* by the Mosque of Sultan Selim; the 6*th* by Tekfûr Serai and the quarter of Egri Kapu; the 7*th* by the Column of Arcadius, *Avret Tash.* Like Rome, the new capital was divided, for municipal purposes, into 14 Regions or Wards, which are described with considerable minuteness in the Notitia. The lines of the *principal streets* were determined, as at present, by the topographical features of the promontory —a range of hills and a level tract between either base and the water. Accordingly there was a thoroughfare along the Marmara, another along the foot of the hills overhanging the Golden Horn, while a third kept on the high ground and ran through the centre of the city. The last was the main street, and was known as the *Mese* (Μέση). Upon reaching the 3rd hill, it formed two branches—one proceeding to the Adrianople Gate (*Edirneh Kapusi*), over the hills beside the Horn, the other to the Golden Gate, over the 7th hill, which overlooks the Marmara. The latter formed the *Via Triumphalis*, down which triumphal processions passed from the Golden Gate to S. Sophia. The streets were in places bordered by *porticoes*, which afforded shelter from sun or rain. Most of the objects of interest near the first two thoroughfares will be noticed in describing the fortifications along the harbour and the Marmara; those on the Mese are mentioned here.

The highest life of the city revolved around the **Forum Augustéon**, now represented by the open area to the south of S. Sophia. This Forum was a quadrangle, surrounded by stately porticoes, and paved with marble. On the N. was *S. Sophia*, with *S. Irene* beyond. On the E. was the *Senate House*. To the S. was the *Great Entrance* (Chalke) leading to the Imperial Residence, which occupied the territory between Sultan Ahmed and the sea; the splendid *Baths of Zeuxippus;* and, beyond, the *Hippodrome.* The square and its porticoes were adorned with statues, among which the following were conspicuous: the Empress Helena, from whose title, Augusta, the place derived its name; the silver statue of Eudoxia, which furnished occasion for the banishment of S. Chrysostom; the colossal equestrian statue of Justinian the Great, on a lofty column. There also was the *Milion*—τὸ Μίλιον —whence distances from Constantinople were measured. It was an arched structure, ornamented with statues, and, so far, unlike the Golden Milestone which served a similar purpose in Rome. North of the Augustéon, which could be closed by gates on the west, were the *Great Courts of Justice,* beside the Cistern of Yeri Batan Serai. A little below was the octagonal building, containing the *Public Library,* whose treasures became more than once a prey to the flames. Still lower was *S. Mary Chalkopratiana,* where the Mosque opposite So'ûk Cheshmeh Kapusi now stands.

Moving westwards, one made for the **Forum of Constantine** (*Tâuk Bazâr,* Fowl Market), an ellipse in shape, and surrounded by two tiers of porticoes. It was entered at either end of its longer axis, through a noble arch of marble. Like the Augustéon it was paved, and hence sometimes called the *Plakoton.* Statues and crosses abounded in every direction. Here was the *Porphyry Column,* carrying the statue of Constantine, and, though shorn of its glory, still keeping its place in the city whose birth it witnessed. Here also was another *Senate House,* and a *Nymphæon,* or hall, in which marriages among the humble classes were celebrated. The *Forum* was the business centre of Constantinople, its porticoes being occupied by traders and merchants. Next came the *Bread Market* or Artopolion (*Boghdaijilar Kapusi*). Further on was the *Anemodoulion,* a beautiful structure, surmounted by a movable figure to indicate the direction of the wind. The *Forum Taurou,* of Taurus, its constructor, came next—a very large public square on the 3rd hill, and now represented by the open area, before the *War Office* (Seraskerat). It was known also as the *Forum of Theodosius* (the Great), because it contained the column bearing his statue, and sculptured with bas-reliefs celebrating his exploits. Here once stood another Senate House; a large fountain, supplied by the *Aqueduct of Valens;* several palaces and churches; and the *Capitol,* which, under Theodosius II., became the seat of the University of Constantinople. Beyond this Forum the *Mese,* as already stated, parted in two branches. Along the branch leading to the

Adrianople Gate were found the *Philadelphion* (near the Shah-Zadeh Mosque), another public place owing its name to statues of the sons of Constantine the Great, in an attitude expressing fraternal love; the *Thermæ Constantinianæ;* the *Church of the Holy Apostles;* and the *Cistern of Aspar.* The branch proceeding to the *Golden Gate* conducted to the *Forum Amastrianon* (Et Meidan, Meat Square, where rations were served out to the Janissaries), where public executions often took place; the *Forum of the Bull,* Boῦs (Ak Serai), named from the hollow figure of a bull, which often served as a furnace for burning the bodies of criminals; the *Forum of Arcadius,* or of Theodosius II. (Avret Bazâr), with a hollow column surmounted by the statue of the former emperor, and sculptured with his triumphs; the *Mint ;* the *Trojan Porticoes;* and the *Monastery of Studius.*

§ 11.—THE WALLS AND GATES—
SEVEN TOWERS.

The **ancient fortifications,** though in a ruinous state, are, next to S. Sophia, the chief object of interest in Constantinople. They consist of the *harbour walls* along the Golden Horn, the *sea walls* along the Marmara, and the *land walls* from the Marmara to the Golden Horn. The last are most picturesque and of great interest as an historical monument and unique example of mediæval fortification.

Travellers wishing to make a complete round of the walls (at least 5 hrs.) should (1) send horses or carriage to Yedi Kuleh (Seven Towers); (2) Take (but not when there is a south wind) a kaïk (P. 20–30) at the outer bridge or at Sirkeji Iskelesi, near the Stambûl railway station, and proceed by water along the Marmara walls to Yedi Kuleh; (3) Ride or drive (4½ m.) outside the land walls to the Golden Horn and along the harbour walls to the outer bridge and Pera. Those who wish to visit only

the land walls can reach Yedi Kuleh by train, carriage, horse, or tram, and drive, ride, or walk thence to the pier of Aivan Serai or to that of Balat, on the Golden Horn, whence steamer or boat can be taken to the outer bridge. This order is recommended when the wind is from the south, and the reverse order, commencing at Aivan Serai, when it is from the north. Horses can be hired when necessary at Yedi Kuleh. Travellers who propose to examine the walls closely, and to visit the interiors of the towers, are advised not to do so alone. A pleasant way of visiting the walls is to ride (5 hrs.) from Pera over the heights of Haskeui (magnificent view of the harbour) to the Sweet Waters, Eyûb, along the walls by Balukli, where visitors stop to see the miraculous fish, to the Seven Towers, and thence through the city by Psamatia to the outer bridge and Pera.

The Harbour Walls.

These walls, situated at a short distance from the water stretch from Seraglio Point on the east to their junction with the land walls at Aivan Serai on the west—a distance of some 3 m. As inscriptions upon them prove, they are mainly the works erected by the Emperor Theophilus (829–842) to replace the inferior and decayed fortifications of Constantine the Great and Theodosius II. His attention to the state of this line of defence was doubtless quickened by the serious naval assaults made upon it, during his father's reign, by the rebel Thomas.

From Seraglio Point to the Outer Bridge.—The **large bones** on the wall beside the first tower belonged to one of the cetacea that have strayed from time to time into the Bosporus. The question has been raised whether they can be the remains of the sea-monster which, according to Procopius, infested the straits during the reign of Justinian the Great. By the local fishermen they are considered the talisman which secures abundance of fish in the waters about the city. The adjacent building is a government storehouse. The **1st gate** reached is *Odun Kapusi*, the Wood Gate, because the wood used as fuel in the residences within the Seraglio enclosure is landed in front of it. The hospital within the gate must be on or near the site of the *Church of S. Demetrius*, highly venerated under the Palaeologi. The Imperial Boat-House (*Kaik Khâneh*), in which the Sultan's old state Kaïks are drawn up, comes next. One of them resembles an old Venetian or Genoese galley. The tower behind the boat-house is regarded as the tower which held the southern end of the chain drawn by Byzantine emperors across the harbour in time of war to keep a hostile fleet out of the Golden Horn. A portion of the chain used for that purpose during the siege of 1453 is preserved in the court of S. Irene.

The **2nd Gate**, *Yali Kiosk Kapusi*, is named after the handsome kiosk of Suleiman the Magnificent, which once stood on the quay a little to the west, and in which sultans gave farewell audience to their chief admirals starting on a naval expedition. Upon the walls to the right is *Sebetjilar Kiosk*, the Kiosk of the Signal, whence signals were made to the fleet. Here the walls separating the Seraglio from the rest of the city reach the Horn. This gate represents the ancient *Porta Eugeniou*, styled also *Marmara Porta*, and, according to some, *Porta Oraia*, the Beautiful Gate. The landing before it was known as the *Scala Timasi*. Within the gate stood the *Great Orphanage* (Ὀρφανοτροφεῖον) of Constantinople and the *Church of SS. Peter and Paul.* The first Saracen settlement and the first mosque in the city were in this vicinity. *Sirkeji Iskelesi*, the pier of the vinegar seller. To the l. is the Railway Station. Here probably was the **3rd Gate**, *Porta Veteris Rectoris,*

and the *Scala Chalcedonensis*, for boats plying between the city and Chalcedon (*Kadi Keui*). Immediately to the rt. is the ancient *Portus Prosforianus*, or *Bosporus*, or *Phosforius*. The first name marks it as the point at which vegetables and fruit were landed for the city markets, as at the present day; the second may be due to the fact that, until the reign of Constantine Copronymus, a cattle-market was held on the quay of this bend in the shore; the third is supposed to refer to the appearance of the moon during the siege of Byzantium by Philip of Macedon. On the level area beyond stood the *Forum Strategion.* The street leading up from *Sirkeji Iskelesi* proceeds to the Sublime Porte. The pier is consequently much frequented by public functionaries, and upon it a new Grand Vizier lands in state on his way from the Palace to the Government offices. The *Genoese colony*, before 1203, was assigned the quarter between the 2nd and 4th Gates. **4th Gate**, *Baghcheh Kapusi*, the Garden Gate, the ancient *Porta Neoriou* (Νεωρίου) of the *Neorium*, the principal harbour of Byzantium and of ancient Constantinople, in the adjoining bay. Some authorities think that this was the *Porta Oraia* —the name being a corrupt form of Neorium. Next comes the Stambûl *Custom House.* At the head of the outer bridge is the *Terminus of the Tramway*, that runs to the Seven Towers, and to Top-Kapusi in the Land Walls. The large mosque is *Yeni Valideh Jami'*, or *Yeni Jami'* (p. 64). The Pisan and Amalfitan merchants, before 1203, were quartered in the district between the 4th and 5th Gates.

Between the Bridges.—**5th Gate**, *Baluk-Bazâr Kapusi*, the Fish-Market Gate, because the principal fish-market of the city is held before it. The ancient *Porta Peramatos* (Πόρτα τοῦ Περάματος) of the Ferry, because the point at which the Horn was crossed, as to-day, by ferry-boats to and from Galata. Most authorities identify it also with the *Porta Hebraica*. At this gate began the quarter occupied by Venetian merchants before 1203. The street from the shore leads to the *Egyptian Spice Bazâr*, an interesting scene of Oriental life. **6th Gate**, *Zindan Kapusi*, the Prison Gate, after a prison formerly in its neighbourhood, the ancient *Porta Carabion*. In the adjoining mosque is a Holy Well, which marks the site of *S. John Baptist de Cornibus* (τῶν Κεράτων). Before the gate is *Yemish Bazâr*, the dried-fruit market. The street leading up into the city conducts one to the *Grand Bazâr*. It is named *Uzun Charshi*, the Long Market, and represents the *Makros Embolos* of Byzantine days. **7th Gate**, *Odun Kapan Kapusi*, the Timber-Yard Gate. Beside it large stores of timber are kept, a practice as old at least as the reign of Justinian the Great. Here was the *Porta Viglæ*, *Porta Drungariou*, which led to the *Central Police Station*, on the height now occupied by the *Offices of the Sheikh-ul-Islâm*. Here the Venetian quarter ended. **8th Gate**, *Ayazma Kapusi*, Gate of the Holy Well, from an Ayazma in its vicinity. Dr. Mordtman regards it as the last gate in the harbour walls erected by Constantine the Great, and as the one styled *Basiliké Pylé*, in the *early* history of the city. In that case the Holy Well probably marked the site of *S. Acacius ad Caryam*. **9th Gate**, *Un Kapan Kapusi*, the Gate of the Flour Depôt. Beside it are flour stores and a flour-mill. It is the ancient gate known as *Mesé*, because of its central position, and as *Platea*, on account of the broad open space about it. The street on the l. leads to the *Church of Pantocrator* (*Kilisse Jami'*, p. 57), the *Aqueduct of Valens* (p. 71), and across the promontory to *Vlanga* on the Marmara. The large mosque to the l. of the Inner Bridge is *Zeirek Jamisi*.

From the Inner Bridge to Phanar.— In the large building on the l. are the offices of the *Tobacco Régie Co.*, which has the monopoly of Turkish tobacco.

10th Gate, *Jub-Ali Kapusi*, the Gate of the Long-Robed Ali, a Turkish saint, buried outside the gate and on its rt. The district within the gate was one of the quarters assigned to Turks resident in the city before the Conquest. Dr. Mordtman regards this gate as the one styled in certain documents *Ispigas*, because parties embarked there to fetch water from the springs which once flowed on the opposite shore at Kassim Pasha. The gate was also known as that of the Glaziers, owing to the workshops of such craftsmen formerly beside it. On the northern face of the gate's eastern tower is a tablet, bearing the coat of arms and the name of Manuel Fakrasè, an officer of the Emperor Cantacuzene. Above this tablet stood another, on which the scene of the Fiery Furnace, described in the Book of Daniel, was depicted. It has been removed to the Imperial Museum. **11th Gate**, *Aya Kapu*, the Holy Gate, the ancient *Gate of St. Theodosia*. It led to the adjacent church dedicated to that saint, now *Gül Jami'* (p. 57). This entrance was also known as *Porta Dexiokratis*, after the name of the quarter. In proceeding from this gate to the next, large blocks of stone, evidently water-worn, will be observed in the base of the walls, proving that here, if not also at other points, the fortifications were once in contact with the sea. This fact explains how the Venetian fleet, in 1204, was able to approach so near the walls as to throw drawbridges from the ships' yards to the ramparts. Here, then, the Latin Crusaders entered the city. **12th Gate**, *Yeni Aya Kapu*, the New Holy Gate, because enlarged after the Turkish conquest. The ancient *Porta Sidhera* (Iron Gate). A few steps within and on the rt. are the remains probably of the *Convent of the Petrion*, in which Anna Delassena, the mother of the Comneni, was confined with her daughters and daughters-in-law. **13th Gate**, *Petri Kapusi*, Gate of Petrus, a patrician who lived under Justinian the Great, and who either resided or held property in this quarter. The gate leads into a close, *Castrum* (τῶν Πετρίων), formed by a wall which, starting from this point, describes an arc, and rejoins the main line of the fortifications a little beyond the next gate. Within the enclosure are the *Residence of the Greek Patriarch* of Constantinople and his *Cathedral Church of S. George.* Upon the loss of S. Sophia, the patriarchal throne was removed to the Church of the Holy Apostles, the site of which is now occupied by the Mosque of Sultan Muhammad II. Thence it was soon carried to the Church of the Virgin Pammakaristos, now the *Fethiyeh Jami'.* In 1586 it was in the Church of the *Vlach Serai* (the Wallachian Palace), now occupied by the representatives of the Patriarch of Jerusalem. Thirteen years later it stood in the Church of S. Demetrius, near the Xyloporta. And at last, in 1601, it ended its wanderings here. The chief curiosities in the church are the iconostasis of olive-wood, the patriarchal throne, the pulpit, and the table for tapers, good specimens of Byzantine ecclesiastical furniture, two Byzantine Icons, one representing the Virgin, the other S. John the Baptist, and various relics. The *Mosque* of *Sultan Selim* crowns the hill. **14th Gate,** *Phanar Kapusi,* Porta Phanariou, from the beacon light placed upon the promontory before the gate. This gate formed the N.W. entrance to the *Petrion Enclosure.* Within, and a few paces to the rt., are the remains of the **15th Gate,** *P. Diplo-Phanariou,* which pierced the inner wall of the close to allow communication between the Petrion and the quarters to the west. Until the early part of the present century the leading families of the Greek community resided at *Phanar,* hence their epithet Phanariots. Many of their members were prominent functionaries in the Turkish service.

From Phanar Kapusi to Aivan Serai Kapusi.—The handsome brick building, surmounted by a dome and situated on the height, is the *Greek National School* for boys, erected in 1880. The small circular church lower down the hill is dedicated to the Virgin, with the style *Mouchliotissa* (p. 57). More to the north is the *Greek National School* for girls. The blue-coloured walls at the foot of the hill enclose the buildings attached to the *Vlach Serai,* the *Monastery* of the *Holy Sepulchre,* once the property of the Wallachian Cantacuzenes. Here the representatives of the Jerusalem Patriarchate reside. The Library contains the collection of MSS., among which Bishop Bryennius discovered a copy of the Epistle of Clement to the Corinthians and the MS. containing the Teaching of the Twelve. These interesting documents are now at Jerusalem. The Library was founded towards the close of the 17th century. **16th Gate,** *Balat Kapusi,* the Palace Gate, a corruption of the Greek παλάτιον, the *Basilikế Pylế* in the *later* history of the city. Here the emperors landed when proceeding by boat to the *Palace of Blachernæ.* **17th Gate,** *Porta Kynigou,* the Gate of the Hunter. It is adorned with a figure of Victory. Under the Palaeologi this quarter was the aristocratic part of the city. It is now occupied chiefly by Spanish Jews, the descendants of the Jews expelled from Spain by Ferdinand and Isabella. *S. Peter and S. Mark* (Khoja Mustafa Pasha Jami'), founded in 458. Its old font lies on the opposite side of the street. **18th Gate,** the small *Aivan Serai Kapusi,* Gate of the Palace with a Balcony. Immediately within the entrance and on the l. are vaults supposed to be the remains of the *Carian Portico,* built by the Emp. Maurice in 587. Within the blue-coloured walls at the farther end of the street is the site of the celebrated *Church of the Virgin* at Blachernæ, founded by Pulcheria, and finally destroyed by fire in 1434. The *Holy Well,* in which the emperors bathed annually, still exists. The narrow street to the rt. of the gate leads to Toklu Dede Jami', *Church of S. Thecla,* founded in the 9th cent., and restored in the 11th. It also conducts to the Gate of

Blachernæ in the Heraclian Wall, and to the space enclosed between that wall and the Wall of Leo the Armenian (p. 38).

The Sea Walls.

These walls defended the city on the E. and on the S., extending for some 5 m. from the *Seraglio Point* to the southern extremity of the land walls, a little below the Seven Towers (*Yedi Kuleh*). In their present condition they afford abundant evidence of the important repairs made at different periods in the walls originally built by Constantine the Great and Theodosius II. The names of the Emperors who took part in the work of restoration are for the most part inscribed upon the walls, and will be noticed as they occur. Extensive repairs have also been made since the Turkish conquest. There are four peculiarities in the construction of these defences, due to the proximity of the open sea: 1. The walls are to a great extent protected at their base by a breakwater formed of large boulders thrown loosely together. 2. The line is exceedingly irregular, turning in and out at short intervals as if to avoid the presentation of a long front to the action of the waves. 3. Fragments of marble have been employed extensively in the lowest courses of the masonry, as better able to withstand erosion. 4. The general profile is slight, because the aid of wind and current could be relied upon to assist in repelling an enemy.

From Seraglio Point to the Seraglio Lighthouse.—This section can be visited on foot. The walls have been demolished for some distance, to make room for the railroad. **1st Gate.** At the point named *Top Kapusi* (the Cannon Gate), now marked by marble steps, stood the ancient *Gate of S. Barbara*, a ch. dedicated to that saint, the patroness of fortifications, firearms, and armourers, being beside it. The *Mangana*, or military arsenal, was in this vicinity. The gate had some architectural pretensions, and was sometimes used as a triumphal entry. Its Turkish name is due to a battery once placed near it to guard the entrance of the harbour, and to fire salutes. **2nd Gate**, *Deïrmen Kapusi* (the Gate of the Mill), after the neighbouring mill. On the wall north of the gate is a long Greek inscription, to the following effect: " Possessing Thee, O Christ, a firm wall, King Theophilus, the pious emperor, reared from new foundations this wall, which guard with Thy might, O Sovereign Ruler, and display to the end of time, standing unshaken and unmoved." On the tower beyond the gate is a cross, with the legend " Jesus Christ conquers." Lower down are the words, " Tower of Theophilus the Faithful Emperor and Great King in Christ." The tower beyond the mosque is also marked as "the Tower of Theophilus, Emperor in Christ." During the Arctic winter of 763–4, the Bosporus and extensive tracts of the Black Sea were frozen hard, and when the thaw came in spring the walls along this shore were crushed and overthrown by the huge masses of ice which the swollen currents drove against them. The repairs, executed immediately after the event, required, as these inscriptions prove, renewal during the reign of Theophilus.

3rd Gate, *Hastalar Kapusi* (Hospital Gate). Possibly this gate represents a postern at the service of the *Church of S. George Mangana*, which stood within. Above a buttress is the small opening through which, it is said, Sultanas were thrown into the sea. Another opening in the face of the walls will soon be observed, revealing a long and sometimes lofty chamber in the body of the fortifications, the precise object of which is not clear. It may have been a covered passage for troops, or a prison. The projecting basement further on once supported the beautiful *Injili Kiosk* (the Pearl Kiosk), a pavilion to which the Sultans resorted, to enjoy the superb view it commanded. High up on the wall, to the rt. of the basement, are three inscribed tablets. The fragmentary inscription upon them has been construed to mean that, while no other emperors who sought to control the sea at this point had raised the wall 20 ft. high, the Emperor Michael III. had done so through Bardas, the Magister and Domestic of the Guards, and thus erected a splendid ornament for the city. Until 1824, a *Holy Well* —the *Ayazma* of the Saviour—flowed in the basement, and was a great resort of devout Greeks on the Festival of the Transfiguration. The excavations made in the Seraglio grounds in 1871 for the railroad, revealed the remains of an imposing Byzantine structure on the ground behind Injili Kiosk. Dr. Paspati regarded them as the remains of the *Palace Bucoleon.* They are rather the ruins of the *Palace Mangana*, built by Basil I. **4th Gate.** Beyond is a small walled-up gateway, surmounted by a cross. It was the small gate leading to the ch. consecrated to the Virgin, *Hodegetria* (Μικρὰ πύλη τῆς 'Οδηγη-τρίας), one of the most highly venerated shrines in Constantinople. Her picture led the emperors in battle. The broken lintel of the gate is now built into the inner face of the wall, and bears the text, " Open to me the Gates of Righteousness, that entering in I may praise the Lord."

From the Lighthouse to Daûd Pasha Kapusi.—The **first tower** bears the inscription: " In the year 1024 the Emperor Basil, the pious sovereign, erected from the foundations this tower, which the dashing of the sea, that battered it for a long time and with much and violent surge, compelled to fall." The shore now forms a small bay,—the ancient *Port Bucoleon* attached to the great Imperial Palace on the hill. With it begins the series of artificial harbours that lined the side of the city along the Marmara. The port was enlarged and protected by two jetties. There are two gates in the walls

bounding the bay. The first is *Baluk Khâneh Kapusi*, the Gate of the Fish-House, which formerly stood here for the fishermen in the employment of the Seraglio. Some regard it as the ancient *Postern of Michael the Protovestiarius.* The other Gate is *Akhir Kapusi*, the Stable-Gate, leading to the Sultan's Mews, once situated here. Its ancient name is unknown. It was the Water-side Gate of the Palace, and was reached from the sea by a flight of steps and a quay of marble. Upon the latter stood the group which represented a lion mastering a bull, and gave the name Bucoleon to the port and to the Imperial Marine Residence beside it. Within the walls from this point onward to the site of the *Seraglio Old Lighthouse* lay the *Imperial Palace Grounds*, stretching up the hill-slope towards S. Sophia and the Hippodrome. Immediately beyond the old lighthouse the walls are pierced by windows in marble casements. We have here the façade of the *Palace of Hormisdas*, so named after a Persian prince who fled to the court of Constantine. It was the residence of Justinian the Great and Theodora before their accession to the throne. On the other side of the railway the walls rest upon five vaults, and support a terrace which bore another Palace, ascribed by some to Leo Macellus. The figures of the two lions now before the School of Fine Arts within the Seraglio grounds came from the façade of this palace. The port at this point was named sometimes the *Port of Hormisdas*, from the residence of that prince upon its shore, and sometimes the *Port of Julian*, having been constructed by that emperor during the visit he paid to the city on his way to his fatal Persian expedition. The port was also known as the *New Port*, to distinguish it from the *Neorion*, in the Golden Horn. The construction of the railroad led to the disappearance of the **7th Gate**, *Chatladi Kapusi* (the Broken Gate), which afforded communication between this port and the city. The gate was sometimes known as *P. Leonis*, from the lions on the adjoining Palace. The Mosque to the west beside the railroad is *Kuchuk Aya Sofia, SS. Sergius and Bacchus* (p. 50).

The quarter *Kadriga Limân,* at the foot of the hill, marks the site of a former harbour, now filled, the ancient *Port of Sophia* (τῆς Σοφίας, τῶν Σοφιῶν), made at the instance of the Empress Sophia, wife of Justin II. At the head of the harbour was the **8th Gate,** *Caterga limanis,* the ancient *Porta Sidhera,* and Porta τῶν Σοφιῶν. Further along the shore is an old breakwater, which protected another ancient harbour, now almost entirely filled, the harbour known as *Kondoskalion,* and *Hepta-skalon.* The walls along its circuit may still be traced to a great extent. In them stood the **9th Gate,** *P. Kondoskalion,* now *Kûm Kapusi* (the Sand Gate). The *Gregorian Armenian Patriarchate and Cathedral* are in the *Kûm Kapu Quarter.* **10th Gate,** *Yeni Kapu* (the New Gate). Here the line of the walls turned inwards and made a curve over a mile in length, so as to skirt the ancient harbour, which occupied the site of the Vegetable Gardens, known as *Vlanga Bostan.* The harbour was called *Portus Eleutheriou,* after its original constructor, under Constantine the Great, and *P. Theodosii,* in honour of the Emperor Theodosius I. It was protected by a mole extending from a point about 50 paces S.W. of Yeni Kapu to the Daûd Pasha Kapusi, just outside the other extremity of the harbour. According to Gyllius, in whose time the harbour was still partially used, the entrance was beside Yeni Kapu. The Lycus empties into the Marmara here. The *quarter* of *Yeni Kapu* rests upon a portion of the mole, and upon the land made by the earth cast into the sea when Sultan Mustafa III. built the *Laleli Jami'.* Thus compensation was given to the Armenian proprietors dislodged by the erection of that mosque.

Daûd Pasha Kapusi, named after the mosque upon the hill. It represents the *Porta S. Æmiliani,* so styled from a church in its vicinity; it was the last gate in the walls of Constantine along this shore. **Psamatia Kapusi,** *Porta Psamathiou* (Ψαμαθίου), retains its ancient name due to the sand cast upon the beach from the bank off this point. **Nârli Kapusi,** Pomegranate Gate. Ancient name uncertain, possibly *Gate of S. John the Baptist,* a gate attached to the domain of the Monastery of Studius (p. 52). On the tower, at the foot of the landing before the gate, is an inscription in honour of the Emperor Manuel Comnenus: "Repaired by Manuel, the Christ-loving sovereign, Porphyrogenitus, and Emperor of the Romans, son of Comnenus, in the year 1164." The last tower of these walls, **Mermer Kuleh,** is largely built of marble. It is a striking and picturesque object, and overlooks a small harbour guarded by a mole. A *water-gate* will be observed. The site of the *Ch. of S. Diomed,* on whose steps Basil I. slept, when he first entered Constantinople as an adventurer, was in the garden near this tower. Upon the occasion of a triumph in honour of a successful campaign in Asia, the troops and trophies appointed to take part in the ceremony were conveyed from Chrysopolis, *Skutari* or Chalcedon *Kadi Keui,* and landed on the tract outside the Golden Gate, through which the triumphal procession was to enter the city.

THE LAND WALLS.

The line of defence, which extends from the Sea of Marmara to the Golden Horn, presents a scene not surpassed elsewhere in the world for beauty and desolation. The line is some 7227 yds. in length, and, exclusive of repairs, consists of: (1) The walls of Theodosius II.; (2) the wall of Manuel Comnenus; (3) the wall of Heraclius; (4) the wall of Leo the Armenian.

1. The Walls of Theodosius II.

General Description.—The fortifications of Theodosius extend from the Marmara to a short distance beyond *Tekfûr Serai*, or 6116½ yds. Originally they ran, further towards the Golden Horn, behind the later walls, which now meet them at right angles. In the reign of Theodosius, if not earlier, the portion of the 6th hill, now occupied by the quarter of Egri Kapu, was surrounded by walls, of which traces remain. These walls ended at the point marked by the Tower of Anemas (p. 38), and were only completed to the Horn after the siege of the city by the Avars in 626. Many authorities, however, maintain that the fortifications of Theodosius were continued from their present termination to the Horn, near P. Kynigou (p. 28).

In 413, the advance of the Huns having rendered it necessary to protect that portion of the city which had spread westward beyond the limits of Constantine's wall, Theodosius directed the Prefect Anthemius to construct a new line of defence in advance of the existing fortifications. That line, which is now represented by the *Inner Wall*, remained through all changes and improvements the chief bulwark of the city. In 447 the wall was seriously injured by an earthquake, and Cyrus Constantine, the distinguished prefect of the city, seized the opportunity to increase the strength of the capital,

Sketch section through the Walls of Theodosius II.

which was also the first fortress of the empire. He not only, under instructions from Theodosius, repaired the work of Anthemius, but built outside of, and parallel to it, a second wall; and beyond this again he constructed a broad, deep moat, with a breastwork on its inner edge. The *Outer Wall* (ἔξω τεῖχος) of Cyrus was lower than the *Inner Wall* (ἔσω τεῖχος) of Anthemius, and was separated from it by a *fausse-braie* (περίβολος), about 20 yds. wide; and between the breastwork (προτείχισμα) and the *Outer Wall* there was a *chemin des rondes* 19½ yds. wide, on which the defenders fought under the protection of the walls and towers in rear.

The **moat** is 63–65 ft. wide; its original depth is unknown, as it is partially filled with soil and occupied by a vegetable garden famous for its lettuce. In front of the Golden Gate the moat is still more than 32 ft. deep. It is divided into several sections by **batardeaux**, or transverse walls (διαταφρίσματα), which were designed to retain the water when the ditch was flooded. The lower portions of these walls are thicker than the upper, and on the sides on which the ground falls they are strengthened by buttresses. **Aqueducts**, some still in use, conveying water into the city, were carried across the moat by the *batardeaux*, and afforded the means of flooding the ditch when necessary.

nts at which the aqueducts
the moat were protected by
>wers. The **Outer Wall** is
. ft. high and 13 ft. thick, and
tected by 78 small flanking
>f square, round, or hexagonal
Each tower stood midway be-
vo towers of the *Inner Wall*,
iains of 71 of them can be
ished. The **Inner Wall** was
ngest part of the fortifica-
:t is nearly 36 ft. high and
5 ft. thick, and was provided
6 flanking towers, of which
ain in a tottering state. The
ary in shape like those of the
'all ; they were entered from
by small doorways, and most
had doors communicating with
sse-braie and the rampart;
ere divided into storeys and
erced by windows and loop-
The **rampart** was reached
e city by ramps of masonry,
hts of steps then led up to the
' the towers on which the en-
>f war were placed. There
; least 14 gates in the Theo-
walls. Seven were " Public
through which communica-
is kept up with the outer
by roads that crossed the
n bridges; and seven were
iry Gates," built for the
ence of the garrison, and
access only to the *chemin
les.* The Public and Military
came in alternate order, and
1 the *Inner Wall* were strongly
ed by towers on either side of
eway. The stone used in the
ction of the walls is a lime-
quarried in the neighbourhood
ri-keui, a village on the Mar-
, few miles from the city. To
ie walls more firmly together,
i of brick alternate with the
i of stone. Until the reign of
ie Isaurian, the building and
of the walls was entrusted to
ctions of the city; but from his
he matter was dealt with by
neral government.

*n the Marmara to Yedi Kuleh-
i.*—The **1st inner tower** was
key.

erected, according to the inscription,
by the Emperors Basil II. and Constantine, 975–1025. A **postern**, with
monogram of Christ above it, follows.
On the **1st outer tower** is the inscription, " John Palaeologus Emperor in
Christ." It is one of 7 similar inscriptions, recording repairs made by
that sovereign between 1433–44. The
4th inner tower was erected from
the foundations by Romanus, "the
great Emperor of the Romans." The
7th inner tower, N. of the line of
railway, is assigned to the Emperors
Leo and Constantine; probably Leo
the Isaurian, and his son Constantine Copronymus, for the walls were
severely shaken by an earthquake in
740, near the close of Leo's reign.
The *Golden Gate* is distinguished
by the large marble towers flanking
its inner portals; it was the **1st
Military Gate**, and formed the "Triumphal Arch," through which the
emperors usually entered the city on
state occasions. Its name is due to
the gilding formerly upon it. The
inner gate has 3 archways, of which
the central one was reserved for the
emperor. The wall on either side
of the outer gate was once adorned
with exquisite sculptures, representing the Labours of Hercules, the
Torture of Prometheus, &c. The two
marble towers beside the gate were
repaired by Cantacuzene and John
Palaeologus I. Within the Golden
Gate, according to some authorities,
stood the **citadel**, known from its
circular form as the *Kyklobion* and
the *Strongylon ;* but that building
was certainly outside the walls on
the shore of the Marmara. The
enclosure of the *Seven Towers*, " Hep-
tapyrgion," was built by Sultan Muhammad II. to guard his conquest
and his treasures. His structure is
famous as the state prison, in which
distinguished foreigners were often
confined for political reasons. Here
the ambassadors of nations at war
with Turkey were sometimes detained.
Inscriptions made by foreign prisoners
may be seen about the entrance to the
dungeon tower, at the E.S.E. corner
of the enclosure. *Yedi Kuleh Kapu-*
r

—Gate of the Seven Towers; according to Dr. Mordtman, the *Small Golden Gate* and the **1st Public Gate.** Within, the Byzantine eagle spreads its wings above the gate. The *Armenian Hospital* lies to the W. of the road.

From Yedi Kuleh Kapusi to Silivri Kapusi.—The *Greek Hospital* is to the W. of the road. The **2nd Military Gate** (τοῦ Δευτέρου): According to Dr. Dethier, the numerals attached to the Military Gates refer to the order in which the divisions of the Gothic Guards were originally quartered along the ground between the walls of Constantine and the Theodosian lines; but this is doubtful. To the W. is the *Greek Orphanage.* The **5th outer tower,** beyond the gate, was erected by John Palaeologus in 1433. The **9th inner tower** bears the names of the Emperors Leo and Constantine. The **10th** and **11th outer towers** are assigned to John Palaeologus, 1433–44. *Silivri Kapusi—***2nd Public Gate—**leading to the ancient *Selymbria.* The inscription on its southern tower styles it the Gate of the Spring (τῆς πηγῆς), because the road to the famous Holy Well at Balukli (p. 53) passed through it. The gate is also stated to have been repaired in 1433 by a certain Manuel Bryennius. The *Mosque of Ibrahim Pasha* within the gate is regarded as the ancient *Church of S. Anna.* The gate's northern tower was erected by Basil II. and Constantine. The Greek force that recaptured the city from the Latins in 1261 entered through this gate. On the W. side of the road are buried the *heads of the famous Ali Pasha of Yanina,* his three sons, and his nephew, A.D. 1827. Opposite the tomb are the remains of an *aqueduct* ascribed by some to Stratego-poulos, the general of Michael Palaeologus.

From Silivri Kapusi to Yeni Mevlevi Khâneh Kapusi.—The **3rd outer tower** beyond the former gate was built in 1439, by John Palaeologus. **3rd Military Gate** in ruins.

Yeni Mevlevi Khâneh Kapusi, so named in honour of a Tekkeh, belonging to the Mevlevi Order of Dervishes, situated to the W. of the road. The **3rd Public Gate,** known in ancient times by several names: *Rhegiou,* because leading to Rhegium; *Rusiou,* either a corruption of the former name, or in honour of some restorer, or, according to Dr. Mordtman, because built by the Red Faction, as the red painted shafts forming the gate's jambs and lintel would indicate; *Melandesias,* or Melantiados, because it led to Melantiade, a village on the Athyra. The *inscriptions* over the gate have special interest. One in Greek proclaims that in the space of 60 days the Eparch Constantine (Cyrus) added wall to wall for the sceptre-loving sovereign (Theodosius II.). The Latin inscription is fuller and more boastful. "By the command of Theodosius, Constantine placed in position these strong fortifications in less than two months. Scarcely would Pallas herself have built a fortress so strong in time so short." These two inscriptions evidently refer to the erection of the outer wall by Cyrus in 447. Another Greek inscription below the first states that the breastwork (προτείχισμα) was repaired under Justin and Sophia, our most pious sovereigns, by Narses, the most glorious Spatharius, and by Sakellarius, and by Stephen, who was devoted to the service of the servants of the most revered sovereigns. Narses is known in connection with other public works during the reign of Justin I. Within an arc of a circle over the lintel is an inscription, referring doubtless to the destroyed figures of the gate's guardian saints. Entering the inner gate, two inscriptions will be seen on the right-hand tower. The higher reads: "The Fortune of Constantine, our God protected sovereign, triumphs." The lower is imperfect. It probably refers to Basil II.

From Yeni Mevlevi Khâneh Kapusi to Top Kapusi.—The **4th Military Gate** is distinguished as that of

Georgius, who repaired it. Within, on either side of it, is a ramp ascending to the ramparts. *Top Kapusi*, the Cannon Gate; its name is a reminiscence of the fact that the strongest battery employed in the siege of 1453 was placed opposite this gate. It is the **4th Public Gate**, the *Gate of S. Romanus*, after an adjacent church dedicated to that saint. Famous as the gate near which the last of the Greek Emperors, Constantine Dragoses, on the fatal 29th May, 1453, sought and found death, so as not to survive the fall of his Empire. Through the same gate, a few hours later, the Turkish Conqueror entered the captured city in triumph. The tower on the N. side of the gate is considered to be the *Tower of Bactagium*, mentioned in the history of the final siege. Near the gate is *Monastir Mesjidi*, an old church dedicated first to SS. Menodoras, Metrodoras, and Nymphodoras, and later, *circ.* 1341, to the Virgin.

From Top Kapusi to Edirneh Kapusi.—The road descends the ravine of the *Lycus*. The walls along the descent are terribly shattered. Here the great breach was opened in 1453, and here was the scene of the stubborn defence made by the Genoese John Giustiniani and his 400 men, until he received the wound which took him from the field of battle, and spread irretrievable panic among the besieged. The **Lycus** is a winter torrent that comes from the heights of *Maltepeh*, and, flowing through the city, enters the Marmara at Vlanga-Bostan. In its bed without the walls is the *fountain of Beyler-bey*. The stream is carried beneath the fortifications, and passes into the city below the 10th inner tower (*Sulu Kuleh*, the Water-Tower) N. of Top Kapusi. The **5th Military Gate** bears a Latin inscription, stating that Pusæus (consul and prefect in 467), who was not inferior to Anthemius, strengthened the walls at this point. The reference is to the strong buttresses which support the inner side of the walls. It was while descending on horseback one of the slopes of the Lycus ravine that Theod. II. fell, and sustained the injuries which caused his death. In pulling down the **2nd tower** beyond the 5th Military Gate, in 1868, twelve slabs were discovered bearing epitaphs of persons who had belonged to the Fœderati, or Gothic troops, in the service of the Empire. Here an **aqueduct**, bringing water from the hill of Halkali, 2 hrs. N. of S. Stefano, enters the city. Some consider it to be the aqueduct of Justinian.

Edirneh Kapusi, the Adrianople Gate, because on the highway to that city. **5th Public Gate**, known, 1st, as *P. Polyandriou*, or of the Cemetery, because in the street leading to the Imperial Cemetery round the Church of the Holy Apostles. 2nd, as *P. Charsiou*, after some person concerned with its construction or repair. The mosque within the gate and to the rt. is *Mihrimah Jami'*, built by Sultan Suleiman in honour of his daughter. It occupies the site of an ancient *Church of S. George*. In compensation for the loss of that church the Greek community received the site on which the present *Church of S. George* stands, to the l. of the gate. In the church are preserved two MS. Lectionaries that once did service in S. Sophia, one containing the Lessons from the Gospels; the other those taken from the Epistles. Through this gate visitors proceed to the *Kahriyeh Jamisi*, the Church of the Chora, containing beautiful mosaics (p. 54). Walk some 8 minutes towards the N.E., the church is easily distinguished by its cupolas and minaret. Visitors to *Tekfûr Serai* also enter here and follow the walls towards the harbour until a glass factory is reached, through which there is access to the interior of the old palace.

From Edirneh Kapusi to the present termination of the Theodosian Walls.—The **6th inner tower** bears the name of Nicholas, a cavalry officer, son of Agalon. The **6th**

D 2

Military Gate is supposed to have stood between the 8th and 9th inner towers. At the inner tower, immediately preceding Tekfûr Serai, the main line of the walls is broken for a short distance. The opening thus made into the city from the *faussebraie* was closed by a transverse wall between the *inner* and the *outer* walls. Most of that structure has disappeared, but in the modern wall, which has taken its place, are traces of a small, ancient gateway. This is supposed to be the **postern**, *Kerkoporta*, which, after having been long closed, was opened during the siege of 1453 to facilitate the movements of the besieged garrison; and through which, when left unguarded, a band of 50 Turks entered the city, and seizing the adjacent tower gave occasion to the belief that Constantinople was in the hands of the enemy, and that further resistance was useless.

Most authorities have placed the famous **Hebdomon Quarter** here, and according to this view, to which there are serious objections, the tower immediately adjoining Tekfûr Serai is the *Tribunal of the Emperor Valens*, in which, during the earlier history of the city, the emperors were proclaimed and received the homage of the army. Valens was the first sovereign thus proclaimed Emperor in Constantinople. Among his successors, Arcadius, Theodosius II., Marcian, Leo the Great, Basiliscus, and Phocas, entered upon their reign in the "Tribunal." The level ground before the walls was, in that case, the *Campus* of New Rome, where soldiers were exercised; and whither, on the occasion of an earthquake, the population of the city often fled to offer litanies for deliverance. In the angle formed by the tower and the wall beyond is a ruined gateway. It represents probably the **6th Public Gate**, the one to which the name *Kerko Porta* or *P. Xylokerkou* strictly belonged, and after which the small postern already noticed was named. It was closed by Isaac Angelus to prevent the fulfilment of the prophecy that through it the Emperor Frederick of Germany would capture the city. The gate led to a *Circus*, constructed of wood, outside the walls. Over the gate was a Greek inscription in honour of Cyrus Constantine, similar to that on Yeni Mevlevi Khâneh Kapusi. The gate further on led into the courtyard of the Palace. Possibly it is the gate known as the *Gate of Porphyrogenitus*, after one of the names of the palace. The windows in the outer wall belonged to buildings attached to the Palace. The **7th Military Gate** and the **7th Public Gate** have disappeared in the changes the walls have undergone.

Tekfûr Serai, the palace of *Tekfûr*, a Turkish designation of the Greek Emperor; the supposed **Hebdomon Palace**. The present building, popularly known as the *Palace of Belisarius*, has been assigned to Constantine Porphyrogenitus. Hence, perhaps, the fact that it is sometimes styled the *Palace of Constantine*, and sometimes that of *Porphyrogenitus*. It had three stories, the lowest being $54\frac{1}{2}$ ft. by $32\frac{1}{2}$ ft. The second communicated with the supposed Tribunal of Valens. The northern façade was decorated with variegated patterns of small pieces of marble and brick. Over the arches, glistening in the sun, are narrow bands of copper, following the lines of the arch, and probably originally gilt. The building deserves inspection as one of the few remaining specimens of Byzantine civil architecture. The palaces of Venice seem to be a development of this style. If this be the Hebdomon Palace, it replaced a much older building, erected by Constantine the Great, or one of his immediate successors, for the convenience of the emperor when reviewing troops on the Campus. In that case it was the favourite resort of Justinian the Great, called Jucundiana, from which several of his laws are dated. The Hebdomon was often occupied by the emperors for its good air and splendid view, and there they usually stayed after a victorious campaign while preparations were made for a triumphal entry through the Golden Gate. There are, however, unanswerable arguments in favour of the view that the site of this famous palace was on the shore of the Marmara, outside the walls, near Makri-keui (p. 86).

II. The Wall of Manuel Comnenus. This wall is often regarded as the work of Heraclius, but according to Nicetas it was built by Manuel Comnenus to give additional protection to the Palace of Blachernæ, which he had made the favourite Imperial Residence. It extended from the present end of the Theodosian lines to the point occupied by the *Tower of Isaac Angelus;* but only the southern portion as far as the foot of the hill belongs to the original wall. The remainder is a restoration at a later date. The new work consisted of a single wall, which, while on the steep slope of the 6th hill, was unprotected by a moat. It was, however, built stronger and higher than any other part of the fortifications, its ramparts were broader, and its towers more closely spaced than elsewhere. At present there are 13 towers, alternately circular and octagonal in the original, and square in the later portion.

Between the 2nd and 3rd towers, from the upper end of the line, there is a small gateway for the convenience possibly of some church. The 3rd tower is probably the one which was ascended by the Emperor Constantine Dragoses and his companion, the historian Phrantzes, to reconnoitre the Turkish camp on the eve of May 29th, whence they heard the ominous sound of preparations for the fatal assault a few hours later. Between the 6th and 7th towers is the gate known as *Egri Kapu*, the Crooked Gate. It is the ancient *P. Caligaria*, so named after a quarter or factory occupied by makers of military shoes (*caliga*). The main ancient conduit, which supplies the city with water from the neighbour-

hood of *Belgrâd*, enters near this gate. It can be seen at the *taksim*, near the fountain on the roadside. During the last siege persistent efforts were made to undermine the walls at this point. Some traces of the Theodosian walls, behind Manuel's wall, will be found inside the gate by following the street running S.E. towards Tekfûr Serai, or the street descending from the Greek Church towards the N.

The site of the **Palace of Blachernæ**, which, like Tekfûr Serai, was between the two walls of Theodosius, can be reached through Egri Kapu by following the street leading to the *Mosque Aivas Effendi*. The foundation of the palace, of which only the substructures remain, is ascribed to the Emperor Anastasius Dicorus (491–518). It was at first probably a villa or kiosk, for the convenience of the emperor, when visiting the shrine of the Virgin in the church of Blachernæ, or when on a hunting expedition in the neighbourhood. But the beauty of its position soon led to its enlargement and more frequent use. In the 9th century it comprised several buildings, and was already of considerable importance. Under Alexius Comnenus it was a favourite Imperial Residence, as the readers of Scott's 'Count Robert of Paris' are aware. The interviews between the Greek Emperor and Peter the Hermit, Godfrey de Bouillon, and other early Crusaders, took place in it. Upon the accession of Manuel Comnenus the palace was further enlarged and improved, and from that time became, with occasional interruptions, the habitual abode of the Court. The negotiations between the leaders of the 4th Crusade and Isaac Angelus were also held here. The palace was injured by its Latin occupants, but was repaired upon the restoration of the Greek Empire, and continued to be the Imperial Residence of the Palaeologi until the fall of Constantinople. The Theodosian walls which surrounded it formed the fortified enclosure known as the *Castellum of Blachernæ*. Between the 2nd and 3rd towers beyond the foot of the hill is a closed gateway, which can be reached through the adjoining candle-factory. It is the *P. Gyrolimne*, the principal gate for the use of the Palace of Blachernæ. It was so named because it looked towards the Ἀργυρᾶ Λίμνη, the Silver Marsh at *Eyüb.* High up, on the *curtain* of the wall, between the 3rd and 4th towers, is an inscription of John Palaeologus, 1441. On the 4th tower is an inscription marking it as one of Isaac Angelus, constructed, in 1188, under the superintendence of Basil. It is a question whether this inscription is in its original position. Some think it once belonged to the next tower, which is undoubtedly that built, according to the historian Nicetas, by *Isaac Angelus*, as an additional protection to the Palace of Blachernæ and as a place of refuge for the Emperor. The material for its construction was obtained from ancient churches. The shafts below the windows supported a balcony. The base of the tower is buttressed by a wall some 14 ft. high.

The next tower, likewise buttressed, is known as the **Tower of Anemas**, because it gave access to the *State Prison of Anemas*, which was situated in the body of the upper portion of the adjoining buttressed wall. The prison appears to have been constructed under Alexius Comnenus, and derived its name from its first inmate, Anemas, implicated in a plot against that emperor in 1107. It was the State Prison attached to the Palace of Blachernæ. Among the more remarkable personages confined here were the Emperor Andronicus Comnenus; the Patriarch Veccus; Andronicus, the son of John VI. Palaeologus; John VI. Palaeologus himself and his two sons, one of whom afterwards became the Emperor Manuel II. Palaeologus. The visitor to the prison must be prepared to face much that is unpleasant. A ladder and lights can be obtained at the large house by the roadside, but the explorer had better provide his own light. The tower is entered through the arched opening on the N., and by following a low passage a vaulted chamber is reached. In this there are three openings, of which those on the rt. and in front lead to different parts of the tower, whence there is access to the court of the *Mosque Aivas Effendi* overhead. The opening on the l. leads to the prison proper, which is about 200 ft. S.-N., 40 ft. high, and 30 ft. wide. It is built of massive masonry and had two storeys, each of which contained 12 cells. The upper floor has disappeared, but the walls and doorways between the cells remain.

III. The Wall of Leo the Armenian.

North of the Prison of Anemas the city is again defended by two walls, sometimes called the *Pentapyrgion*, from their 5 towers. The outer, with a moat, which has disappeared, was built early in the reign of Leo the Armenian (813–20), in expectation of an attack by the Bulgarians under Crum. It has undergone repairs, in the course of which inscribed stones belonging to other structures have been used. One bears the date 793, and another portions of the names of Michael II. and Theophilus, the " Great Kings." The wall has a gate corresponding to a gate in the inner wall, the *Gate of Blachernæ*, which led into that quarter of the city. The inscription on the *Tower of S. Nicholas* beyond states that it was rebuilt from the foundations by Romanus "the Christ-loving Emperor." It derived its name from a *Chapel of S. Nicholas*, between the two walls. The western end of the street outside the harbour walls was closed by a wall that ran down to the water's edge, and was pierced by the *Xyloporta*, the Wooden Gate, of which traces remain.

IV. The Wall of Heraclius.

This, the inner wall alluded to above, can be visited by following the street that cuts through the harbour walls at the Little Aivan Serai Kapusi, and then turns to the rt. The space between the two walls is occupied by a very picturesque *Turkish Cemetery,* held in great veneration as the last resting-place of the Moslems who fell during the first siege of Constantinople by the Arabs. (The guardian requires a fee.) The *wall* was built in 627 for the defence of the Blachernæ quarter, which, being beyond the fortifications, had been recently entered, and partially burned, by a party of Avars at the close of their siege of the city. The venerated shrine of the Virgin in the quarter was strangely spared by the enemy on that occasion. The brickwork forming the upper part of the three towers is evidently a later addition, to raise them above the wall of Leo. The gate is the ancient *Gate of Blachernæ,* which during the civil strifes of the empire was opened more than once by partizans of the faction outside the city to admit their friends and overthrow their rivals. The *Holy Well* before this wall is supposed to mark the site of the *Church of S. Nicholas.*

The **Seven Towers,** *Yedi Kuleh,* built by Muhammad II., 1458, stand near the S.W. angle of Constantinople, where the walls which cross the promontory join the Sea of Marmara. This imperial castle, once a state prison, like the Tower of London and the Bastille in Paris, has ceased to be used as such. Three of the towers have nearly disappeared, and the whole building is in a state of dilapidation. On one of them are several inscriptions, recording the imprisonment of various persons, Venetians and others, in 1600 and 1704. The Janissaries who garrisoned it used, in the height of their power, to bring to this castle the Sultans they had dethroned, and keep them in prison or put them to death. Several Sultans have thus lost their lives in this place, and innumerable heads of Grand Viziers and less illustrious sufferers have hung from the battlements. Foreign ambassadors were always imprisoned here on the Porte's declaring war against the States they represented; the last was the French ambassador in 1798. One of the towers was thrown down by an earthquake in 1768; those remaining are 200 feet high; the whole inner space is unoccupied; stone steps lead up to a platform within the wall, whence there is a fine view of the Sea of Marmara. A small open court in which executions took place, and the heads were piled up, is called *the place of heads.* Close to the tower in which the foreign ambassadors used to be confined is a deep hole, called *the well of blood,* into which the heads of executed persons were thrown; it is now covered with stone slabs. Near this are the *dungeons* where those condemned to die were confined, and a place called *the rocky cavern,* where they were put to the torture. A small *fee* is charged for entrance to the Seven Towers, which can be reached by train to *Yedi Kuleh Station,* by *tram,* by driving, or by riding.

§ 12.—HIPPODROME—COLUMNS.

The **Hippodrome** is now represented by the open space known as the *At Meidan,* " Horse Square," S.W. of S. Sophia. On its S.E. side is the Mosque of Sultan Ahmed ; on the S.W. an Industrial School and the Museum of Old Turkish Costumes ; and on the N.W. Government buildings, the Defter-Khâneh, prisons, &c. These structures have encroached more or less upon the ground once occupied by the Hippodrome. On the N.E. are a public garden and the opening to the square in front of S. Sophia. This famous place of public amusement was commenced by the Emperor Severus when he rebuilt Byzantium, but owing to his departure for the West, the work was stopped and remained incomplete until Constantine the Great founded Constantinople. Then the Hippodrome was finished, and the first races and ceremonies held in it celebrated the inauguration of the new capital of the Empire. The Circus Maximus at Rome served as the model for this racecourse which was an oblong area, with one semicircular end. As the extent of level ground was insufficient, large vaults were constructed on the S.W. to obtain the additional area required. The artificial ground thus formed begins at the monument known as the Colossus (p. 42). By walking toward the S.W., along the W. wall of the Industrial School, a point will soon be reached where the circular end of the Hippodrome rises above the level of the ground, like the stern of a vessel stranded among the rocks. An iron door near this point leads to the vaults in which is a cistern, named in old times the Cold Cistern, on account of the coolness of its water. The master of the Turkish Bath opposite the door keeps the key. The Hippodrome was between 1200 and 1300 ft. in length, and about half as wide. Along a portion of its axis, which ran N.E. to S.W., stood a low wall (*Spina*), that divided the course into two sections, and furnished a platform, upon which numerous valuable works of art were displayed, as the three surviving monuments testify. Beyond either end of the Spina stood the goals (καμπτῆρες), around which the chariots whirled seven times in their giddy course. The semicircular portion of the area, called the *Sphendonè*, was often used for popular amusements on a small scale, and the public execution of criminals.

Along the rectangular end of the Hippodrome stood the *Church of S. Stephen*, from whose upper windows the Court ladies witnessed the games; the stalls (*Carceres, Mangana*) for chariots and horses; and above these the Imperial Tribune (*Kathisma*), which was reached from the adjoining grounds of the Great Palace by a private stairway (*Cochlias*), in which more than one assassination was perpetrated. On the other sides of the Hippodrome were 30 to 40 rows of seats, built of marble after those of wood had been twice destroyed by

fire, in 406 and 498. Above the seats was a long walk or promenade, adorned with statues, and commanding a superb view of the city and neighbourhood. As combats between wild beasts were not permitted, there was no canal of water at the foot of the seats to separate them from the arena, as in the case of the Circus Maximus at Rome. A crowd of statues—gods, heroes, emperors, and charioteers—ornamented the various parts of the building. Among other noble pieces of art the following are mentioned as the most remarkable: A Hercules; the group representing a man and an ass, erected by Augustus in honour of his victory over Antony; the Wolf suckling Romulus and Remus; a man fighting with a lion; an eagle attempting to fly while a serpent coiled round its feet and struck at its wings; a most exquisite statue of Helen of Troy, &c., &c. These works were in bronze, and were melted down by the Crusaders in 1204, and converted into coin.

The Hippodrome was entered by 4 gates—2 on each of its sides—and possibly also by one at its N.E. end. The Gate of the Dead (*Nekra*) stood, probably, near the present southern outlet of the At Meidan. The Hippodrome, besides being a racecourse, served every purpose that could attract a crowd. Here emperors were proclaimed, and victorious generals, like Belisarius, celebrated their triumphs; here criminals were executed and heretics burned; here wild animals were exhibited and athletic sports held. As has been well said, the Spina of the Hippodrome was the axis around which the Byzantine world revolved. Here took place, in 532, the famous struggle between Justinian the Great and the rebellious Factions of the Circus, a struggle that nearly cost him his crown and deluged the arena with the blood of 30,000 citizens. The formidable revolt of the Janissaries, in 1826, was crushed by *Mahmûd II.* in the *Et Meidan*, and not, as sometimes stated, in this place,

Under the Turks the At Meidan was used for horse exercises and for the martial pastime of throwing the *Jerid*, which, since the destruction of the Janissaries, has been persistently discouraged in Turkey.

The **Obelisk**, of Egyptian syenite, came from Heliopolis, where it was erected by Thothmes III. It was placed in the Hippodrome by Theodosius the Great, and is 60 ft. high. It rests on four bronze cubes, placed upon a pedestal formed of two blocks of marble and four of red granite. The *bas-reliefs* upon the pedestal represent scenes witnessed in the Hippodrome. *North side*, lower block—1st. The Obelisk being dragged through the Hippodrome; 2nd. The Obelisk in position. Upper block—two balconies in the Kathisma; the lower, divided by steps leading to a door at the back of the upper, contains 16 spectators; the upper divided into three sections. In the centre, raised above the others, is the Imperial Tribune, occupied by the Emperor Theodosius I., seated, his two sons Honorius and Arcadius, a courtier, and a guard; on either side is a stand, occupied by 3 courtiers and 4 Gothic guards. The groove down the face of the *pedestal* was probably made to carry rain off the monument without injury to the sculptures. At its summit is the *Labarum.*
West side, lower block, a Greek inscription:—

Κίονα τετράπλευρον ἀεὶ χθονὶ κείμενον
　ἄχθος
Μοῦνος ἀναστῆσαι Θευδόσιος βασιλεὺς
Τολμήσας Πρόκλῳ ἐπεκέκλετο· καὶ τόσος
　ἔστη
Κίων, ἠελίοις ἐν τριάκοντα δύω.

Upper block another Kathisma, with 2 balconies: in the lower, 10 Barbarians offering tribute; in the upper the Imperial Family, including the Empress Flaccilla, courtiers and guards. *South side*, lower block, a chariot-race round the Spina and its monuments. Upper block, the Kathis-

ma as on the north. In lower balcony are 16 courtiers; on the steps leading to the upper, 2 tall figures, representing *Mandatores*, through whom the Emperor addressed the Factions. In the upper balcony, the Imperial Family, 5 courtiers and 11 guards. *East side*, lower block, a Latin inscription:—

" Difficilis quondam dominis parere serenis
　Jussus, et extinctis palmam portare tyrannis,
　Omnia Theodosio cedunt sobolique perenni,
　Ter denis sic victus ego domitusque diebus
　Judice sub Proclo su[pera]s elatus ad auras."

On upper block, two balconies: in lower, 57 persons, musicians, dancers, spectators; in upper, the Emperor holding the wreath for the winner of the race, courtiers and guards.

The **Serpent Column** is about 20 ft. high; it is formed of three bronze serpents, the tails downwards, and the bodies twisted spirally as far as the necks; their heads spreading outward formerly supported the golden tripod of the priestess of Apollo at Delphi, whence this singular monument is generally supposed to have been brought. The history of the relic is very interesting. At the celebrated battle of Platæa (B.C. 479), which delivered Greece from the Persian invaders, the Greeks obtained immense booty, one-tenth of which was dedicated to the oracle of Delphi. Out of the gold thus acquired there was made, according to Herodotus, a golden tripod, which was placed on the bronze three-headed serpent that stood close to the altar. The tripod was carried off by the Phocians in the sacred war. The bronze pillar remained at Delphi till the time of Pausanias, but was carried to Constantinople by Constantine, and set up where it now stands. It is one of the most interesting monuments in the world. The three heads are gone, and tradition says that one of them was struck off by Muhammad the Conqueror with a blow of his axe. The head of one of the serpents is preserved in the Imperial Museum. In 1856, after the Crimean War, the base of the column was cleared by British soldiers, under the direction of Sir C. Newton, and the inscription upon the monument was thus restored to view. It commenced on the thirteenth coil of the serpent from the bottom, and extended downwards to the third. The inscription appears to have consisted of a dedication to Apollo, which is in great part effaced, and the names of the 32 Greek States which had taken part in the wars against the Persians. Traces of 31 names remain, written in ancient Greek characters, which bear witness to the antiquity of the monument. The text of the inscription is given in Rawlinson's 'Herodotus,' vol. iv., app. I.

The **pillar** or **obelisk** of masonry (*Colossus*), to the S.W. of the Serpent Column, was once, as the holes for rivets in the stones prove, covered with plates of bronze, that made it gleam like a column of light. It was, when complete, 94 ft. high. The date of the original construction of the monument is unknown, but, according to the inscription on the E. side of the pedestal, it was restored in the 10th century by Constantine Porphyrogenitus:—

τὸ τετράπλευρον θαῦμα τῶν μεταρσίων
χρόνῳ φθαρέν, Κωνσταντῖνος νῦν δεσπότης
οὗ 'Ρωμανὸς παῖς, δόξα τῆς σκηπτουχίας
κρεῖττον νεουργεῖ τῆς πάλαι θεωρίας
ὁ γὰρ κολοσσὸς θάμβος ἦν ἐν τῇ 'Ροδῷ,
καὶ χάλκος οὗτος θάμβος ἐστὶν ἐνθάδε.

The *four Gilt Bronze Horses of Lysippus*, which now adorn the façade of San Marco, in Venice, formed one of the finest ornaments of the Imperial Kathisma. They are said to have been brought to Constantinople from Scio by Theodosius II. After the capture of Constantinople by Dandolo in 1204, they were taken as a trophy to Venice. In 1797 they were removed by Bonaparte to Paris, and placed on the arch in the Place du Carrousel, where they remained till their restoration to Venice in 1815,

COLUMNS.

In the *Seraglio Garden* is a granite column, about 49 ft. high, surmounted by a Corinthian capital, and commonly called the **Column of Theodosius**. According to the much-effaced Latin inscription on the eastern face of the pedestal, it commemorates victories over the Goths : "Fortunæ reduci ob devictos Gothos." Some ascribe the column to Theodosius the Great, but it belongs more probably to the *Emperor Claudius Gothicus*, who gained a victory over the Goths at Nissa, A.D. 269. In that case, it is the oldest monument in the city.

The **Column of Constantine the Great**, at *Táuk Bazâr*, on the summit of the second hill. It is known as the **Porphyry Column**, from its material; the **Hooped Column** (*Chenberli Tash*), because of the metal rings that hold it together; and the **Burnt Column**, in view of the injuries it has received from fire. It is said to have been brought from Rome, and when first erected, consisted of 8 drums of porphyry resting upon a pedestal of marble. It was surmounted by a beautiful bronze *statue of Apollo*, representing Constantine himself, and formed a monument over 120 ft. in height. In 416, a piece of the lowest block having broken off, the drums were bound by hoops of bronze, wrought like wreaths of laurel. As the monument was peculiarly associated with the founder of the city, it was invested with a halo of sanctity and regarded as the pledge of the city's well-being. The *Palladium* of Rome was supposed to have been secretly laid beneath its foundations, as well as a piece of the Cross and other relics, while a nail used in the crucifixion of Christ is said to have formed one of the rays that encircled the statue's brow. At the beginning of every year a solemn service, attended by the Emperor, was performed by the Patriarch at the column's base. Here also public decrees were read, and here, upon the occasion of a triumph, emperors would sit, and, amid acclaiming crowds, place a conqueror's foot upon the head of a prostrate prisoner of war. When the Turks entered the city, it was fondly hoped their advance would be arrested at this point by an angel, who would chase them beyond the empire's ancient boundaries. The statue was injured by lightning during the reign of Botoniates, and afterwards dashed to the ground by a strong southerly gale during the reign of Alexius Comnenus. At the same time the column was injured, a damage which Manuel Comnenus clumsily repaired with the marble masonry now crowning the structure. Upon the restored portion are inscribed the words:—

τὸ θεῖον ἔργον ἐνθάδε φθαρὲν χρόνῳ
καινεῖ Μανουὴλ εὐσεβὴς Αὐτοκράτωρ.

"The pious Emperor Manuel renews the divine work here, wasted by time." The original pedestal is concealed by repairs made in 1701. The column marks the site of the *Forum of Constantine the Great.*

The **Column of Marcian,** in the valley of the Lycus, below the Mosque of Sultan Muhammad II., is popularly known as the *Kiz Tash,* "the Maiden's Stone." It is a granite shaft 33 ft. high, surmounted by a Corinthian capital of marble, bearing a cippus with an eagle at each corner. Upon the cippus, now thrown out of position by earthquakes, rose the Emperor's statue. The pedestal, which stood upon three steps, is ornamented with Victories, wreaths, and a cross, and bears on its northern face an inscription once formed with metal letters:—

"Principis hanc statuam Marciani cerne torumque, Decius ter vovit quod Tatianus opus."

Tatian was prefect of the city.

Near the column is the **Et Meidan,** *Meat Square,* the old Quarter of the Janissaries, where their revolt was mercilessly put down, in 1826, by Mahmûd II. The Quarter was almost demolished by the fire of the Sultan's artillery; and a bare patch of ground still marks the spot on which stood the *Orta Jami'* (Regimental Mosque), in which the Janissaries bound themselves by an oath to revolt.

The **Column of Arcadius,** *Avret Tash,* at Avret Bazâr, on the summit of the 7th hill. Little more than its colossal pedestal, once richly ornamented, remains. It is about 20 ft. high. The column was hollow, with a spiral stairway leading to the top, like the columns of Trajan and Antonine at Rome. Winding round its exterior was a train of figures in bas-relief celebrating the victories of the Emperor Arcadius, whose silver statue glittered on the summit until it was overthrown, in 740, by an earthquake. The monument, about 158 ft. in height, was commenced by Arcadius, and completed in 421 by his son, Theodosius II. It was taken down in 1695, having become dangerous. It marks the site of the Forum, known both as the *Forum of Arcadius* and that *of Theodosius II.* A similar column stood in the Forum of Theodosius the Great or of Taurus, on the 3rd hill. The interior of the pedestal can be visited. On the ceiling of one of its chambers are found the letters A and Ω. A stairway leads to the summit, where remains of bas-reliefs may still be seen. Splendid view of the city and surroundings.

§ 13.—BYZANTINE CHURCHES.

St. Irene. (*Admission by Firman.*) In the first court of the Seraglio, reached either by the *Sôûk Cheshmeh* Gate, or by the *Bâb-i-Humayûn* above St. Sophia. One of the oldest and best-preserved of the Byzantine churches. Originally constructed by Constantine the Great; burnt down in 532 during the sedition of the *Nika,* and rebuilt by Justinian the Great; overthrown, in 740, by an earthquake during the reign of Leo the Isaurian, and rebuilt or restored soon afterwards. During the Arian ascendancy it was for some time in the hands of the orthodox party, but there is no evidence that it was the church in which the second General Council assembled. It has largely preserved its original basilican form, and is a long rectangular building with a nave and two aisles. At the E. end was an apse filled with marble benches, or steps, somewhat similar to the Church of Torcello, near Venice, and at the W. end is a narthex opening into an atrium. The principal dome is carried on a perpendicular drum, pierced with 20 windows, which is apparently the earliest example, in a complete form, of this mode of supporting, and introducing light to, a dome. The decorative details of the interior are simple in character, and the old gilt mosaics and a long Greek inscription are still visible on the walls and vaulted roof of the chancel. The church has never been turned into a mosque, and has been used by the Turks, ever since the Conquest, as an armoury (p. 66).

S. Sophia, *Aya Sofia Jamisi,* was the Cathedral Church of ancient Constantinople, and is now the principal mosque of Stambûl. It was dedicated to Divine Wisdom (τῇ ἁγίᾳ σοφίᾳ), and was also known as "the Great Church" on account of its size and importance. Three buildings have borne the name, and occupied, more or less, the site of this famous sanctuary. First, the basilica, with wooden roof, erected by Constantine the Great, and enlarged and completed by his son and successor, Constantius. It was dedicated with great pomp, 15th February, 360; but, in 404, it was burnt to the ground during the tumult caused by the exile of St. John Chrysostom. Second, the new church which rose on the ashes of the first, and was dedicated in 415, by Theodosius II. It was burnt 15th January, 532, during the sedition of the *Nika.* Third, the present church, of which the foundation-stone was laid by Justinian on the 23rd February, 532, only forty days after the fire. The building was completed in 5 years and 10 months; and the dedication took place on the 26th December, 537. The architects were Anthemius of Tralles (*Aidin*), and Isidorus of Miletus. In 558 the eastern semi-dome and the great dome fell in and crushed the altar, ciborium, and pulpit, but they were rebuilt in the form in which we now find them by Isidorus the Younger; and on Christmas-eve, 561, the church was rededicated, the services on the occasion lasting until the Epiphany. Important repairs were afterwards carried out during the reigns of Basil I.; Basil II.; Romanus Argyrus; Andronicus II.; Anna, the Dowager Empress of Andronicus III.; Cantacuzene; John VI. Palaeologus; and Sultan Abdul-Mejid, who employed the Italian architect, Fossati.

The Church of S. Sophia became, after its restoration under Justinian, the theatre of the greatest and most solemn transactions of state, of the nuptials and public church ceremonies of the emperor. Tradition and history united in pronouncing this place of worship, from the moment of its construction to that in which it was converted into a mosque, to be the most remarkable temple of the whole empire. The building has been described in detail by Paul Silentiarius in a special work; and he has also given the superstitious legends connected with its erection. "A hundred architects superintended it, under each of whom were placed a hundred masons; 5,000 of the latter worked on the right side, and 5,000 on the left side, according to the plan laid down by an angel who appeared to the emperor in a dream. The angel appeared a second time, as a eunuch, in a brilliant white dress, on a Saturday, to a boy who was guarding the tools of the masons, and ordered him to bring the workmen immediately in order to hasten the building. As the boy refused, the gleaming eunuch swore by the Wisdom, i.e. by the Word of God, that he would not depart until the boy returned, and that he in the meantime would watch over the building. When the boy was led before the emperor, and could not find the eunuch who had appeared to him, the emperor perceived that it had been an angel, and, in order that he might for ever keep his word as guardian of the temple, he sent away the boy laden with presents to pass the rest of his life in the Cyclades, and resolved, according to the word of the angel, to dedicate the church to the *Word of God*, the *Divine Wisdom.* When the building was finished as far as the cupola, but when there was not sufficient money to complete it, the angel appeared a third time in the same form, and, leading the mules of the treasury into a subterranean vault, laded them with 80 cwt. of gold, which they brought to the emperor, who immediately recognised the wonderful hand of the angel in this unexpected supply. Thus did an angel give the plan, the name, and the funds for the construction of this wonder of the middle ages." The emperor advanced the work by his presence, visiting the workmen instead of taking his customary siesta, and hastening the progress of the building by extraordinary presents. During these visits he was dressed in coarse linen, his head bound with a cloth, and a stick in his hand.

When the apse, on the E. side of the ch. where the altar was to be placed, came to be finished, and a difference of opinion had arisen between the emperor and the architect, whether the light should fall through one or two open arched windows, the angel again appeared to the emperor, but clad in imperial purple, with red shoes, and instructed him that the light should fall upon the altar through 3 windows, in honour of the Father, and the Son, and the Holy Ghost. The *altar* was to be more costly than gold, and consequently it was composed of every species of precious materials bedded together with gold and silver, encrusted with pearls and jewels, and its cavity, which was called the sea,

was set with the most costly stones. Above the altar rose, in the form of a tower, the tabernacle (*ciborium*), on which rested a golden cupola, ornamented with golden lilies, between which was a golden cross weighing 75 pounds, adorned with precious stones. The 7 seats of the priests and the *throne of the Patriarch*, arranged in a semicircle behind the altar, were of silver gilt. The altar($\beta\hat{\eta}\mu\alpha$) was hidden from the eyes of the people by a wooden wall; and this wall, through which 3 doors covered with a veil led to the sanctuary, was ornamented with gilded pictures of saints, and 12 golden columns. The doors were of ivory, amber, and cedar; the principal door silver gilt.

" Before the structure of the church had risen two cubits above the ground, 45,200*l*. were already consumed, and the whole expense amounted to 320,000*l*.: each reader, according to the measure of his belief, may estimate their value either in gold or silver; but the sum of one million sterling is the result of the lowest computation." The cost weighed heavily on all classes of the community, and even public functionaries and professors were obliged to contribute. The walls and arches were constructed of bricks, but the magnificence and variety of the marble columns surpassed all bounds. Every species of marble, granite, and porphyry—Phrygian white marble with rose-coloured stripes, which imitated the blood of Atys, slain at Synnada; green marble from Laconia; blue from Libya; black Celtic marble, with white veins; Bosporus marble, white with black veins; Thessalian, Molossian, Proconessian marble; Egyptian starred granite and Saitic porphyry—were all employed. Much material was brought from Troas, Cyzicus, Athens, and the Cyclades. Thus many temples of the old religion contributed to the construction of the Church of Divine Wisdom; and the edifice of Sophia was supported on the columns of Isis and Osiris, on the pillars of the Temples of the Sun and Moon at Heliopolis and Ephesus, of that of Pallas at Athens, of Phœbus at Delos, and of Cybele at Cyzicus. When the edifice was finished, and Justinian entered the church, he exclaimed: "Glory to God, who hath counted me worthy to complete such a work. Solomon! I have surpassed thee!"

In *plan* S. Sophia closely approaches an exact square, being 235 ft. N. and S. by 250 ft. E. and W., exclusive of the narthex and apse. Externally the building possesses little architectural beauty; it may have been purposely left plain, like the early Christian basilicas at Rome, or it may have been intended to revet it with marble, and add the external ornament afterwards. All the internal arrangements are com-

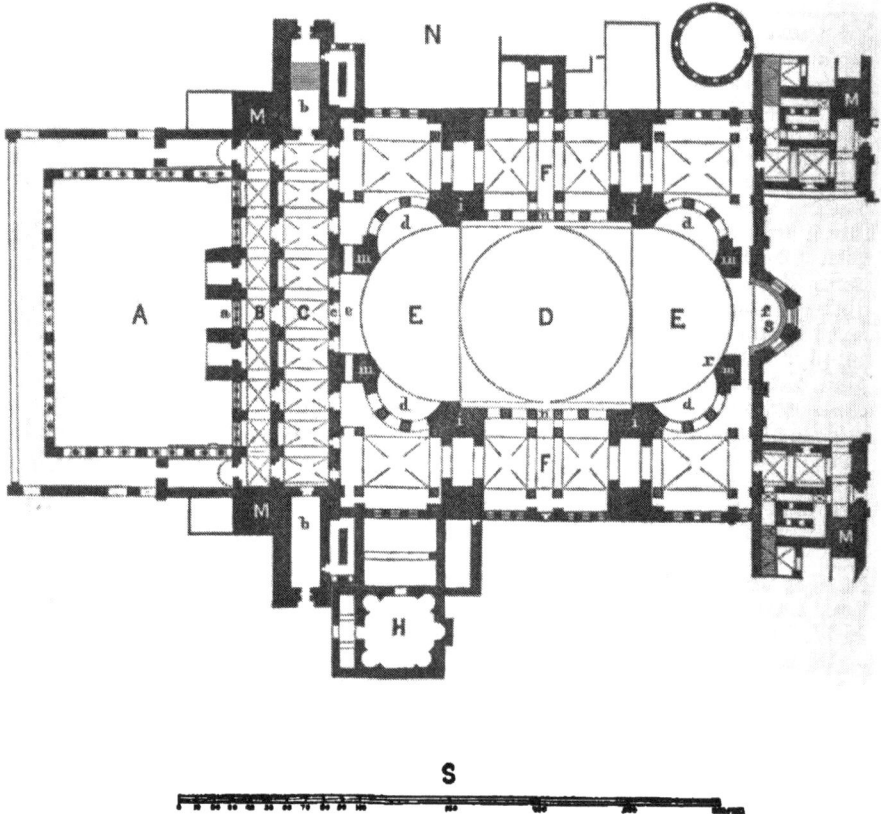

PLAN OF THE MOSQUE OF S. SOPHIA.

A. Atrium.	H. Baptistery (Türbeh of Mustafa I.).	e. Western recess.
B. Exo-Narthex.		f. Apse.
C. Eso-Narthex.	M. Minarets.	i. Piers for Great Dome.
D. Great Dome.	a. Belfry.	m. Piers for Semi-Domes.
E. Semi-Domes.	b. Porches.	n. Screens.
F. Aisles.	c. Porta Basilica.	r. Minber
	d. Exedræ.	s. Mihrab.

plete, and perfect both from a mechanical and an artistic point of view. It is, according to Mr. Fergusson, "the most perfect and most beautiful church which has yet been erected by any Christian people." At the W. end of the building is an open court representing the *atrium* (A), which had on its E. side the exo-narthex, and on its other sides arcades with marble columns and brick pillars. In the centre of the atrium was a large basin of water with the words, "Wash thy sins, not thy face only." This has been replaced by a marble basin of Turkish origin. Five doors gave access from the atrium to the *exo-narthex*, and immediately above the principal entrance rises the ancient belfry (*a*). The exo-narthex (B) is extremely simple, and hardly seems part of the original design; 5 doors lead from it to the *eso-narthex*, which was set apart for penitents and catechumens. The eso-narthex (c) is a splendid hall, 205 ft. in length internally, by 26 ft. wide, and two storeys in height. Its walls are revetted with variegated marbles, and its ceiling glitters with mosaics. At the N. and S. ends are porches (*b, b*), from which the galleries for the women are reached by a succession of ramps. The *S. porch* is said to be that by which the emperor and his court entered the narthex; the *N. porch* is that by which travellers are usually admitted to the church. The entrance to the porch at the S. end of the narthex has a remarkable *double gate of bronze*, of which parts are so beautifully modelled and so chastely ornamented that they would appear to belong to the best period of Hellenic art. In the panels are the words :—

> " O Lord, help Theophilus ;
> O Mother of God, help Theodora Augusta;
> O Christ, help Michael."

Beneath is the date 841. The gates were erected by the Emperor Theophilus, who invokes on them succour for himself, his empress, and his son. The name of the Patriarch John, and the date 838, have been effaced to make room for Michael's name and the date of his nomination as emperor. At the head of the right door is a fragmentary inscription, "Michael Conquerors," which some think refers to the restoration of the use of pictures to Byzantine worship by Michael III. and his mother Theodora soon after the death of Theophilus in 842.

Nine gates lead from the eso-narthex into the body of the church. Over the central gate, *Porta Basilica* (*c*), by which the emperor entered, is figured an open gospel on a reading-desk, surmounted by the form of a dove with outspread wings. On the pages are the words : "The Lord said, 'I am the door of the sheep. By Me if any man enter in, he shall be saved, and go in and out and find pasture.'" In the tympanum above is a mosaic, now covered up, representing Christ upon a throne, his right hand blessing an emperor kneeling low at his feet, his left holding an open volume bearing the words, "Peace be unto you; I am the Light of the world." On either side of the throne are medallion figures of the Virgin and of an archangel.

Visitors should enter the church by the Porta Basilica (*c*), and so obtain the full effect of this marvellous creation of Byzantine art. "The eye wanders upwards from the large arcades of the ground-floor to the smaller arches of the galleries, and thence to the smaller semi-domes. These lead the eye on to the larger, and the whole culminates in the great central roof. Nothing, probably, so artistic has been done on the same scale before or since" (Fergusson, *Hist. of Architecture*, vol. ii.). The Porta Basilica opens directly into *the nave*, which consists of a central rectangular space (D), covered by a dome, with two semicircular spaces (E, E), covered by semi-domes, on the E. and W., the whole forming a grand hall, of quasi-oval shape, 250 ft. in length, 100 ft. wide, and 180 ft. high. Each of the semicircular spaces has three *exedræ*, or recesses, of which those on the sides (*d, d, d, d*) are semicircular and covered by semi-domes, whilst those in the centre are covered by waggon vaults. The central recess on the W. (*e*) is terminated by the narthex; that on the E. is prolonged at a semicircular apse (*f*), which projects beyond the line of the exterior wall, and is lighted by three windows. The *great dome* rises over the centre of the church to a height of 179 ft. It is very little lower than a hemisphere, being 107 ft. across by 46 ft. in height, and its base is pierced by 40 small windows, so small and so low as not to interfere in any way with the apparent construction, but affording an ample supply of light to every part of the dome. The dome of the Pantheon at Rome is 130 ft. in diameter; those of St. Peter's at Rome and Sta. Maria at Florence are each 126 ft., and that of St. Paul's, London, is 108 ft. The dome is supported by four large arches, which abut on masses of masonry (*i, i, i, i*) 75 ft. long and 25 ft. wide. The two arches running transversely, N. and S.; are 100 ft. span, and 120 ft. high to the crown. Beyond the great dome on the E. and W. are two *semi-domes* of a diameter equal to that of the great dome, and these are again cut into by the smaller semi-domes over the *exedræ.* Near the apse and the narthex are four massive piers (*m, m, m, m*), which partly support the larger semi-domes.

On either side of the nave is a *two-storeyed aisle* (F, F), divided into three sections, which are connected by large vaulted openings. The space covered by the great dome is separated from the aisles on the N. and S. by *screens* (*n, n*) built in two storeys. The lower storeys are each formed by four beautiful columns of dark green marble, *verde antico*, said to have been brought from the Temple of Diana, at Ephesus, and five arches; the upper, in front of the women's galleries, have six smaller columns of the same material, and seven arches. Each *exedra* has two large columns, with three arches, and above these six smaller columns with seven arches. The eight lower columns of dark red porphyry (*d, d, d, d*) are said to have belonged to the Temple of the Sun at Baalbek, whence they were carried by Aurelian to Rome. There they came into the possession of a patrician lady, Marcia, as a part of her dowry, and were presented by her to Justinian, to adorn the church,

"for the salvation of her soul." The total number of columns in the church is 107, of which 40 are on the ground-floor and 67 above. The *capitals* are throughout Byzantine, and they are among the most admirable specimens of the style. Many of them bear the monograms of Justinian or Theodora, and upon the capital of the first porphyry column in the exedra to the right on entering the church is the date 534.

The *upper storeys* of the *aisles* and of the eso-narthex formed the women's galleries (*Gynæconitis*). The gallery over the narthex (c) is separated from the nave by a screen, of two double columns, and three arches, over which is a large semicircular window. The galleries are wide and spacious, and afford excellent views of the church, but they are usually closed on account of their unsafe condition. They were reached from the exterior by four gently-sloping ascents, one at each corner of the church, and from the interior by stone staircases reserved for the use of the priests and deacons. Visitors are only permitted to enter the galleries by the ascent at the N.W. corner. In the S. gallery was the seat of the empress. There also is a marble slab with the name of *Henricus Dandolo*, the great Doge who led the assault on Constantinople in 1204, and was, after his death, buried in S. Sophia. In the S. gallery, too, is a closed door leading to a small chapel in one of the buttresses, which communicated with the Baptistery by means of staircases and passages. This *chapel*, which was discovered by Signor Fossati, is supposed to be that into which, according to tradition, a Christian priest fled with the sacred elements when interrupted in his service by the entry of the Turks into the church. He is expected to issue from his hiding-place and resume his functions when the mosque again becomes a Christian sanctuary. All the flat surfaces of the church are covered with a mosaic of marble slabs of the most varied patterns and beautiful colours; the domes, roofs, and curved surfaces with a gold-grounded mosaic relieved by figures or architectural devices. Most of the mosaic pictures are now concealed beneath matting covered with plaster. The forms of the six-winged Seraphim, which Moslems acknowledge under the names of the archangels *Gabriel, Michael, Raphael,* and *Israfíl,* still appear in the four pendentives; and, when the light is favourable, the figure of the Saviour, in the act of benediction, may be seen in the vault of the apse. Copies of the concealed mosaics, and of the architectural details of the church, will be found in Salzenberg, *Alt-christliche Baudenkmale von Konstantinopel;* and Fossati, *Aya Sofia of Constantinople.*

The changes that have been made in the building since it was first appropriated as a mosque are more external than internal. The mosaics have, it is true, been partially covered up, and replaced by inscriptions from the Kurân, but there is no structural change in the interior. Externally it is different, most of the older annexes have been swept away and replaced by buildings of Turkish origin which obscure the original form of the church; lofty minarets (M) rise at the four corners; and the cross which surmounted the great dome has given place to a crescent. The *Mihrab* (*s*), which indicates the direction of the *Kaaba* at Mecca, toward which Moslems turn in prayer, is not in the centre of the apse, but a little to the S., between the central and southern windows. The consequent arrangement of the long rows of worshippers, and of the many mats and carpets in lines oblique to the axis of the church, produces a strangely discordant architectural effect. To the right of the *Mihrab,* and attached to the S.E. pillar of the church, is the *Minber* (*r*), or Friday pulpit, from which the *Khatib* reads the *Khutbe,* or special Friday noon-day prayer for the Khalîf, Sultan, and Islâm. Here, as in all the mosques first dedicated to Islâm through the power of arms, the preacher still mounts the pulpit sword in hand, and on either side of him hangs a flag as a symbol of

victory and conquest. Opposite the Minber is the *Sultan's seat* or tribune, and there are in this part of the mosque several *masbata,* or platforms, for the readers of the Kurân. Beside the Seraphim in the pendentives are immense green shields bearing the names of the four companions of the Prophet, *Abu-bekr, Omar, Osman,* and *Ali,* and round the crown of the dome itself is inscribed the verse of the Kurân: "God is the Light of Heaven and Earth." These inscriptions are the work of a celebrated caligraphist, Bichakji-zadeh Mustafa Chelebi, who lived under Murad IV.; the length of the standing letters is said to be 30 ft. During the nights of Ramazân the verse in the dome is illuminated by a sea of rays from some thousands of lamps, which, suspended in a triple circle above each other, trace out the lines of the dome.

Amongst the relics and curiosities shown in the mosque are: *one of the prayer carpets of the Prophet,* on the wall near the *Mihrab;* two enormous *alabaster water-jars,* said to have been brought from the island of Marmora or from Pergamum, and placed by Murad III. in their present position near the entrance; the *Cradle of Jesus,* of red marble, and a *basin,* in which He is said to have been washed, both, according to tradition, brought from Bethlehem. There are also the *Sweating Column,* in the N.W. part of the N. aisle, which emits damp that is said to effect marvellous cures; the *Cold Window,* close to the *Mihrab,* where the fresh wind ever blows, and where the celebrated sheikh *Ak Shemseddin,* the companion of the Conqueror, first expounded the Kurân; and the *Shining Stone,* a translucent stone in one of the windows of the western gallery. On one of the piers of the nave, in the S.E. bay, is a mark, resembling the imprint of a bloody hand, that is said to indicate the height to which the Turkish Conqueror was able to reach as he rode over the Christian corpses in the church; but the congregation in S. Sophia on the day of the conquest was taken captive and not massacred.

Turkey.

The mosque is illuminated in the most brilliant manner during Ramazân and Bairâm, and in the seven holy nights of Islâm, especially in the *Leilet el-Kadr,* i.e. the night of the Predestination (the 27th of Ramazân), in which the Kurân was sent down from heaven. On this night the Sultan used sometimes to repair, with his whole court, to S. Sophia, and, after having attended the night service, retire amidst a procession bearing innumerable many-coloured lanterns. Travellers who are at Constantinople during either of these nights should make a point of visiting the mosque about 1 hr. after sunset to see the illuminations.

Very few of the ancient annexes of the church are now left. At the E. end are the remains of vaulted chambers, which communicated, by 2 doors, with the body of the church. These probably represent the rooms of the *Diaconicum,* or *Secretarium,* which were used for a variety of purposes, such as retiring rooms for the emperor and court, the meetings of deacons, the holding of synods, and the confinement of refractory priests. On the N. side is a circular building, now used as a store for the neighbouring *imâret,* or "soup-kitchen," for the poor, which appears to be the *Skeuophylakion,* in which the sacred vessels and ceremonial vestments were kept. On the S. side, near the end of the eso-narthex, is the ancient *Baptistery* (H), which is now the *Türbeh* of Sultan Mustafa I. and his nephew Sultan Ibrahim. Externally the building is a rectangle, internally an octagon, in plan; it has an apse on the E. and a narthex on the W., and is covered by a dome. It appears to be of older date than S. Sophia, with which it was connected. On the S. side also were the *Horologion,* the *Holy Well,* and *Metatorion,* or retiring room for the emperors, but of these only the foundations are left. Besides the Baptistery, there are 4 *Türbehs* of Turkish origin on the S. side: that of Sultan Selim II. and his family; Sultan Murad III. and his family; Sultan Muhammad III.; and that of the sons

of Murad III. The doors of the Türbehs and the *faïence* are deserving of notice. Of the 4 minarets, that at the S.E. corner was built by Muhammad II., the Conqueror; that at the N.E. corner by Selim II.; and those on the W. by Murad III.

The western portion of the floor of S. Sophia rests on vaults that cover a large cistern, and in addition to the fountain in the atrium there is one in the street outside of the atrium and another outside the S.E. minaret.

SS. Sergius and Bacchus, *Kuchuk Aya Sofia,* a short distance N.W. of Chatladi Kapu. It can be reached by the street leading to the sea from the W. end of the Hippodrome, or by following the railroad E. from Kûm Kapu station. It was built, in 527, by Justinian the Great, near the palace he had occupied when heir-apparent to the throne (p. 30), and

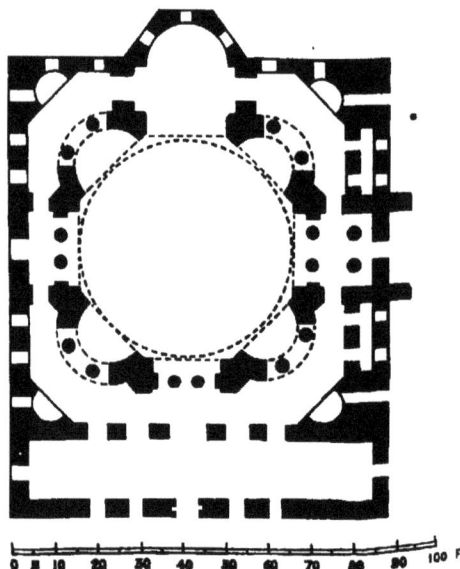

CHURCH OF SS. SERGIUS AND BACCHUS.

was dedicated to the martyrs who were believed to have saved his life and that of his uncle Justin I., when involved in a conspiracy against the Emperor Anastasius. Originally, there were two churches, placed side by side : one, a basilica, dedicated to the Apostles Peter and Paul, has entirely disappeared ; the other, a domical church, remains almost intact. The existing church, which is singularly elegant in design and proportion, is nearly a square in plan, being 109 ft. by 92 ft. over all, exclusive of the apse. The boundaries of the atrium can still be traced, but a Turkish portico has been substituted for the ancient narthex.

The dome, supported by piers arranged in the form of an octagon, is 52 ft. in diameter. "Internally, the arrangement of the piers of the dome, of the galleries, and of the pillars which support them, are almost identical with those of S. Vitale at Ravenna," which was commenced in 526 under Byzantine influence and completed by Justinian. The great difference is, that while S. Vitale is wholly enclosed by an octagonal wall, SS. Sergius and Bacchus is a square, and so gives more accommodation and harmonises better with the surrounding buildings. " The details of this church are generally well designed for the purposes to which they are applied. There is a certain reminiscence of classical feeling in the mouldings and foliage—in the latter, however, very faint. The architrave block had by this time almost superseded the capital, and what was once a classical entablature retained very little of its pristine form, and, indeed, was used constructively only for the support of a gallery, or some such mechanical requirement." — *Fergusson.* On the frieze of the octagon there is a Greek inscription, in honour of Justinian and Theodora. The frescoes and mosaics are concealed by whitewash. This church was used for the celebration of Divine service in Latin by the representatives of the Roman See, when on a mission to the capital of the East. Gregory the Great, when a deacon, spent several years at Constantinople on such a mission. It was to this church that Pope Vigilius fled to escape the dis-

pleasure of Justinian. Its assignment to the Latin clergy was probably due to the existence near it of the Church of SS. Peter and Paul, an acceptable sanctuary for priests from Rome.

Mehmed Pasha Jami', S.W. of the Hippodrome, is regarded by Dr. Paspati as the ancient *Church of S. Anastasia*, famous as the sanctuary founded by Gregory Nazianzen, and in which he preached the orthodox faith while Arianism was triumphant in the city. The ch. was often rebuilt or repaired, and was held in great veneration. Between the ch. and the Cistern Bin-bir-Derek Dr. Paspati places the *Prætorium* of the city and the *Porticoes of Domninus*.

Church of the Convent Myrelaion, *Bûdrûm Jami'.* Reached by the street a little below the fountain of Laleli Jami', and on the opposite side of the tramway ; the church of a convent, founded or restored by the Emperor Romanus Lecapenus in 918. He and many other distinguished persons were interred in it. Good specimen of that period of Byzantine art. Near the church is an ancient Byzantine cistern with 64 columns.

GROUP OF CHURCHES NEAR THE MOSQUE SHAH-ZADEH.

S. Mary Diaconissa, *Kalender Khâneh Jami',* S. of the eastern end of the Aqueduct of Valens. Founded by the Patriarch Kyriakos in 599. The interior is beautiful, and measures 82 ft. by 70 ft. Remains of the "Iconostasis" exist against the eastern piers, and two remarkable coeval panels against the west wall, most classical in their feeling. The square eastern chambers have an upper storey opening into the church. The columns of the central doorway are ancient. As an example of Justinian's age this church is of surpassing interest.

S. Theodore Tyrone, *Kilisse Mesjidi,* up a lane off *Vefa Meidan,* near the Mosque Abûl Vefa. In

E 2

Works upon Art, this church is erroneously designated as that of the Theotokos Lips; it has also been confounded with the Church of S. Theodore Sphorakiou, which was near S. Sophia. The present structure probably dates from the 12th or the 13th century, but, as many of its materials indicate, it stands upon the site of a church as old at least as the 6th century. The façade of its outer narthex is richly adorned, a feature comparatively rare in Byzantine churches, and it may have belonged to the earliest church. The interior is disappointing. In the exo-narthex is an opening to a passage said to lead to S. Sophia. "Taking it altogether," says Mr. Fergusson, "it is, perhaps, the most complete and elegant church of its class now known to exist in or near the capital, and many of its details are of great beauty and perfection" (*Hist. of Architecture*, ii. 327).

Balaban Aga Mesjid, E. of Shah Zadeh mosque. **Sekban Bashi Mesjid**, in a narrow street N. of the aqueduct of Valens and opposite the old Byzantine fountain known as *Kirk Cheshmeh* (Forty Fountains). The Mosque of Sultan Muhammad II. (p. 62) stands upon the site of the **Church of the Holy Apostles**, founded by Constantine the Great, and rebuilt by Justinian the Great with more splendour. Beside it stood the mausoleums, in which a large number of the emperors, empresses, and patriarchs of Constantinople were laid to rest. The conspicuous edifice near the At Bazâr, surmounted by a lofty cupola, and known as *Demirjilar Mesjidi*, was probably the **Church of S. Theophano**, erected by her husband Leo VI.

S. Mary Panachrantos, *Fenari Îsa Mesjidi*, or *Kilisse Mesjidi*. In the valley of the Lycus, to the S. of Sultan Muhammad's mosque. This church was attached to the Monastery of Lips, Μονὴ τοῦ Λιβός, so named because built by a certain Constantine Lips, in the reign of Leo the Wise. It acquired considerable importance

under the Palaeologi, and was repaired by the mother of Andronicus the Elder, who passed the last two years of his life here as a monk, and was buried in its precincts. Its plan is peculiar, a double church, or two churches placed side by side and communicating with each other through a great arch in their common wall. They have the same narthex. On the eastern wall of the building is a fragmentary inscription, in which a part of the founder's name appears. During the Latin empire, in the 13th century, it was used as a Roman Catholic Church.

GROUP OF CHURCHES IN AND NEAR PSAMATIA.

Church of S. John the Baptist, attached to the *Monastery of Studius*, now *Mir Akhor Jamisi*, a short distance S. of the modern Greek Church of St. Constantine, and not far from Yedi Kuleh railway station. The most ancient ecclesiastical fabric left in Constantinople. It was built upon the site of an older church, in 463, by Studius, a Roman patrician, who settled in the new capital. The monastery became the principal home of the order of the Akoemetae, or Sleepless monks, who celebrated divine worship in their monasteries day and night without intermission. The church was repaired in 1293, but was seriously injured in 1782 by fire. It was a three-aisled basilica, 89 ft. by 83 ft., and still retains the characteristic features of a basilica. The narthex is now the oldest portion of the building. Its columns have composite capitals, and support a richly-ornamented entablature. The interior approaches more nearly to the favourite Byzantine square than is usual in the basilicas of the West. The nave had on either side two ranges of columns, one above the other. Only six of the old columns remain. Outside the S. wall is the monastery cistern, with a vaulted roof resting on 23 Corinthian columns. In the base of a wall enclosing ground behind the apse, and at the N.E.

corner of the church, is an old tombstone, with the epitaph: "In the month of September of the year 1387 fell asleep the servant of God, Dionysius the Russian, on the 6th day." The **Monastery of Studius** was held in much honour, and exercised great influence. It was conspicuous during the Iconoclastic controversy (726-842), defending the use of pictures in divine worship. It furnished education to the higher classes, being "an illustrious and glorious school of virtue," and was celebrated for its attention to hymnology.

S. Andrew (ἐν τῇ Κρίσει), *Khoja Mustafa Pasha Jamisi*, in the Chinar Sokak, leading to Silivri Kapusi in the Land Walls. It was dedicated originally to the Apostle Andrew, and later also to S. Andrew, martyr under Constantine Copronymus. It was built by Arcadia, sister of Theodosius II.; and was rebuilt in the 13th century by a distinguished lady, Raoulaina, the cousin of Andronicus II. It is a church of fine proportions, about 67 ft. by 40 ft. The central dome is flanked by two semi-domes, one on the N. and one on the S., not as in S. Sophia, on the W. and E. The church was appropriated as a mosque in 1489 by the Greek renegade, Mustafa Pasha, who accompanied the luckless Prince Jem to Italy. It has a *medreseh*, an *imáret*, and a *tekkeh* of dervîshes attached to it. On the boughs of an old cypress in the court of the mosque hangs an iron chain, which is said to have been able to detect deceit and robbery. On one occasion, according to the legend, a Jewish debtor, who falsely claimed to have paid his debt, was brought here by his Turkish creditor for trial. The Jew, just before taking his station beneath the chain, handed to the Turk a hollow staff, in which the money he owed was concealed, and thus went through the fiction of paying the debt. The chain failed to detect the fraud, and, falling on the Jew's neck, declared him innocent. Upon this the Jew took back his staff and withdrew, but from that day all faith in the chain's insight was lost. The legend is possibly of Byzantine origin.

Site of **Church of S. Mary** (ἐν Σίγματι), marked by the small ancient cistern a little N.W. of the Guardhouse at Alti Mermer (the ancient Exokionion). A very ancient church, often repaired and frequently mentioned in history. **Îsa Kapu Mesjidi,** in the street of that name. It is insignificant, and its Christian name is unknown, but it is interesting as marking the line of Constantine's walls (p. 23). **Sanjakdar Mesjidi.** A chapel attached to the convent τῶν Γαστρίων, N. of the Armenian Church of S. George. An ancient foundation, restored in the 9th century. During the reign of Theophilus it was the headquarters of the strong female opposition to his Iconoclastic policy. The **Armenian Church of S. George,** *Sulu Monastir,* is on the site of **S. Mary Peribleptos,** built in 1031 by Emperor Romanus Argyrus for a large and rich monastery. The ancient church remained in Greek hands until 1643, when it was given by Sultan Ibrahim to the Armenian community. Destroyed by fire in 1782. Nothing of it remains but the cistern whence comes its Turkish name. The Greek **Church of S. George,** ἐν τῇ Κυπαρίσσῳ, situated in this quarter, is a modern building on an old foundation.

CHURCHES NEAR THE LAND WALLS.

For the less important churches, see pp. 34-39.

S. Mary ad Fontem, τῇ Πηγῇ, at *Balukli,* about ½ m. along the road leading from the Silivri Kapusi into the country. The spot is distinguished by groves of trees. The springs of water, and the consequent rich verdure, made the place a favourite resort, and its beauty is always described by Byzantine authors in rapturous terms. One of the springs being regarded as a Holy

Well, a chapel was built beside it at least as early as the time of Leo the Great, and thus the attraction of miraculous cures was added to the natural charms of the locality. Justinian the Great erected a splendid church here with the materials left after building S. Sophia, and subsequent sovereigns either repaired or rebuilt the edifice. Simeon, King of the Bulgarians, set fire to it when he besieged the city. Here also stood an Imperial Palace, with an extensive park stocked with game, which was much frequented by the emperors, especially in spring. It was known as the *Exo-Philopation.* Ambassadors and foreign potentates were often received and entertained in the Palace, as Cardinal Humbert, Luitprand, and Louis VII. of France. Here also was celebrated the marriage of Simeon's son, Peter, with the grandchild of Romanus Lecapenus. The present church dates from 1833. In the cemetery several patriarchs are buried. On the Friday of the Greek Easter-week large numbers of people visit the church and its Holy Well. An interesting description of the *fête* is given by Mrs. Walker, *Eastern Life and Scenery.* In the Holy Well, which is reached by descending a flight of steps, are a few fish, whose light and dark markings have been explained by the following story: A monk was engaged in frying fish beside this well when the Turks stormed the city. Upon tidings reaching him that the assault had proved successful, he incredulously exclaimed, "I will believe that when these fish jump from the pan into the water." They jumped, of course, since the city had indeed fallen, and their descendants have retained the appearance of fish incompletely fried.

Church of the Monastery of the Chora, now *Kahriyeh Jamisi*, popularly known as the Mosaic Mosque. Exceedingly interesting on account of its beautiful mosaics and its plan, which is typical of the later period of Byzantine church architecture. The façade is thought to have served as a model for that of S. Mark at Venice. The name of the church, τῆς χώρας, of the country, "in the fields," carries its foundation back to the period before 413, when Constantinople did not extend beyond the walls of Constantine, and this place was outside the city limits. Later, a basilica was erected here by Justinian the Great. This was followed by a church built by Crispus, the son-in-law of the Emperor Phocas, early in the 7th century. This latter building having fallen into decay was rebuilt by Maria Ducaina, "fairest of ladies," the mother-in-law of Alexius Comnenus, in the 11th or 12th century, when this part of the city assumed a new importance, on account of the partiality of the Comneni for the Palace of Blachernæ. Finally, about the middle of the 14th century, the Great Logothete, Theodore Metochites, restored the side chapels and the narthexes. In this church alternately with that of the Hodegetria was kept the Holy Image of the Virgin, which was wont to be carried in procession when the walls were threatened.

The church is quadrilateral, and has on 3 of its sides semicircular windows, and on its 4th the apse; the interior is small and is covered by a dome resting on a drum, pierced by several windows. It has an inner and an outer narthex; and a side-chapel (*Parecclesion*), which is entered by a door at the S. end of the outer narthex. On the N. side of the church is a small side-chapel of later date, which is connected by a sort of passage with the inner narthex. The *outer narthex* consists of 5 arches covered with an intersecting vault, visible both externally and internally. The two last bays are covered with cupolas, which still retain their mosaics internally. Externally the front was ornamented with courses of stones of different colours, now concealed under a yellow wash. The two narthexes are resplendent with mosaics of singular beauty and brilliance. The *side-chapel* is adorned with *frescoes*, representing, chiefly, saints and angels, also the Imperial family; they are badly damaged, but some noble heads remain. On the *S. wall* is a long epitaph in honour of Michael Tornikes, the friend and companion of the great Logothete. A fine marble doorway is worthy of notice. The subjects of the mosaics in the outer narthex of the church, the southern domed section of the inner narthex, and the two small narthexes of the chapel, are taken from the Gospel History. In the remaining sections of the inner narthex are depicted scenes from the life of the Blessed Virgin, as given in the apocryphal Gospel of S. James. The mosaics will richly repay a close study. Experts are still divided upon the question whether

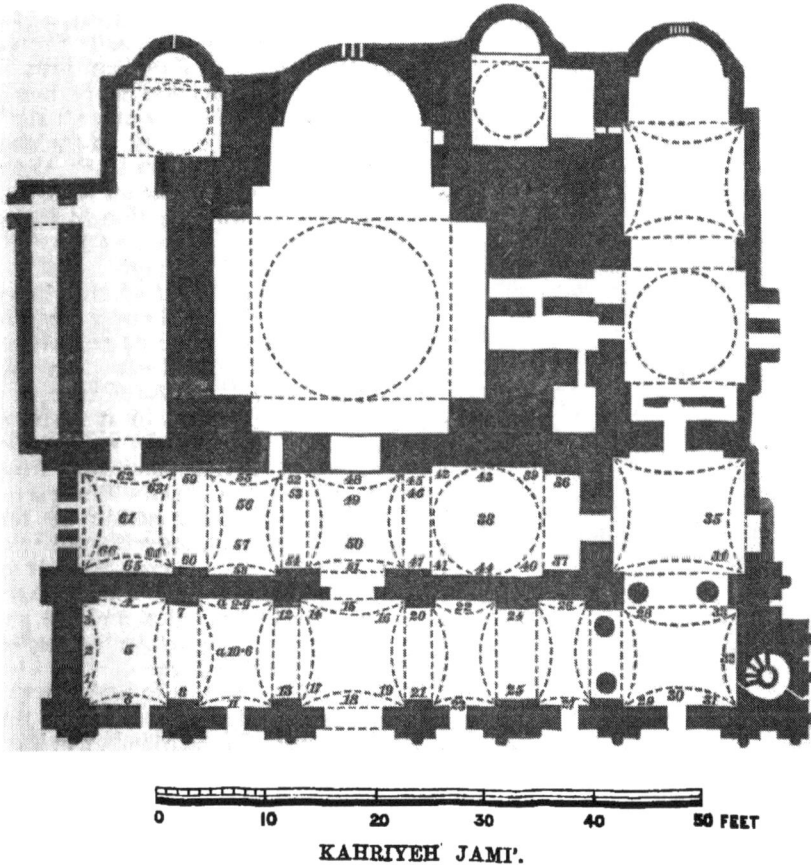

KAHRIYEH JAMI'.

these mosaics were influenced by Italian art, or Italian art was influenced by them.

Outer Narthex (N. end).—(1) Angel appears to Joseph in a dream. (2) Journey to Bethlehem. (3) Elizabeth and Mary. (4) Joseph and Mary having their names regis-tered. (5) Probably, Christ among the Doctors. (6) The Holy Family on the way to Jerusalem for Christ's first passover. (7) S. Andronicus. (8) S. Tarachos. (9) Birth of Christ. Angel appears to Shepherds. (10) Christ's Baptism and Temptation. (11) Return of Holy Family from Egypt. (12) S. George. (13) S. Demetrius.

(14) Miracle of Wine at Cana. (15) The Saviour in the act of benediction as the Giver of Life ('Η Χώρα τῶν ζώντων, "the land of the living"), symbolised in the preceding and the following scene. (16) The Miracle of the Loaves. (17) Sacrifice of a White Bullock. (18) The Virgin in the attitude of Prayer. (19) The 2nd Miracle of the Loaves. (20, 21) Saints, not identified. (22) The Magi, on their way to Jerusalem and before Herod. (23) Hiding of John the Baptist, when a child, by Elizabeth. (24, 25) Saints, not identified. (26) Herod inquiring of the Priests. (27) Mothers mourning the massacred Innocents. (28) Healing of a Paralytic. (29) Christ at Well of Sychar. (30) Massacre of the Innocents. (31) Healing of the Paralytic let down through the opened roof. (32) Herod orders massacre of the Innocents. (33) Healing of the Man sick of the Dropsy.

Inner Narthex (S. end).—(34) Fall of Idols in Egypt at the presence of the Holy Child? (35) Withering of the Fig-tree. (36) Healing of the withered Arm. (37) Healing of the Leper. (38) In the flutings of the Dome, 39 Patriarchal Ancestors of Christ, mostly as given in S. Luke's Gospel. In the crown of the Dome, Christ as Pantocrator. (39) Healing of the Issue of Blood. (40) Healing of the Deaf and Dumb Man. (41) Healing of the two blind Men at Jericho. (42) Healing of Peter's Mother-in-law. (43) Colossal Figures of the Virgin and of Christ. (44) Healing divers Diseases. (45) Mary in the Temple, receiving Bread from an Angel. (46) S. Paul. (47) Mary in the Temple, receiving instruction. (48) Theodore Metochites, the Great Logothete, under Andronicus II., presenting the Church to Christ. The upper inscription reads: "Jesus Christ, the Land of the Living ;" the term Χώρα alludes to the name of the Church. The lower inscription reads: "The constructor, the Logothete of the Chancery, Theodore Metochites." (49) Mary admitted to the Holy of Holies. (50) Proces-

sion of Maidens accompanying Mary. (51) Mary receiving the Wool with which to make a Veil for the Temple. (52) Mary taking her first Seven Steps. (53) S. Peter. (54) Priest praying before the Rods, one of which will indicate the future Husband of Mary. (55) Nativity of Mary. (56) Priests at a Meal. They bless Mary. (57) S. Joachim and S. Anna, the parents of Mary, caressing her. (58) Joseph receiving the Rod which marks him as the favoured Suitor. (59) Meeting of S. Joachim and S. Anna. (60) Joseph takes Mary home. (61) In flutings of the Dome, Christ's royal Ancestors, according to S. Matthew. (62) Annunciation to S. Anna. (63) S. Joachim praying on a Mountain. (64) The Annunciation to Mary. (65) Joseph leaving Mary. (66) The High Priest judging Mary.

The *marble revetment* of the inner narthex and of the church, as also the bas-reliefs which occur at various points, should be noticed. In the panel to the S., within the church, is a mosaic of the Virgin in a garden. Remains of the Greek words for "Land of the Living" appear. Fine carving above the panel. The panel to the N. contains a mosaic of the Saviour, holding an open Gospel that bears the text, "Come unto Me, all ye that labour, and I," etc. *Photographs* of the principal mosaics, and an explanatory catalogue, by André Leval, can be obtained in Pera.

The *minaret* seems to rest on the basement of a turret, possibly of the 14th century. In the chamber is kept one of the *jars* of earthenware used for building the domes of S. Sophia and other churches.

Church of the Monastery of Manuel, a general under Theophilus. *Kefili-Mesjidi*, in the quarter Salma-Tomrûk. E. of the Cistern of Aspar, a basilica. **Odalar Mesjidi,** a little above, was once a Christian church. To the E., in a vegetable garden—*Bogdan Serai*—are the remains of an ancient private chapel. Here, according to some authorities, is the site of the famous **Church of S. John**

the Baptist, in Petra, ἐν Πέτρῳ. For the remains of ancient churches at Aivan - Serai (the Blachernæ quarter), see p. 28.

CHURCHES IN OR NEAR THE PHANAR QUARTER.

S. Mary Pammakaristos, *Fethiyeh Jamisi* (Mosque of the Conqueror), overlooking the valley of Phanar, in the Telah Sokak. This church was attached to a convent, founded in the 12th cent. by Michael Ducas and his wife Maria, sister of Emperor Alexius Comnenus. The apse and the four domes are interesting. On the exterior of the church there is a long Greek inscription. In the dome nearest the minaret are remains of mosaics representing the prophets. Three years after the conquest, on the destruction of the Church of the Holy Apostles, it became the Patriarchal Church, and remained so for 135 years. In 1591 it was turned into a mosque by Murad III., and the tombs of the Emperor Alexius Comnenus and his celebrated daughter Anna Comnena, and the Emperor John Palaeologus, who were buried in the monastery, were destroyed. The Greek Patriarchate, with many of the relics which the church contained, were then removed to the church at Phanar. ·

A little to the S. is S. John the Baptist (ἐν τῷ Τρούλῳ), now *Ahmed Pasha Mesjidi.* S. Mary Mouchliotissa. Founded in 13th cent. by a daughter of Michael Palaeologus, and widow of a Mongolian prince. Hence the title. The Turkish designation, *Kan Kilisse* (Church of Blood), is due to the severe struggle between the Greeks and the Turks at the Gate of Phanar, upon the capture of the city. The church was presented by the Conqueror to the Greek architect, Christodoulos, as a reward for building the mosque of Sultan Muhammad II. The Imperial grant conferred many privileges on the church, and saved it on two occasions from being turned into a mosque; once by Selim I., and again by Ahmed III. S. Theodosia, now *Gül Jami'*, within Aya Kapusi. Its founder is unknown; it probably dates from the 10th or 11th cent. The anniversary festival of the church was being celebrated on the 29th of May, 1453, when the Turkish troops, unknown to the worshippers, were already within the fortifications. The large congregation assembled in the building was surprised at its devotions, and its members were taken captive. The church is finely proportioned, and well preserved, but has little architectural interest. In this vicinity are the remains of three churches, now known as Sinan Pasha Mesjidi, Sheikh Murad Mesjidi, and Pur Kuyu Mesjidi.

S. Saviour Pantepoptes, *Eski Imâret Mesjidi*, on heights above Jub-Ali Kapusi. Founded in the 11th cent. by Anna Delassena, the mother of the Emperor Alexius Comnenus, a good example of a church *built* in the time of the Comneni. Though small in scale it has all its parts of excellent proportions. It is well preserved, and has an outer and an inner narthex. The beautiful polygonal drum which supports the dome is the principal feature of interest. Because of its commanding position the usurper Mourzoufle selected the terrace beside the church as the point from which to watch the assault of the Venetian fleet, in 1204, upon the harbour walls.

S. Saviour Pantocrator, *Zeirek Kilisse-Jamisi*, conspicuous on the height above the Inner Bridge. An imposing structure, consisting of a triple church, founded by Emperor John Comnenus and his Empress Irene, about 1136. According to another view, the Comneni restored a 6th century church, now the central one, and only founded the N. and S. churches. Many fine details about the exterior of the apses, and especially about the pulpit, which is built of Byzantine materials. The *pavements* in the southern and part of the central church are magnificent in material though of late design; they are kept covered up, but will be exhibited to visitors. The *narthex doorway* and the small windows adjoining it, are of very beautiful design in slabs of moulded and polished red and green marbles. The southern church only is used as a *mosque.* Beginning at the south, the three churches measure respectively (without the two narthexes) about 75 ft. by 61 ft.; 68 ft. by 26 ft.; 68 ft. by 55 ft. To the church was attached an important *monastery* with remarkable charitable institutions. Several imperial personages were interred here, among others the Emperor Manuel Comnenus, in a magnificent mausoleum adjoining the edifice. During the Latin occupation the church was assigned to the Roman Catholics, and the monastery was used as a palace. Several relics were kept in the church, amongst others a picture of the Virgin painted by St. Luke, and a block of porphyry, brought from Ephesus by Manuel, on which the body of Christ was said to have been anointed after the descent from the cross. The fine *Sarcophagus* of *verde antico* before the church is considered to be that of the Empress Irene. Underneath it, far below the level of the street, and reached by a long flight of steps, is an *old fountain*, connected with the monastery's ancient cistern. In the vicinity is a small octagonal building, *Sheikh Suleiman Mesjidt*, which is supposed to have been the library of the monastery.

§ 14.—STAMBÛL.

Stambûl, or *Istambol*, from the Greek εἰς τὴν πόλιν, covers the whole area enclosed by the Theodosian walls of Constantinople; and its main streets follow the lines of those of the ancient city. Thus the tramway, from the outer bridge, on reaching the platform of S. Sophia, enters the direction of the *Mese*, now called *Divân Yoli.* The triangular promontory on which it stands is divided into two ridges by the *valley of the Lycus*, which, rising without the city, runs parallel to the Golden Horn, and falls into the Marmara at Vlanga Bostan. One of the hills upon which "New Rome" was built is at the E. end of the southern ridge, and six, defined by ravines falling to the Golden Horn, are on the northern ridge.

Stambûl is the Muhammadan part of the city. Within its walls are the Seraglio, the principal mosques, the *türbehs* or mausoleums of the Sultans, the baths, the *khâns*, the bazârs, the public offices of Government, and the existing remains of ancient Constantinople. It is divided for administrative purposes into three municipal *cercles*, under directors, and into a large number of *mahalles*, quarters. Separate quarters are allotted to the Armenians, the Greeks, and the Jews, but there is less strictness than formerly. The *Greeks* and *Armenians* are to be found in Phanar, Egri Kapu, Yedi Kuleh, Psamatia, and Kûm Kapu; the Jews in the Balat Quarter. The *Persian* Ambassador resides in Stambûl. There have been great improvements during the last twenty years; the quarters destroyed by fire in 1865 have been laid out in good streets on which carriages run with ease and comfort, and many of the streets and squares now surpass those of Pera. The general appearance of the older streets is that of a city built of wood; but a close inspection shows that the *original buildings* were, as at Cairo, of a much more solid construction. At every turn remains of the ancient buildings are to be seen, some of brick, and many with alternate courses of thin bricks and squared stones. The upper storeys usually projected 2 or 3 feet over the ground-floor, and were likewise of brick or stone carried on massive stone corbels in a very bold manner. Most of the private houses stand within their own grounds, and they are more Oriental in construction than those of the suburbs.

It is not prudent for European travellers to pass through the streets of Stambûl during the night, but in daylight they are as safe as in the streets of London. It is usual, however, to visit Stambûl at night during Ramazân, and the streets are then most interesting.

§ 15.—MOSQUES—TÜRBEHS.

The Turks when they captured Constantinople adopted the architectural forms of their new capital, and moulded and modified them so as to bring them into conformity with their special requirements. The admiration which Justinian's great church excited in their minds was reflected in the form of their mosques, which are all more or less copies of S. Sophia. There are about 230 mosques, *jami'*, and 500 *mesjids;* and, of the former, the most important are the great Imperial mosques built by the Sultans. In these the mosque proper, *jami'*, with its forecourt, *haram,* and its "garden," *ruzah,* containing the tomb of the founder, is situated in a large walled court, planted with trees, round which are ranged the various institutions attached to the mosque. These are the *mekteb,* a school where reading and writing are taught; the *medresseh,* or higher theological college, in which the students also

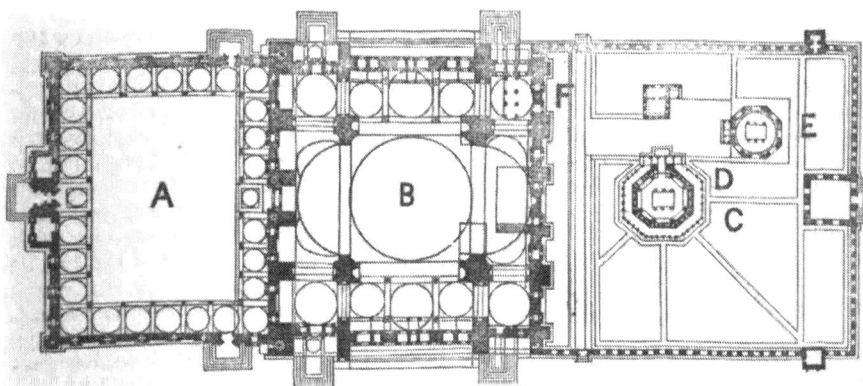

MOSQUE OF SULEIMAN I.

A. Haram or Fore-court.
B. Jami' or Mosque.
C. Rûzah or Garden.

D. Türbeh of Sultan Suleiman I.
E. Türbeh of Roxalana.
F. Tomb of Ali Pasha.

reside; the *imâret,* soup-kitchen or poor-house; the *kitâb-khâneh,* library; and sometimes the *hammam,* bath; and the *khân,* for strangers. The students in the *medressehs* are the Softas, from whom are selected the Ulemas, Kadis, and Mollahs; they are educated, boarded, and get one meal daily out of the *wakûf,* or endowed revenue of the mosques. Many of the mosques are getting somewhat out of repair, for the Government are gradually taking possession of the endowments, promising to pay an equal income, which they withdraw by degrees. The *Türbehs,* or tombs of the Imperial family, are amongst the most interesting sights of the city, and several of them are remarkable for their architectural beauty.

Suleimaniyeh, *Mosque of Suleiman I., the Magnificent.* This, the most beautiful monument of Osmanli architecture, was erected expressly as a mosque, and is the work of *Sinan,* the great architect of the reign of Suleiman I. It was built, between 1550-56, with material taken from the Church of S. Euphemia at Chalcedon, and stands, on a broad platform, on the summit of the "third hill." Like all the great imperial mosques it consists of the mosque proper, *jami'*, with a fore-court, *haram*, in front, and a garden, *rûzah*, behind; and around it is a large open court planted with trees and enclosed on three sides by a wall.

The **fore-court** is rectangular in plan, and surrounded on all sides by cloisters, which are covered by 24 small domes partly resting on an equal number of columns of porphyry, granite, and white marble. It is paved with white marble, excepting at the entrance to the mosque where there is a *slab of porphyry*, to which a quaint legend is attached; and in its centre, under a dome, is the *fountain* for ablutions. On three sides there are marble benches beneath the arcade, and the walls are pierced with windows; on the fourth side is the face of the mosque. At each corner there is a *minaret*, and a good effect has been produced by making the two minarets at the outer corners shorter than those nearest the mosque, and of different design. There are 3 entrances to the fore-court, 2 at the sides, and 1 midway between the 2 smaller minarets, which has directly opposite to it the beautiful portal of the mosque.

The **mosque** is nearly square, 225 ft. by 205 ft. over all externally, and covering between 45,000 and 46,000 sq. ft. Internally the construction rests on 4 great piers of pleasing and appropriate design; and the screen of windows on each side, under the great lateral arches of the dome, is borne by 4 *monolithic shafts* of granite, of great beauty. Each of these is 28 ft. in height, or with the base and white marble capital 35 ft. According to P. Gyllius, one of them crowned the 5th hill about ½ mile from the Mosque of Sultan Muhammad. The original position of the others is uncertain. The columns support a *gallery*, which is reached by two flights of steps near the enrtance, and runs round the building. In a closed portion of the north gallery are a large number of cases and boxes, said to contain treasure of gold ˜nd silver, and articles of great value,

that have been deposited there as in a great national bank. They are all registered, and can only be withdrawn on production of the proper documents. The *dome* "is 86 ft. in diameter internally, and 156 ft. in height. This seems a better proportion than that of S. Sophia, though the dimensions are so much less that it has not, of course, the same grandeur of effect. At S. Sophia the dome is 19 ft. higher, and 22 ft. greater in diameter. These smaller dimensions, as well as the absence in the mosque of all the mosaic magnificence of the church, renders it extremely difficult to institute any fair comparison between the two buildings. On the whole, it may, perhaps, be said with truth, that the mosque is more perfect mechanically than the church, that the constructive parts are better disposed and better proportioned; but that for artistic effect and poetry of design the church still far surpasses its rival, in so far at least as the interior is concerned. *Externally* the mosque suffers from the badness of the materials with which it is constructed. Its walls are covered with stucco, its dome with lead, and all the sloping abutments of the dome, though built with masonry, have also to be protected by a metal covering. This, no doubt, detracts from the effect; but still the whole is so massive—every window, every dome, every projection is so truthful, and tells so exactly the purpose for which it was placed where we find it, that the general result is most satisfactory."—*Fergusson. Internally* the mosque is decorated with all the splendour the Sultan could command. The walls and pillars are veneered with coloured marbles; the *mihrab*, of pure white marble, is bordered with choice Persian tiles, and flanked by enormous gilt candelabra; the *minber*, pulpit, and *maksura*, praying place of the Sultan, are delicately carved in white marble; and the *stained glass windows* are of rich colour and beautiful design. Two of the windows are spoils of the Persian wars; the others are the work of *Sarkhosh Ibrahím*, drunken Ibrahîm, the most celebrated glass manufacturer of the period. Round the dome, as in S. Sophia, is inscribed the 36th verse of the 24th sura of the Kurân, and over the entrance, and on the walls of the mosque are beautifully written inscriptions, all from the hands of the celebrated caligraphist Kara Hissari.

In the **garden** to the W. of the mosque are 2 mausoleums, the *Türbeh of Suleiman I.*, and that of his favourite wife, *Khurrem*, "the joyous one," who from a Russian captive rose to be the all-powerful Sultana known in the West as Roxalana. Both are octagonal buildings, in marble of various colours; and every detail in them is most carefully elaborated. Externally, the **Türbeh of Suleiman I.** is surrounded by an arcade; internally, the walls are overlaid with blue and white tiles, and 8 columns of marble and porphyry support a dome elaborately decorated with arabesques. In the centre are buried 3 Sultans—Suleiman I. (d. 1566), Suleiman II. (d. 1691), and Ahmed II. (d. 1695), and some princesses. The bodies rest in the ground, and over them are tombs, *sandûk*, "box," covered with rich embroidery and costly shawls. Those of the Sultans are distinguished by their turbans and aigrettes, and that of the founder is surrounded by a railing inlaid with mother-of-pearl. Within the türbeh are preserved a *relief plan* of the *Kaaba* at Mecca, and fine old *illuminated MSS. of the Kurân*. The **Türbeh of Roxalana** is also decorated internally with tiles and arabesques, but it has not been kept in such good repair as that of her husband. There are many other tombs in the garden, amongst others that of the Grand Vizier, *Ali Pasha* (d. 1871), on the S. side near the mosque.

The mosque has an annual revenue of P. 300,000, which is chiefly devoted to the support of its dependent scholastic and charitable establishments. These surround the great court, and are reached from it by 10 gates. On *the W.* are the soup-kitchen, *imâret*; the hospital, *Khasta Khâneh*; and the old house of the Agha of the Janissaries. On *the S.* are 4 colleges, *medresseh*; 3 schools, *mekteb*; and a medical school. On *the E.* is the Seraskerat; and on *the N.*, where the ground falls away, are the baths, *hammam*, reached by a flight of steps that leads down from the terrace, whence there is a magnificent view of the city, the Golden Horn, the Bosporus, and the coast of Asia. At the N.W. end of the court is the **Bâb-i-Fetvah**, the official residence of the Sheikh-ul-Islâm.

Ahmediyeh, *Mosque of Ahmed I.* This mosque, situated on the S.E. side of the At Meidan, *Hippodrome*, was built, in 1608–14, by Sultan Ahmed I., who is said to have shown his zeal by working upon it, once a week, with his own hands. It is surrounded by a *great court* planted with trees, and with its six minarets and dependent colleges, soup-kitchens, and tombs forms an imposing pile. When it was built, the mosque at Mecca was the only one in the Moslem world that had six minarets, and, to appease the outcry raised by the Imâm of that place, Sultan Ahmed built a seventh minaret at the Kaaba. The external appearance of the mosque is very pleasing; the mode in which the smaller domes and semi-domes lead up to the centre produces a pyramidal effect that gives an air of stability to the outline, and the six minarets go far to relieve what otherwise might be monotonous.

The **fore-court,** *harâm*, is surrounded on all sides by cloisters covered with small domes, and in its centre is the fountain for ablutions. It is entered by a fine portal, which has exactly opposite to it the principal entrance to the **Mosque,** *Jami'*. This is rather larger than the Suleimaniyeh, measuring 235 ft. by 210 ft., but it is inferior both in design and in the richness or taste of its decorations. Its great defect is that it is too mechanically regular. "In this mosque, as in the Pantheon at Rome, if the plan were divided into quarters, each of the four quarters would be found to be identical, and the effect is consequently painfully mechanical and prosaic. The design of each wall is also nearly the same; they have the same number of windows spaced in the same manner, and the side of the Kibleh is scarcely more richly decorated than the others. Still, a hall nearly 200 ft. square, with a stone roof supported by only four great fluted piers, is a grand and imposing object." — *Fergusson.* The *mihrab*, flanked by its great candelabra, is ornamented with marble slabs which conceal, so it is said, a portion of the black stone of the Kaaba. The *minber*, a masterpiece in marble, is a copy of that at Mecca; it is surmounted by a gilt crown and crescent, and is the pulpit from which the decree that put an end to the tyranny of the Janissaries was read. The box or pew of the Sultan, *mahfil-i-humayûn*, to which a passage leads directly from the fore-court, is in the S.E. corner of the mosque. Kuráns of every form lie on gilded stands, inlaid with mother-of-pearl, and on the wall hangs the last covering of the Kaaba, brought back by the pilgrims from Mecca. The walls beneath the windows are covered with tiles which belong to the best period of Turkish art; but, in striking contrast to this beautiful work, whitewash has been unsparingly employed on the walls above. From the roof hang lamps, some of much value, and ostrich eggs.

The Ahmediyeh has a *revenue* of P. 200,000, and it is used, like the Suleimaniyeh, as a place of deposit for treasure. It is, in some measure, the *state mosque* of Constantinople, for here the Sultan and the chief officers of the Court and State were wont to repair to celebrate the chief Moslem festivals of the *Mevlûd*, or birthday of the Prophet, the departure of the annual caravan for Mecca, and the two Bairâms. In the garden is the **Türbeh of Sultan Ahmed I.**, a rectangular building with au anteroom, and a tomb-chamber covered by a dome, which is decorated with tiles of a good period of art. Within the türbeh are the tombs of Ahmed I. (d. 1617), Osman II. (d. 1622), Murad IV. (d. 1640), and of several princes and princesses. All are covered with costly shawls and embroideries.

Mosque of Muhammad II. On the summit of the 4th hill of the ancient city, and on the site once covered by the *Ch. of the Holy Apostles*, Muhammad, "the Conqueror," erected the mosque that bears his name. It was built, 1463-69, by the Greek architect Christodoulos, who received as payment the whole of an adjoining street. This gift he apparently left to his family, for, under Ahmed III., Cantemir availed himself of the title to protect the Christians who lived in it from expulsion.

The imperial burial-place in the Ch. of the Holy Apostles was called the *Heröon*, and here reposed the rulers of the Byzantine empire in sarcophagi of porphyry, granite, serpentine, and marble. These tombs were desecrated and plundered by the Latins after the capture of Constantinople in 1204, when the holy vessels were converted into troughs for the horses, and the mitres and vestments of the bishops into helmets and halters. The corpse of Justinian, which had reposed for 700 years in the subterranean vault of the church he had built, was robbed of its jewels, and the curtain of S. Sophia, valued at many thousand minæ of silver, was torn into shreds.

The *mosque*, with its fore-court and "garden," stands on an elevated terrace, and around it are 8 colleges, a residence for students, a school, a soup-kitchen, a hospital, a khân, and a bath, the whole forming an immense pile of buildings. The fore-court, *harâm*, is surrounded by cloisters, which are roofed by domes partly resting on ancient columns of marble and granite, and on three of its sides there are marble benches. In the centre, overshadowed by cypresses, is an octagonal *fountain*, with 24 washing places, into which water rushes by many spouts through a bronze grating. The barred windows of the fore-court are ornamented externally with coloured marbles, and above them is written the first sura of the Kurân. The mosque, *jami'*, has several times suffered severely from earthquakes, and after one of these it was almost rebuilt, 1768–71, by Mustafa III., in a semi-Italian style, so that much of the original character is lost. It was intended by Muhammad II. to surpass all other mosques in his kingdom ; but we have little means of judging, now, how far his architect succeeded. Enough of its form, however, still remains to tell us that, like all Turkish mosques, it was a copy of S. Sophia. The principal *entrance*, in Arab style, has some pretensions to beauty, but the *interior* is remarkable only for its vast dimensions. The decoration is of the simplest character, and the flood of light, which pours through numerous windows, on the whitewashed walls produces an almost painful effect. To the rt. of the entrance is a marble slab, set in lapis-lazuli, on which is written, in letters of gold, by the caligraphist *Timurji Chelebi*, the prophecy of Muhammad, "They will capture Constantinople : and happy the prince, happy the army, which accomplishes this." The *mihrab*, *minber*, and *masbata* are of white marble.

In the garden is the Türbeh of Muhammad II., a plain octagonal building, with a porch, and two rows of windows, in which "the Conqueror" lies alone. The interior is ornamented only with verses from the Kurân. The *tomb*, enclosed by a railing inlaid with mother-of-pearl, is surmounted by an enormous turban, and has at its head and foot a large brass candlestick. Near this türbeh is another erected for the Conqueror's wife, who was the mother of Bayezid II.

Mosque of Shah-zadeh, or *of the Prince*, erected, 1543-48, by Suleiman I., in memory of his son, Muhammad, by his Circassian wife, Khasseki. It is the earliest mosque built by Sinan, and the delicacy

and beauty of its outline makes it one of the most pleasing in the capital. The fore-court is of the usual type ; the mosque has a large central dome flanked by four semi-domes, and there are a number of smaller semi-domes, which produce an admirable general effect. The mosque has two minarets of exquisite beauty and lightness. In the garden is the Türbeh of Princes Muhammad and Jehanjir, sons of Suleiman I. The türbeh is an octagonal building covered by a dome with deep flutes ; and its marble walls are richly decorated. A peristyle, ornamented with tiles, leads to the interior, which is of unusual beauty. The Persian faïence, *cloisonné*, with which the walls are covered, belongs to the best period of Persian art, and is particularly worthy of examination. The tombs are those of the two princes, and of one of their sisters.

The Bayezidiyeh, behind the great Bazâr, was built 1497–1505 by Sultan Bayezid II., son of the Conqueror. The fore-court is a fine specimen of Osmanli art. It is surrounded by cloisters, the columns of which are monoliths of *verde-antico*, porphyry, &c. ; the arches are of black and white marble, and the columns rest on marble bases, and have delicately-carved capitals. There are 4 doors in Persian style, and in the centre is an octagonal fountain built by Murad IV. The court contains some fine cypress and plane trees ; and in it, as well as upon cornice, capital, minaret, and dome, are myriads of pigeons, from which it is sometimes called "the Pigeon Mosque." The pigeons are said to be the offspring of a pair bought from a poor woman by Sultan Bayezid, and presented by him to the mosque ; and their lives are held sacred. There is a sort of permanent market in the court, which is generally crowded with buyers and sellers ; and every Friday there is a distribution of food to the dogs of the Quarter. The Jami', with its two free-standing minarets, is of the usual type ; it has a *library* attached to it. The garden contains the **Türbeh of Sultan Baye-zid II.** (d. 1512).

The **Selimiyeh**, built 1520–26, by Suleiman I. in honour of his father, Selim I., stands on the 5th hill of the ancient city, and is a conspicuous object from Pera. The **Jami'** is remarkable for the simplicity of its design, and the general propriety of its proportions. It has attached to it a library, school, soup-kitchen, khân, and bath. In the **garden** are the **Türbehs** of **Sultan Selim I.** (d. 1520), of his wife, and of **Sultan Abdul Mejid** (d. 1861). There is a fine view from the terrace.

The **Yeni Valideh Jami'**, *new mosque of the Valideh Sultan*, was commenced 1615 by the wife of Ahmed I., and completed 1665 by the *Valideh Sultan Tarkhan*, mother of Muhammad IV. The **fore-court** has fine marble cloisters, and a fountain overshadowed by cypresses. The **Jami'** is an imposing building, which has been much whitewashed and otherwise disfigured; it is decorated with blue and white tiles, and has some good stained-glass windows. The two minarets are remarkable for the beauty of their decorative details. Along the walls of the mosque are numerous places for ablution. The external galleries and the apartments reserved for the Sultan are ornamented with tiles of a good period, and in the latter there are some good stained glass and old wood-carving. S. of the mosque the outer court is planted with trees, and forms a regular bazâr, with small shops of all kinds. Here are also an *imâret*, a *medresseh*, and, at the bottom of the court, the **Valideh Sultan Türbesi**, in a small "garden" surrounded by a gilt railing. The building is divided into two chambers, and internally ornamented with very beautiful tiles. In the outer chamber are the tombs of Muhammad IV. (d. 1687), Mustafa II. (d. 1703), Ahmed III. (d. 1730), Mahmûd I. (d. 1754), and Osman III. (d. 1757); in the inner is the tomb of Tarkhan, surrounded by an extremely beautiful inlaid railing, and the tombs of several princes and princesses.

The **Laleli Jami'**, *Tulip Mosque*, built 1760–63, by Mustafa III., stands on a raised terrace, whence there is a fine view of the Sea of Marmara and the Seven Towers. In the interior are 5 fine columns of white marble, which are said to have come from the ruins of the Palace Bucoleon and of the Palace of Theodosius I. in the Forum of Taurus. At the S.W. corner of the enclosure is the **Türbeh of Mustafa III.** (d. 1775) and **Selim III.** (d. 1807); its exterior is highly ornamented, and round the interior runs a long inscription. There are 4 tombs; those of the Sultans are enclosed by railings, one of mother-of-pearl, the other inlaid; all are covered with rich shawls and embroideries. At the ends of the tombs are massive silver candelabra, a large chandelier hangs from the centre of the room, and there are several Kurân stands covered with embroidered silks on the floor.

The remaining mosques which deserve notice are **Rustem Pasha Jami'**, near the Egyptian Bazâr; it was built by the husband of Mihrimah, daughter of Suleiman I., and is profusely decorated with beautiful *faïence* of the best period. **Nûri Osmaniyeh Jami'**, beside the great Bazâr; a fine mosque built entirely of marble, which was commenced by Mahmûd I. in 1748, and completed by his brother, Osman III., in 1755. **Atik Ali Pasha Jami'**, near the Burnt Column, built by the Grand Vizier of Suleiman I., out of the ruins of the Forum of Constantine. **Khasseki Jami'**, in the Ak Serai Quarter; it was built by Suleiman I. in memory of his Circassian wife, whose two murdered sons are buried in the "garden" of the Shahzadeh Mosque, and has a *Lying-in Hospital* attached to it. **Daûd Pasha Jami'**, on the 7th hill; built 1485 by a Grand Vizier of that name. A chronogram gives the date 890 A.H. **Mihrimah Jami'**, near the Adrianople Gate, built in 1555, by *Sinan*, for

Mihrimah, daughter of Suleiman I. and Roxalana. **Yeni Valideh Jami'**, in the Ak Serai Quarter. A small and very beautiful mosque, built in the Renaissance style, in 1870, by the mother of Sultan Abdul Aziz; the porch is of white marble. The **Türbeh** of the Valideh Sultan adjoins the mosque, and is richly decorated internally.

The **Türbeh of Selim II.** (d. 1575) is on the S. side of S. Sophia. It is beautifully decorated; four columns, two of white marble, and two of *verde antico*, support the portico; and within are the tombs of Selim II., of Nûr Banû, "Lady of Light," mother of Murad III.; of 5 sons of Selim, and of several princes and princesses.

The **Türbeh of Abdul Hamid** (d. 1789), a circular building of marble on the rt. side of the wide street leading from the outer bridge, and not far from the entrance to the Seraglio. It contains the tombs of Abdul Hamid and his murdered son, Mustafa IV. (d. 1808), distinguished by the railings round them and their white turbans. There are 15 other tombs, 5 with turbans and 3 with the fez; the remaining 7 are princesses. The tomb of Abdul Hamid is raised higher than the others, and covered with 7 shawls, the small tombs have only one shawl each.

The **Türbeh of Mahmûd II.**, "the Reformer" (d. 1833), near the Burnt Column. This, the latest and most splendid of the Türbehs, is a circular, domed building of white marble, with Corinthian pilasters, lighted by 7 windows with gilded gratings. It contains the tombs of Mahmûd II. and his mother, and of his son, Abdul Aziz (d. 1876), and several princes and princesses. The tombs of the two Sultans are covered with gold embroidered velvet and costly shawls, and surrounded by railings inlaid with mother-of-pearl. At the head of Sultan Mahmûd is the fez, the symbol of reform, with diamond aigrette and plume; and the tomb of Sultan

Turkey.

Abdul Aziz is decorated with the insignia of the order of Osmaniyeh, which he founded. In the apartment there are several massive silver candlesticks, and some Kurân stands, inlaid with silver and mother-of-pearl, on which rest very beautiful MSS. of the Kurân. There is a fine public drinking fountain connected with the Türbeh.

§ 16.—THE SERAGLIO.

The scenes that have been enacted within the walls of the Seraglio make it one of the most interesting places in Constantinople. *Admission* to the *inner court and gardens* is by special order, *irâde*, of the Sultan, which can only be obtained by application, through the Embassy, to the Grand Chamberlain. The order is rarely granted except to distinguished visitors, who are treated as the Sultan's guests, entertained in one of the kiosks, and accompanied by one of the Imperial aides-de-camp. From 5l. to 6l. are given in presents to the palace servants. *No permission* is required to visit the *outer gardens* and the *Court of the Janissaries.*

The **Seraglio**, *Serai*, occupies the E. end of the promontory on which stood the ancient Byzantium and its Acropolis. The situation is lovely. Here were the large public Baths of Arcadius; the palace of the Empress Placidia; the palace of Mangana (p. 30); the churches of S. Barbara, S. Demetrius, and of the Virgin, Hodegetria; and the residences of the notables of the Byzantine Empire. The great Imperial Palace was more to the S., and only partially within the present Serai enclosure. The Serai was protected on the sea side by the *city wall* (p. 29), now partially demolished, and was separated from the city by a *land wall* which ran across the promontory from Yali Kiosk Kapusi to the vicinity of Akhir Kapusi on the Marmara, and still exists. The gates in the land wall are **Demir Kapu**, *Iron Gate*, near the railway station; **Soûk Cheshmeh Kapusi**, *Gate of the Cold Spring*, near the Sublime Porte; **Bâb-i-Humayûn**, *Imperial Gate*, close to S. Sophia; and **Gül-khâneh Kapusi**, *Gate of the House of Roses*, near the shore of the Sea of Marmara. The *Bâb-i-Humayûn* is a lofty portal, on the site of the original gate, built by Muhammad II., on which the heads of decapitated pashas were placed. Above the entrance-door are inscriptions in golden letters. Through this gate the Sultan enters when he visits the Serai in state on the occasion of the festival of the *Hirka-i-Sherif*, or " of the Prophet's mantle," 15th Ramazân, when the mantle, which is preserved in the Serai, is exposed to view.

Within the walls are terraced gardens, planted with cypress, plane, and other trees, amidst which buildings and kiosks, erected at various times and in many styles, are scattered without any attempt at order or method. The earlier date from the reign of Muhammad II., who, however, lived in the *Eski Serai*, " old palace," which stood on the ground now occupied by the Scraskerat. When the Sultans moved to the Seraglio enclosure, the old Serai was given to the widows of deceased Sultans. The Seraglio was the principal residence of the Sultans until Mahmûd II. established himself in the palace of Cheragan, on the Bosporus, N. of the Golden Horn; and when Abdul Mejid moved to the Dolmabâghcheh Palace, and the Seraskerat was built, the Seraglio became the residence of the widows of Sultans and their retinues. In 1863 and 1865 many of the buildings, including a beautiful *Summer Palace* built by Abdul Mejid for his harem, were destroyed by fires; but fortunately the oldest, and the most interesting historically, escaped. *Photographs* of the rooms in the Serai can be obtained in Pera.

The *Seraglio hill* rises in three terraces, of which the two lower are occupied by gardens, and the upper by the Court of the Janissaries, and the Palace with its gardens. The most frequented entrance is the *S'oûk Cheshmeh Kapusi*, which leads directly to the *lowest terrace*. On this, towards Seraglio Point, are the **Military Hospital** and **Medical School**, and towards the S. a **Military School** and a **Cavalry Barrack**. The **gardens**, into which the Yali Kiosk Kapu and Demir Kapu also open, are not well kept, and the ground was much cut up when the railway to Adrianople was made. The *middle terrace* is reached by turning to the rt. after passing through S'oûk Cheshmeh Kapusi. It is well planted, in places, with trees, and on it, in order from the gate are **the Mint**, the **Art School**, in which are casts of the Gigantomachia from Pergamum, now at Berlin, and the Chinili Kiosk, in which is the **Museum of Antiquities** (p. 69). A broad path that passes the **Gül-khâneh Kiosk**, in which Abdul Mejid signed the celebrated *Hatti Sherif of Gül-khâneh*, runs round the hill, and on the S. side leads up to the *upper terrace*.

The Bâb-i-Humayûn opens directly into the **Court of the Janissaries**. On entering there is a grand view over the Sea of Marmara, of Princes' Islands, Kadi Keui, and the distant range of the Bithynian Olympus. On the rt. is the path leading down to the middle terrace, and on the l. the church of S. Irene (p. 43), now used as an **Armoury**. The interior of the ch. is filled with rifles and bayonets of modern pattern; and here are preserved the swords of the conqueror Muhammad II. and of Skanderbeg; an armlet of Tamerlane, and the keys of numerous conquered cities. Here is also a large quantity of chain mail and some fine Circassian helmets. There are 2 effigies in suits of chain mail, one with a remarkably fine head-piece; numerous flags, red and green, are suspended aloft, and two of them, called the flags of Ali, bear on a red field three double-bladed swords with other ensigns.

Outside the ch. are several enormous *sarcophagi* of porphyry from the Ch. of the Holy Apostles, an *obelisk* of porphyry, and a colossal *head of Medusa* from the Forum of Constantine. The **Sarcophagi**, which are quite simple, and without ornament excepting the cross and the monogram of Christ, are supposed to be those of Constantine the Great and other emperors. Beyond S. Irene is the Mint, from the corner of which a path leads down to S'oûk Cheshmeh Kapusi, and here is the celebrated **Plane-tree of the Janissaries.** Beneath this tree the Janissaries hatched mutinies and palace revolutions, and hence they sent in their demands to the Sultan for the dismissal of unpopular Ministers, or the grant of new privileges and concessions.

At the end of the court is the **Orta Kapu**, *Middle Gate*, the entrance to the inner court of Serai, through which no one can pass without an order from the Sultan. It is flanked by towers, and closed by two doors, between which was the *Chamber of Execution.* Here Grand Viziers and Ministers who had incurred the displeasure of Sultans were seized and executed after leaving their presence; and here foreign ambassadors had humbly to await permission to pass the second door. In front of the Gate is the *Mounting Stone*, where everyone except the Sultan was obliged to dismount before entering the inner court. The **Court** is turfed, planted with trees, and surrounded by a low gallery covered with lead, and supported by columns of marble. On the rt. are the kitchens, covered with domes, which have holes in their centres to allow the smoke to escape. The first of these was for the Sultan, the second for the chief Sultanas, the third for the other Sultanas, the fourth for the *kapu aghasi*, or commandant of the gates; in the fifth they dressed the meat for the ministers of the divan; the sixth belonged to the Sultan's pages, *ichoglan;* the seventh to the officers of the Seraglio; the eighth was for the women and maid-servants; the ninth for all such as were obliged to attend the court of the divan on days of session. Formerly, besides 40,000 oxen yearly consumed there, the purveyors had to furnish daily 200 sheep, 100 lambs or goats according to the season, 10 calves, 200 hens, 200 pairs of pullets, 100 pairs of pigeons, and 50 green geese. On the l. a path bordered with cypresses leads to the **Bâb-i-S'âdet**, *Gate of Felicity,* the entrance to the interior of the Serai which was formerly guarded by white eunuchs. The portions of the palace shown to visitors are :—The **Throne Chamber,** or **Hall of the Dîvân,** built by Suleiman I., in which the Sultans gave audience to foreign ambassadors, and the Grand Vizier, assisted by his council, used to determine all causes, civil and criminal, without appeal. The hall is richly decorated with arabesques and *faïence;* and in it there is a large *divân,* with a canopy supported by gilt metal columns richly incrusted with precious stones. An ornamental chimney, and the *latticed window* behind which the Sultan sat when giving audience to ambassadors, should be noticed. The visitor next crosses a flower garden, and passes through courts round which were the apartments of the Sultan's pages, to the **Kitâb Khâneh**, *Library,* which is closed by a very beautifully ornamented bronze door. It contains about 3000 MSS. in Arabic, Persian, and Turkish; a number of Greek MSS.; and a genealogical tree with medallion portraits of the Sultans. None of the MSS. are of exceptional value, according to Prof. Vambéry, the only European who has examined them.

On leaving the Library the **Khazna,** *Treasury,* is to the l.; its façade is covered with tiles, and it has two doors which are opened with great ceremony by the keeper and his assistants. The Treasury consists of 3 rooms, with galleries which are reached by a wooden staircase. In the first room the most conspicuous object is a *great throne*, or *dîvân*, of beaten gold, set with pearls, rubies, and emeralds, thousands on thousands in number. This was a spoil of war taken from one of the Shahs of Persia by Selim I. in 1514. In the gallery of the same room there is a more interesting and beautiful *divân*, which is a genuine work of old Turkish art. The entire height is 9 ft. or 10 ft.; the materials precious woods—ebony, sandal wood, &c.—incrusted or inlaid with tortoiseshell, mother-of-pearl, silver, and gold. The finer decorative details are in mother - of - pearl marquetrie, with splendid cabochon gems, fine balas rubies, emeralds, sapphires, pearls, &c. Pendant from the roof of the canopy, and occupying a position which would be directly over the Sultan when seated on the dîvân, is a golden cord, on which is hung a large heart-shaped ornament of gold, and beneath it again a huge uncut emerald of fine colour, nearly 4 in. in diameter, and 1½ in. thick. Richly decorated arms and armour form a conspicuous feature of the contents of all the three rooms. In the first room is a splendid *suit of mixed chain and plate mail*, wonderfully damascened and jewelled, which was worn by Murad IV., in 1638, at the capture of Baghdad. The hilt and the greater portion of the scabbard of his scimitar close by is incrusted with large table diamonds. A massive *tankard* in solid gold, probably Hungarian, is ornamented with upwards of 2000 flat table diamonds. A *brass bowl*, inlaid with silver, bearing the name and title of Kait Bey, the Mameluk Sultan of Egypt, 1468–96, is a very beautiful specimen of Arab art. The large circular case in the centre of the room contains several thousand *coins*, in bowls, some of which are Roman, Byzantine, and early Arab. The backs of the wall cases are hung with velvet saddle-cloths, embroidered and set with jewels, and there are splendid enamelled jewel-hilted daggers, sabres, scimitars, maces, battle-axes, &c. A great proportion of the objects in the glazed cases are, however, of the commonest and most trivial kind. Side by side with beautiful specimens of Oriental art are modern French and Viennese clocks, gaudy modern china vases with hideous metal mounts, musical boxes, Geneva watches, duelling pistols, re-volvers, knives, forks, silver spoons, card cases, &c. The principal attraction of the second room is a collection of the costumes, or *state robes*, of all the Sultans, from Muhammad II., "the Conqueror" (1453), to Mahmûd II., "the Reformer," who died in 1839. Some of the costumes may really be in part, if not wholly, authentic. All the turbans are enriched with splendid jewelled aigrettes, and each figure has a magnificent dagger inserted in the waistband. Every one of these weapons is a masterpiece of art; one has a hilt of chiselled steel, in perforated work, enriched with gold inlay worthy of Cellini himself; the hilt of another is formed by a huge single emerald. All the outer robes are of magnificent figured brocades, the pattern of each a masterpiece of Oriental design, wrought out in fine silk, gold, and silver, of texture rich, and thick enough to almost stand on end by itself. The under-garments, again, are nearly all of figured silks of the most exquisite and varied patterns.—(*Mr. J. C. Robinson.*)

In the court of the Treasury is the **Kafess**, *cage*, a room in which the imperial children were confined from fear of their aspiring to the throne; and an ancient altar of red porphyry. In a separate building, opposite the Treasury, are kept what may be called the credentials of the Sultans as successors of the early Khalîfs. They are the **Hirka - i - Sherîf**, or, "Mantle of the Prophet;" the **Sanjak-i-Sherîf**, or, "Standard of the Prophet;" the Prophet's staff, sword, and bow; the swords of the first three Khalîfs; and other relics. These are not shown to visitors. From the Treasury visitors pass out to a terrace, with well-kept flower-beds, that overlooks the Bosporus. To the rt. is the **Mejidîyeh Kiosk**, built of marble by Abdul Mejid, and sumptuously furnished in European style. Here coffee and cigarettes are offered to those visiting the Serai. The view from the terraces beside the Kiosk is exceptionally fine, ranging over the peaceful palace garden to the mouth of the Golden Horn, and up the winding Bosporus almost to the Sweet Waters of Asia on the one hand, and over the Sea of Marmara to Princes' Islands and the mountains of Bithynia on the other. To the l. is the lovely little **Baghdad Kiosk**, which is said to have been built by Murad IV. in imitation of one that he saw at Baghdad. It is reached by a flight of marble steps, is thoroughly Oriental in character, and is the finest existing specimen of Turkish decorative art. The walls are covered within and without with beautiful blue tiles; the doors are inlaid with ivory and mother-of-pearl; and the carpets, draperies, and dîvân coverings are most elaborate and costly specimens of Oriental workmanship. The charming manner in which the colours in the interior are blended is very striking. From the Kiosk there is a good view of Galata, Pera, and the harbour crowded with ships. In the inner garden, beneath the Baghdad Kiosk, is the **Column of Claudius Gothicus** (p. 42), often called the *Col. of Theodosius.* Visitors leave the Serai by the way they enter, through Orta Kapu, and across the Court of the Janissaries to the Bâb-i-Humayûn, or by turning to the rt. past the Mint to S'oûk Cheshmeh Kapusi.

§ 17.—Museums.

The **Imperial Museum of Antiquities** is situated within the Seraglio grounds. The State collection of Antiquities, begun in 1850, was kept at first in the Court of S. Irene and other annexes of that Church, but in 1875 was transferred to its present locality. The value and importance of the collection as it now stands are due to the zeal of H. E. Hamdi Bey. The **Museum** consists of two buildings, the Chinili Kiosk, and an Annex just completed. The former is a fine specimen of Turkish architecture. It was once ornamented both within and without with *faience,* remains of which

still appear. It is one of the oldest Turkish edifices in Constantinople, having been built by Sultan Muhammad in 1466. It was, however, repaired and embellished, in 1590, by Sultan Murad III. The interior consists of a cruciform hall, with four rooms between the arms of the cross. As the Museum has not been finally arranged, the position of objects mentioned here is liable to be altered; but the curators are at hand, to furnish information. Among the more interesting objects may be mentioned the following:—

A *statue of Hercules,* from Cyprus, at the left end of the **portico,** along the front of the building; at the right end, a *statue of Jupiter,* from Gaza. In the **vestibule,** and in the room to its right, are found *Assyrian, Egyptian, Kufic,* and *Hittite remains.* Among the last are the *Inscriptions from Hamath,* and the *Lion from Marash.* In the **western transept** is a noble *head and torso of Apollo,* from Tralles. In the **eastern transept,** a bas-relief in three sections, representing *a boar hunt,* from Salonika. Along the eastern wall of the **northern arm** of the cross is a fine head in *bas-relief,* from Cyzicus. Above the medallion is a Decree of the Senate and Demos of that city, in honour of the personage represented, but whose name is lost. On the back of the stone is a later inscription. At the head of the cross is a *colossal statue of Hadrian,* trampling on the figure of a child representing Cyrenaica Victa, from Crete. Behind the statute is the *Stelè from the Temple of Jerusalem,* warning Gentiles, on pain of death, against transgressing the limits of their Court. Near the stelè is the Siloam inscription. In the room to the right are *Cypriote remains.* The room to the left is the **Hall of Bronzes,** containing some beautiful specimens. Especially noteworthy are the portions of the *statues of two athletes,* the *statuette of Hercules,* and the *head of one of the serpents forming the Serpent Column* in the Hippodrome. The case in the centre of the room contains objects found by Schliemann at Hissarlik, and a fine *patera*, from Lamsakos. In a niche in the western wall of the room are *Assyrian* and *Babylonian cylinders* and cones, presented by the Trustees of the British Museum. One of the cylinders belongs to the reign of Sennacherib, and records, among other deeds, that monarch's campaign against Hezekiah, king of Judah. Inquiries should be made for a beautiful *head of Minerva*, from the province of Tripolis; and for a large marble block, upon which are inscribed two decrees issued by the Senate and Demos of Cyzicus, in honour of the queen of Kotys, king of Thrace. Tacitus refers to her, but her name, Antonia Tryphaina, is known only from this inscription.

The **Annex** is a handsome two-storeyed building. In the upper storey will be found a small Collection of *old Oriental carpets* and furniture, an Art Library, and the Director's Offices. The lower storey, consisting of two Halls separated by a Vestibule, is devoted to a very remarkable Collection of 36 *sarcophagi, funereal stelæ, tombstones,* and *cippi,* belonging to various periods, and representing different styles of Art. Here have been placed the superb sarcophagi discovered, in 1887, in an ancient Necropolis, near Sidon. The first division of the Hall to the left, or the Red Hall, forms the Phœnician section, containing 11 *anthropoid sarcophagi.* The most remarkable is that of Tabnith, king of Sidon, the father, or, as others think, the son, of Eshmanazar, whose sarcophagus is now in the Louvre Museum. In the centre of the second division stands the *magnificent sarcophagus,* on one side of which Alexander the Great is represented engaged in battle with the Persians, whilst on the other there is a hunting scene. Painting and Sculpture combine to produce a scene of wonderful realism. The monument belongs to the 4th century B.C., is in the best style, and presents a unique example of polychrome sculpture on so large a scale. It will mark an epoch in our knowledge of ancient Art. The last division contains another beautiful *sarcophagus from Sidon,* in the Lycian style, and of great interest. The central object in the first division of the Hall to the right, or the Green Hall, is a *Greek sarcophagus,* supposed to have belonged to an Asiatic Satrap, and adorned with hunting scenes. It is one of the Sidon find. So is the fine sarcophagus in the middle of the next division, in the form of a temple, and adorned with figures of mourners bewailing the deceased. The central sarcophagus, in the third division, is Byzantine. On the fine sarcophagus to the right are portrayed scenes from the story of Hippolytus, as told by Euripides. Its place of origin unknown. For a full discussion of the historical and artistic questions connected with the sarcophagi from Sidon, see the splendid monograph of Hamdi Bey. Among the objects scattered over the grounds around the Museum, the *inscribed pillars* from Iassos, a large *ancient font* from the Ch. of S. Mary Chalcopratiana, and the escutcheons of the knights of Rhodes may be noticed.

Museum of Ancient Costumes, or *of the Janissaries.* (Open daily; admission P. 5.) In the building, handicraft school, at the S. end of the Hippodrome. It contains a collection of old Turkish costumes on lay figures, which was formed by Sultan Abdul Mejid, and at one time kept in the Seraglio. Here may be seen the Sheikh-ul-Islâm; the viziers; the pashas; the commander of the Janissaries; the Kettles of the Janissaries borne by their proper officers, preceded by another carrying the ladle; the Sultan's dwarfs, his surgeon, executioner, &c.; the chiefs of the black and white eunuchs; representatives of divers trades and professions, and numerous other persons. The figures are poor; the dresses are dusty, and for the most part copies; and the whole place is badly kept; yet in no other place can the visitor obtain such a vivid impression of that strange old Turkish life which passed away for ever when Mahmûd II. introduced his reforms.

§ 18.—WATER SUPPLY—AQUEDUCTS —CISTERNS—FOUNTAINS.

The natural water supply of Constantinople must always have been small and insufficient for the population; and from the time of Hadrian to the present day Emperors and Sultans have endeavoured to secure a good and constant supply by bringing water from a distance. The principle adopted was that of mountain reservoirs and gravitation. The flood water was impounded in winter in reservoirs, and conveyed by aqueducts to the city, where it was stored in open reservoirs and large subterranean cisterns. This system is believed to have been initiated by the Emperor Hadrian, who is known to have improved the water supply of Byzantium, but the principal works were executed by the Byzantine Emperors. The Turks retained the reservoirs, *bend*, and the aqueducts, *kemer*, and even added to their number, but they allowed most of the cisterns to fall into disrepair, and replaced them by a system of water stations, *taksim*, whence water is distributed to the various Quarters of the city for the supply of mosques, baths, public fountains, and private houses.

Before the recent introduction of water from *Lake Derkos*, near the Black Sea, there were three main systems of water supply, two for Stambûl and one for Galata and Pera. (1.) An aqueduct, ascribed to *Constantine the Great*, which passes beneath the walls of Stambûl, near *Edirneh Kapu*, brought water from the springs and streams, near Karamatli and Halkali, to the W. of the city. The water crossed an aqueduct of 11 arches at Kavas Keui. The system was improved by *Valens*, who built the aqueduct which now bears his name. (2.) Water is brought from reservoirs in the vicinity of *Belgrad* — about 15 m. from the city, at the head of the Valley of Sweet Waters—by a conduit which crosses the intervening valleys by

five aqueducts, and finally passes round the heights above Eyûb to *Egri Kapu*, whence it is distributed over Stambûl. One of the aqueducts is ascribed to Justinian. (3.) An aqueduct built by Mahmûd I. conveys water for the use of Pera and Galata from a reservoir constructed by the same monarch at *Baghcheh Keui*, near Buyukdereh. The reservoirs and aqueducts are more fully described below (p. 98); the ancient and modern works connected with the systems within the city are noticed here.

The **Aqueduct of Valens**, *Bosdoghan Kemeri*, spans the upper portion of the valley between the 3rd and 4th hills. It commences a short distance E. of the Mosque of Muhammad II., and ends near the W. wall of the Seraskerat. Its length is 2031 ft., and it has a double tier of arches, the lower $32\frac{1}{4}$ ft. high, the upper $27\frac{1}{2}$ ft. It was built with stones from the walls of Chalcedon, which were broken down by Valens to punish the city for having taken the side of his rival Procopius; and has since been repaired by Justin II., Constantine Copronymus, Basil II., Romanus Argyrus, and Sultan Suleiman, "the Magnificent." At either end steps lead to the summit, whence there is a fine view, and visitors are allowed to walk from end to end. (Small fee to the water-guard at either end.)

The aqueduct forms a picturesque object from many of the points of view round Stambûl, especially when seen towards sunset, when the western rays pouring through the arches, overhung with foliage, tinge the surrounding objects with that inimitable purple and golden haze peculiar to the Bosporus; it is still used to convey water by pipes laid along its summit.

The **Cisterns** constructed by the Greek Emperors were excavated in the ground, and vaulted with brick, the arches being supported by numerous pillars or columns. Ducange gives the names of 19 mentioned by mediæval writers. The most important are:—

The **Cistern Basilica**, *Yeri Batan Serai*, "the Underground Palace," in the street Yeri Batan Serai, leading from the W. corner of the court of S. Sophia to the Persian Embassy. The entrance is in the court of a private house, the owner of which grants admittance. It is the finest cistern in the city, and is ascribed to Constantine the Great; it was enlarged by Justinian, and was under the Portico of the Basilica, in which the great Law Courts of Constantinople sat. The Portico, Στοὰ Βασίλειος, 'Ρηγία, was full of booksellers' stalls, and crowded with lawyers ·and their clients. The cistern is 336 ft. long and 182 ft. wide, and its vaulted brick roof rests on 336 columns, arranged in 12 rows of 28 columns each. The columns are 39 ft. high, and many of them have Corinthian capitals. The cistern always contains water, brought from Belgrad. It cannot be thoroughly explored, and has to be lighted up for visitors. The guide furnishes candles and sets fire to a pile of shavings; this produces a very fine effect, but it only lasts a few moments, and visitors are recommended to take some magnesium wire with them. Caution is necessary in descending to the stone ledge, which projects from the E. side of the cistern and affords standing ground for examining the interior.

The **Cistern of Philoxenus**, *Bin bîr derek*, "cistern of 1001 columns," can be reached from the Hippodrome by the street which ascends the western slope by the *Prison*, or from the *Divân Yol*, by one of the streets opposite the Türbeh of Mahmûd II. It is now dry and occupied by silk-spinners. The entrance is in some waste ground, and there is an easy descent by a flight of steps. Several openings in the roof admit light, but the eye takes some time to accustom itself to the gloom. The cistern belongs to the age of Constantine, and is supposed to derive its Greek name

from one of the senators who assisted that Emperor in the foundation of New Rome. It is 195 ft. long and 167 ft. wide, and its roof is supported by 212 shafts, or; pillars, arranged in 15 rows. These shafts are composed of 3 tiers of columns, which are placed one above the other and tied together by lateral and transverse arches. Owing to the quantity of earth that has been carried into the cistern, only the upper and a portion of the middle tier of columns are visible, but even so the effect is striking and impressive. The upper columns, with their capitals, which are simple with little attempt at ornament, are 27 ft. high, most of them bear monograms. Mr. Fergusson calculates that this cistern would supply a population of 360,000 with water for 10 to 12 days.

Other covered cisterns are :—The so-called **Cistern of Theodosius**, about 137 ft. by 75 ft., with 33 fine columns, to the S.W. of Bin bîr derek. The **Cistern of Phocas**, with 70 columns, N. of Laleli Jami', and near Chukur Cheshmeh. The cistern near **Bodrum Jami'**, with 64 columns. The **Cistern of Pulcheria** (?), with 28 columns, S. of the Selimiyeh Mosque. A **Cistern** with 28 columns, in the Salma Tomrûk Quarter. The **Cold Cistern**, under the S.W. end of the Hippodrome. The **Cist. of Pantocrator**, and the **Cist. of Pantopopte**, beside the churches so named.

The large open *storage reservoirs* of ancient Constantinople are called *Chukur Bostan.* They are the **Cistern of S. Mocius**, 510 ft. by 408 ft., built by the Emperor Anastasius on the summit of the 7th hill, beyond Alti Mermer. The **Cistern of Aspar**, 750 ft. by 261 ft., to the rt. of the street leading from the Mosque of Muhammad II. to the Adrianople Gate. The cistern now occupied by the **Saddle Market**, *Serraj Khâneh*, on the rt. of the street from the Mosque Shahzadeh to that of Muhammad II. The **Cistern Boni**, nearly 500 ft. square, above the Phanar, S. of the Selimiyeh Mosque; the capacity of this cistern is estimated by Andreossy to be at least 6,571,720 cubic feet.

In connection with the water supply, the taksim, suterazi, and fountains deserve notice. The **Taksim** are reservoirs whence the water, brought by the aqueducts, is distributed to the various Quarters of the city. They are generally large masonry constructions, divided into several compartments or basins, and have been built wherever it was necessary to distribute the water through a number of pipes. The most important are that outside Egri Kapu in the Stambûl walls; and that, built by Mahmûd I., 1731, and repaired by Abdul Hamid I., 1786, which gives its name to the Place Taksim in Pera. The **Suterazi**, *water-balance*, or "water-towers," of which many may be seen in Constantinople and the surrounding country, are massive towers shaped like truncated pyramids; they are sometimes ornamented, but oftener quite plain. These towers are designed to eliminate, at certain intervals, the pressure arising from the velocity acquired by the water in the conduits during its fall from a higher level. The water rises through a pipe to the top of the tower, and then descends through another pipe to a reservoir on the opposite side, whence it issues with the loss of the velocity it had acquired. It is uncertain whether the Turks adopted this system from the Byzantines, or introduced it themselves.

The **Fountains** are of two kinds. The *Cheshmeh* is a monument, more or less ornamental, which is usually attached to a wall that conceals a cistern, whence water runs out through one or more spouts like an English public drinking fountain. It has a marble basin beneath to catch waste water, and a projecting eave, *sachak*, above. The *Sebîl* is usually a small, isolated monument in a court, or square, which has been erected by some pious or distinguished person. It consists of a chamber with a water tank from which a man, maintained by the foundation, fills metal cups, attached by chains to the grating of the monument, and places them on the marble slab outside for the use of thirsty passers-by. The larger monuments are sometimes a combination of the cheshmeh and the sebîl, and in the fore-courts of the mosques the cheshmehs are generally isolated structures. The number of fountains, of all shapes and sizes, from a simple arch on a wall to the elaborate structure like that near the Seraglio Gate, is a remarkable feature in Stambûl; and some of them are gems of Osmanli art. "The more important fountains are covered with a coating of marble, and decorated all over with most delicate surface ornament. Where in Western art we should use figures to break the monotony, the Turks employ representations of vases filled with flowers, or dishes with fruit. These fountains, when carved in stone, are coloured and gilt all over; but when of marble, have only a little gilding, and very little colour. The eaves of these fountains have a great projection, are boarded, and decorated with painting. The roof is often composed of a series of domes."—*Builder.*

Water is to the Eastern the symbol of the principle of life; and the words of the Kurân, "By water everything lives," are almost universally inscribed on the great fountains. The most beautiful are the **Fountain of Ahmed III.**, outside the Bâb-i-Humayûn of the Seraglio. It is a rectangular building of white marble, which combines the cheshmeh and the sebîl, and is covered with finely-carved arabesques, and inscriptions in gold letters on blue and green grounds, surrounded by borders of *faïence.* The whole effect is most beautiful and pleasing. On the side facing S. Sophia is one of those chronograms, *tarik,* in which the Turks delight. It is said to have been written by Ahmed himself, and reads: "The date (*tarik*) of Sultan Ahmed flows from the tongue of the water-pipe, open it in the name of God, drink the water, and pray for Ahmed Khân." By adding the numerical value of the Arabic letters together, the date A.H.

1141 (A.D. 1728) is obtained for the completion of the fountain.

The **Fountain of Asab Kapu**, in Galata, near the inner bridge, also combines the two types, and was built by Ahmed III. It is small, but most elaborately ornamented with floral devices and gilt arabesques, and on the street side it has a prettily designed gilt bronze *grille*, divided into compartments by 6 small columns. The *Fountain of Top-khâneh* (p. 19) is of the same date. Other fountains are the *Cheshmeh of Zeineb Sultan*, opposite S. Sophia ; the *S'oûk Cheshmeh*, against the wall of the Serai, by the gate of the same name ; and the Sebîls of *Mahmûd II.*, near his türbeh, of *Hassan Pasha*, near the Seraskerat, of *Abdul Hamid I.*, on the line of tramway near his türbeh, and of *Yeni Valideh Sultan*, prettily ornamented with *faïence*, in the square behind the mosque.

In addition to the water supplied by the State Bends around Belgrâd and Baghcheh Keui the city and the villages on the northern side of the Bosporus, from Mezâr Burnu to Beshiktash, are furnished daily, by the *Compagnie des eaux de Constantinople*, with 10,000 to 12,000 cubic mètres of water brought from Lake Derkos, some 30 miles from Constantinople. The pipes are laid along the heights between the Ali Bey Keui Su and the Kiat Khâneh Su. They cross fifteen ravines by means of as many siphons, and upon approaching the Sweet Waters divide into two branches. Since January 1885, one of the branches has conveyed water to a reservoir at Ferikeui for distribution to the quarters on the northern side of the Horn ; while the other, since May 1889, has supplied Stambûl from a reservoir within the Adrianople Gate. The Company has provided 400 hydrants and 52 free fountains.

§ 19.—BAZÂRS--CICERONI--PURCHASES —SLAVE MARKETS—KHÂNS.

The **Bazârs**, or markets, *Charshi*, are distinguished either by the name of the article made or sold in them, or, as in the case of the *Sali Bazâr*, " Tuesday Market," in Galata, by the day upon which they are held. Some of them are isolated, and situated in the different quarters of the city, as the bazârs near the Golden Horn, in which fish, flowers, fruit, wood, &c., are sold ; the horse market and the saddlers' bazâr, near the Mosque of Muhammad II. ; and the **Misr Charshi**, *Egyptian Bazâr*, adjoining the Mosque Yeni Valideh Sultan. The last is a long vaulted street, in which all manner of drugs, spices, and, those indispensable adjuncts to the toilet of an Oriental beauty, *Henna* and *Kohl*, are sold by solemn bearded Turks, who sit cross-legged in their shops regardless of the throng of passers-by.

The Bazâr *par excellence* is the **Great Bazâr**, which lies between the Seraskerat and the Mosques Sultan Bayezid and Nûri Osmaniyeh, and covers a large area on the hill between the Golden Horn and the Sea of Marmara. It consists of a perfect labyrinth of streets and alleys, and such are their extent and intricacy, that a traveller, unattended by a dragoman, might easily lose himself in them. The Bazâr can be reached from the N. by following either of the streets *Usun Charshi* or *Mahmûd Pasha*, in which are the makers of amber mouthpieces for pipes, the turners, and the workers in brass ; from the Seraskerat, by the *Kasanjilar Kapusi*, or by the steep *Merjan Yol ;* through the Courts of Mosques Sultan Bayezid and Nûri Osmaniyeh ; and by short streets leading down from the *Divân Yol*, through which the tramcars run. The bazâr *proper* is vaulted with stone, and in the roofing there are numerous small domes which admit a subdued light pleasant to the eye, and much in favour of the sellers of soiled or inferior goods. In the centre is an enclosure called the *Bezesten*, in which arms, porcelain, " curiosities," &c., are sold, and auctions are held. The *Bit Bazâr*, in which tents are made, and old clothes are offered for sale, is deserving of a visit; and the traveller who wishes to try *Mohalebi,* a kind of blanc-mange, or Turkish cooking, will find eating-houses in the *Ainajilar Charshi.*

Like the bazârs in London, erected in imitation of them, the covered bazârs of Constantinople are only used as shops, and are all closed and deserted an hour before sunset. Each entrance has an iron door, which is shut at night, when watchmen, *bekjis,* have charge of the bazârs, and are responsible for the safety of the shops and their contents. Not only in the covered bazârs, but in those which more resemble open streets, separate districts are severally allotted to particular trades and merchandise, after the manner of Athens, of Rome, and of the city when under the dominion of the Greeks. The shops of jewellers and engravers of precious stones occupy one quarter; those of the goldsmiths another. The curriers and leather-workers, as well as horse-dealers, all congregate at *At-Bazaru.* *Misr-Charshi* is a long line of drug repositories. All the coffee is ground by hand in *Tahmis-Bazâr.*

The Bazârs have lost much since the influx of European fashions, and the shops in the Grande Rue of Pera have become the resort of the wealthy of both sexes. It is now unusual to see any Turk of rank or wealth in the bazâr. Indeed, they never frequent it, as the articles they purchase are almost always brought to their own houses. As for the ladies, none but those of a certain age are ever allowed to go to the bazârs. Their general appearance before the last war with Russia had impoverished the people was thus described by Albert Smith, in 'A Month at Constantinople':—"To say that the covered rows of shops must altogether be miles in length—that vista after vista opens upon the gaze of the astonished stranger, lined with the varied productions of the world—that one may walk for an hour without going over the same ground

twice, amidst diamonds, gold, and ivory; Cashmere shawls and Chinese silks; glittering arms, costly perfumes, embroidered slippers, and mirrors; rare brocades, ermines, morocco leathers, Persian nicknacks; amber mouthpieces and jewelled pipes—that looking along the shortest avenue, every known tint and colour meets the eye at once, in the wares and costumes; and that the noise, the motion, the novelty of this strange spectacle, is at first perfectly bewildering—all this possibly gives the notion of some kind of splendid mart fitted to supply the wants of the glittering personages who figure in the Arabian Nights' Entertainments; yet it can convey but a poor idea of the real interest which such a place calls forth, or the most extraordinary assemblage of treasures displayed there amidst so much apparent shabbiness."

The wares in which European travellers feel most interest, are the following:—Brûsa and Damascus silks; embroidered table-covers and scarfs; Persian and Indian shawls; Turkish and Persian carpets; old arms; metal pots and vases covered with Persian and Arabic inscriptions; various ornaments of gold and silver; and attar of roses. Modern embroideries, made as much as possible in imitation of the older work, are one of the new features of the bazâr. For all these articles extravagant prices are demanded, and the traveller who wishes to buy any quantity had better employ some local agent who knows their value. When purchasing either by himself, or through a cicerone, he may expect to pay at least fifty per cent. above the real price The best plan for those who have a little time to spare is to visit a number of stalls, observe the prices asked in each, and in the end some little idea may be formed of the real value of the articles sought. It ought to be remembered, however, that those things included under the general name of antiquities have a fancy price, which depends on the demand and supply. A great deal of worthless rubbish is palmed off on travellers under the attractive name of antiquities.

The traveller who has time may employ himself in buying arms, embroidery, porcelain, &c., in the Bezesten, or general articles of Persian and Turkish manufacture in the bazârs; but this is a work of time. The people in the bazârs know by experience that the "Captain" and his ladies have only a few hours in Constantinople, and that they want to buy curiosities at a fancy price to take home.

Unless a traveller knows the language, or can be accompanied by a European resident, he should take a dragoman with him to the bazârs. He should, however, be upon his guard, for though the dragoman will pretend to bid, it is his interest to have as high a price as possible, since he gets a commission from the dealer, and nothing from his employer. If a dragoman is told to take strangers to any particular shop, he will walk the party about, and then propose to them to sit down in the shop of a friend of his, where coffee and pipes are brought in, and the visitors of course buy a lot of rubbish. For special shops, &c., see Index.

The open **Slave Markets,** *Yessir Bazari,* have all been closed, but the traffic in white slaves is still carried on, in a modified form, by the Circassians who live in Top-khâneh, and a diminishing number of black slaves is annually introduced from Africa.

Khâns.—*The* 180 *Khâns of Constantinople* are so many immense stone barracks or closed squares, which have, like the baths, every recommendation except architectural elegance. The court of the *Valideh Khân,* which is reckoned one of the best in Constantinople, is ornamented with trees, and two handsome fountains; and the building, besides warehouses and stables on the ground-floor, has 3 storeys or galleries, one above the other, with ranges of small chambers,

each of which is kept clean by the servants of the *khân,* and fitted up for the time with the carpets and slender wardrobe of the several occupiers. Most of the *Khâns* are near the Great Bazâr; and the larger ones are in the picturesque Chakmakjilar Street. They were originally built for travelling merchants and their wares; but the chambers of many are now let out as counting-houses, stores, and shops to Europeans and natives, whose dwellings are in Galata, Pera, or some distant quarter of the city. These useful edifices are the work of the Osmanli sultans or wealthy private individuals; strangers are, during their residence in the city, masters of their rooms on the payment of the rent, and they keep the keys. They are for all men, of whatever quality, condition, country, or religion soever. The construction of them has contributed to attract the merchants and the merchandise of the furthest boundaries of Africa and Asia to the capital of Turkey. During fires or insurrections their iron gates are closed, and they afford complete security to the persons, as well as the goods of the merchants.

§ 20.—PUBLIC OFFICES — BARRACKS —HOSPITALS—LIBRARIES—SCHOOLS —BIBLE HOUSE.

The **Public Offices** are nearly all modern constructions; the only two deserving of notice are the **Bab-i-'Ali,** Sublime Porte, a building in the Italian style, which stands in a court with a huge marble portal flanked by fountains. It is opposite the W. angle of the Serai Gardens, and contains the offices of the Prime Minister, the Foreign Minister, and the Minister of the Interior; in it the Council of State meets. The **Seraskerat,** or War Office, was erected in 1870 on the site of the Old Serai, built by Muhammad II. after the conquest. It occupies a commanding position in Stambûl, and contains the offices of the several divisions of the War Department. Near it is the **Serasker Tower,** built largely of white marble by Mahmûd II. The view from the top of the tower is perhaps not so picturesque as that from the Galata Tower, but it is more extensive and takes in points not seen from the northern shore of the Golden Horn.

The *Osmanieh Printing Establishment;* the *Turkish Printing Office,* in Galata, where the art of ornamental typography has been brought to great perfection; and the *Telegraph Department Factory,* at the N. end of the Seraglio Garden, though not Public Offices, are deserving of a visit, as the work in them is almost entirely carried out by Turkish workmen.

Barracks.—The large number of Barracks in the immediate vicinity of Constantinople at once attracts the attention of the visitor. They are well worth visiting, and permission is easily obtained from the officer on duty. The rooms are commodious and well ventilated, and order and regularity are observable throughout. In all the great barracks there are schools where the young men are prepared for the military service. The principal barracks are:— *Maltepeh Daûd Pasha,* and *Ramiz Chiftlik,* on the heights to the W. of Stambûl; the *Marine B.,* near the Admiralty, at Kassim Pasha; the *Artillery B.,* at Top-khâneh; the *Artillery and Engineer B.,* at Taksim, N. of Pera; the *Mejidieh B.,* and the *Gümush-su B.* above Dolmabâghchch; and the *Selimiyeh* at Skutari.

Hospitals.—There are several small Turkish hospitals, *khasta khâneh,* in the several quarters of the city; and outside the walls of Stambûl the *Military Hospital* of Daûd Pasha, which is one of the most remarkable of Turkish institutions. The establishment is admirably regulated; the different wards are clean and well ventilated. The laboratory and kitchen are as well organised as any in France or England. The medical men are of the different nationalities of the empire, Turks, Armenians, Jews, and Greeks, and many speak French and Italian fluently. There

are also a *Marine Hospital,* a small hospital at Seraglio Point, a *Lying-in Hospital* for women in Stambûl, and a *Lunatic Asylum* at Skutari. The Greeks, Armenians, and Jews have each their own hospitals; and so have the English, French, Austrians, Italians, and Russians.

There are several **Libraries** at Constantinople, the most important being that in the Serai, those attached to the Imperial Mosques, that of the Medresseh of Abdul Hamid I., the new library near Sultan Bayezid's Mosque, and the Greek libraries in the Phanar and at Pera.

Schools.—The Muhammadan public schools are:—the *Mekteb,* or primary school for boys and girls, in which reading and writing are taught, and portions of the Kurân are committed to memory; one of these is attached to nearly every mosque in the Empire. The *Ibtidaiyeh,* or higher elementary school, of which there are 30 to 40 in the capital. The *Ilushdiyeh,* or secondary school, in which Persian, Arabic, history, geography, and arithmetic are taught; in Constantinople there are 20 Rushdiyeh for boys, and 11 for girls, and in the Provinces 440. The *Medresseh,* in which the students, *Softas,* are instructed in Arabic and Persian, philosophy, logic, rhetoric, and morals founded on the Kurân; with theology, Turkish law, and a few lessons on history and geography. The schools of a higher category are the *Mekteb-i-Sultanieh,* or Lyceum of Galata Serai, which has generally been under French direction, and has produced some distinguished high officials of the Porte and the Palace; a higher *school for civil employés* in Stambûl; a *law school;* a *school of mines and forests;* a *school of languages;* an *art school* (p. 82); a *handicraft school,* in the Hippodrome; a civil *school of medicine;* and an *Orphan's School.* There are also the *Military College* at Pankaldi, with 600 to 700 cadets, who are recruited from 9 military Rushdiyeh in Constantinople, and 17 in the Provinces;

the *Staff College*; the *Artillery and Engineer School*; the *Army Medical School* at Seraglio Point; the *Veterinary School* at Gül-khâneh; and the *Naval College*, on the Island of Halki.

The Greeks, Armenians, and Jews have each large numbers of primary, secondary, and higher schools, maintained by the communities; and of these the *Greek National Training School*, with its fine library, at Phanar, and the *Greek Theological College*, and the *Commercial School* on Halki, deserve a visit. There are also many European colleges and schools, of which the most important are:—*Robert College*, on the Bosporus (p. 92); the *English School for Girls* in Pera; the *American College for Girls* at Skutari; the *German-Swiss School*; the *College of the Lazarists*; the *Jesuit College* of S. Pulchérie; the *French College* at Kadi Keui; and the *Austro-Hungarian School*.

The Bible House, *American Khân*, was constructed, in 1872, with funds collected chiefly in the United States, for the purpose of furnishing permanent quarters to the American Bible and Missionary Societies established in Constantinople. The rooms are leased to the local representatives of the American Bible Society; the British and Foreign Bible Society; the treasury and the Publication Department of the American Board of Foreign Missions, &c. On the premises is a hall where the Trustees of the Bible House maintain Sunday services in Greek and in Turkish.

An extensive publishing business is carried on at the Bible House. The Holy Scriptures are published in all the languages of the Empire by the two Bible Societies, and religious books and tracts, as well as a large selection of school text-books, are published in Turkish, Armeno-Turkish, Greco-Turkish, Armenian, Greek, and Bulgarian, by the American Mission, aided by the Tract Societies of London and America. The Mission also publishes four weekly religious newspapers, and four monthly illustrated papers for children, in different languages. The books of these Societies are subjected to the Turkish censorship before publication, and when authorised by the Dept. of Public Instruction, are sold at a little over cost price in all parts of the Empire.

In laying the foundations of the Bible House walls of the Byzantine period were uncovered, and some of the inscribed bricks are preserved in the building. At the same time graves were found, containing skeletons and Roman coins, covered by large tiles. On the Bible House premises is a small Byzantine cistern, with vaulted roof supported by columns.

§ 21.—GUILDS—DERVSÎHES—HAREMS.

The **Guilds** of Constantinople are trade organisations, and their influence is wholly confined to the trade which their respective members exercise. Under the Byzantine Empire there appear to have been only 35 recognised corporations having their shops in the Bezesten; but after the conquest they rapidly increased till they attained the number of 600, which marched past Murad III., 200,000 strong, in 1635. There are now 275 registered corporations, *esnaf*, each of which consists of masters, workmen, and apprentices, with a Council composed of a governor, appointed by the Prefecture; a president, elected by the members; and a certain number of masters and workmen. Most of the corporations admit persons of every nationality and creed, and all workmen arriving in the capital from the provinces are expected to belong to the *esnaf* of their trade. The funds are derived from real estate, admission fees, and fixed contributions from the members; and they are chiefly expended upon charitable objects, such as assistance to sick brethren, and to the widows and orphans of deceased members. The *esnafs* thus do much good, and the discipline enforced is sufficient to maintain an *esprit de corps* which is not without its advantages. The subdivision of trades is carried to an amusing extent; there is one *esnaf* for the makers of straw-seated stools and another for the makers of straw-seated chairs; one for sedentary barbers, another for ambulant barbers; one for heather brooms, another for rice-straw brooms, and so on. The principal *esnafs* acknowledge a patron, and celebrate a festival in his or her honour once a year. Thus Adam is patron of the Bakers; Eve of the Bath-women; Abel of the Shepherds; Cain of the Grave-diggers; Nimrod of the Farriers; Enoch of the Inkstand makers; Noah of the Shipwrights; and Elijah of the Furpelisse makers. The corporation of the Butchers is the richest, and that of the Bakers the most numerous, having over 1000 members.

THE DERVÎSHES.

The traveller should not omit a visit to the *Tekkehs*, or monasteries of the dervîshes, known to Europeans as the Dancing or Whirling, and the Howling Dervîshes.

The **Dancing**, or **Mevlevi Dervîshes,** have as their founder Mevlana Jelaleddin Hûmi Muhammad, who was descended from Abubekr, and was related to the princely families of Kharezmia and Khorasán. Having succeeded his father as Sultan-ul-Ulema, he publicly taught in Konieh, then the capital of the Seljûk Empire of Rûm. About A.D. 1245 he renounced the world, and, turning dervîsh, founded the order of Mevlevi. His work, 'Mesnevi,' is celebrated, and many of the verses have become proverbs. The head of the Mevlevi at Konieh, who bears the title *Chelebi Effendi,* as lineal descendant of Jelaleddin, appoints the chiefs of other monasteries, and girds the sword of Osman on the Sultan at his accession. Every Mevlevi goes through a hard noviciate of 1001 days before admission to the order.

The Mevlevi, who are not bound by strict rules in regard to drinking, smoking, eating, &c., go through their pecu-liar religious exercise, *Zikr,* or Sem'a, every Tuesday and Friday after the mid-day prayer. The ceremony consists in the dervîshes revolving gently on their toes, and at the same time going round the room, circle within circle. This is done to the music of flute and tambourine, which form the accompaniment to a monotonous chant, on the unity of God and the nullity of earthly existence. Their arms are extended, the right above the head, the left below, with both hands open; their eyes closed, and their heads bent sideways on their shoulders. Many Turkish gentlemen attend for the sake of the music, which has great charms for them. The origin of the dance is obscure; its object, like that of the exercises of the Howling Dervîshes, is to produce the ecstatic state in which the soul enters the world of dreams, and becomes one with God, or the effacement of self in the presence of the Creator. The superior, the chief flute, chief tambourine, and chief whirler are important personages.

For the *Howling* or *Rufâî Dervîshes,* see p. 108.

Turkish Harems.—To lady travellers a visit to one of the principal harems would probably prove interesting, and it can be brought about by getting acquainted with any of the Pera families who are in the habit of frequenting the harems of pashas. The following account of one or two harems is partly from the pen of a lady who had enjoyed opportunities of observing domestic life amongst the higher classes at Stambûl:—

"The harems are of two kinds—those where some European notions and manners have been engrafted on Asiatic splendour, and those which retain with religious scrupulousness all the ancient customs of the Turks. A female dragoman is indispensable, except in the case of those Turkish ladies who speak French, and then intercourse is much freer than through an interpreter. Few Turkish ladies speak French, and still fewer English. Sometimes the husband will come himself to do the honours of his house, when he is a proficient in French, as many of the pashas are.

"As soon as one passes the door of the harem, a number of female slaves show the way to the great lady's presence, two of them supporting each visitor under the arms on the way. At the top of the stairs some near relative of the Hanum will receive the strangers, and accompany them to the door of her room, where she will probably be found standing, if she wishes to do honour to her guests. She salutes them by touching her lips and forehead with her right hand, as a gentleman does, and then she goes back to her divan, where she bids them be seated. Salutations recommence, reciprocal inquiries after the state of each other's health, and various little interrogations as to the fact of being married or not, the number of children existing, if the answer be in the affirmative, and the like, until pipes are brought by female slaves or young negroes, the former having made, in the meantime, a clumsy attempt to divest us of our bonnets and outer garments, smiling all the while with wonder at such strange contrivances. The said pipes are 6 or 8 ft. long, and one does feel rather queer in proceeding to smoke them in real earnest! an English woman is not obliged to do so, but some Levantine women do. Cigarettes are now greatly used in the harem. The tobacco is generally good, although the excise duty has made it an expensive luxury. Then comes coffee in little cups, and *zarfs*, or gold enamelled holders of elegant filigree work, like egg cups, sometimes set with brilliants, as are also the amber mouthpieces of the pipes. The young slaves, fat Georgians, with large black eyes, tall Circassians, slender and fair-haired, and shining negresses, stand in a row at the end of the room in attitudes of respect, watching to take the emptied cups from our hands. Their dress is pretty, being loose and flowing, with wide trousers falling over their slippered feet; but then their faces were so cruelly disfigured by paint of various colours, red and white on their cheeks, black on their eyebrows and eyelids, and a deep yellow tint on their nails, that the charms of feature, figure, and dress were greatly detracted from in our eyes. The robes of the ladies were so long, that it required considerable skill to avoid being tripped up by the folds getting entangled round their inverted feet, giving them somewhat the appearance of feather-toed pigeons. The slaves had more finery about them than their mistresses—gauze figured with satin and gold, gaudy silks, Cashmere shawls of the gayest colours, bright Indian kerchiefs, and pearls and precious stones, being in lavish profusion on their persons, while the Hanums wore dresses of plain silk. The number of these garments was so limited, moreover, that they would require richness and bulk of material to compensate for the total absence of an important proportion of European articles of costume; for these Asiatic matrons and maidens, one and all, wore literally nothing but what was visible, while they displayed an unfortunate predilection for cambric, gauze, jaconnet, and exceedingly gossamer-like silks. The old lady herself was attired with the most appalling simplicity. On her finger, however, she wore a diamond ring, which she told us had cost her father-in-law, Muhammad Ali of Egypt, 2000*l.*, and her head was bound with a plain kerchief, on which an enormous emerald sparkled. The furniture of the room which received us on that occasion consisted merely in divans covered with rich stuffs, some higher, and some lower for humble guests; and handsome chandeliers stood on side tables. After coffee we had sweetmeats offered us in crystal vases on a gold tray, and the visitor must be careful to take a tea-spoon from the goblet on the right-hand side, and put it in that on the left, in which are deposited those that have been used. After drinking a glass of cold water, the mouth is wiped on richly-embroidered napkins which are offered by other slaves. After each of these operations, a salutation of thanks must be addressed to the Hanum by putting the right hand to the lips and forehead, when she will respond, '*áfiet olsun*' (may it be to your health); but salutation after refreshment is now going out of fashion. Then coffee follows again, and the pipes are renewed, while the rambling conversation never flags.

" The next incident was the display of all the Hanum's gorgeous dresses. The visitor must now get up the steam for admiration, yet not astonishment, for she would then be classed as a poor lady, having no fine clothes of her own, and treated during the remainder of the visit accordingly. While this is going on, the slave-girls began to play on wind-instruments resembling clarionets, but longer and more discordant. We went to see the orchestra, and all whose mouths were not otherwise engaged commenced singing. Others began to dance. A sort of maypole was raised in the middle of the room, with many-coloured ribbons attached to its top. The dancers held them by the other end, and went round it, plaiting them as they went by crossing each other, and then un-doing them again. This was slow and measured. The band next struck up a war tune, and the savage instinct of the Circassian mountaineers seemed to awaken. They seized brass shields and short swords, clashing them furiously as they whirled about like young Furies. They threw away their arms and began to romp like hoydens, tumbling over each other, rolling on the floor, throwing pillows at those that fell, laughing and screaming, more as maniacs than as the well-behaved, demure young damsels we took them for.

" Dinner was brought, and our utmost neat-handedness was required to eat with our fingers in so lady-like a manner as our hostess. An interminable succession of little dishes wore out our patience as well as our appetites, and we were glad to make our preparations for departure.

But this was not so easily effected. We must go through the hand-washing process; then drink sherbet. When it was distinctly understood that we never should forget each other, and that we should always be dear friends as long as we lived, the Hanum, her ladies, and our party separated at the top of the stairs, whither she graciously accompanied us. Turkish ladies are generally polite and hospitable, and though they pass over any display of coarseness or rudeness, they are quite able to distinguish between any practice which arises from a difference of manners and that which springs from the want of breeding in a woman. The wives are generally women of rank corresponding to that of their husbands, and the slaves receive some education as to their manners before being sold. The law recognises them as wives as soon as they bear a child to their masters."

It is an error to suppose that Turkish women are imprisoned in their houses like birds in a cage. On the contrary, they have in some respects more liberty than European women. They roam about at will, and they drive through the streets, disguised in a costume which renders recognition impossible. They are veiled, and cover their whole persons with the *ferejeh*, so that it is impossible to distinguish one female from another. The wives of Turks of rank are always accompanied by a eunuch; others who cannot afford that luxury go about alone.

§ 22.—ART—THEATRES.

Art.—The Muhammadan precept, which prohibits imitation of the human form, together with the indolence of the Turkish temperament, have combined to exclude Art from any place in the intellectual life of the Ottoman Empire. It may be argued, however, from individual instances, and from general observation, that the Turks are not insensible to Art. For instance, the late Sultan, Abdul Aziz, spent a great portion of his leisure in watching the work of his painter, Chlebowski, to whom his Majesty gave sketches, drawn with his own hand, of the general design of the pictures he wished to have. These sketches were mostly naval or military battle-pieces, and the artistic conception of them was often remarkable. Some of them are now in the possession of Lord Brassey. Again, the Turkish population is immensely attracted by the picture shops in Pera, and a crowd is always gazing at the coloured prints and oleographs they contain. When the *Ecole des Arts et Metiers* was founded after the return of Abdul Aziz from his European tour (1866), the educational programme included drawing, such as landscape and architecture. But it was neither systematically nor artistically followed up, and now the school itself, like all those institutions which, in a spirit of imitation and in a moment of impulse, have been grafted upon the Turkish system, has dwindled into decrepitude, and is only an example of slovenliness, indiscipline, and disorder. Art has, however, a nursery in the Ottoman capital. Its institution is wholly due to Hamdi Bey, son of Edhem Pasha, an ex-Grand Vizier. Hamdi Bey developed a strong taste for Art in early life, and applied himself to the study of painting, sculpture, architecture, and archæology. From the earliest days of the Imperial Museum (p. 69) he took the liveliest interest in it, and after two successive foreign directors had passed away, he was appointed director about the year 1881, bringing to bear upon his new charge a rare amount of energy. Amongst many other additions and improvements, he induced the Porte to grant permission, and what was harder to obtain, money, to construct a building adjacent to the Museum, to serve as a **School of Art**, under his guidance. The building was opened in 1884, and contains a spacious vestibule filled with casts and models, flanked by four large studios, two on each side, which are used respectively for:

(1) Drawing from casts or models; (2) Painting; (3) Modelling in clay; (4) Architectural designing. The building also contains an elementary studio and a library. For the last three years the number of students has averaged 180, consisting of Moslems, Armenians, and Greeks, mostly youths between 15 and 20 years of age. Many of them display considerable talent, but there is little to encourage them in the pursuit of an artistic career. The school owes its existence and maintenance to Hamdi Bey's indomitable perseverance in combating the prejudice, ignorance, and apathy which he has to encounter. While Hamdi Bey remains, the school will live; but as to its later future it is, to say the least, very doubtful. An annual exhibition of the students' works takes place in the autumn. The school is always accessible to visitors.

The **theatres** in Pera are generally open between November and May, being leased either for Italian Opera, French vaudeville, or Greek comedy, by companies that go the round of the cities of the Levant. The performances are such as are met with in third or fourth rate French or Italian towns, and offer little attraction to tourists. There are several café chantants, where "variety" entertainments are given, and which are in their way as good as in any other place. But they only mask a roulette table, which is kept contrary to law, but with the connivance of the police, and persons who allow themselves to be led into the gambling-room must take the risk of being on unlawful ground. In the summer months two open-air theatres amuse the small bourgeoisie of Pera, but the performances are exceedingly poor.

§ 23.—Baths—Cemeteries—Kaïks—Dogs.

Turkish Baths.—There are about 130 of these establishments dispersed through various parts of the city. The larger ones are near the Great

Bazâr; they have no pretensions to architectural beauty, and are readily recognised by the small "bull's-eye" lights with which their domes are thickly studded. They have the usual three rooms corresponding to the *Apodyterium, Tepidarium,* and *Caldarium* of the Roman baths; and the more frequented ones are clean and well kept. Certain days and hours are set apart for women. Most of the principal mosques have baths attached to them.

There are no remains of the baths of the Byzantine period, but the *Bath of Muhammad II.* is believed by some to have been built on the foundations of the Baths of Constantine. This bath, *Chukur hammami,* now in ruins, lies below the level of the ground, near the Shah-zadeh Mosque, and was discovered in 1833 by M. Texier, who has given a description of it in his 'Architecture Byzantine.' It is a double bath, *chifte-hammam,* having one bath for men and another for women ; and is of great interest as being the oldest bath in the city, and so nearly in conformity with the *data* given by Vitruvius in his description of a Roman bath.

Cemeteries.—The numerous cemeteries scattered through the city and in its vicinity are among its greatest ornaments. The people of every creed have distinct burial-grounds allotted to them. The groves of dark cypresses, with turbaned tombstones of marble, belong exclusively to the Moslems. It was formerly the custom among Oriental nations to plant a tree at the birth, and another at the death, of each member of a family; and a cypress was always planted at each Mussulman's grave; but the custom is not now pursued in every instance. From the antiquity of the burial-grounds, and from the invariable practice of opening a new grave for every one, the disturbing of the dead being regarded as sacrilege, these cemeteries have become forests, extending for miles round the city and its suburbs. That of Skutari (p. 109)

is the largest, and a favourite burial-place of the Turks.

The graves of the poorer Moslems are marked by head- and foot-stones only ; those of the middle class have, in addition, a flat tombstone; and those of the wealthy are distinguished by masonry tombs, which are often so roughly constructed that they fall to pieces in a few months. In some cases, however, the tombs are artistically decorated, and covered by a canopy resting on four columns or pillars. The tombstones are of white marble, and not unfrequently shaped from ancient columns and marbles. A turban or fez surmounting the stone marks the graves of the males; those of the females are distinguished by a conventional leaf, or shell-shaped ornament. The tombs of the ladies and of infant sons are generally the richest. Some tombs are clustered together in the nature of family graves. The rank and condition of the deceased are distinguished by the size of the turban; and its form often indicates the period at which he lived. When the turban leans to one side, it shows that the deceased was beheaded by order of the Sultan. The epitaphs, deftly cut in relief upon the tombstones, are simple and touching. They generally end with a prayer that a *fâtiha* may be said for the soul of the deceased. Nothing is more touching than to see beneath the shade of some dark cypress solitary men absorbed in prayer, or groups of women sitting over the graves of departed friends, with whom, in deep abstraction, they seem to hold communion; or supplying with water the flowers planted in cavities left expressly for them in the tombstones. Multitudes of turtle-doves frequent these gloomy cemeteries, and hold divided sway with bats and owls. The aromatic odour of the cypress is supposed to neutralise all pestilential exhalations.

The Turks suppose the soul to be in a state of torment from the period of death to that of burial. The funerals, therefore, take place as soon as possible. The only occasion when a Turk is seen to walk at a quick pace is when carrying a body towards the cemetery. The Kurân declares that he who carries a body for 40 paces procures for himself the expiation of a great sin. Coffins are not used when the body is deposited in the grave. Thin boards are placed over it, to prevent the earth from pressing on it.

The largest cemetery on the Stambûl side is that mighty death-field which extends outside the land walls, from the Seven Towers to Eyûb; at Skutari a far-stretching cypress forest covers the remains of countless myriads; at Pera are the great and little fields of the dead for the true believers (p. 19); and at Pankaldi are cemeteries for the Armenians (p. 19).

The *Protestant burial-ground* is at Feri-keui, and is held by the representatives of England, Prussia, Holland, Sweden, and the United States. There was an old cemetery above Dolmabâghcheh, and when that at Feri-keui was acquired in 1864, the remains of the dead were removed to it, and the old tombstones are now ranged along the walls. The place deserves a visit. The *Roman Catholic* cemetery is also at Feri-keui; the *Greek* and *R. C. Armenian* cemeteries are at Chichli; and the *Jews* have burial-grounds at Chichli, Has-keui, Orta-keui, and Kuskunjuk.

The British Cemetery at Skutari (p. 110), where so many of our countrymen lie, who met their deaths by wounds or sickness during the Crimean war, is an interesting spot. The adjoining hospital is that in which Miss Nightingale laboured with such heroic devotion. A portion of it is now used as a barrack, but Miss Nightingale's rooms are preserved intact. The cemetery is kept by an official appointed by the English Government.

Kaïks, or **Caiques.**—The number of kaïks that ply on the waters of Constantinople has been estimated at 30,000; they may be hired like hackney coaches in a European capital.

The *Kirlangich*, "Swallow-boats," are formed of thin planks of beech-wood, neatly finished, and elaborately carved. The elegance of their construction, the extreme lightness of the wood of which they are composed, and the dexterity of the boatmen, *Kaïkjis*, cause them to glide over the smooth surface of the waters with great rapidity. A little *caution* is necessary on entering kaïks, as from the nature of their construction they are easily upset; but once seated in them they are safe enough, and, next to gondolas, the easiest and most comfortable of all boats. They have no seats; the passengers sit at the bottom, and when once seated should not move about or lean over the side. A row down the Bosporus in a kaïk, on a fine summer evening, or on a calm moonlight night, is one of the most beautiful and enjoyable of excursions.

Dogs. — There are two popular errors concerning the dogs that throng the streets of Constantinople; the one, that they are ferocious; the other that they are scavengers, and thus instruments of cleanliness. The Constantinople dog is a mild, sociable creature, never aggressive, and always thankful for small mercies. But he is anything but an instrument of cleanliness; on the contrary, he contributes in no small measure to the uncleanliness of the streets, and his scavengering is limited to rummaging for edible morsels in the heaps of rubbish which householders throw out before their doors for the dustman to clear away in the morning. The pure-bred dog, when in good care, is a handsome animal, not unlike the Australian Dingo, of a tawny colour, with a furry coat, a bushy tail, and pointed ears. But few of them now are pure bred, and fewer in good condition. The majority suffer from mange, and a large proportion are maimed by the tramways and hack carriages which have replaced the *suruji* horses of twenty years ago. The dog's existence is precarious; depending on the produce of dust heaps aforesaid, on the scraps and offal of the butchers, and on the stale loaves which bakers cut up and distribute. It is the scarcity of provisions which renders the dogs jealous of intruders in their quarter, and it is a fact that the dogs know the boundaries of their respective quarters. The dog that has strayed into a quarter not his own is visibly conscious of the weakness of his moral position, and the dogs of the quarter spare no pains to remove any doubt that may exist in the intruder's mind on the subject; but they never pursue him over the boundary line of the quarter. The principal inconvenience of the dogs to mankind is their nocturnal barking and howling. The number of them, however, has perceptibly diminished of late years; the waste spaces in which they used to bask and breed have been enclosed or built over, and gradually the Constantinople dog is being improved away.

§ 24.—SPORT.

Game is fairly plentiful in districts within easy reach of the city. There is good *quail shooting*, the best begins about the 1st September, at San Stefano and along the Marmara coast to Silivri, and on the Black Sea coast near Kilios, and Domuzdereh. With dogs and a N. wind, good *cock shooting* on the Black Sea coast, both sides, at Alem Dagh, along the shores of the Gulf of Ismid, at Kara Bogha on the Marmara, and at the Dardanelles. *Snipe, duck,* and a variety of *wild fowl* at Kuchuk Chekmejeh. In the forests that cover the hills on either side of the Gulfs of Ismid and Mudania are *red deer* and *bear;* and round the shores of Lake Sabanja, easily reached by the railway from Ismid, are boar, deer, pheasants, snipe, duck, woodcock and other game.

It is advisable not to shoot without a companion, nor without some one who speaks the language well.

§ 25.—BOOKS.

Salzenberg, *Alt-Christliche Baudenkmale von Constantinopel.* Paspati, Βυζαντίνα Μελεταί. Von Hammer,

Constantinopolis und der Bosporus. Andréossy, *Constantinople et le Bosphore.* Mordtmann, *Belagerung und Eroberung Constantinopols.* Walker, *Eastern Life and Scenery.* Bryce, *Constantinople.* Curtis, 'Constantinople,' in *Encyc. Brit.* Meyer. *Türkei und Griechenland.*

§ 26.—EXCURSIONS.

i. **The Sweet Waters of Europe.**—The place known by this name is the lower part of the valley of the *Kiat Khâneh Su,* where, for some 2½ m., the river, spanned by rustic bridges, meanders through green meadows dotted with clumps of trees. This lovely spot was formerly the favourite spring residence of the Sultans, but the Imperial Kiosk is now rarely used. There are several pretty villas, but the great attraction is the Friday promenade in May and June, which, though not the gay scene that it was before the last Turko-Russian War, is still much frequented by Turkish society. The Sweet Water Valley can be reached by *steamer* from the outer bridge to Kara Agatch at the head of the Golden Horn, or by *kaïk* in 1½ hrs.; and *by land* in a carriage or on horseback. The carriage-road, from Pera, is the same as that to Buyukdereh as far as Chichli, where it turns off to the l., and, leaving the Christian village of Feri-keui to the l., descends over undulating ground to **Kiat Khâneh Keui,** *paper mill village,* where the promenade commences. Dist. 3¼ m. On horseback one can ride by S. Dimitri, Piâle Pasha Jamisi (p. 21), and the Ok Meidan (p. 21), to the valley, and return by the carriage-road.

ii. *Pera to Therapia and Buyukdereh by land.*—A drive or ride of about 10 m. over a good carriage-road. After leaving the Grande Rue of Pera, follow the tramway past the *Taksim gardens* (p. 19), and *Pankaldi,* to *Chichli,* where the road to the Sweet Waters turns off to the l. The road now passes the new *Greek Cemetery,* and crosses bare hills to the small village of **Sinasli Kuyuk** (3 m.). At the entrance to the village, a road on the rt. leads to Kuru Cheshmeh and Orta-keui; and beyond the *Kulluk*, "guardhouse," there is on the rt. a road to Bebek, and on the l. a large country house, *chiftlik*. The road now crosses undulating ground, on which French troops were encamped during the Crimean War, and keeps near the conduit of Mahmûd I., which is visible in several places. Shortly after passing a road on the l., to Ayas Agha and Dermen Dereh, **Mashlak** (6¼ m.) is reached. Here there is a growing village with several *chiftliks*, and a road, rt., to Emirghian and Stenia. From Mashlak the road continues along the crest of the hills to a point at which it divides into three branches; that on the rt. runs down to Therapia (9 m.); that on the l. follows the conduit to Baghcheh Keui (10 m.); and that in the centre descends into the Buyukdereh valley, and passes through Kefeli Keui to Buyukdereh (10 m.).

iii. *Pera to the Forest of Belgrád by road.*—*Guides* should be taken for the forest roads, and luncheon should be carried. For description of forest, aqueducts, and reservoirs, see p. 98. The following routes may be followed on horseback:—(*a*) To Baghcheh Keui and Belgrad by the Pera-Buyukdereh road. (*b*) To Kiat Khâneh Keui (3¼ m.), Ayas Agha (3¼ m.), and Baghcheh Keui, by Dermen Dereh (4½ m.), total 11 m.; or from Kiat Khâneh direct to Baghcheh Keui (6¾ m.), total 10 m. This route may be varied by following the Pera-Buyukdereh road, and turning off to Ayas Agha before reaching Mashlak. (*c*) To Kiat Khâneh Keui (3¼ m.), Ali Bey Keui (1¾ m.), Pyrgos, by the aqueducts (5 m.), Belgrád (2½ m.), and Baghcheh Keui (3 m.), total 15½ m., or including return by direct road to Pera, 25½ m. (*d*) To Ayas Agha and Pyrgos, through the forest (9½ m.); and (*e*) To Kiat Khâneh Keui, and by the valley of the same name to Pyrgos (11 m.).

iv. *Constantinople to Makri-keui, San Stefano, and Kuchuk Chekmejeh.* —By *rail* from Stambûl:—frequent trains daily to San Stefano in about ¾ hr., and several times to Kuchuk Chekmejeh in about one hour. (Time-tables in daily papers.) From the station at **Sirkeji Iskelesi** the railway follows the shore line round the eastern edge of the Seraglio gardens, and past the church of SS. Sergius and Bacchus, to **Kûm Kapu** Stat., near the Armenian Patriarchate. It then keeps near the shore of the Marmara to **Yeni Kapu** Stat., and after crossing Vlanga Bostan, runs along the inner side of a very fine portion of the old sea wall to **Psamatia** and **Yedi Kuleh** Stats. From the last place Yedi Kuleh and the land walls may be visited. Beyond Yedi Kuleh Station the railway cuts through the walls of Theodosius, and, passing the vill. of Yedi Kuleh, and a gun factory (*demir-khâneh*) on the shore (l.); and the Armenian Hospital, and the Daûd Pasha Barracks (r.), reaches

Makri-keui, a small vill. on the shore with a Greek, Armenian and European population. Here, and not at Tekfûr Serai, Prof. A. van Millingen, with great probability, places the famous *Hebdomon Palace*, which is said by ancient writers to have been beside the Sea of Marmara, and seven miles from the "Milion" near S. Sophia. The plain close to the village was the *Campus*, on which the legions of the Eastern Empire were marshalled; and to the east, apparently where the gun factory now stands, was the *Kyklobion*, or *Castrum Rotundum*, where important visitors were welcomed by the State authorities before entering the city. Leaving Makri-keui, the line passes (l.) the *Government Powder Mills*, and crosses a level plain to

San Stefano Stat., whence a road runs to the pretty village of the same name on the shore of the Marmara. There are several villa residences, and the place is a favourite Sunday resort of the people of Constantinople.

Here, after the occupation of Bulgaria and Rumelia (1877–78), the Head-Quarters of the Russian Army were established for several months; and here, on the 3rd March, 1878, the preliminaries of the Treaty of San Stefano were signed. From San Stefano the railway follows the shore of the Marmara to

Kuchuk Chekmejeh, *little drawbridge,* a Turkish vill. on the bank of a large lagoon much frequented by duck, and other wild fowl. Beyond the village are the *Lines of Chatalja,* laid out at the commencement of the war of 1877, which stretch from the Marmara to the Black Sea and protect Constantinople from an attack by land.

§ 27.—THE BOSPORUS.

Everyone who visits Constantinople should take the steamer (*see* Index) up the European shore of the Bosporus as far as Buyukdereh, and return thence down the Asiatic shore to Skutari.

Nothing can exceed the beauty of the scenery along the banks of the **Bosporus,** but, to feel the full beauty of this real earthly paradise, the views must be seen at different times of day, and under varied conditions of light and shade. The slopes on either side are clothed with verdure, and studded with magnificent palaces, or picturesque wooden houses; and the shores, broken into numerous bays, are washed by swiftly-running waters of the deepest blue.

This extraordinary channel, *Stambûl Boghasi,* which separates Europe from Asia, and connects the Euxine with the Marmara, is said to have derived its name βόσπορος, *Ox-ford,* from the passage of Io, transformed into a cow, from one continent to the other. It commences at *Seraglio Point* on the European, and *Skutari* on the Asiatic shore, and has a tortuous course of about 19 m. from the Sea of Marmara to the entrance to the Black Sea between *Rumili Fanar* and *Anadoli Fanar.* The *breadth* is from about

810 yards at *Rumili Hissar* to 2½ m. at *Buyukdereh Bay;* and the *depth* is from 120 ft. to 396 ft.; the general *direction* is S.S.W. and N.N.E. The Bosporus resembles a river with abrupt and angular windings, the projecting points of which break the impetuosity of its stream, and quiet its surface. The *European* shore presents an almost continuous line of palaces, summer residences, and villages; but on the Asiatic side they are separated by wide intervals of rich vegetation. At the N. end there are numerous forts and batteries, on either side, mounting heavy guns. From the Black Sea southwards, to Yeni Mahalle and Fîl Burnu, the shores are composed of *igneous rocks,* such as trachyte, dolerite, and basalt, but along the remaining course of the channel the prevailing formations are *Devonian* and consist of schists, limestones, sandstones, marls, quartzose conglomerates, and calcareous deposits of various kinds. Between Demirji Keui and Yerli Keui, and also between Arnaût Keui and Balta Limân, *dioritic porphyry* is found, and the strata of the Devonian rocks are crumbled up and bent. Immediately outside the walls of Stambûl *tertiary rocks* commence, and near Makri-keui there are good limestone quarries.

The **current** almost invariably sets from the Black Sea to the Marmara. This is due to the prevalence of N.E. winds in the Black Sea; to the excess of water received from the large rivers over the amount lost by temperature at some seasons; and to the difference of specific gravities in the Black Sea and the Mediterranean. Of these the wind has by far the greatest influence. There is as general a **counter current,** setting up under the surface stream, in an opposite direction, from the Mediterranean to the Black Sea; its strength is over one knot. The *current* runs at an average rate of 2½ knots an hour; but its speed varies from hour to hour, and the numerous windings produce a variety of counter currents and whirling eddies under the points.

Between Rumili Hissar and Anadoli H. it runs at the rate of 5 knots, and past Arnaût Keui at 4 knots: at this part it is called the **Devil's current**, *sheitân akindisi.* The Seraglio Point divides it into two branches — one falling into the Marmara; the other running up the Golden Horn to the Inner Bridge, where it is met by the current from the upper basin. It then turns round to the E., and washing the quays of Galata and Topkhâneh leaves behind it a zone of eddies which vary every six hours. The current is quicker in the afternoon, when the N.E. breeze is strong, than in the forenoon; sometimes it ceases altogether; and occasionally it has been known to run in the opposite direction.

The prevailing **winds** are from N. to N.E. in summer, and from S. to S.W. in winter. Sometimes in summer the wind is from the S.W. at the southern end, and from the N.E. at the northern end of the channel. At the time of the equinoxes the winds are variable, and sharp changes of temperature are experienced. In winter sudden shifts of wind are frequent, and strong N.E. winds are always accompanied by rain and snow. The *Barometer* rises for northerly and falls for southerly winds. The average *temperature of the water* hardly differs from that of the air, but it rarely reaches the atmospheric maxima and minima. The surface is rarely frozen over; only 17 instances are recorded during more than 14 centuries, the last being in Feby., 1755. The Golden Horn was, however, partially frozen over in 1849 and 1862. During the Arctic winter of 762–63 the Black Sea and the Bosporus were frozen over for several weeks, and people crossed on foot from the European to the Asiatic shore; when the thaw came the ice carried away a portion of the sea-wall of Constantinople.

From October to early March **fogs** are common, but they clear off at sunrise, or, if the wind be S.W., in the afternoon. From the middle of April to the middle of May fogs from the Black Sea enter the Bosporus, and rarely clear off till mid-day; these fogs are cold and unhealthy. Though lighthouses have been built on the European and Asiatic sides, the approach to the B. from the Black Sea is still dangerous. Numerous wrecks occur, and the work of the life-saving stations at Kilia and Shileh is sometimes severe. To the mariners of classical times the dangers of a passage through the straits were very real: they gave rise to some of the legends that gathered round the Expedition of the Argonauts to Colchis, and are attested by the crowd of temples and votive altars raised on either shore.

The Bosporus, Euxine, and Marmara abound in **fish**. The principal are the porpoise, sword-fish, large and small *bonita* (tunny), mackarel, pilchard, turbot, brill, sole, plaice, sea-salmon, grey and red mullet, *loufer* (a kind of herring), gurnard, whiting, smelt, and three other sorts of fish unknown in British waters. Lobsters, prawns, oysters, mussels and cockles are abundant; the lobsters of Rumili Hissar, and the oysters of Arnaût Keui are famous. The lagoons of the Marmara and Black Sea furnish pike and eels, and to them the grey mullet resort in winter and become enormously fat. The sword-fish and the *loufer* are the best eating, though both are rather rich and heavy food. The most important fisheries are the sword-fish, the bonita, and the pilchard, the last-named shoaling in vast numbers up the Bosporus in August. All these fish are salted and packed, and a considerable export trade is done in them. The Pilchard is also dried in the sun and used grilled as a relish to raki. Table-fish, excepting turbot, are mostly caught in the fishing stations which are provided with an elaborate system of nets, hanging from lofty spars, which can be let down and hoisted up at pleasure. The nets are placed with reference to the set of the currents, and intercept the ascending and descending shoals. They are the property of the

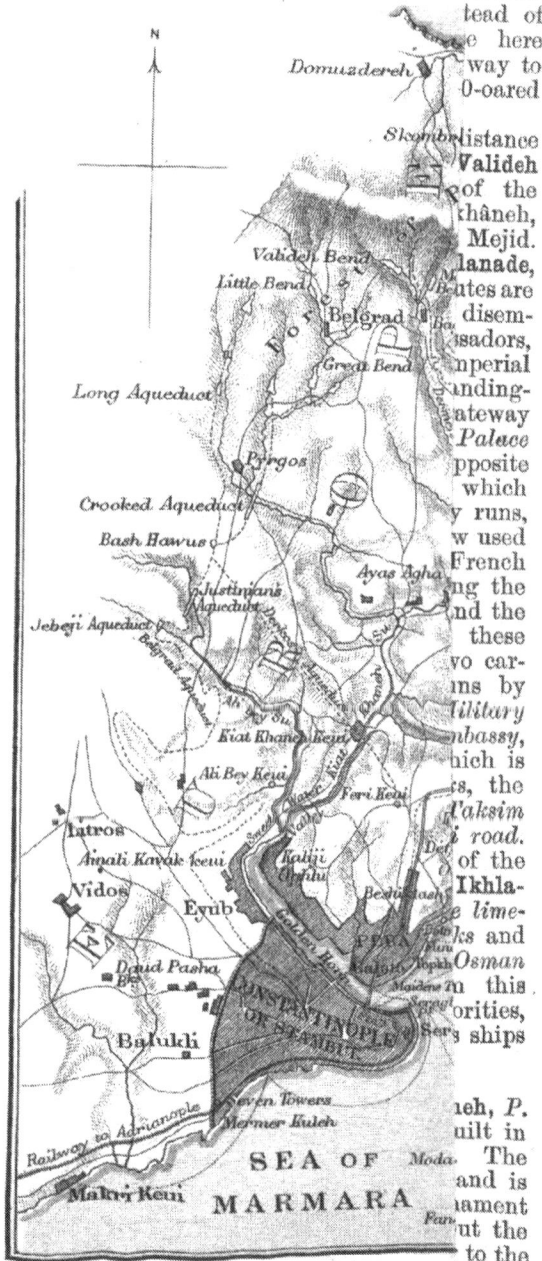

ition of
guished
t whose
Pente-
tead of
e here
way to
0-oared
distance
Valideh
of the
khâneh,
Mejid.
lanade,
B utes are
disem-
ssadors,
mperial
anding-
ateway
Palace
pposite
which
y runs,
w used
French
ng the
nd the
these
vo car-
ns by
Military
mbassy,
hich is
s, the
Taksim
road.
of the
Ikhla-
e lime-
ks and
Osman
n this
orities,
ships

eh, *P.*
uilt in
The
and is
ament
ut the
to the
at

Betwee
H. it r
past A
part it
sheitân
divides
falling
runnin
Inner
current
then tu
ing th
khânel
eddies
The c
noon,
than i
ceases
has bee
directio
  The
to N.I
S.W. in
mer th
souther
norther
time o
variabl
peratur
sudden
and st
accomp
Barom
for so
tempere
from t
reaches
minime
over ;
during
last b
Golder
frozen
ing th
Black
frozen
people
pean t
thaw
portion
nople.
  Fron
are co
sunris
the af
Apri

BLACK SEA

Kilia

Rumili Kalessi
Demirji keui Fanaraki Ft
Keui
Yeni Keui
Kuribjeh Ft
Buyuk Liman Ft

Rumili Fanar
Kabakos B
Jim Burnu
Anadoli Fanar
Riwa

Poiraz Dt
Ft. Burnus Ft

Sekeriyeh keui
Kechili B.

Mahmud B.
M! Kabatash Ft
Rumili Kavak
ncheh keui
Yeni Mahalleh
Mezar Burnu
Buyukdereh Ft

Anadoli kavak

Giants Mt
Umuryeri *Akbaba*

Beteli Keui
Deresi Keui
Arnaut Keui

Therapia
Kalender
Sunken Lakelesi
Vali keui

Beikos
Beikos Bay

Yeni Keui
Jashlak *Stenia*
Emirghian
Balta Liman
Sultanieh
Injir keui
Pasha Baghcheh

Kanlijeh

Rumili Hissar
Castle of Europe
Robert College
Bebek

Anadoli Hissar
Castle of Asia

Kandili
Arnaut keui
Vani Keui

ara Chesmeh
erdar Burnu
stakeui

Chengel Keui

Beyterbey
Istavros
Kuzgunjuks

Sultans Pal?
Baghcheh
bukli
an
Demirje kuni
Emir
M! Bulgurlu
Bulgurlu

SKUTARI
Neft Validet
Jami

Selimiyeh
Barracks

Haidar Pasha

THE
BOSPORUS

Kadi Keui
Chalcedon

Burnu

Road to the Islands

English Miles

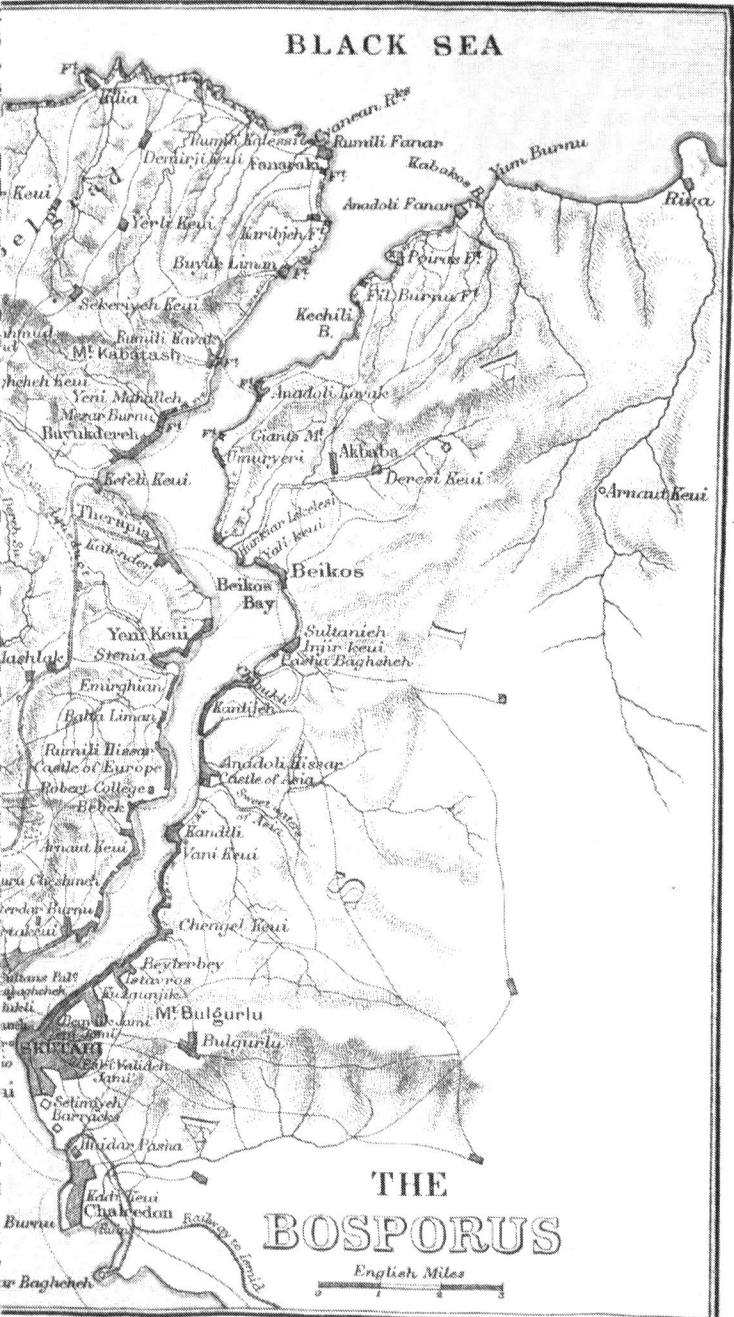

Jan Murray, Albemarle Street.

F.S.Weller.

guild of fishermen, but several of them are leased to Neapolitans. Besides these stationary nets — which are huge fish-traps — fishermen use the harpoon for the larger fish, which they seek mostly by night, attracting them by a fire lighted in the bows of their boats. They use the line in various ways for the *loufer*, grey mullet, &c., and the seine and casting-net for smaller fish. Amateur fishermen find amusement in angling for the *loufer*, which is done lounging in a kaïk in the cool of the summer mornings or evenings. Trolling for jack in the upper waters of the Golden Horn is said to afford fair sport. All fish brought to market pays tithe to the State; the fishing tithes of the whole Empire amount to nearly 40,000*l.* per annum. This tax is one of those assigned to assure the dividend on the Public Debt.

Books.—Von Hammer, *Constantinopel u. d. Bosporus*; Tchihatchef, *Le Bosphore et Constantinople*; Miss Pardoe, *The Bosphorus and the Danube.*

EUROPEAN SHORE.

The steamer on leaving the *outer bridge* crosses the *outer port of commerce*, and passes by *Galata*, with its imposing tower, *Kilij Ali Pasha Jami'* (p. 20), the *Arsenal* of Top-khâneh (p. 19), *Sali-bazâr*, and *Fundukli* (p. 20). The Embassies of Sweden, Russia, Holland, France, Austria, and Germany; Galata Serai, the Greek Church of the Holy Trinity; and the cypresses of the Grands Champs des Morts, are visible on the heights to the l.

1. **Kabatash**, *rough stone*, a small harbour formed by a mole, on which there is a fountain. Merchant ships are generally moored opposite Kabatash, whilst, higher up, towards **Beshiktash**, *cradle stone*, the ships of war lie at anchor previous to sailing from Constantinople.

The two words, *Kabatash* and *Beshiktash*, undoubtedly refer to the celebrated *Petra Thermastis*, noticed by Dionysius, in his description of the Bosporus, as a rock distinguished for its form. This is the rock whose roadstead was formerly called *Pentecontoricon*, that is, the roadstead of the 50 - oared ships, because here Taurus the Scythian, on his way to Crete, anchored with his 50-oared vessels.

Amidst the trees a short distance beyond Kabatash is the **Yeni Valideh Jami'**, built, in the style of the Mahmûdiyeh Jami' at Top-khâneh, by the mother of Sultan Abdul Mejid. Adjoining the Mosque is an **esplanade**, planted with trees, whence salutes are fired on the embarkation or disembarkation of princes, ambassadors, ministers, and honoured Imperial guests. There is a private landing-place, and an ornamental gateway leads to the grounds of the *Palace of Dolmabâghcheh*. On the opposite side of the main road, along which the Galata-Orta-keui tramway runs, are a small **Court Theatre**, now used as a *Military Depôt*, in which French Comedies were performed during the reign of Sultan Abdul Aziz; and the **Imperial Stables**. Between these buildings is the junction of two carriage-roads, of which one runs by *Gümush-su Barracks*, the *Military Hospital*, and the *German Embassy*, to *Taksim*; and the other, which is less steep, by the *Gas - Works*, the *Mejidieh Barracks*, and the *Taksim Gardens*, to the *Pera-Pankaldi road*. A third road, on the other side of the stables, runs up the **Kuchuk Ikhlamûr ¡Deresi**, *Little valley of the lime-tree*, past the *Machka Barracks* and *Depôt*, and the *Konak of Osman Pasha*, to **Nishantash**. From this point, according to some authorities, Muhammad II. transported his ships overland to the Golden Horn.

The **Palace of Dolmabâghcheh**, *P. of the filled-in garden*, was built in 1853 by Sultan Abdul Mejid. The *building* is a mixture of styles, and is overlaid with a profusion of ornament not always in the best taste, but the general effect is not unpleasing to the eye. On the Bosporus side the great pile of buildings, with its *marble quay* and flights of steps leading down to the water, is a striking feature from many points of view. On the land side the palace is hidden by high walls, in which there are two richly-decorated *portals*—one opening on to the esplanade, the other on to the main road. The *interior* is fitted up in a luxurious manner with large mirrors, crystal chandeliers and candelabra, chimney pieces of malachite and Sévres china, gaudily-painted ceilings, and cupolas of stained glass, through which a flood of rich, warm light pours down into the various apartments. The great *central hall*, or *Throne Room*, is one of the largest and most profusely decorated halls in Europe. It is only used on State occasions, such as the Sultan's Bairâm reception; and in it was held the inaugural sitting of the first Turkish Parliament on the 19th March, 1877. The *bath*, with its alabaster walls and marble floor, is very beautiful; and there is a small *picture gallery*, with pictures by Gérome, and French and native artists. Adjoining the central hall is the *Harem*, and beyond it are the apartments of the Court functionaries and servants. The *gardens* of the palace are celebrated for their beauty; they are reserved for the use of the ladies of the Harem. The Sultans Abdul Mejid and Abdul Aziz made this palace their residence, and from it the latter, after his dethronement in May, 1876, was carried off with his family to the Seraglio in Stambûl. A few days later he was removed at his own request to the Palace of Cheragan, where his life came to a tragic end.

2. **Beshiktash**, *cradle stone*, the ancient *Jasonion*, called by the later Greeks *Diplokionion*, or " double column." It was here that the Venetian fleet, under the command of Dandolo, landed the troops that besieged Constantinople in 1203. Here also, according to some authorities, and not near Galata, was the point from which the boats prepared by Muhammad II. were transported overland to be launched on the waters of the Golden Horn. Ducas thus describes this remarkable operation:—" He ordered a road to be made through the valleys lying at the back of Galata to the end of the horned bay (the harbour), opposite to *Kosmidion*, Eyûb. They levelled the road as much as they could, and when they had placed 80 galleys of 50 and 30 oars on rollers, he ordered their sails to be hoisted, and the ships to be drawn over the dry land from the passage to the mouth of the harbour in the Keratic Bay, which was immediately carried into execution."

The *landing-place* at Beshiktash is one of the most frequented on the Bosporus; numbers of *kaïks* are always to be found there plying for hire, and the Galata-Orta-keui *tramway* runs past it. Near the guardhouse is the **Türbeh** of the red-bearded Sea King, **Ghâzi Khaireddîn Pasha**, d. 1546, who conquered Algiers and Tunis, and defeated the combined Christian fleet off Prevesa. During the reign of Suleiman the Magnificent, **Barbarossa** was the terror of the Mediterranean, and he successfully opposed two expeditions sent against him by Charles V. On the other side of the main road is the **Mosque of Beshiktash**, built by the celebrated Admiral Sinan Pasha in the 16th century. Near the sea is a **Tekkeh of Mevlevi Dervîshes**, one of the most beautiful and most frequented spots in the vicinity of Constantinople; and close to it is the *burial-place* of the pious Sheikh, *Yahia Effendi*, which is visited every Wednesday by numbers of people from the city.

Between the suburbs of Dolmabâghcheh and Beshiktash is the **Beuyük Ikhlamûr Deresi**, *Large valley of the lime-tree*, a beautiful rocky ravine, in which the Sultan has a *Kiosk*. A public pathway, much frequented by the people of Beshiktash, leads up the ravine to the Chichli Guard House, on the Pera-Buyukdereh road; and there is a *pleasure ground*, laid out in the usual

Turkish style of terraces on the steep slope of the hill, planted with limes and other trees, and adorned with fountains. It is a favourite resort of all classes of the people on their respective holy days. The *walk* from Pera to the Chichli Guard House, and down the "Valley of the Lime-tree" to Beshiktash, returning thence by the Grands Champs des Morts, is a very beautiful one in spring when the fruit-trees are in full blossom. Half of it may be done by tram or kaïk.

Beyond Beshiktash is the **Palace of Cheragan**, built by Sultan Abdul Aziz on the site of the palace of the Grand Vizier of Ahmed III., in which Mahmûd II. took up his residence when he left the Seraglio in Stambûl. This, the finest of the palaces on the Bosporus, extends along the shore to Orta-keui, and is entirely of marble. The *interior* is remarkable for the beauty of the sculptured ornament in marble and wood; and the apartments are fitted up with even greater luxuriance than those of Dolma-bâghcheh. In the building nearest Orta-keui the life of Sultan Abdul Aziz ended tragically on the 13th June, 1876. The palace is now the residence of the deposed Sultan Murad V., and is inaccessible to visitors. A *bridge* over the main road connects the grounds of Cheragan with those of *Yildiz Kiosk;* and not far from it, on the road to Orta-keui, there is a small open square with a handsome iron gateway leading to the park of the present Sultan's favourite residence. To the l. of the square is a *guard-house,* and to the rt. the **Mejidîeh Jami'**, to which the Sultan sometimes proceeds in state on Friday, on the occasion of the *Selamlik* (p. 11).

Yildiz Kiosk, *Star Kiosk,* the residence of Sultan Abdul Hamid II., was occupied, until her death, by the mother of Sultan Abdul Mejid. It is *beautifully* situated on the heights above Cheragan, and has a large park surrounded by lofty walls. The *palace* of Yildiz, in which the Sultan receives his Ministers, gives audience to Ambassadors, and occasionally en-

tertains them at dinner, is small, but fitted up with much elegance and taste. The views from the windows over the park and the Bosporus to the Asiatic Coast are very beautiful. Near the palace are buildings in which the Sultan's Secretarial Staff, the high Court officials, the Imperial Aides-de-Camp, and others have their offices. The *park* is charmingly laid out, and contains several picturesque kiosks and sheets of ornamental water. The *Harem* is in the midst of a flower garden, and close to it there is a small *Court Theatre.* In this charming retreat, far removed from the noise and bustle of the city, the Sultan passes his days engaged upon the weighty affairs of the State. The only occasions upon which he leaves it are to attend the public Friday prayer at Mosque, to hold the official Bairâm receptions, and to pay the customary visits to the Seraglio and S. Sophia. A large force under the command of Ghâzi Osman Pasha, the hero of Plevna, is always kept in the Barracks in the immediate vicinity of Yildiz Kiosk, and no visitors, except those proceeding to an audience with the Sultan, are allowed to pass the gates. In front of the principal entrance, from which a carriage-road runs to the Pera-Buyukdereh road, there is a small but pretty mosque, built by the present Sultan and called after him **Hamidieh Jami'**. It is usually selected for the ceremony of the Selamlik.

3. **Orta-keui,** *middle village,* or "Middleton," called by the Greeks *S. Phocas,* is a large and not very clean village inhabited principally by Armenians and Jews, and celebrated for its gardens. It is the terminus of the tramway. Near the landing-stage is a picturesque mosque, **Yeni Valideh Jami'**, built by the mother of Sultan Abdul Aziz in the modern florid Turkish style. Above Orta-keui the shore is fringed with the summer residences, *yalis,* of Turkish Pashas; and on the point called **Defterdar Burnu,** ancient *Klidion,* off which a heavy sea and strong current run

during northerly winds, there was until quite recently a fine old Turkish palace, painted yellow, with oriental colonnades, which was formerly occupied by Esmah Sultan, sister of Sultan Mahmûd II.

4. **Kuru Cheshmeh,** *dried fountain,* lies between Defterdar Burnu and Akindi Burnu, and is inhabited by Greeks and Armenians. Here stood a laurel-tree, said to have been planted by Medea on landing at this spot with Jason on his return from Colchis. The hill nearest to the laurel was called the Berry of Isis, and is possibly the projecting point of land on which the village of Kuru Cheshmeh begins.

5. **Arnaût-keui,** *Albanian village,* is the ancient *Hestiae,* or *Anaplus,* which was later called *Vicus Michaelicus,* from the celebrated ch. of the Archangel Michael which was built there by Constantine the Great, and repaired by Justinian. The church was destroyed by Sultan Muhammad II., and the material was used in the construction of the castle at Rumili Hissar. Arnaût-keui, originally an Albanian colony, is now peopled by Greeks and a few Jews. It is built on the S. side of **Akindi Burnu,** *current cape,* where the current runs so strong, 4 knots an hour, that small vessels and kaïks generally land their crews and track round the point. Trackers, *yedekjis,* can always be obtained on payment of P. ¼ each. In stormy weather the passage round is dangerous for kaïks, and the current here as well as below Rumili Hissar is called **Sheitân Akindisi,** *Devil's Current.* There is a pretty *fountain* near the shore, built during the reign of Murad IV., and a road along the quay which is much frequented by the pleasure-seeking crowd on Sundays and holy days. On the Greek *festival of the Epiphany* (18th January N.S.) a strange sight may be witnessed here, and also higher up the Bosporus in the cove of Therapia. A vast crowd of Greeks, of both sexes, assemble on the promontory, regardless of the most pitiless storm or heaviest snow. A bishop comes forward holding a crucifix, which he blesses, and then throws into the sea. Numerous bold divers eagerly plunge into the rushing current after the sacred relic, and the fortunate survivor of the fierce submarine struggle of waves and men receives an ample reward, as well in hard cash as in acquired sanctity of character, both of them sufficient inducements with a money-loving and fanatical people to outweigh their habitual dislike of cold water applied externally.

6. **Bebek,** *the baby,* the anct. *Chelae.* This lovely bay, on which once stood a temple of Artemis Dictynna, soon attracted the attention of the Ottoman Sultans, and Selim I. built a summer residence, *yali,* on its shores. In the graceful building called *Kiosk of the Conferences,* the Sultans used at one time to receive Ambassadors in secret audience. The Konaks of Prince Halim Pasha, and of the late Grand Vizier Ali Pasha, are also here; and there is a well laid-out *public garden.* Bebek is much frequented by the European residents of Constantinople, and there is a large British and American community. The latter form a Protestant Evangelical Union, and have *Divine Service* on Sundays. The houses on the shore have watergates through which the kaïks of the proprietors are drawn up to subterranean boat-houses. As the water is shallow the landing-stage is some distance above the village. At Bebek the *carriage-road* from Pera along the shore of the Bosporus ends.

On an eminence projecting from a hill 300 ft. above the Bosporus, between Bebek and Rumili Hissar, stands a handsome stone edifice of 5 storeys, the **Robert College,** an admirable institution founded in 1863 by C. Robert, Esq., of New York. It gives an excellent education to sometimes more than 200 students, under a staff of well-instructed Professors, and confers degrees of B.A. The education is in English, and on the general plan of the course of studies pursued in Colleges in the United States. That plan is however modified in many respects to meet the exigencies of students drawn from the various nationalities of the East. The College has exercised a marked influence on the educational progress of Turkey. It contains a *Library* and small *Museum*, in which will be found collections of the birds of Turkey, of the geology and fossils of the Bosporus, and an enormous hornets' nest! There are magnificent *views* of the Bosporus from the College grounds and flag tower, to which strangers are admitted, and from the neighbouring hill crowned by a **Tekkeh** of **Bektash Dervîshes.**

We now arrive at one of the most picturesque parts of the Bosporus, where the continuous line of villas and streets is for the first time broken since leaving Top-khâneh, by a very *ancient cemetery*, situated on a bold rocky promontory, and crowned with *a grove of* cypress and pine. Along its craggy sides run the winding walls of *R-umili Hissar*, or the Castle of Europe, whose massive towers and fantastic shape, rising high from the surrounding wood, and with here and there a gaily-painted house nestling under its buttresses, defy adequate description with the pen. The Bosporus is here only 810 yds. wide, and the stream which runs past at 5 knots an hour has obtained the name of **Sheitân Akindisi,** the *Devil's Current.*

7. **Rumili Hissar,** *Castle of Rumelia,* was built by Muhammad II. in 1452, as a preliminary to the siege of Constantinople. It was erected upon the site of the State Prison of the Byzantine Emperors, called the *Towers of Lethe,* which was destroyed to make room for it; and immediately opposite to the Castle, *Anadoli Hissar,* erected by Bayezid I., on the Asiatic shore, during the reign of Manuel II. Palaeologus. The Greek Emperor sent an ambassador to remonstrate with the Sultan against such evident preparation for the blockade of his city, and infraction of existing treaties; but the only answer he received was, that if another ambassador were sent he would be flayed alive. Muhammad employed 1000 masons, 1000 lime-burners, and a multitude of labourers on the construction of the castle; stones, lime, and tiles were collected from the ports of Anatolia; and the Christian churches in the neighbourhood were despoiled of their altars and pillars to complete the walls. By a caprice of the Sultan the plan was ordered to be an imitation of the Arabic letters of the word Muhammad; each *Mim* (M) was represented by a tower; and the final result was one of the most quaint and picturesque of fortresses. The building of the 3 great towers was assigned to the three generals, Khalîl Pasha, Chagan, and Sarijeh; and to each of the 1000 masons was assigned the task of building two yards of wall. The castle was completed in 3 months, the walls being 30 ft. thick, and high in proportion. The tower built near the water's edge, by Khalil Pasha, was armed with enormous guns which threw stone shot of more than 6 cwt.; and the Turks, having thus obtained complete command of the Bosporus, levied toll upon all ships passing up or down the straits. For this reason Muhammad called the castle **Boghaz Kessen,** *throat* or *strait cutter;* a translation, apparently, of *Lamokopion,* the Byzantine name of the promontory. Within the castle are several modern Turkish houses; and in its walls may be seen numerous fragments of columns, capitals, and sculptured stones, which were taken from Byzantine and perhaps earlier buildings. In the Turkish *village* of Rumili Hissar there are also many fragments. Two *submarine cables* are laid between Rumili Hissar and Anadoli Hissar, and connect Pera with Skutari.

It was at the foot of the **promontory of Hermaeon,** once graced by a Temple of Hermes, and now occupied by the "Castle of Rumelia," that Mandrokles of Samos built the celebrated *bridge* over which Darius led the Persian armies to Scythia. The actual site of the bridge was probably above the direct line between Rumili Hissar and Anadoli H., as the current is there too rapid to admit of the easy construction of a work of such magnitude. But the rock, hewn into the form of a throne, on which Darius sat and watched the march of his army over the bridge from Asia to Europe, was on the promontory itself. This rock was called the *Throne of Darius*, and close to it stood the celebrated pillars of white marble on which were inscribed in cuneiform and Greek characters the names of all the nations that formed part of the army. The pillars appear to have been afterwards removed by the Byzantines to their own city. (*Herod.* iv. 87.) The **promontory** gradually rises to a lofty height, about ¾ m. from the shore, which is called **Shehîdlar**, *place of martyrs*, because some Moslem soldiers who fell in battle were buried there. This is a favourite ride from Pera, and pic-nicking ground for the foreign residents on the Bosporus.

North of the promontory is **Balta Limân**, *harbour of Balta*, the anct. *Portus Mulierum*, a small village which takes its name from Balta Oghlu, the Admiral of Muhammad II. who lived there, and commanded the Turkish fleet anchored in the bay, anct. *Gulf of Phidalia*, prior to the attack on Constantinople.

At this place, where a small stream falls into the Bosporus, is the splendid villa, built by the eminent statesman and reformer Reshid Pasha, which was purchased by Sultan Abdul Aziz and presented to his daughter Fatmeh, who married Reshid's son. Here were signed the Commercial Treaty of 1838, the Treaty of the Five Powers in 1841, and the Convention of 1849 relative to the Danubian Principalities.

8. **Boyaji Keui**, *village of the dyers*, on the shore of the bay, is occupied by Greeks and Armenians.

9. **Emirghian.** — The shore here curves into a small bay beautifully planted with cypress-trees, whence the spot was formerly called *Kypa-*

rodis, or "the cypress grove." Its Turkish name is derived from Emirghian Oghlu, a Persian prince, and Governor of Erivan, who was brought prisoner to Constantinople by Murad IV. after the capture of Erivan. As he was an accomplished musician he won the favour of the Sultan, who allowed him to live in this place. The *village* is charmingly situated amidst plane and cypress trees, and is almost entirely occupied by Turks. There is a good *carriage-road* to Mashlak on the Pera-Buyukdereh road; the *pathway* from Bebek along the shore of the Bosporus ends here. A little above the landing-stage are the beautiful **summer palace** and charming gardens belonging to **Ismail Pasha**, the ex-Khedive of Egypt.

10. **Stenia**, *the straits.*—The fairest, largest, and most remarkable harbour of the whole Bosporus, a bay formed by nature for building and preserving ships, and celebrated on this account from the remotest times as the scene of numerous sea-fights and nautical enterprises. It bore amongst the Byzantines the names of *Leosthenius* and *Sosthenius*. The first name is derived from its founder Leosthenes, the Megarian; the second from the temple of safety, *Sosthenia*, erected by the Argonauts, out of gratitude for their deliverance from the hands of the oppressor Amycus. After Amycus, the king of the Bebryces —who ruled at the foot of the Giant's Mountain on the opposite side of the Bosporus—had forcibly refused the Argonauts a further passage, they ran into the woody bay of Stenia, where, encouraged by the heavenly apparition of a genius with eagle's wings, they recommenced the struggle with Amycus; and in memory of their victory dedicated the temple (Sosthenia) with the statue of the heavenly face. Constantine the Great, who found here the temple and the statue of a winged genius, converted the former into a church; and the winged genius, who appeared as a saviour to the Argonauts, into the

Archangel Michael, as the commander of the heavenly host. When the barbarians pressed onwards to the capital of the sinking empire of Byzantium, their fleets more than once appeared in the Bosporus, where Stenia became their resting-place; and, in 941, the town was destroyed by the Russians, who left not a vestige of its former edifices. A pretty walk or ride leads up the valley from hence to *Mashlak* (p. 86). There is also a beautiful *walk* over the ridge, by Kosref Pasha's estate and the wood, to Baltalimân; and on the rt. a short cut leads by the vineyard of the Logothete Aristarchi to Therapia. On the S. side of the harbour is the *summer palace* of the Persian Ambassador.

11. **Yeni Keui**, *new village*, the ancient *Cautes Bacchiae*, has a Greek and Armenian population, some of whom are rich, and have handsome houses on the seashore. The N. part is called *Keui-bashi*, "head of the village." The heights behind, especially where clothed with vineyards and pine-trees, offer pretty walks. There is a beautiful walk along the shore to Therapia, and a little less than half-way there is an *Imperial Kiosk*. A short distance further is a much-frequented, shady spot, with a café, which is called **Kalender**, and a "Holy Well," *ayazma*. The bay, which is extremely picturesque, is the rendezvous of all the lovers of fishing from the neighbouring villages. As the sea is always tranquil and still, and therefore favourable to navigation, this romantic little bay was called by the Byzantines "the bay of the quiet sea."

12. **Therapia**, *healing*, was formerly called *Pharmakia*, "poisoning," from the poison which Medea threw upon the Thracian coast. The euphony of the Greeks changed the poison into health. Therapia deserves its name from the salubrity of the air; for the cool winds, which blow directly from the Black Sea, temper the heat of the summer, and render it one of the most charming residences on the whole of the Bosporus. It was at one time the favourite summer resort of the great Phanariot families, Ypsilanti, Soutzo, Mavrikordato, &c.; but their residences and beautiful gardens have gradually passed into other hands. Therapia is now a Greek village, of more than 4000 inhabitants, with a small sheltered harbour in which the men-of-war attached to the British, French, German, and Italian Embassies, steam launches, and pleasure boats, are anchored. At the head of the harbour there is a small *public garden*, the gift of M. Zarifi, and thence the road to Pera runs up the pretty **Valley of Krio-Nero**, *cold water;* there is a pleasant walk to the clear, cold spring, which gives its name to the valley. During the summer months *Therapia* is filled, almost to over-flowing, with the European residents of Constantinople, who live at the *hotels*, or take houses or lodgings for the season; and no pleasanter place could be selected by the traveller for making excursions to the *Forest of Belgrâd* (p. 98) and other places of interest in the vicinity. The Ambassadors of Great Britain, France, Germany, and Italy have their summer residences at Therapia. The **German Palace** is on the S. side of the harbour, in a richly-wooded park which, having passed from the Soutzo family into the hands of the Sultan, was presented by H.I.M., in 1880, to the German Emperor. The other ambassadorial palaces are on the quay that runs N. from the landing-place. The **French Palace** is remarkable for its beautiful garden and park; it formerly belonged to the Ypsilanti family, but was confiscated by Selim III., and given by him to France in return for the assistance rendered by Gen. Sebastiani, in 1807, when Admiral Duckworth's fleet appeared off Constantinople. The **British Palace** is a conspicuous wooden building, with balconies overlooking the Bosporus, built in pretty grounds presented to England during the Embassy of Lord Stratford de

Redcliffe. The grounds formerly belonging to Prince Mavroyani, who is mentioned in Hope's *Anastasius*, are very picturesque; the house is not remarkable. One of the prettiest spots is the terrace of the garden of M. Zohrab, looking immediately down upon the port. The harbour of Therapia, like that of Stenia, has often been the theatre of the sea-fights of maritime powers, and especially between the Genoese and Venetians. It was the place of retreat chosen by Nicolo Pisani, after having fought, during the 13th and 14th of February, 1352, with the enemy and the storms at Stenia. There are several very pretty walks in the neighbourhood of Therapia. The best time to spend a few days here is in May or June, when, in the soft twilight of a calm evening, one can wander about amongst cypresses and pine-trees with the glassy Bosporus spread out beneath.

13. **Kirech Burnu,** *lime-point*, so called from its limestone rocks; it was formerly called *Klithra*, "the key" of the Euxine, because from thence the first view of the Black Sea is obtained. There is here an *Ayazma*, or "Holy Well," dedicated to S. Euphemia, some fine old plane-trees, and a battery for the defence of the B. The spot is much frequented by those who are fond of water parties, and especially during the fig-season. Beyond Kirech Burnu lies the deep **Bay of Buyukdereh,** the ancient *Sinus Profundus* (Βαθύκολπος), well sheltered from all winds, and offering the best anchorage in the Bosporus. A good *carriage-road* leads from Therapia, past Kirech Burnu, and through **Kefeli Keui,** on the S.W. shore of the bay to Buyukdereh on the N. side.

14. **Buyukdereh,** *large valley*, one of the pleasantest places on the Bosporus, takes its name from the great valley which stretches 3 m. inland from the head of the deep bay to the wooded heights beneath the aqueduct of Baghcheh Keui. The "Great Valley," which terminates in verdant meadows, is not less resorted to as a promenade than the cemetery at Pera. At its lower end is the most splendid group of trees on the Bosporus, consisting of 7 plane-trees, which form the **Seven Brothers,** *Yèdi Kardash.* The tradition that Godfrey de Bouillon was encamped here during the winter of 1096-97 is not alluded to by any of the historians of the Crusades; and it is contrary to the statement of Anna Comnena that his camp was near the city between the bridge, *Kosmidion*, and S. Phocas. On the other hand the same lady says that Count Raoul and other crusaders occupied the district between the convent of S. Tarasius, on the shore of the "deep bay," and Sosthenius, *Stenia*.

Buyukdereh has the advantage of being sheltered from the N. winds, and is therefore warmer than Therapia in spring and autumn; many of the rich merchants of Constantinople reside there, and go down to their business every morning by steamer. There is also a *carriage-road* from B., by Mashlak, to Pera (p. 85); the drive takes about 1½ hrs. The **village,** which contains good *hotels* and a *café,* stretches along the shore for some distance. To the l. of the steamboat pier, towards the "great valley," are the houses of the poorer Greeks and Armenians; and to the rt. is a fine quay bordered by the summer residences and gardens of the American, Austrian, Russian, Spanish, Belgian, and Roumanian Ambassadors and wealthy natives. Amongst these the finest is the **Russian Palace,** with its forest-like park. Behind the buildings rise the picturesque wood-clad heights of *Kabatash,* from which fine views may be obtained. The **Quay** forms the promenade of the inhabitants of Buyukdereh. On fine moonlight nights, when the dark-blue sky mingles with the deep blue of the Bosporus, and the twinkling of the stars with the phosphoric illumination of the sea; when kaïks full of Greek singers and guitar-players glide along the banks, and the balmy air of the night wafts the softest melodies over the waters; when the silence of the listeners is interrupted by soft whispers, *lenesque sub noctem susurri,* the quay of Buyukdereh merits the enthusiasm with which its admirers are wont to proclaim its praises. On summer evenings a band plays from 9 to 11.

The walks and rides about Buyukdereh are numerous and beautiful, and it is the best base of operations for the traveller who is desirous of visiting the forest of Belgrâd, its reservoirs and aqueducts (p. 98), the wilds of the Upper Bosporus, "the Giant's Mountain and Grave" (p. 103), "the Genoese Castle" at Anadoli Kavak, and the lovely valley of Hunkiar Iskelesi, near Beikos No one, therefore, visiting the capital between May and November, who can afford the time, should omit to spend a week or more here. Those who cannot stay so long may still find means of visiting any one of these places by spending a night at the Hotel at Buyukdereh, and making an excursion on the next day before returning by the steamer to Constantinople in the afternoon. Carriages, horses, kaïks, and boats can always be obtained.

Walks.—A favourite walk is to the plane-trees known as the *Seven Brothers* (p. 96), and the adjoining meadow-land on which the black tents of some of those curious people, the gypsies. *chingeni,* may generally be seen. Some beautiful *private gardens* close by are sometimes shown to visitors. Another very favourite walk is in the opposite direction, along the quay and through the small village of Sari-yar (p. 100) to the **Kesstâne Dereh**, *chestnut valley,* or **Valley of Roses**. In this lovely valley there are three springs highly prized by the Turks for the superior quality of their water. They are much visited on Fridays by Turkish, and on Sundays by Greek and Armenian ladies from Buyukdereh, Sariyar, and Yeni Mahalleh. The position of one of them, the **Kesstâne Suyu**, *chestnut*

water, is very beautiful; and the contrast between the wooded, rocky slopes of **Mt. Kabatash,** and the bare yellow hills on the opposite side of the valley, is very striking. From Kesstâne Suyu one can return over the hill, and, when leave is obtained at the gate, through the garden of the Russian Embassy; some fine views are obtained during the descent. The walk from Sariyar up the "V. of Roses" was a favourite one of Lord Stratford de Redcliffe. A third walk, with fine views, is to the summit of Kabatash, 855 ft., returning by the "V. of Roses."

Excursions. — (1.) *To Baghcheh Keui, Belgrâd, and Pyrgos.*—A good carriage-road leads up the "Great Valley" to the *aqueduct* of Mahmûd I., and, passing under one of the arches, goes on to **Baghcheh Keui** (3 m.), a village much frequented during the spring by wealthy Greek and Armenian families. The **view** from the road, where it passes beneath the aqueduct, over the wooded valley and the Bosporus to the hills on the Asiatic coast, is particularly fine. The **aqueduct** was built by Mahmûd I., in 1732, to supply the suburbs of Pera, Galata, and Foghiktagh, and it rivals in magnitude the works of a similar kind constructed by the Byzantine Emperors. The winter rainfall is impounded in two large reservoirs, or *bends*, which are situated in the forest about ¾ m. above Baghcheh Keui, and are known as **Sultan Mahmûd's Bend** and the **Valideh Bend**; they have been formed by building solid dams of masonry across the valley. In spring the *bends* are quite full, but their capacity is not sufficient for the growing wants of Pera and Galata, and they sometimes run dry in summer and autumn. The water is carried across the Buyukdereh valley by the **aqueduct**, mentioned above, which is 560 yds. long, and has 21 arches; and it then runs through a conduit to the *Taksim,* at the entrance to Pera (p. 18), whence it is distributed to the different quarters of the city. There are

Turkey.

several *su-terazi*, or "water-towers" (p. 73), on the line of the conduit, and 4 of them may be seen close together in the valley about halfway between Pera and Buyukdereh.

From Baghcheh Keui there is a good carriage-road to the village of **Belgrâd** (2½ m.), situated in the midst of the forest between the "Great" and "Little" Bends. The village is inhabited by Greeks and Bulgarians, and was called by the Byzantines *Petra.* The **forest of Belgrâd** is 15–18 m. in circumference, and contains a large variety of trees—oak, beech, birch, elm, plane, pine, &c.—which are covered in summer with dense foliage of every shade of green. On the preservation of these woods depends the supply of the great reservoirs; and the villagers of Belgrâd and other hamlets in the forest, who are called *su-yoljis*, have the double care of cleaning the *bends* and preserving the woods. The forest of Belgrâd, the only one in the neighbourhood of Constantinople, on the Thracian side of the Bosporus, is therefore, in the fullest sense, a sacred grove, whose trees are never touched by the axe, and whose springs are not allowed to dry up.

Besides the importance which the village of Belgrâd derives from its aqueducts and reservoirs, it is remarkable for possessing the loveliest walks and rides on the whole of the Thracian side of the Bosporus; the thick woods are the resort of a great variety of game, among which deer and wild boar are the chief. The beauty of Belgrâd is perhaps over-praised: the woods are not of large growth; the reservoirs are filled with turbid water, brought from the neighbouring brooks, and are the resort of myriads of frogs, whose croaking, in the spring, drowns every other sound. Yet these woods, in the fair days of spring, form a favourite resort for Franks, Greeks, and Armenians. The latter spend weeks together in the spring in the uninterrupted enjoyment of the happiest indolence, giving to the spot the name of *Defet-gamm*, i.e. care-dispeller; and, in-

deed, a more delightful *sans-souci* cannot be imagined than the wood-crowned lawns of Belgrâd. The beautiful village fountain has long since been celebrated in the letters of Lady Mary Wortley Montagu, who made this her summer residence; and the house which she occupied is still shown by the villagers. Formerly several of the European envoys lived at Belgrâd, as well as at Therapia and Buyukdereh, during the fine season; but as fevers prevail at the end of the summer, Buyukdereh and Therapia have been preferred, for their ever pure and wholesome temperature.

From Belgrâd a forest road runs on the W. side of the Great Bend, past the Bash Hâwuz of Belgrâd, and under the Devil's Aqueduct, to **Pyrgos**, *Tk. Burgas* (3 m.), a village which derives its name from the tower, Πύργος, erected there by Andronicus Comnenus. From Pyrgos the *Aivat Bend* and the *Long Aqueduct* may be visited, or the ride may be continued S. to the aqueducts in the valley of Ali Bey Su, and thence to Pera. The ride from Buyukdereh by Baghcheh Keui, Belgrâd, Pyrgos, and the aqueducts to Pera is 22–25 miles.

The **Aqueducts** and **Bends** connected with the water supply of Stambûl.—There are 4 *Bends* or reservoirs in the vicinity of Belgrâd, and of these the largest is the **Great Bend** about ¾ m. S. of the village; it is really a small lake, and the fine masonry dam and sluice gate are deserving of notice. The water from the Great Bend and the **Little Bend**, which lies N. of Belgrâd, runs into a large tank, called the **Karanlik Hâwuz**, *dark tank*, or the *Bash Hâwuz* of Belgrâd, that is said to have been made by Andronicus Comnenus, 1183-85. From this point a conduit runs S.W. to the valley of the Kiat Khânch Su, receiving on its way the water of a *Bend* in *Pusha Dereh*, 1¾ m. W. of the Great Bend, which passes over the small **Sheitân Kemeri**, *Devil's Aqueduct.* The joint stream crosses the valley, about ¾ m. below

Pyrgos, by the **Egri Kemer**, *Crooked Aqueduct*, which derives its name from its construction in two sections almost at right angles to each other. One section is 670 ft. long, and 106 ft. high, where the valley is deepest; it has 3 tiers of arches, and the piers of the 2 upper tiers are pierced with arches, transversely, so that it is possible to walk from end to end above the lower and middle tiers, as well as along the top. The second section is 300 ft. long, and has only one tier of 12 semicircular arches. This fine aqueduct is apparently Byzantine, and the work of Andronicus. From this point the water is conveyed by conduit, 1½ m., to the **Bash Hâwuz**, *principal tank*, of Pyrgos, also called *Sultan Osman Hâwusi*, excavated on the wooded height S. of the village; it is said to have been made by Andronicus Comnenus, and repaired by Osman II., 1618-22. In the *V. of Evhad-eddin*, about 2¼ m. N.W. of Belgrâd, is the **Aivat Bend**, constructed in 1766 by Sultan Mustafa III. The water from this *bend* crosses the V. of the Kiat-Khaneh Su, about 1 m. above Pyrgos, by the **Usun Kemer**, *Long Aqueduct*, which was built by Suleiman the Magnificent; it is 2200 ft. long, and 80 ft. high, and has two tiers of arches, but it is not so well built as the "Crooked Aqueduct." After crossing the aqueduct, the water runs through a conduit to the *Bash Hâwuz* of Pyrgos, where it joins that brought from the Great Bend. From the Bash Hâwuz the united stream flows off towards the V. of the Ali Bey Su, which it crosses by the **Muallak Kemer**, *Hanging Aqueduct*, commonly known as *Justinian's Aqueduct*. This is the finest example of Byzantine work of this description; it is 720 ft. long, and its greatest height is 108 ft. There are two tiers of pointed arches, which have a span of 55 ft. in the lower, and 40 ft. in the upper tier. The piers are pierced, laterally and transversely, by arches, and the appearance of lightness thus given to the structure, as if the water channel were suspended in the air, probably

gave rise to its Turkish name. Andreossy assigns the aqueduct to Constantine, but it is more probably the work of Justinian. The water next runs S. and crosses the *V. of Jebeji Keui* by an aqueduct which has 2 tiers of arches, 11 in the upper, and 8 in the lower tier. In a small Hâwuz, at the S. end of the aqueduct, the water from Pyrgos is joined by water brought from springs in the Jebeji Keui valley; and from this point a conduit winds round the hills to the *Taksim* (p. 37) at Egri Kapu. From the Jebeji Keui aqueduct to Pera, by the "Sweet Waters," is about 9¼ m. N.B.—Travellers visiting the forest and aqueducts should take luncheon with them, as little but bread, eggs, and coffee can be obtained in the villages; they should obtain a good *guide*, and make up parties of 3 or more, as it is sometimes unsafe to ride alone.

(2.) *To Baghcheh Keui, Kilia, Rumili Fanar, and the Bosporus.*—To *Baghcheh Keui*, 3 m. (p. 97), thence through the forest to *Domuzdereh*, 4 m., and along the Black Sea Coast to *Kilia*, 3 m. (p. 101), or through the forest direct, *viâ Skombre Keui*, 2¾ m., to Kilia, 1¾ m.; along the Black Sea Coast to *Rumili Fanar*, 3¾ m. (p. 101), opposite the Cyanean Rocks; and by the Bosporus shore to *Karibjeh Keui*, 1½ m., *Beuyuk Limân*, 1¼ m., *Rumili Kavak*, 2 m. (p. 100), and *Buyukdereh*, 3 m. This is one of the most delightful rides in the vicinity of the Bosporus; the total distance is 19-22 m., and, with a halt of 2 hrs. at Rumili Fanar to rest the horses and visit the Cyanean Rocks (p. 101), the tour occupies about 9 hrs. There is also a *direct road* from Buyukdereh to Kilia, 6 m., *viâ Sekeriyeh Keui* and *Demirji Keui*. Luncheon should be taken.

(3.) *To the Genoese Castle* (p. 102), by water to *Anadoli Kavak*; no one should omit this excursion. (4.) *To the Giant's Mountain and Grave* (p. 103), by water to *Majiar Kalesi, Umur Yeri*, or *Hunkiar Iskelesi*, and then on foot.˙ (4.) *To Beikos and the Valley of Hunkiar Iskelesi* (p. 104), by water to *Beikos*, and thence on foot. By sending horses across in the steamer, or previously arranging for their hire at Beikos, excursions may be made inland to *Arnaût Keui* (p. 104), or to Riva on the Black Sea Coast.

15. **Mezâr Burnu**, *Cape of Tombs*, so called from the cemetery upon it, is the ancient promontory of *Simas*, on which stood a statue of Venus Meretricia, to which the sailors offered sacrifice. Beyond the promontory is the village of **Sari-yar**, *yellow cliff*, at the mouth of the lovely valley of the *Kesstâne Su* (p. 97). The bay of Sari-yar is the ancient *Skeletrinas*.

16. **Yeni Mahalleh**, *new quarter*, a village of Greek sailors and fishermen, a short distance above the Kesstâne Su. Beyond Yeni Mahalleh the channel of the Bosporus narrows, and there are forts on both shores to protect the straits from an attack from the north. Those on the European side commence with **Deli Tabia**, a reconstruction of a fort erected by a French engineer, in 1783, at the foot of the promontory called, in ancient times, *Milton*, from the colour of the rocks; and they continue to Rumili Fanar. From Yeni Mahalleh, where the Devonian strata are replaced by igneous rocks, there is a pleasant walk along the top of the cliff to

17. **Rumili Kavak**, *Rumelian poplar.*—This, the last station of the Bosporus steamers, is a picturesque village at the mouth of the ancient *Chrysorrhoas*; the valley is *geologically* interesting. On the hill N. of the village are the ruins of a castle, **Imros Kalesi**, built by Murad IV., in 1628, on the site of the earlier Byzantine fortress, *Polichnion*. Here, or in the immediate neighbourhood, was the *Serapeion*; and here Jason, after having offered sacrifices on the Asiatic shore to the 12 great gods, erected an altar to Kybele. *Yoros Kulesi*, or "the Genoese Castle," on the hill

above Anadoli Kavak on the Asiatic side, corresponds to Imros Kalesi on the European; and from each of these castles a wall ran down to the shore, where a projecting mole, on either side, reduced the width of the channel. In times of danger the moles were connected by a chain, so that the castles, walls, moles, and chain formed a continuous line of defence from hill to hill across the straits. Remains of the walls and dams may still be seen; and the chain was used by Murad IV. to keep out the Russians, who had ravaged the shores of the Bosporus in 1626. The width of the straits here is about 1100 yds., and the batteries on either side are connected by a submarine cable. Beyond, and not far from the dam, there is a ravine with a spring, and the ruins of the monastery of *S. Mary of Mavromolo*, built by the wife of Constantine Ducas (1059–67); and on the hill at the head of the ravine is **Ovid's Tower**, the ancient *Turris Timæa*, which formerly served as a watch-tower. This was the old Pharos, from which torches were held up at night, whose light, placed in a straight line with those at the mouth of the Bosporus, saved the ships navigating the Black Sea from being wrecked on the Cyanean rocks or the Thracian coast. The ancient inhabitants, a barbarous and cruel people, used often to light fires in the most dangerous places, in order to embarrass the mariners, who took them for the lighthouse, and who, after suffering shipwreck, were robbed. This crime was more particularly indulged in by the inhabitants of the coast of *Salmydessus*, now called *Midia*.

Beyond Rumili Kavak the scenery changes; cliffs of dolerite and basalt rise abruptly from the sea, and form an iron-bound coast especially dangerous to ships approaching the Bosporus from the Black Sea in foggy weather; and the road to Rumili Fanar runs inland over barren igneous rocks, which are quite devoid of the rich vegetation that clothes the Devonian strata to the S. The first break in the coast-line is **Beuyük Limân**, *large* *harbour*, the ancient *Portus Ephesiorum*, which offers shelter to ships running into the Bosporus from the heavy swell of the Black Sea. At the S. end of the bay there is a battery; and on **Tashlanjik Burnu**, *stony cape*, the ancient *Aphrodision*, to the N., there is another, called **Karibjeh Kalesi**, which was built, in 1773, by the French General Tott. This mass of rock was formerly called *Gypopolis*, i.e. Vulture town. Here was the fabled court of King Phineas, where he entertained the Argonauts, who defended him from his troublesome guests the Harpies.

Beyond Karibjeh the Bosporus widens out until the extreme point of the European shore is reached at **Rumili Fanar**, *Rumelian Lighthouse*, near the village of **Fanaraki**. The lighthouse stands on a rocky promontory, and about ½ m. to the N. is the battery of **Rumili Kalesi**, mounting heavy guns. Opposite to the lighthouse are the **Cyanean rocks**, or Symplegades, through which Jason steered the Argonauts with no less good fortune than danger. There are 12 islets, or rocks, called by the Turks *Oraji Tash*, but only one, *Kyani*, upon which are the fragments of a column and altar, deserves the name of island. It is flat on the top, and of the same height as the cliff of the coast, and is composed of doleritic conglomerates. The inscription, "Divo Caesari Augusto," which Gyllius saw on the altar, has disappeared. The rocks were called the *Cyanean*, i.e. the bluish rocks, from their colour, and the *Symplegades*, i.e. the rocks which strike together. Jason, who sailed to capture the golden fleece, or (to rescue historical truth from the garb of poetic fable) to obtain the precious sheep's wool of Colchis, dared, and happily performed, the dangerous passage, after having followed the advice of the good king Phineas, not to make the attempt until he had previously sent out a dove. The *Dove* was probably the name of a small craft, of a similar description to that which the Turks make use of at the present day, bear-

ing the name of another bird, *Kirlangich*, i.e. the *Swallow*, and was sent forward to examine the dangerous passage. When the poet relates that the vessel, by the separation of the Symplegades, happily passed through, but lost a portion of its tail, which the islands, striking together, caught hold of and jammed, the meaning is no other than that the ship, hastening onward, was injured by a rock in the stern, and lost its rudder. The island is considered by some, when seen on coming from the Black Sea, to have the appearance of the hull of a vessel between two rocks.

In a bay of the Euxine, to the W. of Rumili Fanar, is the village of **Kilia**, and near it a *fort*, designed to protect the European defences of the Bosporus against an attack from the rear. There is here a life-boat and rocket service, organised by the late Capt. Palmer, which has saved many lives. The bay itself is a famous fishing station. The next place after Kilia on the shore of the Black Sea is **Derkos**, the ancient *Derkon*, or *Denelton*, a day's journey from Constantinople. Between Derkon and Selymbria, *Silivri* on the Marmara, was the great Anastasian Wall, intended to protect the capital against the attacks of the barbarians.

Of late efforts have been made to diminish the risks of ships navigating the section of the Black Sea near the entrance to the Bosporus. A lightship has been anchored 15 m. outside the entrance, and lights and beacons, with distinctive marks, have been erected along the neighbouring coasts of Europe and Asia. Rocket batteries and refuge houses have been established at 14 stations, 6 m. apart; there are fog-guns at Rumili Kalesi and Yum Burnu, and 6 life-boats on the European and Asiatic coasts. Since the establishment of the service, in 1867, 2527 lives have been saved.

ASIATIC SHORE.

The extreme point on the Asiatic shore is **Yum Burnu**, called in ancient times *Ancyraeum*, "Anchor Cape," from the anchor which Jason took from thence and left behind at Phasis. Eastward of Yum Burnu, on the shore of the Black Sea, is **Riva**, at the mouth of the **Riva Su**, the ancient *Rhebas*, a stream celebrated, by poets and geographers, for its beauty. There is here a life-boat and rocket station. On the other side of Yum Burnu is **Kabakos Bay**, where the basaltic cliffs are broken by caverns and hollows, in which numberless sea-birds breed, — including the *Yelkovan*, which are almost constantly on the wing skimming, in flocks, the surface of the Bosporus. The largest of these caverns is 72 ft. broad, ɔ9 ft. deep, and 40 ft. high. Some rocks in this bay, now covered by water, were supposed by some of the older travellers to be the Cyanean rocks. On the next promontory stands **Anadoli Fanar**, *Anatolia lighthouse*, about 2 m. S.E. of the sister lighthouse on the European side. Hence the dangerous rocky coast continues to **Poiras Point**, from *Boreas*, on which there is an old castle, and a battery facing that of Karibjeh in Europe; **Fil Burnu**, *Elephant Cape*, the ancient *Coracium Prom.*, with its battery and

1. **Anadoli Kavak**, *Anatolia poplar*, the most northerly station of the Bosporus steamers on the Asiatic side. The village is inhabited by Turks, and is celebrated for its figs and grapes. The promontory of A. Kavak, with the heavily armed battery of *Kavak Kalesi* at its foot, and *Yoros Kalesi*, or "the Genoese Castle," on its upper slopes, lies immediately to the N., and protects the gardens from the cold winds. The **Genoese Castle** is of Byzantine origin; its ruins are picturesque and interesting, and from them there is perhaps the finest **view** on the Bosporus; one which Darius, ˙˙ᶜᵒrding to Herodotus, turned aside

to enjoy. On the E. side there is an old gateway, built of marble from the temple. From the castle there is a pleasant walk, about 1¼ hrs., along the crest of the ridge to the top of the *Giant's Mountain*, whence a descent may be made to Hunkiar Iskelesi, or Beikos, where travellers staying at Therapia or Buyukdereh can take a kaïk or one of the Bosporus steamers.

In ancient times the place where the castle stands was called *Fanum*, or *Hieron*, from the temple of the 12 gods, to whom, first of all, the Argive *Phrygos*, and then Jason, on his return from Colchis, dedicated altars and instituted sacrifices. Besides the altars of the 12 gods, we find the temple of Zeus Urius and Poseidon, frequently alluded to by the ancient writers as standing on this side of the strait, whilst the temple of Serapis and Kybele stood opposite. Probably this was the same temple in which stood the altars of the 12 great gods. The *straits of Hieron*, or the "sacred opening" of the Bosporus, as it was called, were always regarded as the first line of maritime defence of the capital against the attacks of northern barbarians, and as the most suitable place for levying tolls on vessels sailing in and out of the Euxine. They were consequently fortified at a very early date, and became the scene of many hard-fought naval actions. In A.D. 248 the Heruli appeared before Byzantium with a fleet of 500 boats, and invested Chrysopolis, *Skutari*, whence, after an unsuccessful sea-fight, they were compelled to return to Hieron. At the same period the Goths passed over at this point from Europe to Asia, and ravaged Bithynia as far as the walls of Nicomedia. In 865 the Russians appeared for the first time in the Bosporus, and advanced with a fleet as far as Hieron. They again appeared in 941, in the 28th year of the reign of the Emperor Romanus, when they burned Stenia, the Greek fleet, and Hieron. With 10,000 swift-sailing vessels (Dromites) they made for Constantinople, when Theophanes, the patrician, attacked them and drove them back. The custom-house of the Bosporus was at *Hieron*, as that of the Hellespont was at *Abydos*. The Empress Irene reduced the tolls in the 4th year of her reign. When the Genoese began to threaten the Byzantine emperor in his palace, and to aspire to the dominion of the sea, they were particularly anxious to obtain possession of Hieron, and so become masters of the straits and the duties. In the 14th century they had gained possession both of *Hieron* and *Serapeion*, i.e. of the 2 tollhouses on the Asiatic and European sides of the Bosporus. In 1350 the Venetians sent 33 galleys to dispute their possession of the Bosporus, and the straits of Hieron became the frequent scene of Genoese and Byzantine contest. In subsequent times, when the Turks threatened the gates of the capital, a Byzantine garrison occupied Hieron, to prevent their passage of the Bosporus. From the ruins of the ancient temple Justinian built a church, which he dedicated to the Archangel Michael, leader of the heavenly hosts, who was looked upon as the special guardian of the straits of the Bosporus.

S. of Anadoli Kavak, at the foot of the " Giant's Mountain," is **Majiar Kalesi**, one of the most important batteries on the Bosporus; and beyond it are the small landing-place of **Sudluje**, and **Majiar Burnu**, *Cape of the Hungarian*, from a Magyar who was kept prisoner there for some years.

The **Giant's Mountain**, 650 ft. high, is the highest hill on the shores of the Bosporus, almost exactly opposite Buyukdereh, and it is well worth ascending for the sake of its glorious *view*—thus described by Byron:

The wind swept down the Euxine, and the wave
 Broke foaming o'er the blue Symplegades.
'Tis a grand sight from off " the Giant's Grave "
 To watch the progress of those rolling seas
Between the Bosphorus, as they lash and lave
 Europe and Asia, you being quite at ease ;
There's not a sea the passenger e'er pukes in
 Turns up more dangerous breakers than the
  Euxine.

It is called by the Turks **Yosha dagh**, *Mountain of Joshua*, because *The Giant's Grave* on the top is, according to the Moslem legend, the grave of Joshua. The grave was formerly called the *Couch of Hercules ;* but the classical story is that it was the tomb of Amycus, king of the Bebryces. Amycus challenged all who landed to a trial of strength with the cestus, in the use of which he excelled, and was killed by Pollux, who accepted the challenge, on the return of the Argonauts from their Colchian expedition. The *grave*, which is guarded by dervîshes, is 20 ft. long, and 5 ft. broad ; it lies within a stone enclosure, and is planted with flowers and bushes. It is much visited by Moslems, who, in accordance with a very wide-spread Oriental superstition, hang rags and shreds of their garments on the bushes as a sort of votive offering to secure immunity from fever and other diseases. Amidst the trees near the tomb is a *mosque*, with a white minaret, built by the Grand Vizier of Osman III. on the site of Justinian's Church of S. Pantaleon, which is served by the dervîshes who guard the tomb. The *view* from the terrace S. of the mosque is fine. The **ascent** may be made by short, steep footpaths from Sudluje in 20 min., and Umur Yeri in $\frac{1}{2}$ hr. ; from Hunkiar Iskelesi, by an easy road through the woods in about 1 hr. ; and from Beikos. At the foot of the Giant's Mountain, between **Majiar Burnu**, the ancient *Argyromium Prom.*, and **Selvi Burnu**, *Cypress Point*, the ancient *Aëtonichon*, and immediately opposite the Bay of Buyukdereh, is the **Bay of Umur Yeri**, with the village of the same name. The bay is the quarantine ground for vessels from the Black Sea, and on the shore probably stood the leper hospital built by Justinian.

To the S. of Selvi Burnu is the village of **Hunkiar Iskelesi**, *landing-place of the Manslayer*, i.e. the Sultan, situated at the extremity of one of the most beautiful valleys on the Asiatic side of the Bosporus. In this valley, which, near the sea, is a wide grass-covered plain, dotted with clumps of plane-trees, a Russian army was encamped in 1833; and here, on 26th June, 1833, was signed the celebrated *Treaty of Hunkiar Iskelesi,* which closed the Dardanelles to foreign fleets. A pyramidal block of granite, bearing an inscription in Turkish, commemorates the event. The village is a favourite resort of the Armenians; and the chief families were assembled here to celebrate the 10th anniversary of the Armenian Constitution when the great fire of 1870 broke out in their quarter at Pera. The Byzantine emperors had a summer palace here, called *Miloudion,* and the place has always been a favourite resort of the Sultans. Suleiman the Magnificent built a summer palace here, which, having gone to ruin, was rebuilt by Mahmûd I., in 1746, in all its splendour, with springs, fountains, cisterns, &c. The existing palace, the **Palace of Beikos,** was built by Muhammad Ali, the Pasha of Egypt, and presented to the Sultan by his son Ibrahim Pasha. It is built of marble above a series of terraces that rise from the sea, and afford good views of the straits. *Admission* by a small fee to the guardian.

The plain at the mouth of the **Valley of Hunkiar Iskelesi** is watered by two streams, of which the most northerly issues from a valley called **Tokat Dereh,** from a kiosk erected there by Muhammad II., "the Conqueror," as a memorial of the capture of Tokat. The other flows through the Hunkiar Iskelesi valley proper, which gradually assumes the character of a wild ravine. In this latter valley, 2¾ m. from Hunkiar Iskelesi, is the village of **Akbaba,** celebrated for its chestnuts and cherries, and for the tomb of Akbaba, who was a companion of "the Conqueror"; and ¾ m. further, at the head of the ravine, is **Deresi Keui,** with its famous chalybeate spring. From this point it is about 5 m., over a wooded ridge, to the large village of **Arnaût Keui,** in a romantic valley, through which a stream runs down to the Riva Su

(p. 102); there is a direct road, 6 m., from Arnaut Keui to

2. **Beikos,** a large Turkish village, and seat of a Kaimakam. It is surrounded by gardens and vineyards, and stands on the shore of the largest bay in the Bosporus, formerly called the *Bay of Amycus,* or *P. laurus insanae.* In this bay the British and French fleets assembled in 1854 before entering the Black Sea. In the time of the Argonauts, Amycus held his court at Beikos, and here he was slain in his combat with Pollux. The spot was known as Δάφνη Μαινομένη from the laurel, planted where he fell, that caused insanity in those that wore the branches. Here is the great park of Abraham Pasha, agent to the ex-Khedive of Egypt, Ismail Pasha; it extends inland for several miles, and affords good shooting. Beikos Bay is celebrated for its sword-fish, which are caught in great numbers in August and September. A *good road* leads from Beikos, through Yali Keui, the valley of Hunkiar Iskelesi, and Akbaba, and thence over the hills to Tavlajik Chiftlik, Anadoli Fanar, and Riva on the Black Sea coast. *Horses* may be hired or brought across from the European side for the *tour* from Beikos to the Giant's Mountain, Hunkiar Iskelesi, Deresi Keui, and Arnaût Keui.

Southward from Beikos is the village of **Sultanieh,** so called from the famous gardens of Sultanieh planted by Bayezid II. No trace remains of the summer palace built, in the Persian style, by Murad III., on the banks of the **Gümush Su,** *silver water,* with the spoils of the palaces captured by Usdemir Oghlu Osman Pasha, during the war with Persia. Next follows **Injir Keui,** *fig village,* celebrated for its figs and gardens; and close to it is

3. **Pashabaghcheh,** *Pasha's gardens,* with a *mosque* built by Mustafa III., potteries, and a glass manufactory. **Chibûkli,** *pipe village,* on the shore to the S., was noted in the 5th century for the great *Monastery of the Sleepless,* ἀκοιμήτων, founded by the

Abbot Alexander, in which Divine service was celebrated uninterruptedly day and night. It is now the *petroleum depôt* of Constantinople.

4. **Rifât Pasha**, close to Chibûkli, has some fine gardens.

5. **Kanlijeh,** *bloody village.*—A large Turkish vill., with the summer-houses of many Turkish grandees, including that of the late Fuad Pasha. Nothing can exceed the beauty of this vill., as seen from the water, with its graceful kiosks, its terraced gardens, and its pine-clad heights. Between Kanlijeh and Injir Keui there are traces of a paved road along the shore, and remains of Byzantine chapels, holy wells, and landing-places. Kanlijeh Burnu was formerly called *Oxyrrhoon Prom.*, and the small bay, **Peha Kürfez,** to the S., *Phiala.*

6. **Anadoli Hissar,** *Anatolian Castle,* a vill., with the ruins of a castle, exactly opposite *Rumili Hissar* (p. 93). The castle was built by Bayezid I. before that on the European side, and was called **Güzel Hissar,** *beautiful castle;* but it was afterwards known as the *Black Tower,* from the number of prisoners who died in it of torture and ill-treatment. The *mosque,* built by Muhammad II., is interesting from its peculiar construction. On the S. side of the vill. runs the **Geuk Su,** *blue water,* the ancient *Aretas,* known to Europeans as the **Sweet Waters of Asia.** At the mouth of the stream is the *Imperial Kiosk,* built by the Valideh Sultan, mother of Abdul Mejid, in the same style as the Dolmabâghcheh Palace, on the site of an earlier kiosk erected by Mahmûd II., and restored by Selim III. Near it is a beautiful *fountain* of white marble, which is profusely ornamented with arabesques and gilt inscriptions, and covered by a projecting roof with small domes surmounted by gilt crescents. The smooth turf, overshadowed by plane-trees, sycamores, and ash, which borders the *Blue River,* is the favourite Turkish promenade on Friday after-

noons during the summer months; and here, as at the "Sweet Waters of Europe," may be seen groups of gaily-dressed Turkish ladies seated on Oriental carpets, drinking coffee, eating sweetmeats, smoking cigarettes, and enjoying the luxury of doing nothing. The beauties of the Geuk Su Valley have been sung by the poet Malheni, who places them above those of the 4 most beautiful spots in Asia, viz., the plain of Damascus, the meadows of Obolla, near Busorah, the plain of Sogd, and the valley of Shaab Bewan in southern Persia. About 1 m. up the valley, near an Ayazma, or Holy Well, some curious theatrical demonstrations take place on Sundays; and a short distance to the S. is the pretty valley of the *Little Geuk Su.*

7. **Kandili,** *beacon village,* built above and below a promontory of the same name, is noted for the loveliness of its site and the purity of its air. Its ancient name was περίββους, the "stream-girt," from the violent, "Devil's," current (p. 92), which sweeps round the promontory, *Echea Prom.*, with great impetuosity. From the landing-place, and also from the Vani Keui pier, lovely walks between country houses and gardens lead to the upper terraces which command views, embracing at the same time both the upper and lower mouths of the Bosporus, the Black Sea, and the Sea of Marmara. Kandili is a Turkish village, with a *mosque* built by Mahmûd I.; but several European families, principally English, have taken up their residence there. From Kandili there is a beautiful *walk,* presenting new views of the Bosporus at each turn, to the *fire signal station,* at an old Imperial Kiosk, on the heights above Vani Keui. This is a *celebrated point of view,* and here signal guns are fired on the outbreak of fire (p. 9). Near this spot there was an encampment of British troops during the Crimean war. The walk may be continued to Kulehli. Next to Kandili is,

8. **Vani Keui,** on the shore of a

small bay; the *pier* is to the N. of the village. Then follow a large *Barrack*, and the village of **Kulehli**, or **Kuleh Baghcheh**, *Tower garden*, which derives its name from the following legend.

Sultan Selim I., incensed against his son Suleiman, ordered the Bostanji Bashi, "Chief Gardener," to strangle him. The latter, however, at the risk of his life, saved that of the prince, by concealing him for 3 years in a tower at this spot. It was only after the return of Selim from Egypt, when he repented of his cruel order, and the want of children fell heavily on his heart, that the Bostanji Bashi agreeably surprised him by the announcement of his having disobeyed it. When Sultan Suleiman came to the throne, he changed the tower into a garden. Formerly the ch. of the Archangel Michael stood here, exactly opposite to the one built on the European side at Kuru Cheshmeh. The Archangel Michael was regarded as the special guardian of the Bosporus; and hence churches were dedicated to him at Anaplus, Hieron, Kuru Cheshmeh, and Kuleh Baghcheh.

9. **Chengel Keui**, *Hook village*, because the shore makes a "bight" or "hook" there; a Greek vill. with some good country houses. The *Imperial garden* on the shore was the scene of the bloody executions of Murad IV.

10. **Beylerbey**, a purely Turkish vill. with a fine *mosque* built, in 1778, by Abdul Hamid I., and enlarged by Mahmûd II. Under the Byzantine emperors it was distinguished by the magnitude and splendour of its edifices. In the time of Gyllius it was called *Chrysokeramos*, from a ch. covered with golden tiles. From Beylerbey there is a road to the summit of *Bûlgurlû* (p. 109). Adjoining the village on the S. are the gardens of **Beylerbey Serai**. This, the most beautiful of the summer palaces on the Bosporus, was built, in 1865, entirely of white marble, by Sultan Abdul Aziz, on the site of a palace erected by Mahmûd II. The *façade* on the Bosporus side is very fine, and in front of the palace there is a marble quay with flights of steps leading down to the water. The *interior* is profusely decorated, and the great hall of columns on the ground-floor with a fountain playing into a marble basin in the centre, the staircase, and the large reception room on the first storey, are masterpieces of modern Oriental decorative art. This lovely palace, which is generally placed by the Sultan at the disposal of his royal guests, is surrounded by a terraced garden, laid out with much taste, and here and there, at points from which good views can be obtained, there are picturesque kiosks. In an adjoining garden was the *Menagerie* of Abdul Aziz, who was passionately fond of animals. The tiger and leopard houses, which were large enough to allow the animals great freedom of action, were most interesting; in a separate enclosure there were over 100 ostriches; and in another place a large number of game cocks were kept. A few animals are still left, but since the death of the late Sultan the menagerie has been much neglected.

No special permission is needed to see the Beylerbey Palace. Visitors are shown round by the palace servants, who expect a present of about P. 20 per head if there be a party, or P. 50-60 for a single visitor.

S. of the Palace is the small village of **Istavros**, *the cross*, where Ahmed I. built a mosque and a royal garden in 1613.

11. **Kuzgunjik**, *little raven*, immediately after Istavros, and close to Skutari, has a large colony of Jews and Greeks. It received its name from Kuzgun Baba, a Turkish saint who lived in the time of Muhammad II. There are here 3 Jewish synagogues, and the residence of the Chief Rabbi. In the name of the small adjoining port of **Ukeuz limân**, *Ox-haven*, the original name of the Bosporus (Oxford), as regards its meaning, has been

preserved. With the village of Kuzgunjik, or rather with the neighbouring cape of Chrysopolis, the straits of the Bosporus terminate; for the sea on the other side is already called the Propontis or Sea of Marmara.

SKUTARI—MOUNT BULGURLU—KADI KEUI.

A *day* is needed to visit Skutari, Mount Bulgurlu, Kadi Keui, and the Turkish and British Cemeteries; and as there are no European hotels luncheon should be carried, and eaten on the summit of Bulgurlu. *Half-a-day* is sufficient for Skutari and Bulgurlu, or for Skutari and Kadi Keui. Skutari to Bulgurlu, 1 hr.; Bulgurlu to Kadi Keui, 1½ hrs.; Kadi Keui to Skutari, 1 hr. *Carriages* and *riding horses* can be hired at Skutari (*see* Index), or sent across from Constantinople by ferry boat. *Steamers* run at short intervals from the outer bridge at Galata to Skutari, Haidar Pasha, and Kadi Keui (*see* Index); and *steam ferry boats* between Sirkiji Iskelesi (Stambûl), Kabatash, and Skutari. In fine weather the passage may be made by *kaïk.*

On leaving the Golden Horn the steamer crosses the Bosporus obliquely, and passes near the rock on which stands **Kiz Kulehsi,** *Maiden's Tower,* called by Franks *Leander's Tower,* apparently from a transference of the Dardanelles legend of Hero and Leander. The existing *tower,* built by Mahmûd II., is about 90 ft. high, and is used as a signal station and lighthouse. The ancient name of the rock was *Damalis,* from the wife of Chares, the general sent by the Athenians to help the Byzantines against Philip of Macedon, who died at Chrysopolis. Her husband built a mausoleum in her honour, and the Byzantines erected a column, which was surmounted by the figure of a heifer, as a play upon the name Damalis, "heifer," and as an illustration of the legend of Io, who, changed into a

cow, swam across the Bosporus, "Oxford," at this point. The *Turkish name* probably comes from the same source, and not, as popularly believed, from the legend that Mahammad II. built the tower as a residence for a beautiful daughter who a gypsy had predicted would die from the bite of a snake. The steamer next passes the promontory of Skutari, on which is the fine **Ayazma Jami',** built in 1760 by Mustafa III., and, after passing the curious little octagonal mosque, **Shemsi Pasha Jami',** reaches the **Beuyük Iskelesi,** or principal landing-place.

Skutari or **Uskudar,** the largest suburb of Constantinople, is beautifully situated on the western slopes of Bulgurlu, and the houses, intermingled with gardens and trees, rise, tier above tier, after the manner of an amphitheatre. It has a population of about 45,000, including some 5000 Greeks and Armenians, and forms the 9th "Cercle Municipal," or administrative division of the capital. The streets are narrow and ill paved, and the whole town is more thoroughly Oriental in character than Stambûl. Skutari has a large number of mosques, of which no less than 8 are Imperial; several Medressehs, Imârets, Khâns, Baths, and Tekkehs of Dervîshes; a *Lunatic Asylum,* a *Turkish printing office,* and an *American College for Girls,* which does a noble work for young ladies belonging to the various communities of the East; but perhaps the object of greatest interest is the large Moslem cemetery.

Uskudar, of which Skutari is a corruption, means in Persian a courrier, who conveys the royal orders from station to station. Skutari was the first station of the Asiatic courriers; the place whence all travellers from Constantinople to the East, by land, started upon their journeys; and the depôt for all caravans arriving from Asia. The *ancient* name, *Chrysopolis,* "golden town," was derived, according to some, from Chryses, the son of Agamemnon and Chryseis, who died here, and, according to others, from its being the place of deposit for the gold collected by the Persians from the tributary cities. Chryso-polis was seized by the Athenians, who, by the advice of Alkibiades, were the first to levy tolls on ships passing into and out of the Pro-pontis. Here Xenophon and the Greek auxiliaries, who he had brought back from the campaign against Cyrus, halted for 7 days, whilst the soldiers disposed of their booty; and here the Byzantines erected 3 co-lossal statues in gratitude for the help they had received from the Athenians against Philip of Macedon. Under Turkish rule it was the centre of the disorders during the first year of the reign of Suleiman II.

Immediately in front of the princi-pal *landing-stage* is an open space, with a Turkish fountain, in which carriages and horses stand for hire. To the l. a road runs along the shore past the little port of **Ukeuz limân** to *Kuzgunjik* (p. 106); and in face is the *main street*, full of Oriental life. At the commencement of this street, to the l., is the **Beuyük Jami'**, *Great Mosque*, built in 1547 by Mihrimah, daughter of Suleiman, " the Magnifi-cent." A few yards further is the corner of a road which leads through **Bülbül Deresi**, *valley of nightingales*, and *Ishyadiyeh* to Bulgurlu (p. 109); and, opposite to it, is **Yeni Valideh Jami'**, built in 1709 by the Valideh Sultan, mother of Ahmed III., whose *Türbeh* is within the enclosure. Close to the mosque are the *Bit Bazâr* and 2 Khâns. From Yeni Valideh Jami' a street, on the rt., runs to the **Doghan-jilar Meidân**, *Square of the Falconers*, on which the Janissaries assembled prior to a campaign in Asia; and thence through the Quarter of *Pasha Kapusi*, in which is the **Konak**, or *Government House*, to Selimiyeh and the large Turkish cemetery. A short distance beyond Yeni Valideh Jami' the *main street* forks; one branch, on the l., running, between the Christian Quar-ters of *Selamsiz* and *Yeni Mahalleh*, direct to Bulgurlu; the other, on the ٭., leading past the **Ahmediyeh**

Jami', built in 1721, and a small cemetery and mosque to the

Tekkeh of the **Rufâî**, or *Howling Dervishes*, who belong to the Order of Dervîshes founded by Saïd Ahmed Rufâî (d. 1182). The peculiar devo-tional exercises of the Rufâî, which take place every Thursday between 1 and 2 P.M., attract numerous visi-tors, for whom a place is specially re-served, and who are expected to make a present on leaving. Besides the Dervîshes, Moslem visitors often take part in the exercises, and it is not unusual to see men foaming at the mouth, and so overcome by religious excitement as to be quite helpless. The *mosque* is a rectangular chamber, with a simple *mihrâb*, and no orna-ment, except a few verses from the Kurân. After the usual midday prayer, *Namaz*, the Sheikh takes his seat on a carpet near the Mihrâb, whilst the Dervîshes seat themselves in a circle in front of him, and re-peat the *Fatiha*, or 1st Sûra of the Kurân. This is followed by the recitation of several pious formu-læ, and all then stand up and re-peat slowly the profession of faith, "*La ilâh illa 'llah*," which they divide into the six syllables, *la-i-lâh-il-la-lah*. Whilst pronouncing the first syllable they bend forward; at the second they raise themselves up again, and at the third they bend backward; this motion is repeated at the 3 follow-ing syllables, or they change the di-rection of the bowing, by inclining the body at the first syllable to the rt., standing erect again at the second, and bending at the third to the l., repeating the motion at the other syllables. This chorus begins slowly, and continues with increasing ra-pidity, so that the motion always keeps time with the words, or rather with the cry; the motion soon be-comes so quick that the singer is obliged to pronounce two syllables in one bend, and, as the rapidity of the motion increases, the two syllables are rolled into one, and nothing can be distinguished but a wild cry of *il* and *lah*. During this chorus 2 singers with melodious voice sing passages out of the *Borda* (the celebrated poem in praise of the prophet), or out of other poems in praise of the great Sheikh Abdul Kadir Jilani, or Seyd Ahmed Rufâî. The signal for the quickest movement is when the Sheikh begins to stamp. They then all bend themselves like possessed; one hears but the single sound *lah*, interrupted by an outcry of *hû! yâ hû!* meaning He, O He [is God]. But the whole services more frequently consist, after the recitation of the Fatiha, of the reiteration of the 99 names of God 99 times; this is done sitting, while the Sheikh counts the 99 beads on his long chaplet. When they come to the last name, *Hû*, they rise in a frenzy of excitement, and forming a ring by holding each other's hands, they swing to and fro, whilst the Sheikh encourages them, by voice and gesture, until some fall down foaming, and others are carried away swooning. The name Hû or Allah Hû is supposed to be a great talisman. As such it is inscribed on religious buildings, and when recited, it is supposed to give the Rufâî miraculous powers.

From the Tekkeh, a street to the l. leads past the *Barracks;* the **Eski Valideh Jami'**, built by Nûr Banû, mother of Murad III., in 1582, with a college, soup-kitchen, and hospital; the **Chinili Jami'**, *Fayence Mosque*, built, in 1640, by the Valideh Sultan, Mahpeiker, mother of Murad IV., and Ibrahim, and remarkable for the tiles with which it is ornamented within and without; and the Christian Quarter of *Yeni Mahalleh*, to the Bulgurlu road (p. 108). This road passes the Armenian cemetery, with its fine plane and beech trees, and ascends to the village of **Bûlgurlû**, *vill. with fromenty*, on the saddle between the two peaks of the mountain, between rows of Turkish villas and vineyards, from which come the luxurious *Chaous grapes*, the most prized of all the grapes of Constantinople.

The macademised road continues to

Sultan Chiftlik, but, after passing through the village, a road runs off to the l., to a group of large plane-trees, beneath which gushes forth the far-famed **Spring of Chamlejah**, the best and purest of all the springs in the vicinity of the capital. The spot is much frequented by Moslems, on Fridays, and by Christians, on Sundays, from Skutari and the neighbourhood; and the scene is almost as picturesque and interesting as the better known promenades of the Sweet Waters of Europe and Asia. Close by is an *Imperial Kiosk*, built by Muhammad IV., who also erected a cupola over one of the springs. At Chamlejah, visitors wishing to enjoy the grand view from the N. peak of Bulgurlu, or **Beuyük Chamlejah Tepeh**, must leave horses and carriages. The ascent takes about 15 min., and from the summit, 850 ft. above the sea, there is a most extensive prospect over both the shores of the Bosporus and the sea of Marmara, embracing the city and all its suburbs. The advantages of view and water enjoyed by this mountain, the ancient *Damatrys*, were fully appreciated during the Byzantine period, and several hunting-boxes or *chateaux* were erected upon it for the convenience of the Emperors whilst hunting in the neighbourhood, or when commencing or completing an Asiatic journey.

From Bûlgurlû there is a direct road by the valley of the *Kurbali Su* to Kadi Keui, whence one can return by steamer to Constantinople, or by Haidar Pasha and the cemeteries to Skutari; another road runs through *Baghlarbashi* to Haidar Pasha; and a third through *Yeni Mahalleh* to the

Beuyük Mezâristan, the *Great Cemetery*. This the largest, the most beautiful, and the most celebrated of Oriental cemeteries, is a great forest of cypress-trees, extending for some 3 m. between Skutari and Haidar Pasha. It is traversed by several roads and pathways, amongst others by the main road to *Ismid*, which run between high walls built of broken tombstones; and here and there may be seen stone-cutters deftly fashioning the white marble from the Isle of Marmara into turbaned headstones. The cemetery is a favourite burial-place of the Turks, who love to be buried in the land of Asia, from whence they came, and in which are the sacred cities of Mecca and Medina; and there are many fine tombs. One that always attracts the attention of travellers is a dome, resting on six columns, which marks the resting-place of the favourite charger of Mahmûd II. The form of the tombs, and of the inscriptions upon them, is similar to that already described (p. 83), but there is something peculiarly soothing and impressive in the Skutari cemetery, where the visitor wanders amongst countless tombs, and hears no sound but the soft moan of hundreds of doves, that find a home in the overshadowing branches of the cypress-trees. On St. George's Day, 23rd April (o.s.), 5th May (N.S.), the cemetery is visited by large numbers of Moslems and Greeks.

To the W. of the cemetery, on *Kavak Burnu*, are the great yellow **Selimiyeh Barracks**, with square towers at each angle. Originally built as a summer palace by Suleiman I., they were turned into barracks by Selim III., in 1807, for his *Nizâmi jedid*, "new regular troops;" burned by the Janissaries when they murdered Selim, and afterwards rebuilt by Mahmud II. In front of the Barracks is a *parade ground*, and near them are the *Selimiyeh Jami'*, and the pier, *Harem Iskelesi*, at which the Skutari steamers touch. S. of the Barracks are the Haidar Pasha **Military Hospital**, the scene of Miss Nightingale's labours, and, on the shore, the **British Cemetery**, in which a large number of officers and men who died during the Crimean war are buried. Here, amid the more costly tombs of the officers, may be seen the simple grass-covered mounds, beneath which rest in peace 8000 British soldiers, who died in the service of their Queen and

country. In striking contrast to the Oriental burial-places, the British cemetery is admirably kept by Mr. Lyne, late Serjeant R.E. The enclosure is planted with trees and shrubs, and there is a large granite *obelisk*, supported by four angels, by Baron Marochetti, which is seen from a long distance.

Adjoining the British cemetery are *Haidar Pasha Railway Station*, which is also the W. terminus of the Ismid line, and a good pier, to which passengers from Constantinople are conveyed by steamer. Close to the station is a grove of trees, in which is the spring called in ancient times the *Spring of Hermagoras;* and on the plain of Haidar Pasha beyond, the Turkish troops assembled before starting on an Asiatic campaign. On the same plain, or near it, was fought the decisive battle between Constantine the Great and Licinius in 324. Between Haidar Pasha and the extreme point of the promontory of *Moda Burnu*, lies the thriving suburb of

Kadi Keui, *village of the judge*, the ancient *Chalcedon*, which forms the 10th "Cercle Municipal" of Constantinople. It is a bright healthy place, with a large Greek and Armenian population, and, as there is frequent communication with Galata by steamer, many Europeans, whose business takes them daily to the capital, reside there. Since the fire of 1883 the town has been greatly improved; the houses are well built, and those of the wealthy are surrounded by gardens. There are fine Greek and Armenian churches, a Greek lyceum, a Jesuit school, and a training college of the Mekhitarist Armenians. There is also a large English colony and a pretty chapel. In summer the excellent bathing, and the fine view from the esplanade of Moda Burnu, attract many visitors from Constantinople. Horses and carriages stand for hire at the pier.

Chalcedon was founded 17 years earlier than Byzantium by colonists from Megara. The answer which the oracle gave to the founders of Byzantium, when they applied for the decision of the gods, is well known (p. 1). Chalcedon became the chief town of *Chalcedonia*, a district that extended to the Euxine, and included Chrysopolis, *Skutari* and it was celebrated throughout the ancient world for its Temple of Apollo, whence distances in Asia Minor were sometimes reckoned. During the reign of Darius it was taken by the Persians, who are said to have entered the town through a subterranean gallery that they had driven beneath the walls to the central market place. Chalcedon came to the Romans under the will of Nikomedes III. of Bithynia, and it was afterwards besieged by Mithridates, who defeated the Roman Governor of Bithynia beneath its walls. It was the birthplace of the philosopher Xenokrates, the most distinguished of the disciples of Plato; and in Church history it is celebrated as the city in which the 4th General Council, that condemned the Monophysite heresy of Eutyches, was held in 451. The Council sat in the Ch. of S. Euphemia, which was built by Constantine on the site of the Temple of Apollo. Chalcedon was taken and sacked by Hellenes, Byzantines, Goths, Arabs, and Persians, who on the last occasion occupied the place for 10 years, A.D. 616-26. But its final destruction is due to the Turks, who found it a convenient stone-quarry when building the mosques of Constantinople, and nothing now remains of its former grandeur. The columns of the Ch. of S. Euphemia were used in the construction of the Mosque of Suleiman I.

Beyond **Moda Burnu** is **Kalamish Kürfesi**, the *bay of reeds*, from the quantity of reeds that grow near the Ayazma of S. John Chrysostom, also called *Moda Bay*, the ancient *Port of Eutropius*, which receives the waters of the Kurbali Su. On the opposite side of the bay is **Fanar Burnu**, better known as **Fanar Baghcheh**, *Lighthouse gardens*, one of the favourite resorts of the pleasure-loving people of Con-

stantinople. It can be reached by *train* from Haidar Pasha in 20 min., or by *katk* from Kadi Keui pier in 30 min. The railway leaves the Ismid line a little beyond *Kizil Toprak station*, and there are frequent trains on Sundays and holydays. The *gardens*, amidst which nestle many villas, are very beautiful, and there is a fine view over the Marmara from the lighthouse. There is a fair *hotel*, and furnished *apartments* may be hired. Fanar Burnu was formerly called the *promontory of Heræon*, from a Temple of Hera, and an isolated rock in the sea is still known as Hereki Tash. A palace built on the promontory of Justinian was a favourite summer residence of the Empress Theodora; no traces of this or of the temple remain.

---

§ 28.—THE PRINCES' ISLANDS.

The *Princes' Islands* are served by steamers of the *Mahsûse Company*, which start from the Outer Bridge, Galata (*see* Index). Starting by the early boat, it is easy to visit Prinkipo, and possible also, with a push, to see Halki, in one day. It is pleasanter, however, to spend the night at Prinkipo, where there are good hotels. A *tezkereh* is not necessary.

The **Princes' Islands**, in the Marmara, are so called because they were, during the Byzantine period, a favourite summer resort of the Emperors, and also a place of exile or imprisonment for deposed sovereigns and troublesome princes. Their ancient name was *Demonesi*; to the Byzantines they were known as *Papadonesia*, from the number of monasteries on them; and they are called by the Turks *Kizil Adalar*, "Red Islands," from the ruddy colour which the presence of a large amount of iron gives to the rocks. They are 9 in number, and the 4 that are inhabited are noted for the mildness and salubrity of their climate, and for the excellent sea-bathing on their shores. The only *water supply* is rain water, stored in tanks. The islands constitute a *Kaza*, under the Prefecture of Constantinople.

After leaving the bridge, the steamer calls at Kadi Keui (p. 110), and in about an hour reaches the steep, rugged island of **Proti**, *the first*, which is inhabited by a few Armenians. On the highest point, 375 ft. above the sea, was the monastery built by Romanus IV., Diogenes, and in which he died, after his eyes were put out, A.D. 1071. In a second monastery, near the ruins of a large cistern, Michael I., Rangabe, lived for 32 years, 813–45, after resigning the crown and embracing a monastic life; and to the same place Romanus I., Lecapenus, was deported by his sons, A.D. 945, and compelled to become a monk. A third monastery was built by Bardanes, and became his residence after his eyes were put out, A.D. 803. There are few traces of the monasteries, as, on their destruction, the stone was carried off to Constantinople for building purposes. Soon after leaving Proti, the two rocky islets, **Oxeia**, "the pointed," and **Plate**, "the flat," are visible to the rt. On both were monasteries, which were at once homes for ascetics and prisons for political offenders. *Oxeia*, a marble rock, 300 ft. high, is now the home of sea-birds. On *Plate* are a few fruit-trees and other traces of former cultivation, the ruins of a Byzantine guard-house, some subterranean chambers, and a dilapidated *Anglo-Saxon Castle*, built by Sir H. Bulwer, who purchased the island, and afterwards sold it to the ex-Khedive of Egypt.

The next island, **Antigone**, formerly called *Panormos*, ends on the S. in a fine cliff, 500 ft. high. The village, on the E. side, is entirely Greek. In a small pine wood on the highest point is the ·*Monastery of the Transfiguration*, built by Basil I., the Macedonian (restored 1869), in which the Regent, Stephen, was confined by Romanus Lecapenus. The *Ch. of S. John the Baptist* is said to occupy the site of the church built by Theodora, A.D. 842, over the dungeon in which Methodios, afterwards Patriarch of Constantinople, was confined, and chained between 2 robbers for 7 years. To this island the Emperor Stephanos was banished by Constantine Porphyrogenitus. The steamer next passes the barren rocky islet of **Pyti**, which retains a trace of the old name, *Pityusa*, of Prinkipo, and stops at the quay of

Halki, the ancient *Chaleitis*, so called from a famous copper mine. Donkeys may be hired at the landing-place to visit the monasteries,—an hour's ride, without counting halts; the hotels are indifferent. The island is partly covered with dwarf pine, and there are some pretty walks, especially one to the picturesque little bay of *Cham Limân*. The population is Greek. Close to the landing-place is the *Ch. of S. Nicholas*, with a curious belfry; and to the rt. are the *Turkish Naval College*, and, above it, the *Monastery of S. George*. On the highest point, 445 ft., is the *Monastery of the Holy Trinity*, originally founded by the Patriarch Photius, and rebuilt, in 1844, as the principal *Theological College* of the Greek Orthodox Church. There is a good *library*, and the number of students is from 80 to 100. The view from this point is very fine. The *Monastery of the Panagia* (*Virgin*), founded by John Palaeologus and Maria Comnena in the 15th century, was rebuilt in the 17th century, and restored in 1796, by Prince Ypsilanti. It is now a *Commercial School*, with a large library and about 150 students. Here is the tombstone of Sir E. Barton, Ambassador from Q. Elizabeth to Sultan Muhammad III., who died in the monastery in 1598 from disease contracted whilst attending the Sultan during his campaign in Hungary. No less than 8 Patriarchs of Constantinople are buried in this monastery.

Prinkipo, the ancient *Pityusa*, "abounding in pines," and the largest of the islands, is only separated from Halki by a narrow channel. The steamers stop at a long projecting mole, and here carriages, horses, and donkeys can be hired to make the round of the island (2 hrs.). Kaïks can be hired for crossing to Halki, or to Kartal, or Pendik, on the mainland. There is one good hotel, and other fair ones.

The *island* is celebrated for its healthy climate and excellent sea-bathing, and it is much frequented in spring and summer. It is about 2 m. long, and ¾ m. wide, and is divided into two parts by a depression in the hills. On the summit of the S. hill, 655 ft. high, is the *Monastery of S. George,* whence there is a very beautiful and extensive view; and on the N. hill, which is lower, and partly covered with pines, is the *Monastery of Christ,* built in 1597. In several places there are traces of ancient mining and smelting works. The *village,* with its well kept streets, and the prettily scattered villas and gardens of wealthy Europeans, Greeks, and Armenians from Constantinople, is on the N. slope of the N. hill. There are several bridle-paths, and a good carriage-road round the N. hill. After leaving the village, the *carriage-road* passes through vineyards and olive groves to a small valley, up which it runs to the saddle, *diaskelo,* between the two hills. From this point a steep bridle-path leads up, through bushes of myrtle and terebinth, to the Monastery of S. George; and a second path ascends through the pine woods to the Monastery of Christ on the N. hill. The carriage-road descends to the *Monastery of S. Nicholas,* on the E. coast, and then follows the shore line to the landing-place. A pleasant way of seeing the island is to ride on a donkey through the woods to the Monastery of Christ, and thence to the Monastery of S. George, returning by the carriage-road.

Close to the shore, on the W. side of the S. hill, are the ruins of the convent, to which the great Empress Irene, the contemporary of Charlemagne, and Harûn er-Rashîd was banished after her dethronement, in 802, by Nicephorus, the Chancellor of the Empire. Her presence here being considered dangerous, she was removed to Lesbos, where she died soon afterwards, and her body was then brought back, and buried in the convent. From this convent Michael II. married Euphrosyne, who had taken the veil; and to it the Empress Zoe was banished by Michael V. Kalaphates (A.D. 1042); and the Empress Anna Delassena, mother of the Comneni, by John Ducas, in 1071.

In 1878, when the Russian army was at San Stefano, the British fleet was anchored off Prinkipo.

About 2 m. E. of Prinkipo is the islet of **Antirobithos,** with the ruins of a monastery, to which the Emperor Constantinos was banished by Constantine Porphyrogenitus (A.D. 945).

Some of the steamers continue the voyage to *Mal-tepeh, Kartal,* and *Pendik,* stations on the Haidar Pasha-Ismid Railway, but they do not run in connection with the trains.

EXCURSIONS FROM CONSTANTINOPLE

§ 1.—THE SEA OF MARMARA.

The **Sea of Marmara**, *Propontis*, measures about 110 m. from E. to W., and 40 m. from N. to S. in its widest part. Eastward it terminates in the two deep gulfs of Ismid, 30 m., and Mudania, 20 m., long; whilst on the S. is the hilly peninsula of Kapu Dâgh, which according to Strabo was once an island. The small *steamers* of the Mahsûse Company call at all important points; they run regularly in summer, but irregularly in winter.

The steamers start from the Golden Horn, and, after rounding Seraglio Point, follow the coast line past *Makrikeui, San Stefano* (p. 86), and the bay of *Beuyük Chekmejeh* to **Epivatos,** or *Boyados,* a small place surrounded by vineyards, with an old Byzantine tower and an ancient mole which forms a harbour for *kaïks.* The next stopping-place is **Silivri,** *Selymbria,* near the S. end of the wall built by Anastasius Dicorus for the defence of Constantinople. Selymbria was occupied by the Athenians under Alcibiades (B.C. 410); and is mentioned as being in alliance with them by Demosthenes (B.C. 351). In the reign of Arcadius it received, in honour of the Empress, the name of Eudoxiapolis, which it retained for some time. The walls on the top of the cliff are conspicuous, and to the W. of the town there is a long Roman bridge. The shore to the W. is low, with a sandy beach, and the ground rises gradually to an altitude of about 700 ft. It is treeless, and little cultivated; and the only marked feature is a table-topped hill, upon which are two large *tumuli.*

Eregli, *Heracleia, Perinthus,* a small town on the N. slope of a small hilly peninsula. Perinthus, a colony of Samos, founded about B.C. 599, was the residence of Alcibiades during his second exile, and was noted for its obstinate defence against Philip of Macedon (B.C. 341). About the 4th century A.D. it assumed the name of Heracleia, and was called Heracleia Perinthus (*Eregli Bartin*). Justinian restored the palace and the aqueducts of the city. Several roads from the interior led there, and it was the seat of extensive commerce. There are many fragments of masonry and traces of the old city. A large part of the *Russian Army* embarked here after the campaign of 1877–78. Near the coast W. of Eregli are many *tumuli.*

Rodosto (Tk. *Tekfûr,* or *Tekir-dâgh*), *Bisanthe,* a large town built on the slopes of a hill and presenting an imposing appearance from the sea. There is a good trade in cereals, cotton, wool, and silk; and most of the European States are represented by Consuls. There is a large mixed population; the Greeks show great commercial activity, whilst the Armenians are wealthy and have most of the banking business in their hands. Bisanthe was founded by the Samians, and at a later period its name was changed to *Rædestus.* It was restored by Justinian, and afterwards destroyed by the Bulgarians in A.D. 813 and 1206; and was an important town of the later Byzantine Empire. There are a few fragments of masonry dating from the ancient city; and an old

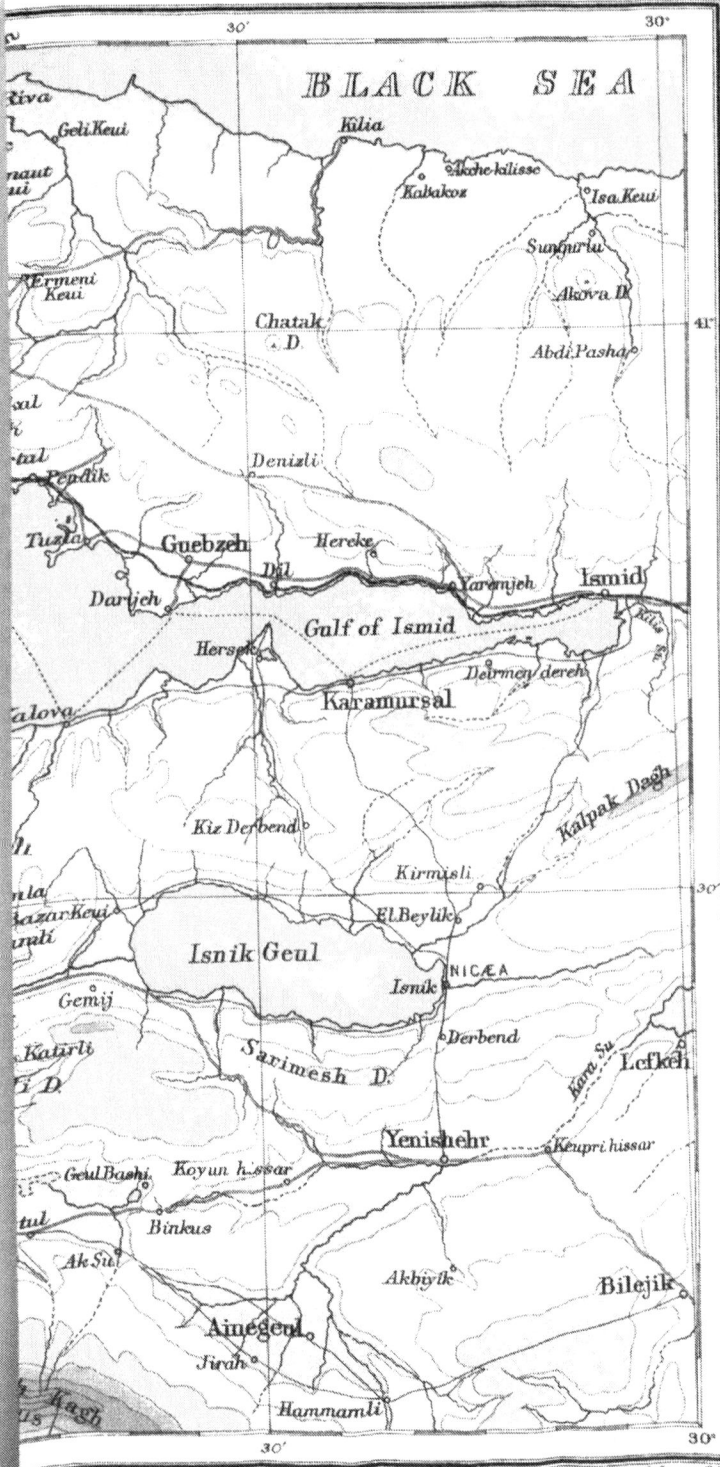

BLACK SEA

Riva
Geli Keui
Kilia
Akche kilisse
Kalbakoz
Isa Keui
naut ui
Sungurlu
Ermeni Keui
Akova D.
Chatak D.
Abdi Pasha
sal
ri
tal
Denizli
Pendik
Tuzla
Guebzeh
Hereke
Dil
Ismid
Darijeh
Yaranjeh
Gulf of Ismid
Hersek
Deirmen dereh
Karamursal
alova
Kalpak Dagh
Kiz Derbend
Kirmisli
azar Keui
mli
El Beylik
li
Isnik Geul
NICÆA
Gemij
Isnik
Derbend
Lefkeh
Katirli
i D.
Sarimesh D.
Kora Su
Yenishehr
Keupri hissar
Geul Bashi
Koyun hissar
Binkus
tul
Ak Su
Akbiyik
Bilejik
Ainegeul
Jirah
Dagh
us
Hammamli

30'
30'
41°
30'
30'
30'

Greek church of the Virgin, in which the Hungarians exiled to Rodosto at the beginning of the 18th century are buried.

Soon after leaving Rodosto the ground begins to rise rapidly, and the fine headland, *Khoja Burnu*, is passed. The steamer then calls at **Ganos**, a village standing on a spur about 100 ft. above the sea; at **Khora**, a small village at the mouth of the deep ravine of *Kerasia derehsi*; and at **Merefte** (Gk. *Myriophyto*), a thriving Greek village with a large export of wine. Behind the village is the fine peak of *Elia Tepeh* (2255 ft.), and to the west are *Heraclitza*, with its dangerous low sandy spit and shoal, the conspicuous village of *Arapli*, and the large village of **Shar-keui** (Gk. *Peristasis*), with a mixed population. From this place the steamer crosses to

Kara-bogha (p. 134), on the Asiatic coast, at the end of the plain of the Granicus, and thence to **Kûtali** (Tk. *Ekinik*) Island, with its Greek population and rounded hill of S. Elias; and **Marmara**, a small village on the site of the ancient town of Proconnesus. The island of Marmara, **Mermer adasi**, *Proconnesus*, is about 10 m. long from E. to W., and 5½ m. wide; a double chain of hills runs from E. to W., and one of them attains an altitude of 2320 ft. The northern half of the island is white marble with scarcely any soil; the southern is slaty rock, with patches of granite, and here the valleys are fertile and cultivated. The celebrated quarries which supplied most of the ancient towns in the vicinity with marble are on the N.E. side, and are still worked. There are 6 villages, all Greek. The sail through the islands to the vine-clad island of **Pasha Limân**, where a French Company has an establishment for making wine, and a distillery; and along the coast of the *Kapu Dâgh* peninsula to **Erdek**, Gk. *Artaki* (p. 134), is very beautiful. From Erdek the steamer returns across the Marmara to Constantinople.

§ 2.—THE GULF OF ISMID.

The *Mahsûse* steamers run daily to Ismid at the head of this beautiful arm of the sea, calling at several places on the way. .The shores of the gulf are very picturesque, presenting a charming alternation of tree-clad mountain, valley, and plain; villages are numerous, but much rich land still lies waste. After passing Skutari and Princes' Islands (p. 111), the steamer crosses the mouth of the gulf to the thriving village of

Yalova, leaving to the right the fine range of *Mons Arganthonius*, which terminates in *Boz Burun*. From Yalova a path leads up the Samanli Dereh to the *hot baths*, which are romantically situated in a cool secluded valley, at the foot of a sharp peak, and were formerly much esteemed and visited, especially during the cherry season. There are some remains of the palace and other buildings erected by Helena and Constantine. Another path runs up *Darli Dereh*, and crosses a high pass near *Yellû Dâgh* to Geumlek (p. 120); and a third runs up *Balaban Dereh* and over the ridge to the villages on the N. side of the Isnik Lake.

Darijeh, on the N. shore of the gulf, is prettily situated near the point of the same name; to the W. is the fine bold point of *Yelkenkaya Burnu*, apparently the promontory *Satyrus*, near which was the famous monastery of *Nicetiata*; and to the E. are the ruins of an old castle, *Eski-hissar*, and behind them on the high ground, two isolated cypresses mark the reputed tomb of Hannibal. The steamer now passes between Kaba Burnu and Dil Burun and crosses to **Kara-mursal** on the S. shore, where horses can be hired to proceed to Isnik and Brûsa (p. 121). She then keeps to the S. coast, calling when necessary at *Eregli, Ghanja, Kadikli, Deirmendereh,* and *Seyban,* and finally crosses the shallow head of the gulf to *Ismid* (p. 116).

§ 3.—CONSTANTINOPLE TO ISMID AND ANGORA, BY RAIL.

Steamers run frequently between Constantinople and the *railway station* at *Haidar Pasha* (25 min.). (*See Time Tables in the daily papers.*) The line as far as Ismid runs close to the shores of the sea of Marmara, and gulf of Ismid, and follows generally the course of the great road which for centuries was the most important military and commercial route in the country. The views across the bright blue water to Princes' Islands, and the wooded heights of Bithynia with Olympus rising above them are ever changing and always beautiful.

On leaving the station the train crosses the plain of Haidar Pasha, and passes the small stations of **Kizil To-prak** (1½ m.); **Geuz Tepeh** (3 m.); **Eren-keui** (3¾ m.); **Bostanjik** (5¼ m.), beyond which (1¼ m.) are the remains of a subterranean church; **Mal-tepeh** (8¾ m.); **Kartal** (12¼ m.), probably *Kartali-men*, where part of Yezid's fleet lay when he was besieging Constantinople, A.D. 717; and **Pendik** (15¼ m.), *Panti-chium*, which was destroyed by fire in 1891. The three last places are largely inhabited, especially in summer, by merchants and others who have daily business in Constantinople; and they contain many charming villa residences surrounded by gardens. **Tûzla** (21¾ m.), a village, with a mixed, Turk and Greek, population, on the shore of Tuzla Bay, probably the ancient harbour of *Kalos Agros.*

Guebzeh or **Ghevzeh** (27½ m.), anct. *Dakibyza*, on a hill ½ hr. from the station, has some picturesque groves of cypress, and a fine mosque of white marble, containing some good *faïence*, built in the 16th century by the celebrated architect Sinan. Some writers identify Guebzeh with *Lybissa*, famous for the tomb of Hannibal; but the latter place was certainly nearer Nicomedia, and probably not far from **Dil Iskelesi** (34¼ m.), where there is a station and a *ferry* to Hersek, whence a road leads to Isnik and Brûsa (p. 121). **Tavshanjik** (36¾ m.); on the hill above the station is the large village of *Tavshanjik*, noted for its mineral springs, which are much resorted to in summer. **Hereke** (39½ m.), on the top of a hill clothed with orchards and vineyards, there is a small village, and below, near the line, are the Imperial silk factories with machinery worked by water-power. **Yaremjeh** (45¾ m.), near the landing-place of *Kuchuk Iskelesi*. **Tutun chiftlik** (49¾ m.). Here there are a kiosk and tobacco farm belonging to the Sultan. **Derinjeh** (52¼ m.), now the port of Ismid. The *Anatolian Railway Company* have established their workshops here, and built docks and a quay, alongside of which the largest ships can lie.

Ismid, from εἰς Νικομήδειαν, Nico-media (56¾ m.) stands on rising ground much seamed by watercourses, near the head of the gulf of Ismid, anct. *Sinus Astacenus*. This portion of the gulf is being gradually silted up by the mud brought down by the *Kiles Sû*, and had become so shallow in 1879 that the dockyard was closed. At the head of the gulf there is a low swampy plain which makes the town unhealthy in summer. There is an export trade in wood, and in salt from the *salines* on the plain.

Nicomedia, the capital of Bithynia, was founded on the site of an earlier town, Astacus, which had been destroyed by Lysimachus. It was a large and flourishing place when bequeathed to the Romans by Nico-medes III., and under the Roman Empire it became one of the greatest cities in Asia Minor. Pliny, in his letters to Trajan, mentions a senate-house, an aqueduct, a forum, a temple of Cybele, and other public buildings; and a later writer alludes to thermæ, basilicæ, gymnasia, public gardens, &c. Nicomedia was taken and pillaged by the Goths; but it was soon restored, and Diocletian made it his residence and one of the capitals of the Roman world. Here he commenced his persecution of the Christians, and here he afterwards abdicated. Constantine frequently visited the city, and it was at his villa of *Ancyron*, in the suburbs, that he died. In A.D. 358, all the public buildings were thrown down by an earthquake; but the town was rebuilt and adorned with churches, baths, &c., by Justinian. In 1326 it fell into the hands of the Osmanli Turks.

Ismid is the chief town of the Sanjak of the same name, and is the residence of a Mutessarif, a Greek Metropolitan, and an Armenian Archbishop. It has an arsenal, and imperial factories for the manufacture of fezes and cloth.

On the top of the hill are the remains of the *Acropolis*, and on the hill-sides are fragments of the Bithynian, Roman, and Byzantine *walls* and towers. There are remains of the Roman drains for carrying off the flood water; and on the E. side of the town, in the Jewish cemetery, is the large **cistern**, *Imbahr*, which may possibly be the work of Justinian. There is a fine **mosque**, built in the 16th century by Sinan, on the same plan as the Suleimaniyeh which he erected at Constantinople; and an older mosque which was once a Christian church. The arsenal and dockyard, closed in 1879, were established by the celebrated Grand Vizier Md. Kiuprili in the 17th century. There is a *kiosk* built by Sultan Abdul Aziz, but it is now in a dilapidated state. The gardens which surround most of the houses, and the numerous plane-trees and cypresses, give the town an appearance of beauty and importance which vanishes when the walls are passed and the narrow, dirty streets are reached.

The *monastery* and *tomb* of S. Pantalemon, who suffered martyrdom under Maximin, are ¼ m. W. of the town.

After leaving Ismid the character of the country changes. The gently sloping hills are covered with rich vegetation, and the land is well cultivated and fertile. In the vicinity are several colonies of Circassians.

Beyond **Beuyûk Derbend** (68 m.) the line passes through a forest to which a tangled mass of creepers gives an almost tropical character. It then follows the shore of Lake Sabanja, anct. *Sophon*, a pretty sheet of water, 10 m. long and 3 m. broad, to **Sabanja** (76¾ m.). Various schemes, commencing with that of Pliny the Younger, have been proposed for connecting the Lake with the Gulf of Ismid, but none of them have been carried out. There is good shooting in the vicinity of Sabanja: deer, wild boar, pheasant, duck, snipe, woodcock, &c., and fair accommodation can be obtained. On leaving the shore of the Lake, the line runs over the plain to

Adabazâr Station (81¾ m.), where horses and carriages can be hired to visit the fine bridge built by Justinian over the Sangarius, *Sakaria*, 1¾ m. distant, or the thriving town of Adabazâr, 5¼ m. to the north. The famous bridge *Pontogephyra*, or *Pentegephyra*, now called *Besh Keupri*, "Five Arches," was built A.D. 553–560, to replace a bridge of boats on the important road from Nicomedia to Ancyra and the northern provinces. The bridge has now no connection with the Sangarius, which has changed its course, and flows about 2 m. to the E. It spans the *Chark Su*, anct. *Melas*, which flows out of Sabanja Lake and joins the Sangarius some miles to the N. It has eight arches, is about 1350 ft. long, and is in a very perfect state of preservation.

On leaving Adabazâr Station the line turns south, and ascends the fertile valley of the *Sakaria*, which is gradually hemmed in by lofty heights well wooded with sycamore and oak. It then enters the wild defile of *Balaban*, about 12 m. long, and after crossing the river twice, and passing through a small tunnel, reaches **Geiveh Station** (97 m.). The long straggling village of *Geiveh*, with its mulberry gardens, lies on the opposite side of the Sakaria, here a deep muddy river, 325 ft. wide, and is reached by a stone bridge built by Sultan Selim III. It is close to the site of *Tottæum*, a station on the ancient road from the Bosporus to Ancyra, and the centre of a large cotton and silk industry. The line now crosses a fertile plain, which produces large quantities of opium, cotton, and silk, to **Ak-hissar** (104 m.), and **Mekejeh** (112½ m.), passing, near the latter place, a tomb with a Greek inscription. At Mekejeh horses and arabahs can be obtained for the journey to Nicæa (7 hrs.).

Beyond Mekejeh the valley again closes in, and the line crosses the river twice before reaching **Lefkeh** (121¼ m.), which occupies the site of *Leucæ*, "White Town," an important station on the Byzantine military road from Nicæa to Dorylæum. Lefkeh is a neatly-built town, with several silk spinning factories, and horses and arabahs can be hired for visiting Nicæa (6 hrs.). About 7½ m. S. of Lefkeh the Sakarîa issues from a deep *cañon*, so narrow that there is not room for a footpath between the water and the rock, and here the line turns up the tributary valley of the *Kara Su*. The valley is very fertile, and every inch of it is covered with mulberry-trees, fruit-trees, and vegetable gardens as far as **Vezir-khân** (133 m.), where there are quarries of good variegated marble. Above Vezir-khân, the valley of the Kara Su becomes a narrow defile, at one point only 91 ft. wide, and here there is barely room for the rapid stream, and the railway that follows its tortuous course as far as

Bilejik Station (144 m.). Near the station is an *hotel*, and on a hill, 2½ m. distant, is *Bilejik* (alt. 1901 ft.), the chief town of Ertoghrul Sanjak. Bilijik, possibly the Byzantine *Belocorne,* has good streets, large khâns, a bank, silk spinning factories, and several manufactories. It is a good centre from which to visit the beautiful country in the neighbourhood. An old sarcophagus in the market-place serves as a fountain. On leaving Bilejik Station, the line rises 1 in 40 for about 7½ m., and, passing the large village of *Keuplu*, ascends the *Sorgun*

Dereh, which it crosses at *Pekdemir* on a fine viaduct about 590 ft. long. It afterwards re-enters the valley of the Kara Su, and running through 12 tunnels, and over two important viaducts, reaches **Kara-keui** (154½ m.), situated between high hills. This section of the line is a remarkable piece of engineering and construction, and the viaducts of *Bash-keui* and *Yaïla* are specially worthy of notice. Leaving Kara-keui, the line crosses the Kara Su several times and then follows a small tributary to **Boz-yuk** (163½ m.), where there are an old mosque with good *faïence*, and a khân. Soon after leaving Boz-yuk, the water-parting is crossed (alt. 2878 ft.), and **In-eunu Station** (174 m.), in the valley of the Sari Su, is reached. The village of *In-eunu* is some distance S. of the station; it is prettily situated at the foot of a cliff, in which there are several natural and artificial caverns, and a few fragments of old columns have been built into the houses. The line now runs, with a very slight incline, down the valley of the *Sari Su*, anct. *Bathys*, to **Chukur Hissar** (182¾ m.), near a curious mound 100 ft. high, and

Eski-shehr (194½ m.), anct. *Dorylæum*. The modern town is well situated at the foot of the hills that border the great treeless plain which stretches E. towards Angora. It has been built near the junction of the Sari Su with the *Pursak Su*, anct. *Tembris*, and is divided by a small stream into a commercial quarter, on the low ground, in which are the bazârs, the khâns, and the hot sulphur springs (temp. 122° F.); and a residential quarter on the higher ground. It is the centre of the meerschaum trade, which is largely in the hands of the Christians; and meerschaum pipes, *istife lulesi*, are made there. There are no remains of antiquity excepting a few inscriptions and the hot-bath, in the lower town, which, with its large basin and fine columns, appears to be Byzantine. The Pursak Su swarms with fish, but they have a muddy taste and are hardly fit for food.

Dorylæum, so called from Dorylas, a Phrygian personal name, was of Phrygian origin, and was always a place of importance. It is mentioned by most of the ancient geographers, and, as late as A.D. 451, was autocophalus. Under the Byzantine Emperors it was one of the great military stations, and its plain is often mentioned as the place of assembly of the armies of the Eastern Empire in their wars against the Turks. It was famous for its natural hot-baths, for its delightful climate, its fertile soil, and for the abundance of fish in its river. About 1074 it fell into the hands of the Seljûk Turks; and on the 1st July, 1097, it was the scene of the memorable battle in which the Crusaders, under Godfrey, defeated the Seljûk Sultan, Kilij Arslan. About 1175 it was rebuilt by the Emperor Manuel; but it soon afterwards fell again into the hands of the Turks. At the foot of an isolated hill, about ¾ m. N. of Eski-shehr, are the ruins of *Shahr Euyuk* which apparently mark the site of Roman Dorylæum; and 5 m. to the S.W., on a spur of the plateau that borders the Tembris valley, is *Karaja-shehr*, a fortress which was probable built by Manuel.

[From Eski-shehr the traveller can proceed in 3 days, viâ Kutaya, to *Chivril*, the terminus of the Smyrna-Aidin Railway.]

Beyond Eski-shehr the line runs down the valley of the Pursak to Ak-bunar (208¾ m.), where there is a fine spring, and an *inscription*. North of Ak-bunar are the *meerschaum mines* which give employment to the inhabitants of numerous villages at the foot of the *Jumdikian Dâgh* (5500 ft.).

The meerschaum, or silicate of magnesia, occurs in nodules which are found in a bed of clay from 30 to 60 ft. below the surface. The meerschaum bed extends E. for about 35 m., almost to the junction of the Pursak with the Sakaria, and it is worked by sinking very narrow shafts, and then driving low galleries. Above this bed is one of *Fuller's Earth*, about 3 ft. thick. which is extensively worked and is locally known as *kil*. The nodules of meerschaum are of irregular shape, usually the size of a man's fist, and rarely as large as his head. They are first washed, and trimmed with a sharp knife to remove holes and excrescences, and then dried gradually in the air, waxed, and polished with a cloth. Before being sent into the market they are sorted according to grain and colour.

From 3 to 4 m. beyond Ak-bunar the line passes close to the shapeless ruins of *Kara-euyuk*, which probably mark the site of *Midæum*, where the son of Pompey was taken prisoner by the generals of M. Antony, and afterwards put to death. The inscriptions seen here by a traveller in the 16th century appear to have disappeared. The next station is Alpi-keui (219 m.), which takes its name from a small village on the opposite bank of the river in which there are a few inscriptions. A couple of miles lower down the line crosses to the N. bank of the Pursak and runs on to Beylik Akhur (232½ m.), and Sari-keui (252 m.), the present terminus. The line is being continued to Angora, and will soon be opened.

Provisions should be taken from Constantinople; sleeping accommodation may be obtained by inquiry of the station-masters.

§ 4.—BRUSA AND NICÆA.

No visitor to Constantinople who can afford the time should omit a *visit to Brûsa*, the first capital of the Osmanlis. For this 3 days are required, or, if Mt. Olympus be ascended, 4 days. A longer stay is, however, recommended, for the old Turkish mosques and tombs are worth a long journey to see, the bazârs are well stocked, the environs are lovely, and the hot iron and sulphur springs are celebrated throughout the east.

Travellers visiting Brûsa require a *Yol tezkereh*, which must be shown on embarkation at Constantinople, where *baggage* is also examined. The *Mahsûse steamers* leave the Golden Horn three times a week, early in the morning, for *Mudania*, which is connected with Brûsa by a good carriage-road, and a railway or steam tramway. At Mudania, where the *Yol tezkereh* has to be shown, and *baggage* is examined, *carriages* and *horses* await the arrival of the steamer. The *passage* is 6 hrs., more with a head wind, and the *drive* is 3 hrs. *Trains* run in connection with the steamer, and take 1¾ hrs. Return tickets from Constantinople to Brûsa are issued. *Food* can be obtained on the steamer, but it is better to take luncheon from the hotel. A Constantinople *dragoman* is useful, especially when there are ladies, but he is not necessary. On the *return journey* it is usual to leave Brûsa very early, so as to catch the steamer at Mudania and reach Constantinople the same day. *Yol tezkerehs* are shown, and baggage examined at Mudania and Constantinople.

The sail across the Marmara is very enjoyable in fine weather. After passing Skutari, the steamer leaves the Princes' Islands to the left, and crosses the *Gulf of Ismid* to **Boz Burun**, anct. *Posidium*, which formed the termination of *Mons Arganthonius*. To the W. of the cape is the Island of **Kalolimno**, anct. *Besbicus*, with a small Greek population. After rounding Boz Burun the steamer enters the **Gulf of Mudania**, or **Geumlek**, *Injir Limân*, "gulf of figs,' anct. *Cianus Sinus*, and either runs along the coast to *Armudli*, "place of pears," and *Kapukli*, or crosses to *Trilia* and *Syki* on the S. coast, to the W. of Mudania. At these places passengers are landed and embarked in boats. The steamer then proceeds to the wooden pier of

Mudania, anct. *Myrlea*, a colony of

Colophon, which was afterwards renamed by Prusias, after his wife, *Apamea*, is now the port of Brûsa. It was taken, A.D. 1351, by the Turks under the leadership of the pious dervîsh Hajji Bektash, who was afterwards the patron saint of the Janissaries. The town consists of a row of poorly built houses along the shore, intermingled with vineyards, and mulberry groves, and a large proportion of the population is Greek. The climate is much milder and drier than that of Constantinople. There are large olive gardens, and a large production of oil.

[From Mudania the steamer goes on (1 hr.) to **Geumlek**, anct. *Cius*, at the head of the picturesque gulf. The small town, which is still called *Kio* by the Greeks, is said to have been founded by one of the Argonauts

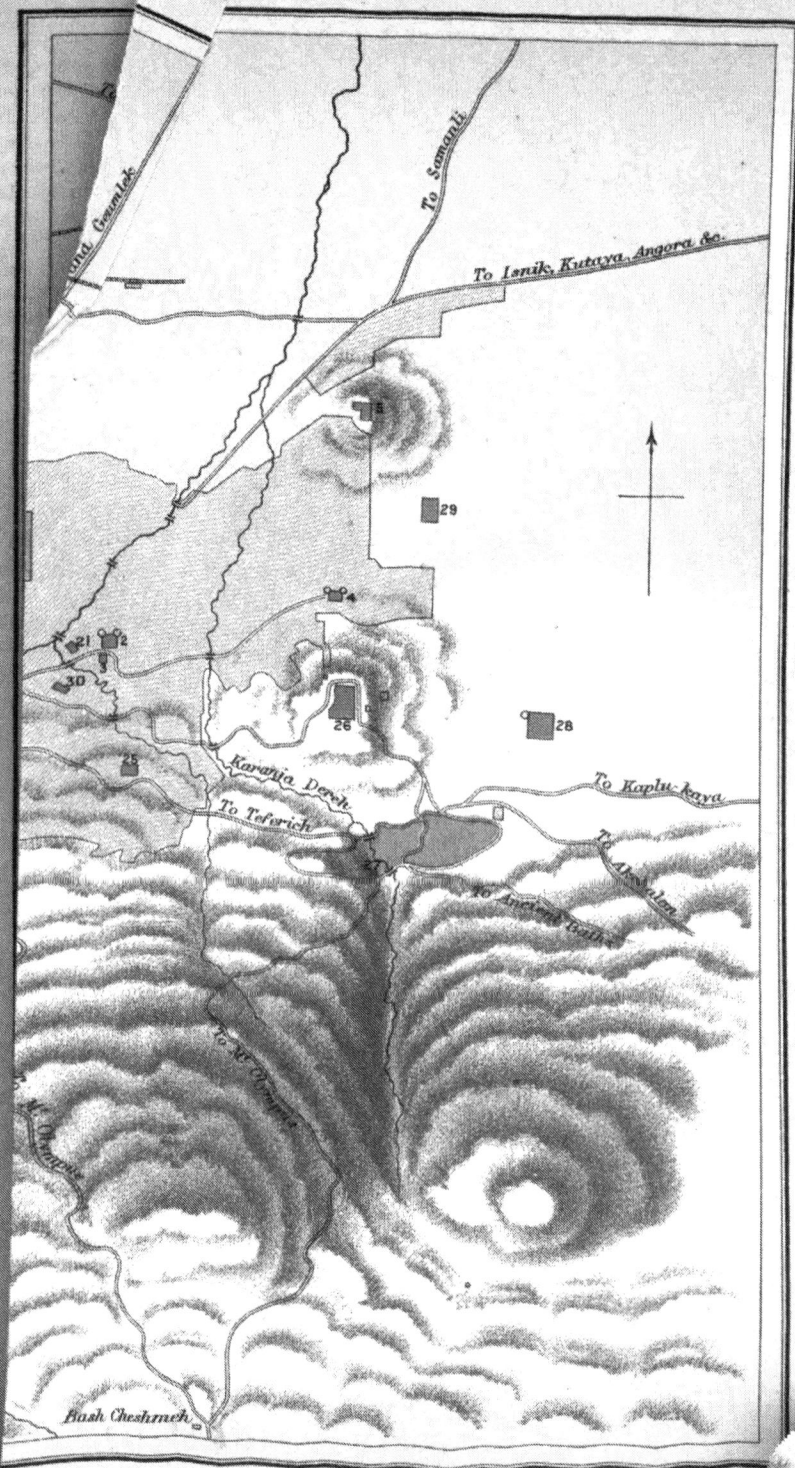

To Samanli

To Isnik, Kutaya, Angora &c.

29

4

28

Karanja Dereh

To Kaplu-kava

To Teferich

To Abulabad

27

Bash Cheshmeh

J. Bartholomew, E

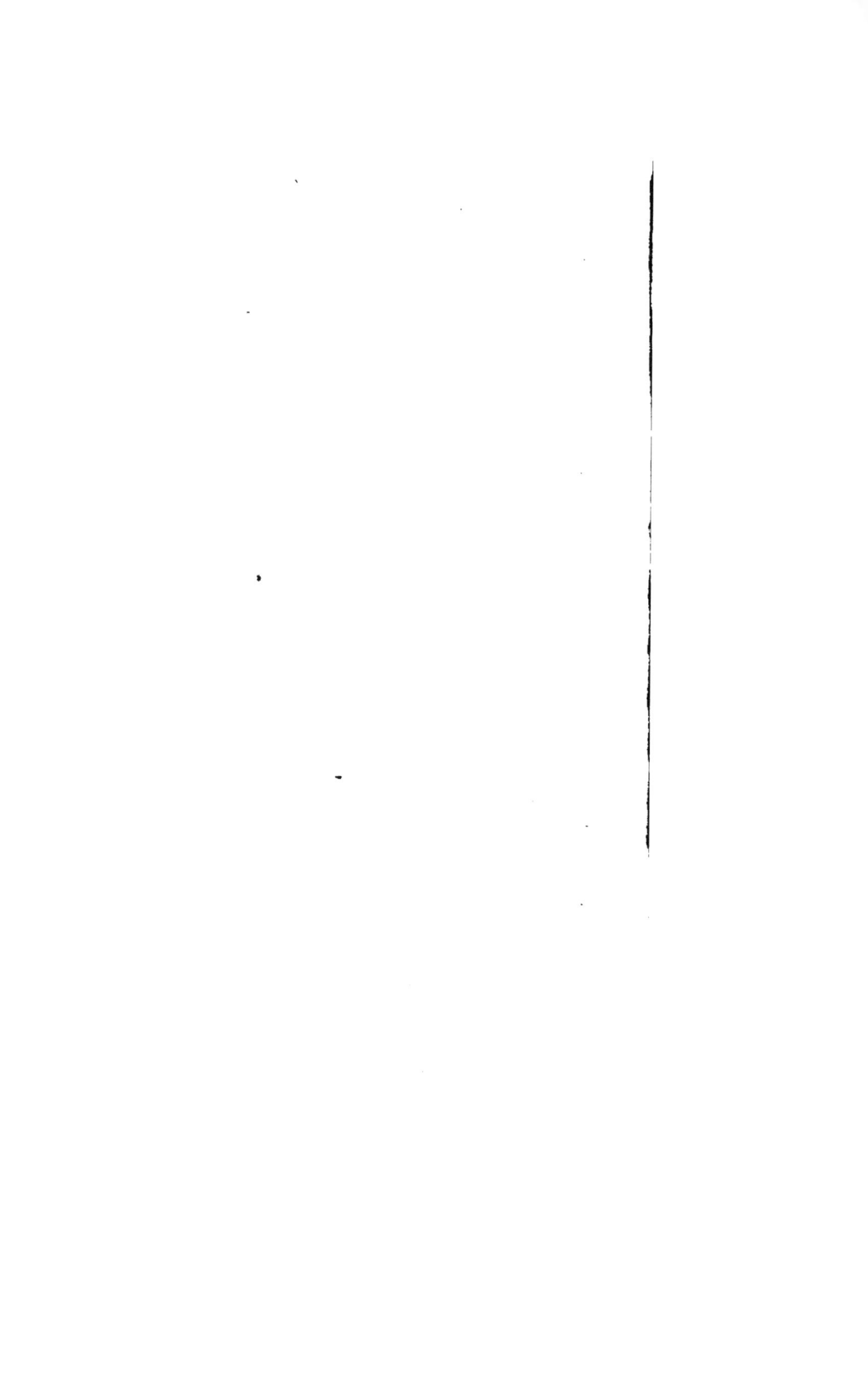

Cius, on his return from Colchis; it was afterwards rebuilt by Prusias, and its name changed to *Prusa ad Mare.* The Crusaders, who called it *Civitot*, made it their principal point of disembarkation in A. Minor. The place is prettily situated at the foot of Mt. Arganthonius, and on the right bank of the *Geumlek Su*, anct. Ascanius; and there are some interesting fragments of the old walls. There are the remains of a naval yard, and a pier at which chromium and other articles of commerce are shipped. There is a carriage-road, in bad repair, to Brûsa (4½ hrs. drive), and an easy road to Isnik, *Nicæa* (10 hrs.).]

ᵖ The road from Mudania to Brûsa at first follows the shore of the gulf, and then winds upwards, through vineyards and mulberry groves, in which lie the Greek villages *Yerdeli* (r.) and *Misopoli* (l.), to a guard-house, alt. 900 ft. (*tezkereh* shown). Hence there is a fine view of Olympus, with Brûsa nestling amidst a wealth of verdure at its foot, and of the broad, fertile valley through which the waters of the Nilûfer, maddest of rivers, find their tortuous way to the Rhyndacus and the sea. From the guard-house there is a sharp descent to the **Nilûfer**, or **Ulfer Chai**, anct. *Odrysses*, which is crossed by a bridge, and here there is a half-way house, and resting-place in a grove of plane-trees. The road now runs through well cultivated ground, and leaving *Chekirgeh* and the Mosque of Murad I. to the right, passes between the baths of *Kara Mustafa* (l.) and *Yeni Kaplija* (r.), and enters Brûsa through an avenue of trees.

The railway keeps to the right of the road; and the trains stop at *Yorgoli*, *Koru*, and *Ajemlar* (for Chekirgeh and the baths). At Brûsa the trains stop at the entrance to the town below the Muradîyeh Quarter, in which are the best hotels; and then go on to the terminus further east.

Brûsa, the chief town of the Vilâyet of *Khudavindighiar*, is one of the most beautiful and interesting places in Turkey; and according to a popular saying it has a mosque and a walk for every day of the year, so that none need pray or walk in the same place more than once a year. It stretches in a long line from E. to W. along the lower slopes of Olympus, and its situation overlooking the valley of the Nilûfer is not unlike that of Great Malvern above the vale of the Severn. The town is naturally divided into three Quarters by two ravines that come down from the heart of Olympus. In the centre on a bold terrace of rock stands the *citadel*, occupying the site of the ancient town, and containing within its walls the tombs of Osman and Orkhan, and the old palace of the Osmanli sultans; and on the low ground the *Ulu Jami'*, the *bazârs*, and the houses of Moslems and Christians. On the E., and parted by the deep ravine of the *Geuk Su*, "blue water," from the citadel, is the Emir Sultan Quarter with the mosques and tombs of Muhammad I., Bayezid I., and Emir Sultan; and the Set Bashi Quarter of the Armenians. On the W. is the *Muradiyeh* Quarter, with the mosque of Murad II., the hotels, and the Greek Quarter. Further W. are *Chekirgeh* and the hot springs and baths. The streets of Brûsa are clean, and the roads made by Ahmed Vefyk Pasha enable visitors to drive to all the points of interest. One of the most *picturesque views* is that from the *bridge* which spans the ravine of the Geuk Su. The environs are of great beauty; the mountain, with its marked zones of vegetation, rises up from the town, and there are many charming drives and walks in the chestnut, oak, and other woods.

Brûsa, alt. 600 ft., is the residence of a Vali (Governor-General), and the administrative centre of the Vilâyet. Its **population**, including a large number of refugees from Bulgaria, is about 70,000, of whom 35,000 are Moslems, 12,000 Greeks, 11,500 Armenians, 2000 Jews, and 500 Protestants. The Greeks live chiefly in the Muradîyeh and Kaya Bashi

Quarters; the Jews in the low town; the Protestants at Set Bashi and Kaya Bashi; and the Armenians in the Set Bashi and Emir Sultan Quarters. There are a Greek Metropolitan, an Armenian Bishop, a R. Catholic Armenian Bishop, and a Chief Rabbi.

The **climate** is good throughout the year, but is most pleasant in the months of April, May, June, September, and October. The town is healthy, and since the cultivation of rice has been stopped there has been very little fever.

Brûsa, anc. *Prusa*, long the capital of the kings of Bithynia, was built by Prusias, the protector of Hannibal, or, according to some authorities, by Hannibal himself. In B.C. 75, Nicomedes III., King of Bithynia, left his kingdom to the Romans, and Prusa became the residence of the governors of the province. From the letters of Pliny the Younger, when governor, to Trajan, we learn that the city was then prosperous, and possessed a gymnasium, thermæ, an agora, and a library in which stood a statue of the Emperor.

During the Byzantine period Brûsa was by turns in the possession of the Christians and the Muhammadans. In 950 it capitulated to the Arabs under the Hamadan prince Seif ed-Devlet, but soon reverted to the Christians. Towards the close of the 11th century it fell into the hands of the Seljûk Turks, who evacuated it after the capture of Nicæa by the Crusaders, A.D. 1097. After the conquest of Constantinople by the Latins, 1204, Theodore Lascaris retired to Brûsa, and here he was unsuccessfully besieged by the Count of Blois, who had received Bithynia as his share of the plunder. The walls were repaired by Theodore, and the place so strengthened that it was only after a siege of ten years that it passed into the hands of the Osmanlis under Orkhan in 1326. Brûsa now became the residence of the Osmanli sultans. Artists, poets, historians, soldiers of fortune, dervîshes, and holy men

thronged to the new capital, from Persia, Khorassan, and far-distant Bokhara; mosques, colleges, and other public buildings speedily arose; and a palace, upon the size and grandeur of which Osmanli historians love to dwell, was erected. The circular church of S. Elias, turned into a mausoleum, became the last resting-place of Osman, and here were also buried Orkhan and his brother Alaeddîn, Orkhan's son, Suleiman, who carried the Osmanli arms across the Hellespont, and lost his life at Gallipoli, and the earlier princes and princesses. The town was sacked by Timûr (1402), and by the Prince of Karaman (1413); and in modern times it has suffered severely from fire (1801–2), and from earthquake (1855). During the fire of 1802 the tomb of Osman was seriously damaged, the dome with its silver plates fell in, and the insignia of office granted by the Sultan of Iconium to Osman were destroyed. The great earthquake, which threw down nearly all the mosques and houses in the town, and caused the death of more than 1000 people, completed the destruction.

Brûsa has few remains of Roman and Byzantine times, but it contains a large number of old Turkish monuments of the greatest beauty and interest. The **Citadel**, *Hissar*, or "Old Town" was at one time strongly fortified, and there are still many well-preserved portions of the walls of Theodore Lascaris, and, in places, of the Roman masonry upon which they were built. There is a fine view over the town, and the rich valley of the Ulfer Chai from the **Esplanade**, constructed at the E. end of the walled town by Ahmed Vefyk Pasha, who also rebuilt the *Tombs of Osman and Orkhan*. The interior of the tombs which stand on the esplanade are profusely decorated in the modern style. The *Mosque of Orkhan*, also rebuilt by Ahmed Vefyk, is near the W. end of the old town, and close to it may still be seen a few remains of the *palace* in which the early Sultans held their brilliant court. In this quarter, by the clock-tower, are the ruins of an old Byzantine Church called *Daûd Monastir.* In the citadel is also the Mosque of *Uftadi Effendi.* Outside the south wall of the town is **Bunar Bashi** or **Bash Cheshmeh,** "chief spring," a fine spring bursting forth from the rock, beneath the shade of ancient plane-trees, which formerly supplied the fountains in the palace gardens. Here there is a much frequented *café,* to which Moslems and Christians alike resort, and not far from it is a *Tekkeh* of "Dancing" Dervîshes. From a field above the spring there is a good view of the Byzantine walls.

Mosques and Türbehs.—No order is necessary to visit the mosques, but the guardians expect a small fee. Visitors should always be accompanied by a dragoman, and take slippers with them.

The **Ulu Jami',** "Great Mosque," is close to the bazâr near the centre of the town; and is the work of three Sultans,—Murad I., Bayezid I., and Muhammad I., each of whom also built a separate mosque. It is a square of about 100 paces, and in plan resembles the earlier Arab mosques. The interior is divided by square pillars into five aisles, each containing four bays covered, except in one instance, by flat domes. In the central aisle, that leads from the main entrance, one of the bays has no roof; and beneath the opening, which admits the direct rays of the sun, there is a large water basin well stocked with fish. The *mimber* and *karsi* are beautifully carved, and the latter is only equalled by the *Karsi* at Sinope. The mosque was once very rich, and it still has some fine *carpets,* and 700 lamps which, when lighted at Ramazân, produce a fine effect. The pillars were formerly gilt to the height of a man, and the walls decorated with tiles, but these have been replaced by whitewash, and written sentences from the Kurân. On either side of the façade is a free-standing *minaret.* Both were originally decorated with blue or green tiles, and that on the

left had a *tank,* on its upper story, which was supplied by a spring on the slopes of Olympus. The aqueduct and the water-pipes within the minaret have been destroyed. The *haram,* or court, contains a fountain erected by the celebrated Mufti, Aziz Effendi.

The **Yeshil Jami',** *Green Mosque,* built by Muhammad I. in 1420, stands upon a terrace whence there is a fine view over the valley. In completeness of design, artistic taste, and costliness of material it excels all other Osmanli buildings. The exterior is plain, but until the earthquake of 1855 there were two minarets, covered with green *faïence,* at the north end. The entrance door is ornamented with arabesques and inscriptions delicately carved in white marble, and in excellent taste; and there is a finely carved door of wood. The interior is covered by two large domes, and two smaller ones richly ornamented. The internal walls are decorated with *faïence.* Green is the prevailing colour, but there are many floral designs of great beauty. The best specimens will be found at the *mihrab,* in the gallery at the N. end, in the chambers beneath it, and in the entrance passage. The tiles are of Persian design, and were probably made at Cotyaeum, *Kutaya,* or at Nicæa, *Isnik,* where there was a Genoese factory in which Persian tiles were copied. The mosque appears to stand upon the site of a Byzantine church, of which some fragments remain.

The **Yeshil Türbeh,** *Tomb of Muhammad I.,* is the gem of Brûsa. It is an octagonal building with a dome, and a fine doorway, much damaged. Formerly it was decorated externally and internally with *faïence,* but when the tomb was repaired by the late Ahmed Vefyk Pasha, the exterior was covered with the modern green tiles of Kutaya. In the interior most of the old work remains, and the floral designs are of exquisite beauty. The *mihrab* and the *cœnataph* of Muhammad I. are particularly good. There are also cœnataphs of two Sultanas, a Prince, and a Grand Vizier.

Not far from the Green Mosque is the **Mosque of Emîr Sultân**, rebuilt by Selim III. at the beginning of the century on the site of that erected by Bayezid I. The mosque, which gives its name to this quarter of the town, was once equal in wealth to the mosques of Medina and Kerbela, and it is still one of the great places of pilgrimage in Turkey. Emîr Sultân was the celebrated *dervish*, Shemseddîn Muhammad, from Bokhara, who always accompanied Bayezid I. in his campaigns and saved Brûsa from destruction at the hands of Timûr. Below the green mosque is the *Jami' Morsella* with a fine spring, the water of which is so highly prized that it is sent to Constantinople. Lower still, near the road to Kutaya, is the

Yilderim Jami', *Mosque of the Thunderbolt*, i.e. of Bayezid I., standing on a mound apart from all buildings, excepting a few hovels. It is built of stone, and, though it has only one door and one minaret, as in the oldest mosques, it is striking from its simplicity and grandeur. The mosque which was being built when Bayezid was defeated by Timûr, was completed by his son Musa Chelebi during the Interregnum; and was consequently badly endowed. Some beautifully painted floral ornaments on the wooden panelling of the *mihrab*, and some very old carpets are the chief objects of interest. Close to the mosque is the *Türbeh* of the ill-fated Bayezid who, after making Constantinople and Western Europe tremble, was overwhelmed by the Mongolian invasion. His lonely, forsaken tomb is in the simplest style, and it is said that Murad IV., when returning from his successful campaign in Persia, gave the cœnataph a contemptuous kick which injured his foot and brought on the ailment from which he soon afterwards died.

The **Mosque of Murad II.**, *Muradi-* *yeh*, is a large building standing on a rock terrace in the west quarter of the town to which it gives its name. The plan is not unlike that of the mosque of Bayezid I. There is a beautiful porch with some good *faïence*, but the interior is plain, and the *mihrab* and *mimber* are in the simplest style. Attached to the mosque are a Khân, Imâret, and Medresseh. Close to the mosque is one of the prettiest and most secluded spots in Brûsa :—the walled enclosure in which are the **Tombs of the Sultans,** surrounded by rose gardens and overshadowed by gigantic plane-trees, of which one is said to be 400 years old. The *Türbeh of Murad II.* is a plain building surmounted by a dome, without ornament of any kind. Beneath the dome is a simple grave of earth, edged with marble. It was the special wish of the Sultan that his grave should be exposed, like that of a poor man, to rain and snow, and an opening was consequently left in the centre of the dome. The columns round the grave stand on overturned capitals. In an adjoining tomb chamber lie his sons Ahmed and Alaeddîn. Amongst the other tombs in the enclosure are those of the luckless *Prince Jem,* who was poisoned at Naples; of his brother *Mustafa;* of *Mahmûd,* son of Bayezid II.; of the *Servian Princess,* wife of Murad II., who, alone of the four Christian Sultanas, preserved her religion; of other Sultanas, princes and princesses; and of many of the poets, holy men, and philosophers, who were attracted to Brûsa by the brilliant court of the first Sultans. All these tombs are of simple construction, built of brick and stone; and in some of them there are good specimens of Persian tiles.

The **Mosque of Murad I.,** *Ghâzi Hunkiar Jami',* erected in the suburb of *Chekirgeh,* in the 14th century, is different in form to all other mosques, and is said to have been built by Christian architects. The mosque is largely constructed from the remains of older buildings, and in the main façade there are several different kinds of capitals. The façade, which bears "an extraordinary resemblance to one of the earlier Sienese palaces," consists of a two-storied vestibule with pillars and pointed arches; and a fine view is obtained from the upper story. The masonry is in courses of different colour. The interior is simple and shows more traces of Byzantine influence than the later mosques of Bayezid and Muhammad I. The most remarkable feature of the mosque is that its *Medresseh* forms an integral part of the building. From the vestibule a flight of steps leads up to a passage that runs right round the mosque without any communication with the interior; on the outer side of this passage, doors open to the cells of the students. Thus, when the Imâm led the prayers before the mihrâb, each student could pray in his cell, and at the same time in the mosque. There are now no students, and a small elementary school, in one of the lower rooms of the vestibule, is the representative of the college founded by Murad I.

In front of the mosque is a terraced garden in which is the **Türbeh of Murad I.**, surnamed *Khudavendkiar,* "over-lord," who was treacherously assassinated on the field of Kossova, and is the only Sultan who has won the title of *shehid,* "martyr." Khudavendkiar, from whom the vilâyet of Brûsa takes its official name, lies in the centre of the building beneath the dome, and on either side of him lie the sons of Bayezid I., Suleiman and Mûsa. Here also are the tombs of Murad's son Yakûb, and of four princesses. Near the tomb stands a fine inscribed bronze bowl in which corn is blessed and then sold to the villagers to mix with the corn they sow. In the building, which has been repaired in recent years, are kept a portion of Murad's chain armour, his prayer-carpet (apparently of deerskin), a green, well-patched garment, said to have been worn by him on the fatal field of Kossova, his turban, a very old lock and key from some captured city, and other relics.

From the terrace, on which a mar-

ble *fountain* gives forth jets of hot and cold water from alternate mouths, there is a fine *view* over the valley of the *Ulfer Chai,* and of the hills beyond it. But the grandest view is that obtained from the minaret of the adjoining mosque.

Other **mosques** at Brûsa are those of *Mollah Abu Jebbari,* on the plan of the Ulu Jami', but on a smaller scale; *Mollah Abdul Attif,* on the slopes of Olympus, &c. The tombs of "Babas," "Dedehs," "Abdals," and "Sultans" are innumerable. Amongst the most celebrated are those of *Geyikli Baba,* "father of stags," who accompanied Orkhan on his campaigns; *Ramazan Baba,* a Bektash dervish; *Abdal Murad,* "Simple Murad," who was present at the capture of Brûsa, and whose wooden sword is still shown; *Abdal Mûsa,* who came with Hajji Bektash from Khorassan; *Emir Sultan* of Bokhara, whose tomb is still a place of pilgrimage; *Chekirgeh Sultan,* "Locust Sultan," who gave his name to the suburb of Brûsa; *Hajji Khalfa,* chief of the Bairam dervîshes, &c. Here also are buried the learned commentator *el-Bostan;* the great legal authority *Khosrev ibn Khisr;* the poets *Khiali* and *Mollah Khosrev,* and the prose writer *Wassa Ali,* whose classic works were largely inspired by the running waters, and sylvan beauty of the slopes of Olympus.

Churches.—The Greeks have churches at Bolukbazar and Kaya Bashi; the Armenians at Set Bashi; and the Roman Catholic Armenians and Protestants at Set Bashi. None of them possess any historical or architectural interest.

There is a station of the American *Western Turkey Mission* at Brûsa; and, in connection with it, a very successful *school* for Greek and Armenian girls. The **Brûsa Orphanage** was founded in 1875 as a home for children left orphans and destitute during the terrible famine that ravaged Asia Minor in that year. It is supported by contributions from England, America, and Switzerland; and a suitable building was erected in 1883 with funds collected by the late Mrs. Baghdasarian. Between 500 and 600 orphans from all parts of the empire and of all religious denominations have been brought up at the orphanage under the care of Mr. Baghdasarian.

The bazârs are good, and in them, as well as in the numerous khâns, may be purchased Brûsa gauze, silks, Brûsa towels, carpets of camels'-hair felt embroidered with silk, Kutaya pottery, gold and silk embroideries, &c. Good wine made locally can also be obtained.

The principal industry of Brûsa is connected with the production and *manufacture of silk.* There are several *fabricas,* or spinning factories, in which silk is spun for export to Lyons, and home consumption, but since the appearance of the silkworm disease some years ago most of the silk has been obtained from villages at a distance from Brûsa. The silk is woven in private houses chiefly by women. The girls in the "fabricas" are mostly Greeks, but there are many Turkish girls wearing an apology for a *yashmak.* Silk spinning is a very delicate and beautiful process, and a visit to one or more of the factories in the Muradiyeh Quarter is strongly recommended. Those under French management are the best. The beautiful *silk gauze* is woven in very rough hand-looms in private houses; it is very narrow and a great number of yards are required to make a dress. The cost is P. 6 to 7 the pic, or 1s. 4d. to 1s. 6d. a yard. In spite of its light, diaphanous texture it is very strong; and when washed, though losing its evenness, it acquires a silkiness and softness preferred by many. The prettiest are those with white or maize-coloured stripes; as the silk has always a yellow tinge, blue and pink stripes are never so clear and true in colour. Very good *handkerchiefs* are made, and a mixture of silk and cotton which is cool and strong and much used for light summer clothing for men. The soft fluffy *Brûsa towel* is made in the rudest and most primitive-looking looms in the cottages. The towels when of a superior kind cost about P. 30 a pair; their great beauty lies in their soft, spongy, absorbent texture. The bath towel or *takm,* about two yards long, and the bath *burnûs* are also made; and so is *burunjik,* a beautiful material that looks like thick cream-coloured crape with silky stripes, and is used for the best sort of *katkjis* shirts. Visitors can obtain admission to private houses in which there are looms through the landlord of the hotel, or through members of the American Mission.

Excursions.—The environs of Brûsa are of great beauty, and the new roads that have been made enable visitors to ride or drive to several points of interest.

About 1½ m. westward of the town is the village of **Chekirgeh,** "Locust," anct. *Pythia,* celebrated for its hot iron and sulphur springs, and for the mosque and Tomb of Murad I.(p. 125). Here and in the vicinity are the **Baths of Brûsa** which are much frequented during the season (May) by visitors from Constantinople. In addition to three or four smaller springs there are two large sulphur springs, one supplying the baths of *Beuyük* and *Kuchuk Kükürtlu,* the other those of *Yeni Kaplija* and *Kainarja;* and two iron springs, one at *Kara Mustafa,* the other, *Eski Kaplija,* at Chekirgeh. The sulphur waters are like those near Vienna and near Zurich; the iron waters like those of Toplitz, Wildbad, Gastein, &c. The lowest of the baths is *Kara Mustafa,* below the road from Mudania to Brûsa; the water has no taste or smell, and from its clearness is called the *Gümush Su,* "silver water"; temp. 112° F. On the hillside, about 120 ft. above Kara Mustafa, is the spring that supplies *Yeni Kaplija,* the water is clear, limpid, and tastes a little "flat"; it gives off gas in bubbles and rises at a temp. of 195°

F. Three hundred paces to the W. is the spring of *Kükürtlu*, which rises violently at a temp. of 178° F., gives off larger quantities of gas, and has a slight smell. Half an hour from these baths is *Eski Kaplija* at Chekirgeh; the source is said to be unknown, but the water is brought down by two conduits at a temp. of 117° F. Chekirgeh is apparently the place at which Justinian built a palace, and a public bath, and to which the Empress Theodora came, in 525, with a suite of 4000 persons. The importance of the place in the early Moslem period is shown by the erection of an Imperial mosque there by Murad I. Besides the public establishment there are *hotels* and several houses in the village which enjoy the privilege of having water laid on for baths. These are much patronised by invalids who wish greater privacy than can be obtained in the public baths.

The baths are handsome structures, containing several apartments, and they are supplied with hot and cold water. Those of *Yeni Kaplija*, erected by Rustem Pasha, Grand Vizier of Suleiman I., are the finest. The central basin, about 25 ft. diameter, is covered by a lofty dome; the domes and vaults are decorated with *faïence*, and the floor paved with marble. There is a separate bath for ladies. The dome of the *Eski Kaplija* bath is said to have been built by Murad I. The baths were greatly improved by Ahmed Vefyk Pasha, and, with increased facilities of communication, they will no doubt become better known, and more frequented.

Other excursions are to **Inkaya** (1 hr. drive), whence there is a fine view over the lake of Apollonia. To **Aksu** (3½ hrs. drive) on the Kutaya road. Half an hour's walk from Aksu there is a good view of the eastern end of Olympus, and horses can be obtained to visit a *waterfall* (1 hr.) beautifully situated in a forest of oak and fir. This excursion requires the whole day. The picturesque villages *Deirmenli Kizik*, and *Jumali Kizik*, can be visited on horseback (1 hr.). A very beautiful ride is up the left bank of the *Geuk Su*, by *Karakli* (2600 ft.), and over the shoulder of Olympus to *Baghli* (4½ hrs.), a whole day excursion.

The **ascent of Olympus**, *Keshish Dagh*, "Monk's Mountain," alt. 7600 ft., presents no difficulties, and can be made in about 6 hrs. (5 on horseback, 1 on foot); the descent takes 4 hrs. The best season is from the middle of May to the middle of October when, except in the ravines, there is little or no snow. By starting before daylight the ascent and descent can be easily made in one day. A *guide* is necessary, and one or two *zaptiehs* should be taken. The hotel landlord will make arrangements, and provide food for the day, as none can be obtained on the way. The expense for one person is about 25*s*. (Index). Travellers wishing to spend the night on the summit to see the sun rise must make special arrangements.

The best route for the ascent starts from Set Bashi and leads up the right bank of the *Geuk dereh* (2½ hrs.) through chestnut, oak, hazel, and beech to the 1st plateau, *Kadi Yailasi*, a beautiful "alp" with a fine spring. The road is a rough bridle-path, so steep in places that it is better to dismount and lead the horses. From Kadi Yailasi there is a fine view, and every visitor to Brûsa should try and ascend thus far. From the 1st plateau a rocky path leads up through a pine forest to the 2nd plateau, *Saralan* (1½ hr.). This is the roughest part of the ascent. The road now leaves the forest and ascends gradually through scattered pines and junipers to the 3rd plateau (1 hr.), crossing the heads of numerous streams of clear cold water well stocked with *trout*, which are much prized at Brûsa. At *Kirk Bunar*, "forty springs," on the 3rd plateau the horses are left and the remainder of the ascent (1 hr.) is made on foot.

The view on a fine day from the summit of Olympus, a perfect panorama, is almost unrivalled. The *Sea of Marmara*, the gulfs of *Mudania* and *Ismid*, Constantinople, the Dardanelles and the Black Sea on the N.; the lake of *Isnik*, the plain of *Yeni-shehr*, and the valley of the *Sakaria* on the N.E.; the peninsula of Cyzicus, the lake of Apollonia, *Mániás Geul*, the valley of the Rhyndacus, and the chain of Mount Ida on the W.; and the vast plains of Mysia and Bithynia on the S. and E.

Botany of Olympus.—" Contrasted with the Greek Archipelago, evergreen oaks were almost entirely absent, and replaced by several deciduous species; indeed, there are few evergreen shrubs on Olympus. The common laurel and Daphne pontica, the Eastern form of Daphne laureola, were the main exceptions. Bulbous plants were remarkably abundant. Fritillaria pontica in profusion almost everywhere, with a range of altitude of nearly 4000 ft. I obtained also 7 or 8 species of ornithogalum, a galanthus out of flower, and 6 or 7 species of crocus. I was just in time to see Crocus aerius in full beauty, at a height of from 4000 ft. to 5000 ft., the flowers at its highest limit appearing amongst the melting snow, and lower down under the pine-trees, intermixed with crocus gargaricus, a charming little yellow species. At a height of from 3500 ft. to 4000 ft. the floral display was like a garden. The purple aubrietia deltoidea, with a yellow alyssum on the rocks, and the yellow and blue crocuses, intermixed with hypericum calycinum, a handsome doronicum, and large tufts of a handsome purple primula, varying with white flowers, identical with a plant in cultivation under the name of primula altaica, but closely allied to our common primrose. Two or three species of gagea, and the lovely glaucous low-growing hypericum olympicum, were also conspicuous, intermixed with a blue muscari. The summit of the plateau, at a height of about 5500 ft., the limit of the pines, was comparatively barren, and afforded nothing but tufts of a juniperus, a sort of ' savin,' a small potentilla, crocus aerius, and a

little gagea among the snow patches; but it was evidently too early on April the 16th for the higher region of Olympus, which in June would probably afford a further set of species.

" The number of species of the plants of Olympus named after the mountain expresses the extreme richness of the flora. In addition to those already named I found a dentaria closely allied to bulbifera, viola olympica, a handsome species coming between the Alpine calcarata and tricolor. Cistus laurifolius and C. salviæfolius, anemone blanda, the eastern representative of A. apennina, Ruscus aculeatus, and R. hypophyllum, a sedum allied to telephium, a gentiana allied to asclepiadea, saxifraga rotundifolia, a handsome lamium allied to L. longiflorum, a number of conspicuous species of lathyrus and orobus, including one with yellow flowers. Boraginaceous plants are extremely abundant, including several symphytums, a borago, and lithospermum purpureocæruleum; also a digitalis not yet in flower, campanula persicifolia, an alpine myosotis, a corydalis, a geranium, a convallaria, and asphodelus luteus.」

" Amongst the shrubs were ligustrum vulgare, cercis siliquastrum, gorgeous with its rich rosy-crimson flowers, intermixed with a handsome white-flowered fraxinus, which was very conspicuous above Brûsa; also juniperus oxycedrus, jasminum fruticans, and viscum album on the chestnut.

" Vaccinium arctostaphylos is an abundant shrub on the flanks of Olympus; the leaves are collected and used in lieu of tea. They are gathered in spring, and, after being laid in the shade on a straw mat, are rolled in the hands and dried by a slow fire in an oven. The vaccinium leaves are sold under the name of ' Brûsa Tea ' and make a very palatable beverage.

" Ferns were tolerably abundant, but I observed none but the following British species : scolopendrium vulgare, asplenium adiantum-nigrum, A. acutum, A. trichomanes, cystopteris fragilis, polystichum angulare, pteris aquilina, and athyrium filix-fœmina."

Roe, and red deer, bear, wolves, jackals, and foxes are found on Olympus, as well as quail, red-legged partridge, &c.; but game is not plentiful, and is difficult to find. In the lower ground there are wild boar. There are plenty of woodcock in winter; and, near Lake Apollonia, there is good wild pheasant shooting.

BRÛSA TO ISMID, BY NICÆA.

	hrs.
Brûsa—	
Kustul	3
Binkus	3
Yeni-shehr	6
Isnik (*Nicæa*)	4
Mekejeh	6
Ismid (by rail).	

On leaving Brûsa the road to Kutaya, up the valley, is followed until the foot of the hills is approached. The Yeni-shehr road here turns to the left and passes *Kustul* (3 hrs.), a Moslem village with a small castle and a fine stream; it then skirts the side of a large morass, crosses the Delikli Chai, which runs into a prettily situated lakelet, and ascends sharply to *Binkus* (3 hrs.) on the ridge (700 ft.) that separates the waters of the Marmara from those of the Black Sea. Between Brûsa and Kustul there are good views of Olympus, and of the picturesquely situated villages on its slopes; and beyond Kustul there are traces of an ancient, probably Roman, road. From Binkus the road descends through a well-wooded glen, and passes out through a curious *Bâb*, or natural gateway, to the great plain of Yeni-shehr with its large fever-breeding swamp. It keeps near the foot of the hills on the N. as far as a fine spring (3 hrs.), and then runs across the plain to *Chaûshlar*, a village with a conspicuous white min-

aret, and Yeni-shehr (3 hrs.), which it enters over a long causeway said to have been made by Selim II.

Yeni-shehr was the head-quarters of the Osmanli army during the war with the Byzantines prior to the capture of Brûsa. It is a large town with a good *khân*, and several interesting *mosques*, erected by Osmanli princes during the 14th century. The mosques are built of brick and stone, and are of the simplest character—a single chamber with a porch, a dome, and a minaret. Each mosque had its imâret, and medresseh, occupying two sides of the haram, and a fountain in the centre of the enclosure. The *Mosque of Sinan Pasha* has a very large imâret, and a minaret on which some good tiles still remain; in its court are some fine marble columns, lying on the ground. On a mound, apparently a tumulus, near the town is the tomb of Baba Sultan, an Indian saint; an imâret; and a large number of graves with fragments of columns, &c. The plain was formerly better drained, but it must always have been liable to floods in winter. The water supply is regulated by small *suterazi* (p. 73). The people are all Moslem, and the men are amongst the finest in Western Anatolia.

From Yeni-shehr the road crosses the plain and then climbs a ridge about 1100 ft. high, to the village of *Derbend* (2 hrs.). During the ascent a good view is obtained of the whole range of Olympus, which looks grand and imposing from this side. The descent is through trees and shrubs of the most varied foliage, and the blue waters of the lake, lying between well wooded hills, with the old walls of Nicæa on their margin, make up a charming picture. From the foot of the hills the road runs across the plain to the south gate of

Isnik (2 hrs.), a contraction of εἰς Νἰκαιαν, *Nicæa* (alt. 400 ft.). It stands on the shore of Lake Ascania, in a plain which is bordered on three sides by high wooded hills. The plain was formerly celebrated for its fertility, but its summer climate was never considered healthy, and fever, due to the large swamps, is now very prevalent during the hot season. The position of Nicæa, at the foot of the pass by which the Roman road from the Propontis crossed the hills to the valley of the Sangarius, was one of considerable importance; and the town was strongly fortified. The fortifications are well preserved, and are almost equal in interest to those of Constantinople, which they closely resemble in design. The modern village of mud houses, which is almost lost in the ruins that surround it, has a small Moslem and Greek population, whose chief occupation is the growth of silk. Fair accommodation can be obtained in the house of a Greek priest.

Nicæa was founded, about B.C. 316, on the site of an earlier town (Helicore or Ancore) by Antigonus, and called Antigonia; but, not long after, Lysimachus changed the name to Nicæa in honour of his wife. It soon became a city of importance and disputed with Nicomedia, *Ismid*, the honour of being the metropolis of Bithynia. Hadrian rebuilt the walls after an earthquake (about A.D. 120), and erected the existing gateways on the E. and N. In A.D. 259 the city was captured and burnt by the Goths; but it soon rose from its ashes, and its walls were strengthened by Claudius (Gothicus), who built the S. and W. gates. In 325 Nicæa was the seat of the celebrated Council, called together by Constantine, at which the creed called Nicene was drawn up and the heresy of Arius condemned; and here, during the regency of Irene (A.D. 787), was held the "Second Council of Nicæa," at which the veneration of sacred pictures was sanctioned. Attacked several times in vain by the Arabs, whose defeat on one occasion, about A.D. 910, is recorded in an inscription in the walls, the town at last fell into the hands of the Seljûk Turks, about A.D. 1080, and became the residence of the two first Sultans of Rûm, —Suleiman and Kilij Arslan. Poets, astronomers, artists, and men skilled in the science of the day, flocked to the capital from Persia, and Arabia; and for a few years the Court rivalled in brilliancy those of Baghdad and Cordova. In 1097 the town was besieged by the Crusaders, and after a memorable siege, full of picturesque incident, it surrendered to their Byzantine allies, who had transported boats from Civitot, *Geumlek*, and blockaded the sea front. In 1203, after the capture of Constantinople by the Latins, Theodore Lascaris made it the seat of the Empire of Nicæa; but in 1330, it was taken by the Osmanli Turks under Orkhan who, whilst granting the Niceans liberty to retain their religion, turned several of the churches into mosques, and erected mosques, schools, and public buildings. Orkhan made it the capital of the Sanjak of *Khoja Ili*, but Muhammad II. removed the capital to Nicomedia, and from this transfer dates the decadence of Nicæa. The once flourishing city is now a miserable village; but the imposing walls, and the ruins of theatre, baths, churches, mosques, &c., remain to attest its former grandeur.

Nicæa, according to Strabo, was built with great regularity; it was quadrangular, and measured 16 stadia in circumference; it had 4 gates, and all its streets intersected each other at right angles, so that, from a monument in the gymnasium, in the centre, all the 4 gates could be seen. The place has largely preserved its original form, but the circuit of the walls is now about 23 stadia. The enlargement is probably due to Hadrian, but, excepting the two gates, little of his work remains. The *existing walls* and towers, built in courses of brick and mortar of almost equal height, are of later date. They consisted of a strong inner wall with flanking towers; and of an outer wall, about 50 ft. in advance, which had similar flanking towers, and was protected by a ditch that could be filled with water on the approach of an enemy. The towers are at unequal distances in the wall; most of them have semicircular fronts, but some are square, and one near the S.E. angle has ten sides. The walls were frequently restored, and additional towers were erected by Byzantine Emperors and Turkish Sultans, who, with slight regard for the public monuments of earlier generations, made free use of columns, friezes, architraves, and official inscriptions which lie embedded in the masonry. The *ditch* is now partly filled in and covered with mulberry gardens and fruit-trees.

Travellers are recommended in the first place to ride round *the walls,* and afterwards to reach the parapet of the inner wall, by one of the flights of steps, and to follow the *chemin des rondes* on foot. The line of the *south wall* is broken towards the lake by a deep re-entering angle; and it was at the projecting S.W. angle that the Crusaders attacked the city. Here was the tower which they undermined, and close to it, within the walls, was the palace of the Seljúk Sultan. A little further east the parapet of the wall has been built with the seats of a theatre; and not far from this spot is a mutilated inscription bearing the name of Theodore Lascaris. In the centre of the wall is the *Yeni-shehr Gate* by which Orkhan entered the city in triumph. It is approached by a causeway and is well fortified. The gate of the outer wall is flanked by large round towers of later date than the gate, and that of the inner wall has a flanking tower built on shafts of columns. There are also remains of a third or inner gate, over which there was at one time an inscription of Claudius (Gothicus). The parapet of the *east wall,* near the S.E. angle, contains fragments of cornices, and pedestals of columns that must have been taken from a large building, temple or basilica, close at hand. In the centre of the wall is the *Lefkeh Gate,* with a handsome Roman gateway, partially concealed by later additions, which, according to an inscription, was erected in the reign of Hadrian. In the outer wall are some mutilated bas-reliefs, and near the gateway is a long inscription. The ancient *aqueduct,* which still supplies Isnik with water, enters at the Lefkeh Gate, and with its small *suterazi* (p. 73), overgrown with ferns and creepers, is

a most picturesque object. The road to Lefkeh runs out through the principal *cemetery,* and after a slight ascent reaches an enormous sarcophagus, whence there is a view over the city and lake that should not be missed. In the centre of the *north wall* is the *Stambúl Gate.* The lower portion of the outer wall, at this point, is possibly as old as the Greek period; the upper portion is a reconstruction and contains several mutilated bas-reliefs and fragments of friezes. The gate of the inner wall is a fine portal with classic mouldings, and is probably of the same date as the Lefkeh Gate. Between the Stambúl Gate and the lake a portion of the wall is built of large finely-dressed stones taken from some important building, apparently a church, in the vicinity. A few yards to the E. of this masonry is a tower with an *inscription* stating that it was built by Leo (the Philosopher) and his son Constantine. The *west wall,* which has suffered more than the others, is now separated from the lake by about 50 yards of swampy ground. The water gate was near the N.W. angle.

The ground *within the walls* is partly occupied by gardens and partly overgrown with brushwood. Following the street from the Yeni-shehr Gate, the traveller has on his left the ruins of the *theatre,* possibly that mentioned by Pliny the Younger, in his letters to Trajan; and on his right an *Imáret* and *Tekkeh,* and then the **Greek Church,** which is certainly older than the 12th century. The apse has a raised stone bench running round it, and in its centre is a stone chair or throne for the bishop, built into the wall and reached by six steps. In the semi-dome over the apse are some well preserved mosaics representing the Virgin and other figures; and in the pavement of the floor are fragments of mosaic and marble, and a tablet from the walls, inscribed "Tower of Michael the Great King, Emperor in Christ." A rude picture of the first Council is deserving of notice; and so is the design of the brickwork of the narthex. Near the Lefkeh Gate is the **Yeshil Jami',** *Green Mosque.*

κ 2

built by Khaireddîn, the Grand Vizier of Murad I., and restored by Ahmed Vefyk Pasha. It is a fine building of white and bluish marble, with a minaret that was once simply but effectively ornamented with green, red, and purple tiles. In the *interior* two fine marble columns support a gallery, and the remaining space is covered by a well-constructed dome. The walls are lined with various kinds of marble. The *porch*, of white marble, is one of the finest specimens of early Turkish art in Asia Minor. The façade consists of three pointed arches, springing from two piers, and two columns of red granite; and each side has two arches and one marble column. The capitals of the columns, and the dome in the centre of the porch, of Persian or Arab design, are very beautiful; and the delicate carving of some of the details could scarcely be surpassed. Over the door is a long inscription. Near the mosque are its *medresseh* and *imâret.* The latter, with its three large and two small domes, and its fine porch, is a striking building, and well deserves a visit.

To the W. of the Yeshil Jami' is the **Mosque of Eshref Zadeh**, which was once a famous place of pilgrimage. Internally its walls are covered to a height of about 4 ft. with tiles of the best period. A little farther is the **Church of S. Sophia**, *Agia Sofia Jami'*, which is supposed by some writers to have been the place in which the First Council was held. The existing church, however, could not have been built before the latter half of the 6th, and it may be as late as the beginning of the 8th, century. The First Council was probably held in the imperial palace, but the second may have been held in the church, which was once used as a mosque, and is now a ruin. The only perfect portions are the small domed chapels at the ends of the side aisles; in these fragments of plaster still adhere to the walls, and some of the figures of the old frescoes can be seen. Near the church are *Chatal Cheshmeh Jami'* and an old cemetery.

From Isnik the road crosses a high ridge to the gorge of the *Sakaria*, anct. Sangarius. On the western slope there are the ruins of a fortified camp, supposed to have been built by the Crusaders during the siege of Nicæa; and from the summit there is a fine view of the lake district and Olympus. At the foot of the eastern slope is **Mekejeh** (7 hrs.), a station on the Ismid-Angora Railway (p. 118).

[A road, now little used, but during the first five centuries A.D. of great importance, runs N. from Isnik, and, passing the *obelisk* of Cassius Asclepiodotus, erected towards the close of the first century, and the villages of *el-Beylik* and *Kirmisli*, ascends the valley of the *Uzun Chai* to the crest of the ridge. It then descends to the plain of the *Kilis Su*, and crosses it to Ismid (14 hrs.). On this road were the Roman stations of Liada, Libus, and Eribolus. *Libus* was half-way between Nicæa and Nicomedia, and *Eribolus* was on the S. shore of the gulf 10 M.P. from Nicomedia, but neither have yet been identified.]

Isnik to Geumlek and Brûsa.—The road to Geumlek (10 hrs.) follows the line of the Roman road along the S. side of the lake and the left bank of the river *Ascanius*, and is good throughout. About 3 hrs. from Isnik is an *inscription* recording the fact that the road was improved by Nero. It was whilst advancing along this road that Walter the Penniless and 22,000 knights and pilgrims lost their lives in battle with the Seljûks (A.D. 1096). From Geumlek (p. 120) there is steam communication to Mudania and Constantinople; and a road, in bad repair, over the Katerli Dâgh to Brûsa (4½ hrs.).

Isnik to Constantinople, by Hersek.— This is a section of the important road that, during the Byzantine period, led from Constantinople to Asia through Nicæa and Dorylæum. It was much used as late as the early part of the present century, and is an interesting route to follow. After leaving Isnik the road runs, for 3 hrs., over the plain, making a circuit of the N. end of the lake and passing through olive and mulberry groves and vineyards. It then ascends for 2 hrs. through a forest of ilex and other evergreens, and, after crossing the ridge, descends in another hour to the small Greek village of *Kiz-derbend* (6 hrs.). The road now descends for 3 hrs through the beautiful valley of the **Kirk Gechid**, "Forty fords," anct. *Dracon*, crossing the stream twenty times, and passing a ruined castle with many towers. It then runs for an hour along the projecting tongue (*dil*) of land which terminates in **Dil Burun**, *Cibotus*, passing close to *Hersek*, on, or near the site of *Helenopolis*. This town, which was founded by Constantine, A.D. 318, and adorned with baths and public buildings by Justinian, became the usual landing-place for the emperors and others who, on their way to the interior, came by water from Constantinople instead of by the land road and ferry. From Dil Burun or Hersek there is a ferry (about 2 m.) to *Dil Iskelesi*, anct. Ægialoe, a station on the Haidar Pasha-Ismid Railway (p. 116).

[Another road runs from Isnik to *Kara-mûrsal* (9 hrs.), near the site of *Prænetus*, which was sometimes used as a landing-place instead of Heleno-polis. From Kara-mûrsal, a large village which takes its name from one of Osman's leaders, who was granted the district in 1326, there is steam communication with Constantinople.]

§ 5.—CONSTANTINOPLE TO THE DARDANELLES, BY CYZICUS AND PRIAPUS.

	hrs.
Panderma (str.)	8
Cyzicus	2
Edenjik	1
Dimetoka	10½
Karabogha (*Priapus*)	3
Kemer (*Parium*)	5½
Lapsaki (*Lampsacus*)	9
Dardanelles	7

Steamers leave the Golden Horn three times a week for Panderma. They start in the evening, and the

sail across the Marmara usually takes about 8 hrs., including a call at *Perama*, a small village on the peninsula of Cyzicus.

Panderma, *Panormus*, a large town, with a mixed population, occupying a lovely situation on the slope of the hill in a small bay. It has a trade in cereals, cotton, opium, valonia, salt fish, sheep, cattle, wool, marble, bora-cite, &c. The road from Panderma runs along the coast for 2 hrs. to the ruins of

Cyzicus, now *Bal-Kiz* (Παλαία Κύζικος), situated at the S. end of a peninsula that projects into the Marmara. The peninsula, *Kapu Dâgh*, is a hilly district, 16 m. from E. to W., and 8 m. from N. to S., which culminates in the sharp peak of **Adam Kaya**, *Mt. Dindymus* (2620 ft.). It is now joined to the mainland by a sandy isthmus one mile wide, but was originally an island, separated by a narrow and probably shallow channel. The origin of Cyzicus is doubtful. According to one story it was settled by Pelasgians from Thessaly, and to another by Milesians. After the battle of Mycale it belonged alternately to the Persians, the Athenians, and the Lacedæmonians. The peace of Antalcidas (B.C. 387) gave it to Persia; but, after the battle of the Granicus it passed to Alexander, who connected it with the mainland by two bridges. It was afterwards subject to the kings of Pergamum, but retained its own form of government. In B.C. 74 the town was besieged by Mithridates; but the strength of its walls enabled it to hold out until Lucullus compelled the king of Pontus to raise the siege. For its services on this occasion Cyzicus was made a free city by the Romans, and it attained a high degree of prosperity, especially during the reigns of Hadrian and Marcus Aurelius. It was celebrated for the beauty of its buildings; for its great temple dedicated to Hadrian; for its mint at which the "Cyziceni" were coined; for its oysters; and for its perfumes. Constantine removed several of its statues to his new capital, and, after having been ravaged by the Goths, it was finally destroyed by an earthquake in A.D. 943. It was amidst the ruins of Cyzicus that Orkhan's son, Suleiman, dreaming of conquest one moonlight night, formed the bold determination to carry the Osmanli arms across the Hellespont to Europe.

The ruins lie partly on level, and partly on rising ground at the foot of Mt. Dindymus. They were for years the quarry from which marble was obtained for the erection of mosques and other buildings at Constantinople. All the large buildings have consequently disappeared; and the site is so overgrown with brushwood, and covered with cherry orchards and vineyards, that it is difficult to see what is left. There are remains of the *walls*, two fine octagonal towers, and extensive substructures with numerous massive vaults. One of the *towers*, called Bal-kiz, apparently commanded one of the bridges built by Alexander, About 1 m. from the shore are the remains of an *amphitheatre*, built in a wooded valley. Some of the massive masonry is not less than 60 ft. high; and the interior, overgrown with trees and shrubs, is most picturesque. A small stream flows through the centre of the arena; and possibly the building was sometimes used as a Naumachia. There are also the ruins of a large *theatre* almost overgrown with shrubs and luxuriant vegetation. The houses of the village of *Hammamli*, near the apex of the city walls, and the walls separating the vineyards, are built out of the ruins; but there is nothing of importance in them.

[About 2 hrs. W. of the ruins, at the N. point of a small sandy bay, is **Erdek** or **Artaki**, anct. *Artace*, a small town, with a mixed population, which exports a wine much esteemed at Constantinople. Artace was a Milesian colony, and was burnt during the Ionian revolt in the reign of Darius I. In the reign of Justinian it had a Church of the Virgin, and was a suburb of Cyzicus. There are a few fragments of ancient sculpture from Cyzicus in the town, and, in a vineyard above it, a wall of white marble of an early period.]

The road from the ruins at first runs inland to the Turkish village of **Edenjik** (1 hr.), where are many fragments of columns, cornices, and marble blocks, and a few inscriptions from Cyzicus. It then follows the coast line, passing through the villages of *Chaush* and *Musacha*, to the *Geunen Chai*, anct. Æsepus (4½ hrs.), which rises in Mount Ida and flows to the sea through a swampy plain that teems with wild-fowl in winter. After crossing the Æsepus it gradually turns inland to the small village of **Dimetoka** (6 hrs.). [The town of **Bîgha**, *Pegae*, which gives its name to the Saujak, is 1 hr. to the S.W. It was formerly an important centre of commerce, but is now little more than a village.] From Dimetoka the road runs over the plain, and after about 1½ m. crosses an old bridge over the *Granicus*, now the *Bigha Chai*—a stream memorable for the victories gained on its banks by Alexander over the Persians (B.C. 334), and by Lucullus over Mithridates. It then continues over the plain to

Kara-bogha, or **Kara-bîgha**, *Priapus* (3 hrs.), the port of Bîgha, whence corn, sheep, and cattle are exported to Constantinople (steamer 3 times a week). Priapus, which derived its name from the god of gardens, was noted for its harbour and its wine. It was a naval station, and surrendered to Alexander after the battle of the Granicus. Across the promontory terminating in *Kaleh Burnu*, there are remains of fine Byzantine walls and towers, and on its S. side the form of the ancient port can be traced. The road onward runs N. over the hill and descends the *Chinar Dereh* to *Shah Melik Liman*, possibly *Linum* (2¼ hrs.), celebrated for its cockles. It then keeps near the coast and passes through the villages of *Aksas* (Gk.) and *Deirmenjik*, and the gorge of *Chanakli Boghaz* to

ARCHIPELAGO

N

Bulair

Yenikeui

Sheitan Keui

Koraman

Bergaz

GALLIPOLI

Chardak Pt.
Chardak Keui

Taifur Keui

Sahin Keui

Lampsacus

Jemali Keui
Burnan Keui

Galata

Inji Liman

Avapus
Mermedia B.

Turkhan Keui

Selvileri

Chanak Dere

H E L L E S P O N T

Palova

Bokali Kalesi

Kilk Bashi Liman

Yapildak

Musa Keui

Abydos

Nagara Burun
Kefed

Kilia Liman

Kaba Tepeh

Maito

Cham Kalesi

Chanak Kalesi

Dardanelles
Sultaniyeh
Kalesi

Kilid Bahr

Tekkeh

A S I A   M I N O R

Burgas

Sari Siglar
Bay

Kepez Kalesi

Saghan Dere

Ilkri
Baba

Dardanus

Water

Krithia

Kus Keui

Domus D.

Quarantine

Eski Hissarlik
Elaeus

Eren Keui

Morto B.

C.
Helles

Sidd el Bahr

Kum Kaleh

Yalova Burun
Ophryneum

Kum Keui

Janct Rhoeteum

THE

DARDANELLES

Sigeum
Yeni shehr

Dumbrek
(Simois)

Dumbrek

Kalil eli

Hissarlik

Chiplak

Sigeum
shehr

Kum

Plain of Troy

Kalifatli

English Miles

0   5   10

Kemer, *Parium* (3¼ hrs.). The village of Kemer, called by the Greeks Kamaris, from the subterranean vaults (Καμάραι), which still exist, is situated a short distance from the coast beneath a high cliff. Parium was colonised from Miletus, Erythræa, and Paros, and was enlarged by the kings of Pergamum. It was afterwards made a Roman colony, and adorned with public buildings by Marcus Aurelius; it was noted for an altar, decorated with much magnificence, which was the work of Hermocreon, and measured a stadium each way. The ruins consist of the city walls of white marble, a theatre, an aqueduct, and fragments of masonry.

The road now runs along the coast to *Kiresli Iskelisi,* where it turns up to *Geurijeh* (3 hrs.), a large village in a fertile valley which supplies much charcoal to Constantinople. It then descends to *Boz Burun,* and follows the coast through *Dikileh* (3 hrs.), and *Chardak,* pleasantly situated on the well-cultivated plain, to **Lapsaki,** *Lampsacus* (3 hrs.). From this place there is a lovely ride along the shore of the Hellespont to *Abydos* and the *Dardanelles* (7 hrs.).

---

§ 6. THE DARDANELLES AND THE PLAIN OF TROY.

1. THE DARDANELLES.

All steamers leaving Constantinople for Mediterranean ports call at the Dardanelles; they generally start in the evening and reach the strait early next morning. As the steamers keep to the European coast, which is wanting in beauty, there is little to be seen in the Sea of Marmara.

The **Dardanelles,** which derived its ancient name, *Hellespont,* from the well-known legend of Phryxus and Helle, and takes its modern name from the town of *Dardanus,* is a winding strait having a general S.W. and N.E. direction. Its length is 33 m.; its breadth varies from 1400 yds. to 4 m., and averages about 2 m.; and its depth in mid-channel is 25 to 55 fathoms. There is a marked difference between the two shores of the Dardanelles. On the Asiatic side, low wooded hills, intersected by fertile, well-cultivated valleys, stretch away to the foot of Mount Ida; whilst on the European side the high hills, which rise somewhat abruptly from the water, present a uniformly yellow, and apparently arid aspect. The general direction of the *current* in the Dardanelles is from the Marmara to the Mediterranean; and its average strength is about 1½ knots. After strong northerly winds, however, it has been known to be as much as 5 knots between Chanak Kalesi and Kilid Bahr. After entering the Dardanelles the first place of interest is

Gallipoli, anct. *Kallipolis,* on the European shore, at the mouth of the Sea of Marmara, where the strait is over 5 m. in breadth. It is 25 m. from Chanak Kalesi (Dardanelles), and is situated on the Peninsula known to the Greeks as the *Thracian Chersonese;* it has a small but convenient harbour which is generally full of boats. The *anchorage* in Gallipoli bay is good, and here the British squadron lay in 1878-9. The town, in spite of its large population, and its commercial importance, is a wretched place. It was once fortified, but all that is now left is a tower generally ascribed to Bayezid I. The *bazârs* are well supplied, and usually filled with a picturesque crowd of Turks, Albanians, Greeks, Armenians, &c. On rising ground, on a projecting spit, is a *hospital* built during the Crimean war. The cemeteries are extensive and contain the tombs of many of the Turks who first crossed to Europe, including those of Ajeh Bey, and Ghâzi Fasil, who captured the town, and other Moslem worthies.

Gallipoli was the first European town that fell into the hands of the

Osmanlis, having been taken by them nearly a century before the fall of Constantinople, A.D. 1357. The Emperor John Palæologus, to comfort himself for the loss of Kallipolis and of Choiridocastron (Pig's Fort) said, " he had only lost a jar of wine and a sty for hogs," alluding to the magazines and cellars built by Justinian and to the fortress at Sestos. Bayezid I., knowing the importance of the post for passing from Brûsa to Adrianople, caused Gallipoli to be repaired in 1391, strengthening it with a huge tower, and making a good port for his galleys. Gallipoli, with the lines of Bulair to the N., is the key to Constantinople, the Bosporus, and Black Sea, and was occupied by the English and French as the first step to the Crimean expedition, 1854. Fortifications were thrown up by them across the Isthmus to the Bay of Saros. On the S. side of the city are some tumuli, said to be the sepulchres of the ancient Thracian kings : and N. of the town are some undefined ruins, supposed to be the remains of the ancient city.

On the Asiatic side, nearly opposite Gallipoli, is the vill. of *Chardak*, with its mosque, and 2½ m. lower down, on the same side, is **Lapsaki**, *Lampsacus*, occupying a beautiful position amidst olives and vineyards, with a fine background of wooded hills. The present town is small, and, with the exception of a handsome mosque, offers nothing worthy of notice. Lampsacus was one of the towns given by Xerxes to Themistocles; Magnesia was for his bread, Myus for his meat, and this for his wine.

On the European side, opposite Lapsaki, the bay of Galata ends in *Galata Burnu*, and lower down, on the hills, are the Greek villages of *Galata* and *Bahir* with their numerous windmills. A little beyond Galata is the valley of the **Kara-ova Chai**, anct. *Ægospotamos*, memorable for the victory over the Athenian fleet which Lysander won off its mouth (B.C. 405), and so terminated the Peloponnesian war.

A little below this, on the Asiatic side, is the mouth of the *Burgaz Sû*, Percotes or Praktius (?), draining the rich valley of the same name. On the left bank of the stream, about 3 m. from the coast, is the large vill. *Burgaz* with its 3 minarets; and on the right bank are the ruins of *Percote*. Lower down is the mouth of the *Yapildak Sû*, Praktius (?); and, on the European side, are the valley, *Chamli Dereh*, and, 4 m. lower, **Ak-bashi Liman**, the ancient port of Sestos. On the hill above the bay are the ruins of the Byzantine fortress of *Choiridocastron*, ' Pig's Fort,' built on the site of **Sestos**. It was here that the Osmanli standard was first planted in Europe by Suleiman Pasha, son of Orkhan, A.D. 1356 ; and the spot where the bold adventurer with his little band, landed on the Thracian shore is still called *Ghâzilar Iskelesi*, ' the landing-place of the victors.' Near the old fortress is a *Tekkeh* surrounded by plane-trees and cypresses. A little lower, on the Asiatic side, is *Nagara Kalesi*, a large white fort, from which a long low sandy spit projects to the westward. The high mound, *Mal Tepeh*, at the back of Fort Nagara, is supposed to be the height from which Xerxes surveyed his army and fleet. This was the acropolis of **Abydos**; and the Hellespont, at this place, was called the *Straits of Abydos*.

The Thracian side of the strait, immediately opposite to Nagara Point, is a strip of stony shore projecting from between 2 high cliffs; and to this spot, it seems, the European extremity of Xerxes' bridges must have been applied; for the height of the neighbouring cliffs would have prevented the Persian monarch from adjusting them to any other position. This part of the Dardanelles is likewise memorable as the place where the army of Alexander, under Parmenio, crossed from Europe to Asia; and as that, where the first Osmanlis, under Suleiman Pasha, crossed from Asia to Europe. Here Leander used to swim across to visit Hero. The same feat was performed by Lord Byron, and in recent times by some officers of H.M.S. *Shearwater*, and by Mr. John Thacker Clarke of the

Assos expedition. The *tekkeh* in which Lord Byron resided still exists.

Lower down on the European side are the [deep inlet of *Kilia*, Koelos, and the bay of *Maito*, Madytos; and lower still, where the strait is narrowest, are the famous **Castles of the Dardanelles**, *Boghaz-hissarlari*, erected by Muhammad II., 'the Conqueror.' On the European side, on the slope of a projecting hill, called by the Greeks Kynossema, 'Tomb of the dog,' from the belief that Hecuba, who had been metamorphosed into a dog, was buried there, is **Kilid Bahr**, 'Key of the Sea,' —the 'Castle of Europe.' The fort is of a heart or trefoil shape in plan, with a tall keep, rising in its centre, of a similar shape. Under the Keep there are 8 enormous brass guns of ancient date, which throw stone shot from 20 to 29 inches in diameter. Close to the fort is the vill. of Kilid Bahr, and to the south of it there is a heavily armed modern battery. Towards the close of the Peloponnesian war a naval action was fought off the promontory between the Athenians and Spartans.

On the Asiatic side, at the mouth of the *Rhodius*, is **Sultaniyeh Kalesi**— the 'Castle of Asia'—a massive stone fort with modern batteries, armed with Krupp guns. Inside the fort there are still some of the large brass guns, and stone shot that used to form its armament. Adjoining the fort is the town of **Kaleh Sultaniyeh**, called by Europeans **Dardanelles**, and commonly known as **Chanak Kalesi**.

Situated in the narrowest part of the great channel between the Mediterranean and the Sea of Marmara, as a sort of advanced post to Stambûl, it is visited almost every day by vessels of one nationality or another, which are compelled to stop to show their papers. Consequently, it has opportunities of carrying on a considerable trade in valonia, grain, wine, and pottery, the chief products of the place. The pottery, from which it takes its name, 'Chanak,' though coarse, has a great reputation throughout the Levant. The minarets, the houses painted in various colours, and the flags of the consuls, give the long line of edifices which borders the sea-shore a very gay and lively aspect.

Chanak Kalesi, originally a Genoese settlement, is now the chief town of the Sanjak of Bîgha, and the headquarters of the General commanding the troops in the forts defending the straits, and in the islands of the Archipelago. It is the starting-point for the Troad, and every one landing to make that excursion should try to visit the site of Abydos, whence there is a fine view over the narrowest portion of the Hellespont, and of the numerous batteries on either side. There is a carriage-road from Chanak to Fort Nagara beneath Abydos. Boats can be hired to visit points of interest in the straits.

Below Chanak the European shore is bare and wanting in interest, whilst the Asiatic shore is bordered by rich plains, wooded hills, and picturesque villages. Immediately south of Chanak is the bay in which the British fleet anchored on its way to the Bosporus in 1853; and then follow the site of Dardanus; Eren Keui; Rhoeteum; the tomb of Ajax; the mouth of the Mendere (Scamander), with the plain of Troy and Hissarlik behind it; *Kûm Kaleh*, an old stone fort, with a few houses round it; the tombs of Achilles and Patroclus; and *Cape Yeni-shehr*, the Sigean promontory, with many windmills on the higher ground, from which the low point projects. Between this last point and the Rhoetean promontory to the north was a deep bay, now filled with mud brought down by the Scamander and the Simois, on the shores of which, it is said, the Greeks hauled up their ships during the Trojan war. Opposite Kûm Kaleh, at the extremity of the Thracian Chersonese, and distant $2\frac{1}{4}$ m., is the large fortress of *Sidd elbahr*, with a lighthouse, and a modern battery near it. These two forts, the new castles of Asia and Europe, were built by Muhammad IV., in 1659, to defend the entrance to the Dardanelles, and secure his fleet from the insults of the Venetians who used to attack it in sight of the old castles.

Near Sidd el-bahr is a tumulus, said to be the tomb of Protesilaus, the first Greek who was killed, on landing, in the Trojan war. About 1½ m. higher up the strait is *Eski Hissarlik*, with the ruins of Elaeus, a place often mentioned in the history of the Peloponnesian war. In A.D. 323 the fleet of Constantine was at Elaeus, whilst that of Licinius was anchored off the tomb of Ajax.

2. PLAIN OF TROY.

Dardanelles—	hrs.		hrs.
Eren Keui . .	3	Ujek Tepeh . .	2
Chiplak . .	2¼	Yeni Keui . .	1¼
Bûnarbashi (by		Kûm Kaleh . .	2¼
Thymbra) .	2¼	Dardanelles . .	5

An *excursion to the plain of Troy* can best be made from the Dardanelles (Chanak Kalesi, or Kaleh Sultaniyeh). Three days are required for a visit to all the places of interest in the historic plain, but two will suffice for Hissarlik (Troy) alone. Leave Constantinople in the evening; arrive Dardanelles early next morning. *1st day.* Visit Abydos, and in the afternoon ride to Eren Keui; *2nd day.* Hissarlik, Bûnarbashi, Ujek Tepeh, Yeni Keui · *3rd day.* Yeni-shehr, Kûm Kaleh, Rhoeteum, Palaeo Kastro, Dardanelles. Travellers not sleeping at Eren Keui and unprovided with tents must cross the plain from Hissarlik to Yeni-shehr and find quarters there. The excursion is one that can only be recommended to students of Homer, antiquarians, and archæologists. The scenery is wanting in grandeur; the interesting articles found by Dr. Schliemann are in museums at Berlin, Athens, and Constantinople : and the untrained eye will find little that is attractive in the confused mass of ruins at Hissarlik.

Travellers visiting Troy from Constantinople will find daily communication with the Dardanelles; those continuing their journey to Smyrna must arrange to catch the steamer at the Dardanelles or at Tenedos. Spring or late autumn is the best time for the excursion, as in summer and early autumn the malaria from the marshy plains occasionally causes intermittent fever. After the middle of November the swollen streams generally make travelling difficult.

A *dragoman*, knowing the roads and localities, and a little English or French, who will procure lodgings in the villages and act as a sort of personal attendant on the traveller, can be found at the Dardanelles for 8 to 10 francs per day. Nothing more, except a little superior knowledge of European languages, can be looked for in the dragoman obtained at Constantinople, whose terms will generally be higher. In neither one nor the other must the traveller seek for any acquaintance with antiquarian subjects. Mr. Frank Calvert, the American Consul, is a great authority on the local antiquities, and would, no doubt, give all travellers, who are properly introduced, any information they may require before going into the interior, should he happen to be on the spot.

The traveller would do well to take a camp bed, blankets, mosquito *net*, preserved meats, candles, lantern, and English saddle and bridle with him from Constantinople. Fair quarters can be obtained at Eren Keui, Yeni Keui, and Yeni-shehr, but a tent will be found cleaner and more comfortable. Horses for the excursion should be hired at the Dardanelles. They are to be had for about P. 30 to 40 a day, including their keep, and the food and pay of the *suruji* who accompanies them. Horses can be obtained sometimes at Yeni Keui, Yeni-shehr, and Kûm Kaleh. A coasting steamer which runs once a week from the Dardanelles to Mitylene touches at Yeni Keui, and a boat can be hired to go to Kûm Kaleb, from either of which places the plain may be visited if horses can be obtained. A *yol-tezkerch* is necessary, and if it be intended to spend more than a week in the country a *buyuruldu* should be obtained from the Governor of the Dardanelles through the Consul. A mounted policeman (*Zabtieh*) affords similar protection, and can be obtained through the Consul.

MAP OF THE
PLAIN OF TROY.

English Miles.

Br. Bridge; C. Cemetery; F. Fountain;
R. Ruin; T. Tumulus; W. Well.

H E L L E S P O N T

Ancient Mole

Site of
Ancient Cap.

Erenkeui

Ophrynium

Rhoeteum

Bunarbaschi Kogu

Dumbrek R.

Simois R.

In Tepé

Chablak

C.

C.

Kalifatli

Sana Br.

Kum Kaleh

Avigaou Gate

Aeanteum
Tomb of Ajax

Old Bunarbaschi

W. Ilus

W. Major

Wooden Br.

Sana Br.

Marsh

Kurukeui

Bostazi

Ancient Ruins

W.

P   L   A

Tombs of Achilles
and Patroclus

Sigeum Pr.

Sigeum?
Yeni Shehr

Tomb of Antilochus

Sigeum?
(Site of ancient City)

A

E

Geukyeri Pr.

GEUKYERI
BAY

Longitude 26°10' East of Greenwich.

London; John Murray, Albemarle Street, W.

F. S. Weller.

On leaving the Dardanelles the road crosses the *Sari Chai*, anct. Rhodius, by the side of which there is a promenade shaded by plane-trees. It then runs along the plain, by the edge of the sea, to a slight eminence upon which stood *Dardanus*—a city formerly called Teucris. Mal Tepeh, a small truncated hill rising on the extremity of a spur of land, marks the site of the ancient Acropolis, and foundations may be traced round it on all sides. This town, an Æolian settlement, was never a place of importance. It was here Cornelius Sylla, the Roman general, and Mithridates, surnamed Eupator, terminated the war by a treaty of peace. The Romans made it a free city in honour of the Trojan descent of the people. Its autonomous coins are rare. The old town of Dardanus, which was more ancient than Ilium, appears from the Iliad to have been at the foot of Mount Ida. After crossing a low spur, a few houses on the shore of a small bay (2¼ hrs.), where there was a British hospital during the Crimean war, is reached. Here the road leaves the sea, and strikes up a hill to the left, winding round a deep gorge, and gradually revealing a lovely view of the entrance to the Hellespont, and of Imbros and Samothrace beyond the Thracian Chersonese. On the top of the hill, about 550 ft. above the sea, is *Eren Keui*, or Ren Keui (¾ hrs.), a very rich Greek village, called by the Turks *It Geulmez*. It is surrounded by vineyards and orchards, and figs, peaches, pears, apricots, &c., grow in the greatest profusion. There is a fine view over the plain of Troy to the cone of Tenedos. From Eren Keui the road descends through scattered park-like wood to the valley of the Dümbrek Sü, *Simois*, crosses the river (1¼ hrs.), below the Turkish village of *Halil-eli*, and then ascends to Chiplak (1 hr.), a small village, containing many fragments of Greek and Roman buildings brought from Ilium. Hence a path leads over ground covered with brushwood to Hissarlik (½ hr.).

[The following route may be taken from Eren Keui:—Ophrynium, Rhoeteum, Tomb of Ajax (1 hr.), Küm Keui (¾ hr.), Hissarlik (½ hr.).]

The **Plain of Troy** comprises that angle of the Troad which is bounded by the Hellespont on the N., and the Ægean Sea on the W. Away to the S.E., 30 m. distant, rises Mount Ida, covered with snow during the entire winter and early spring. From it long, rugged spurs, mostly clothed with forests of valonia oak, extend to the sea, intersecting the plain of Troy, and enclosing valleys through which flow three principal streams, the Dümbrek or *Simois*, the Kemer or *Thymbrius*, and the Mendere or *Scamander*. The Scamander runs through a broad marshy vale northwards into the Hellespont, and, owing to the nature of the ground and winter torrents, has evidently changed its bed more than once. The Dümbrek and the Kemer fall into the same vale; the latter joins the Scamander; the former has a separate mouth near In Tepeh (tomb of Ajax), though probably it joined the Scamander in classic times. All of them, however, are winter torrents, which are usually dry in autumn. Along the western side of the valley of the Scamander, separating it from the Ægean, is a low bare ridge, dotted here and there with *tumuli*, and having upon it several villages; at the southern end of this ridge is the now celebrated anchorage Besika Bay. Still farther S., some 3 m. from the shore, is the island of Tenedos.

The plain of Troy, like most plains in Asia Minor, is marshy. Its soil is naturally fertile. The miasma rising from the swamps occasionally produces fever during summer and autumn. Were the plain drained and properly cultivated, it would become healthy; and with the green brushwood on the lower hills, and the park-like groves on the mountain sides, the aspect of the whole country would be improved. A large amount of draining has been done on his estate by the late Mr. Consul Calvert. The traveller can avoid fever generally by a few precautions. He ought not to expose himself to the dew or to bathe in rivers, and to be careful the water he drinks be pure. A grain or two of quinine is a great prophylactery.

The view from the higher points on the plain of Troy is wide and grand. On the E. is Ida, with its snowy crest, encircled by peaks and dark ridges that cluster round it: on the W. is the coast-line, flanked all along by undulating high land, beyond which are the bright waters of the Ægean, studded with islands. Nearest us Tenedos; farther off, Lemnos, vast and mountainous; more to the N. the low ledge of Imbros, over which Neptune looked down upon old Troy from the peaks of "far off" Samothrace. On the N., across the plain, is the Hellespont, and beyond it the low, bleak coast of Thrace; and far away, dimly seen on the horizon, the pyramid of Mount Athos. Such was the grand panorama over which Priam may have looked from the citadel of Troy.

The halo which Homer's great poem cast round the city and territory of Troy caused them to be reverenced in all ages; Alexander the Great visited the tumuli of the Trojan heroes on his passage, and conferred honours on Ilium Novum, believing that it stood on the foundations of Old Troy. He also founded on the coast of Troy the city of Alexandria, which flourished under both Greeks and Romans. Constantine the Great entertained at one time the idea of founding the capital of his future empire on the shores of the Hellespont instead of on those of the Bosporus.

The Troad does not appear to have been of equal importance in the Byzantine period, to judge from the few ruins of that epoch to be met with in it; nor are there many notices in the Byzantine historians or mediæval writers respecting it.

The position of Troy itself has always indeed engaged the attention of scholars, but it is not our province to go deeply into the question in these pages; we can but broadly state the facts of the case, leaving others to form their own conclusion from an examination of the localities.

There are in the plain two claimants for the site of Troy—*Hissarlik* and *Bûnarbashi.* The former is on the E. bank of the Scamander, 3 m. from the Hellespont; the latter is on the W. bank, 5 m. further S. The claim of Hissarlik is maintained by Dr. Schliemann, Mr. Frank Calvert, and Mr. Gladstone; while the advocates of Bûnarbashi number, among others, Leake, Texier, Forchhammer, and Tozer.

To Bûnarbashi it has been objected that it is too far from the sea to accord with descriptions in the 'Iliad,' and that the ground around it is too rugged to allow of chariot races being run in its immediate vicinity, or of Achilles chasing Hector round the walls of the city. On the other hand, it has been objected to Hissarlik that it lacks the rugged features mentioned by Homer, that its citadel is too low, and that the site is much too small for a great city. In judging of the site, several things must be borne in mind; taking it for granted that there was such a city as Troy, and that the descriptions given by Homer are not altogether imaginary. Primæval cities, as a rule, were very small—they were, in fact, castles rather than cities; and the ancients, especially poets, were wont to exaggerate their size, the numbers of their armies, and of their assailants. Then, again, the natural features of the plain of Troy must have undergone a great change in the course of 3000 years. The ancient cities are buried deep beneath the soil; craggy steeps have been rounded off, and ravines filled up, as at Jerusalem. The excavations of Schliemann have shown what an immense accumulation of rubbish covers the remains of the earliest buildings. The beds of rivers, too, have changed their places; and even fountains which once sent forth copious streams may have dried up, or become choked with *débris.*

TROY.

Hissarlik† has been long known as the site of *Ilium Novum*, and the most recent researches, especially those of Dr. Schliemann, seem to identify it with the Troy of Homer. "The site of Ilium is upon a plateau lying on an average about 80 ft. above the plain, and descending very abruptly on the N. side. Its north-western corner is formed by a hill, about 26 ft. higher still, which is 705 ft. in breadth and 984 in length, and from its imposing situation and natural fortifications, this hill of *Hissarlik* seems specially suited to be the Acropolis of the town." The stream of the Dûmbrek or *Simois* flows past a short distance from the northern base of the hill, and joins what appears to be the ancient bed of the Scamander about half a mile to the N.W. The Scamander runs to the W. of Hissarlik. The view from the top of the hill is very extensive, embracing the whole plain of Troy, the mountain ranges on the S.E., with the islands that stud the Ægean Sea.

Ilium Novum was founded, according to some—rebuilt as successor of the *Old Ilium*, according to others—by an Æolian colony long after the Trojan war. It was greatly embellished by Alexander the Great, Lysimachus, and the Cæsars; all of whom believed it to be the site of Troy. Under the Byzantine Emperors it fell into decay, but did not entirely perish; for when Suleiman halted at this place in 1357, before crossing the Hellespont, he found some fine edifices still standing. Dr. Schliemann says, in regard to the disputed sites of Troy: —" In my work, *Ithaca, the Peloponnesus and Troy*, published in 1869, I endeavoured to prove, both by the result of my own excavations and by the statements of the Iliad, that the Homeric Troy cannot possibly have

† Consult 'Asie Mineure,' by Texier, 8vo. Didot Frères, 1862; Leake's 'Plains of Troy,' 1 vol., with map; Lord Derby's translation of the 'Iliad'; Tozer's 'Highlands of Turkey,' Murray, 1869; and Schliemann's Ilios, 1880, and 'Troy and its Remains,' 1875, and his 'Ithaca, the Peloponnesus and Troy,' 1869.

been situated on the heights of Bûnarbashi, to which place most archæologists assign it. At the same time I endeavoured to explain that the site of Troy must necessarily be identical with the site of that town which, throughout all antiquity, and down to its complete destruction at the end of the eighth or the beginning of the ninth century A.D., was called Ilium, and not until 1000 years after its disappearance—that is, 1788 A.D.—was christened Ilium Novum by Le Chevalier, who, as his work proves, can never have visited his *Ilium Novum*; for in his map he places it on the other side of the Scamander, close to Kûm Kaleh, and therefore 4 miles from its true position. Ever since my first visit, I never doubted that I should find the Pergamus of Priam in the depths of this hill."

Previous to Von Hahn, Mr. Frank Calvert made excavations at Bali Dagh (Bûnarbashi). His discoveries proved the remains to be of later date than he expected to find. He was led to change his belief as to the identity of the site with Troy, and to place here the ancient city of *Gergis*. He then commenced excavations at Hissarlik, which he now held to be the veritable site of Troy. The heavy expense of removing the large mound put a stop to the excavations, which were fortunately resumed with such success by Dr. Schliemann.

Dr. Schliemann's discoveries at Hissarlik, whatever may be thought of the conclusions he has drawn from them, must be regarded as among the most remarkable in modern times. He began his excavations in 1870, and continued them, amid great difficulties and opposition, for nearly 4 years, entirely at his own expense. He found an accumulation of rubbish and ruins on the top of the hill no less than 52 ft. in thickness; through this he dug down to the native rock, laying bare four successive strata of remains, each representing a distinct city, which had been erected successively on the same site. Of these strata, Mr. Smith remarks in his introduction to Schliemann's work:—

" First, Homer recognises a city which preceded the Ilium of Priam, and which had been destroyed by Hercules; and Schliemann found a primæval city of considerable civilisation, on the native rock, below the ruins which he regards as the Homeric Troy. Tradition speaks of a Phrygian population of which the Trojans were a branch, as having apparently displaced, and driven over into Europe, the kindred Pelasgians. Above the second (Trojan) stratum are the remains of a third city, which, in the type and patterns of its terra-cottas, instruments, and ornaments, shows a close resemblance to the second; and the link of connection is riveted by the inscriptions in the same character in both strata. And so, in the Homeric poems, every reader is struck with the common bonds of genealogy and language, traditions and mutual intercourse, religion and manners, between the Greeks who assail Troy and the Trojans who defend it. If the legend of the Trojan war preserves the tradition of a real conquest of the city by a kindred race, the very nature of the case forbids us to accept literally the story, that the conquerors simply sailed away again. It is far more reasonable to regard the ten years of the war, and the ten years of the return of the chiefs, as cycles of ethnic struggles, the details of which had been sublimed into poetical traditions. The fact that Schliemann traces in the third stratum a civilisation lower than in the second, is an objection only from the point of view of our classical prepossessions. There are not wanting indications in Homer that the Trojans were more civilised and wealthy than the Greeks; and in the much earlier age to which the conflict (if real at all) must have belonged, we may be sure that the Asiatic people had over their European kindred an advantage which we may venture to symbolise by the golden arms of Glaucus and the brazen arms of Diomed. Xanthus, the old historian of Lydia, preserves

the tradition of a reflux migration of Phrygians from Europe into Asia, after the Trojan war, and says that they conquered Troy and settled in its territory. This migration is ascribed to the pressure of the barbarian Thracians; and the fourth stratum, with its traces of merely wooden buildings, and other marks of a lower stage of civilisation, corresponds to that conquest of the Troad by those same barbarian Thracians, the tradition of which is preserved by Herodotus and other writers."

Schliemann considers that the *First Settlement* on Hissarlik was of the longest duration, as its ruins cover the rock to a height of from 13 to 20 ft. Its houses and walls were built of stone, joined with earth. The vessels and other objects of terra-cotta found among these ruins were of a quality superior to those in the upper strata. They are of black, red, or brown colour, ornamented with patterns incised and filled with a white substance. The people, Schliemann supposes, belonged to the Aryan race, as Aryan symbols were found on the pottery.

The *Second Settlement* was composed, according to Schliemann, of the Trojans; and the *débris* of their city lies from 23 to 33 ft. below the surface. This stratum bears marks of having been exposed to intense heat, consisting largely of red ashes of wood, which rise from 5 to 10 ft. above the tower of Ilium, the Scæan Gate, and the enclosed wall: they show that the town was destroyed by a fearful conflagration. A farther proof of the action of fire is a stratum of scoriæ of melted lead and copper, from ⅓ to 1½ of an inch thick, extending nearly through the whole hill. Among the *débris* were found human bones, skeletons with helmets, vast quantities of terra-cotta in fragments, and, most wonderful of all, " The Treasure of Priam." This treasure was discovered by the side of the palace, at a depth of 27 ft., covered with from 5 to 6 ft. of ashes, above which was a post-Trojan wall,

19 ft. high. The articles, packed in a small cist made of slabs of stone, consist of vases, bottles, cups and dishes of gold, silver, and electrum; caldrons and shields of copper; bracelets, rings, chains, and many other ornaments of gold; battle-axes, spear-heads, swords, and daggers of copper; and many other articles, some of which are fused together by fire. The intrinsic value of this treasure is very great, and its archæological value is, of course, much greater.

None of the articles in the treasure contain inscriptions; but inscriptions were found on vases of terra-cotta, seals, and other objects, the purpose of which is unknown. Among the latter are great numbers of little disks of pottery, called "whorls" by Schliemann, and supposed to be either household idols or votive offerings, others imagine them to have been used in spinning. The letters of the inscriptions resemble to some extent those upon tablets and terra-cottas in Cyprus, and seem to be allied to the ancient Phœnician: but they have not yet been satisfactorily deciphered.

The *Third Settlement* on Hissarlik was by Greeks. The ruins of their city make up a stratum 10 ft. or more in thickness, containing pottery of a coarser kind than the Trojan, marked with religious symbols; also containing fragments of copper implements and weapons, and musical instruments made of stone and ivory. The architecture was not so massive as the Trojan, the walls being of small stones mixed with clay; and also occasionally of sun-dried brick. The *débris* presented one peculiar feature: it contained immense quantities of small mussel-shells, bones, and fish-bones. Then follow two other settlements of similar character. The sixth Dr. Schliemann supposes to be Lydian. Mr. Calvert from the style of pottery believed this settlement to be Æolic Greek.

Schliemann adds, regarding an upper or surface stratum, the seventh, which covers Hissarlik:—"When the surface of the hill was about 2 mètres lower than it is now, Ilium was built by a Greek colony; and we have already endeavoured to prove that this settlement must have been founded about the year B.C. 700. From that time we find the remains of Hellenic house-walls of large hewn stones, joined without cement. . . . We also meet with great numbers of copper coins of Ilium, of the time of the Roman Empire, from Augustus to Constans II. and Constantine II., likewise older Ilian coins with the image of Athena, and medals of Alexandria Troas. . . . In my three years' excavations I have not found a single medal of a later date than Constantine II. . . . And as there is here not the remotest trace of Byzantine masonry or of Byzantine pottery, it may be regarded as certain that the Ilium of the Greek colony was destroyed towards the middle of the fourth century after Christ, and that no village, much less a town, has ever again been built upon its site." He adds:—"To judge from the area of the Ilium of the Greek colony, it may have possessed 100,000 inhabitants. It must have been rich, and the plastic art must have attained a high degree of perfection. The site is strewn with fragments of excellent sculptures."

As to the extent of the Troy of Homer, Schliemann says it was confined to the small area of the hill of Hissarlik, and could not, therefore, have contained more than 5000 inhabitants; but, he adds, it could always raise a considerable army from among its subjects, and as it was rich and powerful, it could obtain mercenaries from all quarters. Mr. Smith suggests that Hissarlik contained simply the palace and permanent citadel, while the houses of the great body of the citizens were scattered over the surrounding region. Be this as it may, there seems to be good ground for believing that we have here the real site of the Troy of Priam, which Homer has immortalised. According to ancient tradition, Troy was founded by Tros, B.C. 1462. He was succeeded by Ilus, and by Laomedon, under the latter of whom the walls were built. The fall of Troy, according to the chronology of Herodotus, was in B.C. 1270; according to the inscription from Paros in 1209; and according to Eratosthenes in B.C. 1184.

Returning to Chiplak and continuing towards the S. the road passes near an oval barrow and a Turkish cemetery. To the E. of the barrow are the ruins of a temple, possibly that of Venus, consisting of a few frusta of columns and some portions of walls half-buried.

Akchi Keui, or Batak, 1½ hr.—A former village on an eminence, now occupied by a large Chiftlik, called *Thymbra Farm.* This place is considered by some to be Callicolone, whence Mars and Apollo, the protectors of Troy, watched the operations of the rival armies. Mr. Calvert makes this the site of *Thymbra.*

The road to Bûnarbashi leads near two tumuli. The largest of these, on the river Thymbrius, is a truncated cone 30 ft. high and about 100 ft. diameter at the base. It is called *Khanai Tepeh,* and is supposed by some to be the tomb of Troilus, son of Priam. Recent explorations have brought to light remains contemporary with the earlier settlements at Hissarlik. It was next used as a prehistoric cemetery, the bodies being buried on their left side with the hand under the head, resting on a stone (sometimes a quern), and the legs doubled up. Next it served as a sacrificial enclosure; the wood ashes are to be seen several feet in depth with circular flat altars of sun-dried brick at different levels. Again it was turned into a cemetery in Hellenic and Byzantine times. It marks probably the site of pre-historic Thymbra, as Akchi Keui does the later town. The other, Harman Tepeh, is a natural mound. A quarter of an hour after passing the tumuli, the Scamander is forded close to its junction with the Thymbrius. The temple of Apollo Thymbrius, where Achilles was smitten by the arrow of Paris, is supposed to have stood here.

Bûnarbashi, 1 hr.—A small Turkish village at the foot of a gentle ascent which terminates in an elevated plateau, formerly supposed to be the Pergamus of Troy.

[From Chiplak to Bûnarbashi by the direct road is 2 hrs.; and the latter place can be reached in the same time from Hissarlik, passing by *Pasha Tepeh,* excavated without results by Mrs. Schliemann in 1873.]

Mr. Frank Calvert considers Bûnarbashi to be the site of Gergithus, or, as it is also called, Gergis. But Mr. Tozer suggests it is quite possible that Gergithus was the Greek city which replaced the more ancient one. Gergithus was handed over to the people of New Ilium, 188 B.C.

To reach the hill, ascend the rising ground S.E. of the village towards a barrow which is visible from it. This tumulus will be found to be one of three standing near one another. The first is composed of small stones, and measures 20 paces from top to bottom. This goes by the name of the *Tomb of Hector.* It was excavated by Sir John Lubbock without result. The second tumulus is the largest: it has been excavated by Mr. Frank Calvert, who carried a shaft through it, and discovered in the centre a square structure built of irregular masonry, measuring about 14 ft. by 12, apparently the base of an altar or shrine. The third, which is smaller than the other two, and flat on the top, has the appearance of a mere mound of heaped earth. It was excavated by Dr. Schliemann but nothing was found. A fourth tumulus, apart from the rest on the road from Ezinch to Bûnarbashi, was also excavated. A square-built Greek tomb was found in the centre of the mound. A golden crown in the form of oak leaves and acorns and other objects were found. These relics are now in the Imperial Museum at Constantinople. The view from the tomb of Hector is more extensive than from any other spot. It embraces the whole plain of Troy to the sea, which is 7 m. distant.

Farther to the S. the ridge is crossed by a low mound; beyond this, the ridge contracts to a narrow neck, and a short steep ascent leads to the site of the so-called Acropolis, which is bounded by precipices 400 ft. deep on three sides. At the foot of these rocks winds the Scamander. On the opposite side of the river rise high banks, intersected by deep valleys.

In the spring of 1864 important excavations were made on the Acropolis by Von Hahn, the Austrian Consul at Syra, an indefatigable explorer of the antiquities of Turkey. He traced the line of the outer walls throughout their whole circuit, except on the southern side, where the natural defences of the position rendered them unnecessary. At the western extremity of the area he discovered a bastion and a gateway, constructed like those at Assos, on the principle of the horizontal arch. The older portions of the walls (those on the N.) were of Cyclopean masonry, and point to a period of the highest antiquity.

Mr. F. Calvert discovered the ancient Necropolis outside the walls. The tombs consisted of large earthen jars, πίθοι, which contained unburnt bones. He considers them to be of a later period than the heroic age. Those he examined contained pottery of the 5th century B.C.

[From Bûnarbashi the traveller, if he is bound for Smyrna, and does not wish to return to the Dardanelles, may go on to Geyikli Scala (3½ hrs.), and thence cross to Tenedos (1 hr. by boat with a favourable wind), and meet the fortnightly Austrian steamer from Constantinople to Smyrna which touches there every alternate Friday morning, or from Smyrna to Constantinople every alternate Monday. The Hellespont Tug Company runs a weekly steamer, from the Dardanelles to Aivali, calling at Yeni Keui, Tenedos, Petra and Molivo (ancient *Methymna*, island of Mitylene), and Behram (*Assos*), when there are passengers. Information as to these and other lines of steamers which touch at Tenedos can be obtained at the

Dardanelles, or from the quarantine official at *Geyikli*, which village is on the way to the *scala*.]

From Bûnarbashi a road leads in 10 minutes to the springs called by the Turks *Kirk Geuz* (forty eyes); they issue from a conglomerate, and, after watering several gardens in the vicinity, swell into a small stream, which is conducted by an artificial channel to turn some flour mills, and finally fall into the Ægean, at Besika Bay. There are two distinct sources, about a quarter of a mile apart, each consisting of several springs. According to Le Chevalier, these are the hot and cold sources of the Scamander, but recent observations have proved that they are both of the same temperature.

The path now follows the Bûnarbashi stream for abour 2 m., passing along the foot of the *Throsmos*, and then turns up the hill to **Ujek Tepeh** (2 hrs.), the highest and most conspicuous tumulus in the Troad. It is more than 60 ft. high, and stands on a natural mound. According to some authorities the tumulus is the tomb of Ilus son of Tros; but Dr. Schliemann who excavated it and found a core of masonry in the centre considers that it was erected by Caracalla in honour of his friend Festus, who died in the Troad. From Ujek Tepeh the path descends to the Bûnarbashi stream, and after crossing it passes traces of a bath and well, built by Alexander the Great with stones brought from Troy. A little further, near the north end of Besika Bay, are *Besik Tepeh*, and *Palaeo Kastro* (1 hr.), the site of *Agamia*, built in memory of Hesione, daughter of Laomedon and the young girls of Troy, who were exposed on the shore to the violence of the pirate Ceton, who was incited by Neptune. Hercules, however, arrived in time to rescue Hesione. In ½ hour more **Yeni Keui**, *Neochori*, a Greek village in which fair quarters can be obtained, is reached.

From Yeni Keui the road runs along the ridge of Sigeum, whence there are fine views over the plain, to an artificial trench called the *Trench of Hercules*, from the tradition that Hercules made it as a defence against Ceton. A few minutes to the N. are the *Tepeh*, and *Church of S. Demetrius*. The latter is built out of the ruins of a temple, the former is natural rock.

Yeni-shehr, *Sigeum* (1½ hr.), is situated on a high headland on the border of the sea. It is called by English sailors "Janissary Point," and is readily identified by the row of windmills near it, which are conspicuous objects from the sea.

Sigeum is said to have been an Æolian colony, founded by Archæonax of Mitylene, who used the stones of old Troy for its construction. The Athenians expelled the Mityleneans, and a war sprang up in which Pittakus of Mitylene, one of the seven sages, slew Phrynon, the Athenian leader. The poet Alcæus was engaged in this war. At length the matter was referred to Periander of Corinth, who decided in favour of Athens. From this time the Peisistratidæ possessed Sigeum. After the overthrow of the Persian kingdom, Sigeum was destroyed by the people of Ilium. The church is built on the ruins of a Temple of Minerva, of which some traces exist. Two important inscriptions were found here in the 18th century.

About 20 minutes N. of Yeni-shehr are the two tumuli called the *Tombs of Achilles and Patroclus*. The smaller tumulus is perhaps that of Antilochus, as the ashes of Achilles and Patroclus were apparently deposited in the same tomb. Their tumulus is described by Homer as being a landmark for sailors passing the headland. The tomb of Achilles was much venerated in ancient times and a small town seems to have sprung up near it under the name of Achilleum. There is said also to have been a temple dedicated to Achilles, but no traces of it remain. The tomb was visited by Alexander the Great, Julius Cæsar, and Germanicus. From the tumuli the road descends through gardens and vineyards to

Kûm Kaleh (¾ hr.), "Sand Castle," a small town, which derives its name from the adjoining castle. Hence the road runs westward crossing by bridges the several channels, including the *Kalifatli Asmak*, through which the flood waters of the Scamander find their way to the sea. The sterile tract of land through which the streams run occupies the place of the bay on the shores of which the Greeks hauled up their ships. At the eastern end is *In Tepeh* (1 hr.), or *Tomb of Ajax*, a conspicuous tumulus on the slopes of the Rhœtean promontory. An opening in the mound leads to a double-vaulted chamber in the interior; and on the top of the tumulus are the ruins of the Heroön of Ajax, which was restored in Roman times. About ½ m. farther is *Rhœteum*, where are the traces of the Acropolis and other ruins. **Palaeo Kastro,** the anct. *Ophrynium* (40 min.), is near the shore. It derives its name from ὀφρύς, as it is on the "brow of a hill" where was a grove sacred to Hector. A few traces of the Acropolis walls are visible, and foundations of buildings extend down the hill to the Hellespont, where the remains of a mole may be seen under water on a calm day. There are autonomous but no imperial coins of Ophrynium. Hence the road continues to Eren Keui (20 min.) and Dardanelles (3 hrs.).

INDEX AND DIRECTORY.
1894–95.

———◦◦———

(P.) = ·Pera. ·
(G.) = Galata.
(S.) = Stambûl.
P. = Piastre.
The first number after the name indicates the page on which the place is described.

A.

Abdul Hamid I., Sebîl of, **74.**
Abdul Hamid, Türbeh of, **65.**
Abdul Mejid, Türbeh of, **64.**
Abûl Vefa Mosque, **51.**
ABYDOS, **136, 103, 137.**
Achilles, Tomb of, **146.**

ADABAZAR, 117.
  Station : Anatolian Rly.
  Carriages run to the town 5¼ m. distant.
ADALIA, **[2].**
ADAM KAYA, **133.**
Adileh Sultan, Türbeh of, **22.**
Admiralty, **20.**
ADRIANOPLE, **[5], 4, 66.**
Adrianople Gate, **24, 25, 72, 74.**
ÆGEAN SEA, **140, [18].**
ÆSEPUS RIVER, **134.**
AFRICAN TURKEY, **[19].**
Agia Sofia Jami', **132.**
Agriculture, **[24].**
Ahmed I., Türbeh of, **62.**
Ahmed I., Mosque of, **61, 4.**
Ahmediyeh Mosque, **61, 4, 108.**
Ahmed Pasha Mesjidi, **57.**
Ahmed III., Fountain of. **73.**
Ainajilar Charshi, The, **75.**
AINALI KAVAK, **14.**
Ainali Kavak Palace, **21, 4.**
AIVALI, **145.**
  Turkey.—viii. **95.**

AIVAN SERAI, **14, 17, 18, 25, 57.**
Aivan Serai Kapusi, **28, 39.**
Aivas Effendi Mosque, **37, 38.**
Aivat Bend, **99, 98.**
Ajax, Tomb of, **146.**

AJEMLAR, 121.
  Station : Brûsa Rly. for Chekirgeh and the baths.
AKBABA, **104.**
AK-BASHI LIMÂN, **136.**

AK-BUNAR, 119.
  Station : Anatolian Rly.
AKCHI KEUI, **144.**
Akhir Kapusi, **30, 65.**

AK-HISSAR, 118.
  Nahieh of Geiveh.
  Station : Anatolian Rly.
AKINDI BURNU, **92.**
AKSAS, **134.**
AK SERAI, **25, 64, 65.**
AKSU, **127.**
ALBANIA, **[18].**
ALEM DÂGH, **85.**
ALEXANDRETTA, **[2].**
ALI BEY KEUI, **86.**
ALI BEY KEUI SÛ RIVER, **14, 74, 98, 99.**
ALTI MERMER, **23, 53, 72.**

ALPI-KEUI, 119.
  Station : Anatolian Rly.
American College (for girls), **78.**
American Khân, **78.**
ANADOLI FANAR, **102, 87, 104.**
ANADOLI HISSAR, **105, 6, 88, 93, 94.**
ANADOLI KAVAK, **102, 103, 97, 99, 100.**
ANAPLUS, **106.**
ANATOLIA, **[18].**

Ancient Costumes, Museum of, **70.**
Anemas, Tower of, **38, 32.**
ANGORA, **119.**
  H. B. M. Consul ; H. A. Cumberbatch, Esq.
ANTIGONE, **112.**
ANTI-LEBANON, MOUNT, **[19].**
Antiquities, Museum of, **69, 66.**
ANTIROBITHOS, **113.**
ANTI TAURUS MOUNTAINS, **[18].**
APSUS RIVER, **[18].**
Aqueducts, **98, 99.**
ARABIA, **[18], [19].**
Arab Jami', **16, 18.**
ARAPLI, **115.**
ARARAT, MOUNT, **[18].**
Arcadius, Baths of, **65.**
Arcadius, Column of, **43, 23.**
Arcadius, Forum of, **25, 43.**
ARGANTHONIUS, MOUNT, **115, 120.**
ARGÆUS, MOUNT, **[18].**
Argonauts, The, **101, 88, 92.**
ARMENIA, **[2].**
Armenian Cemetery, **19, 84.**
Armenian Church, **53, 11.**
Armenian Hospital, **34, 86.**
Armoury, **66.**
ARMUDLI, **120.**
Army, **[23].**
Army Medical School, **78.**
ARNAÛT KEUI, **104, 87, 88, 92, 100.**
Arsenal, **20.**
Art, **81.**
ARTAKI, **134.**
Artillery Barrac'cs, **77, 19.**
Artillery School, **73.**
Art School, **82, 66, 77.**

M

Constantine, Column of, **42**, 11.

Constantine, Forum of, **24**, **64.**

CONSTANTINOPLE, [1], 1–87.

Arrival: *By sea.* As the steamer approaches her moorings she is surrounded by a fleet of boats and kaïks ; and, directly the Quarantine officials allow communication with the shore, she is boarded by a crowd of Hotel dragomans and boatmen, all clamorous for employment. The principal hotels send dragomans to await the arrival of the steamers ; they carry hotel cards, and have the names of their hotels on their caps and generally on their boats. The traveller should look sharply after his small hand-packages until he has handed them over to the dragoman of the hotel he has selected ; he may then trust all the arrangements for landing to the dragoman, and pay him on arrival at the hotel. If there be no hotel dragoman the traveller should pick out the most respectable looking of those on the ship, tell him the hotel he wishes to go to, and pay him nothing until all the baggage has been safely delivered. On leaving the ship the boat goes to the *Galata Custom House*, near the outer bridge, where passports have to be shown before permission to land is granted. The passports are generally retained by the police, and sent later on to the Consulate of the country to which the travellers belong, and there they remain until the owners send for them. Baggage is examined either at the Galata Custom House or at the special *Custom House* beside the landing-place of the Messageries Maritimes which, being less crowded, will be found more convenient by European travellers. A *bakhshish* of 1–2 francs will usually smoothe the way through the Custom House, but searchers are sometimes troublesome, and seize books and printed matter for reference to the censor (see *Custom House*, p. [6]). After passing the Custom House

the luggage is placed on the backs of porters (*hammâl*), and the traveller walks or drives to his hotel ; if it is his first visit he had better walk and keep with the porters carrying his baggage. The *cost of disembarkation* depends partly on the amount of baggage, and partly on the rank of the traveller, and the class of hotel to which he is going ; it varies from 5–10 fr. a head, for boat, dragoman, porters, and bakhshish. The ordinary charges are :—*Boat* from ship to shore, 2 fr. a head, an extra payment is expected when there is much luggage ; *carriage* Custom House to hotel, 2 fr. (P. 10) ; *porter*, 1–2 fr. (P. 5–10), according to weight.

N.B. Do not be in a hurry to land ; and do not pay the dragoman until all baggage is safely deposited at the hotel.

2. *By land.* Dragomans or representatives of the principal hotels await travellers arriving by train. The dragoman of the hotel selected will engage carriage and porters for transport to the hotel. *Carriage* from Station to Hotel (including bridge toll), 5 fr. (P. 25) ; *porter*, 2 fr. (P. 10).

Departure: The formalities on departure are almost the same, in reverse order, as those on arrival. It is well to allow plenty of time in case of the occurrence of any *contretemps*.

Custom House at Galata, near the Outer Bridge, and at the Agency of the Messageries Maritimes. Rifles, revolvers, foreign cigars, and tobacco are prohibited. Books, newspapers, and all printed matter are submitted to the censor ; if not returned within a day, application should be made for them through the Consulate. Books such as the ' Handbook ' and the ' Continental Bradshaw ' have, on occasion, been seized. A present of one or two francs to the inspector usually simplifies matters.

Hotels : The principal hotels—indeed all those frequented by European travellers—are in Pera, and in or near the *Grande Rue*. The situation is high and

good ; and nearly every part of the city can be visited from it by carriage. The terms are from 14–20 francs a day according to the room occupied ; they include board, lodging, and attendance, but exclude wine and extras. No reduction is made for travellers who do not take their meals in the hotels. Those who require good accommodation at the best hotels during the seasons, April to June, and October to November, should telegraph for rooms. During the slack seasons, July to September, and December to March, arrangements can generally be made to live *en pension* at the hotels on reduced terms. Travellers should inspect their rooms, and ascertain terms before finally engaging them. In the best hotels the servants are men, generally Greeks, who expect a *pourboire* when the traveller leaves ; there are no chambermaids. Washing is charged from 3–4 francs a dozen ; for articles requiring care, it is sometimes advisable to employ one of the *blanchisseuses* in the city.

H. Royal, Petits-Champs, near the British Embassy. Good situation, fine view over Golden Horn, and western portion of Stambûl. Kept by M. Logothetti. Good rooms. 16–20 francs a day. *Pera Palace*, a large new hotel, on high ground, opened 1895. *H. de Londres*, Petits-Champs. *H. Bristol*, Petits-Champs. *H. de Byzance*, 388, Ge. Rue de Pera, opposite the Dutch Legation. Clean and well kept. 12–17 francs a day. *Grand Hôtel* (*H. de Luxembourg*), 128, Ge. Rue de P., a large and well-managed hotel, kept by a Frenchman. 15–20 francs a day. *Grand H. Français et Continental*, 47, Boulevard des Petits-Champs. 15–20 francs a day. *H. Bellevue*, 27, Boulevard des Petits-Champs. *H. Impérial*, 45, R. Asmali Mesjid. Austro-Hungarian proprietor. *H. Kittrey*, 2, R. Dervish. Proprietor and management German. Much used by Germans. *H. de la Chambre de Commerce*, 7, R.

Omar. A family private hotel, kept by Mrs. Skelton. *H. de Pest*, 455, Ge. Rue de P. Same Proprietor as *Hôtel Impérial*. Frequented by commercial travellers. *H. de la Paix*, 429, Ge. Rue de P. 10–12 francs a day. *H. de la Grande-Bretagne*, R. Vénédik. 10–12 francs a day.

The above Hotels are recommended in the order in which they are placed. The first six are good and comfortable ; the three last are second-class hotels in which rooms can be hired without boarding. The smaller hotels and boarding-houses in Galata and Stambûl cannot be recommended

For Hotels in the neighbourhood of Constantinople, see Therapia, Buyukdereh, Prinkipo, &c. &c.

Lodgings : Travellers who intend to make a long stay sometimes take furnished lodgings, and have their meals at clubs, hotels, or restaurants. All the furnished lodgings are bad, and very few respectable. The sanitary arrangements and the attendance are wretched. The average charge is £1 per week for two rooms. There are a few respectable houses in which lodgers are taken, and information as to these should be obtained through a resident or some member of the Consular Staff.

Houses : The rent of an unfurnished house of 9 or 10 rooms in Pera is from £80 to £125. There are few good houses, and these command a high rent. Rents on the Bosporus are determined by situation and accident. In Therapia and Buyukderch rents fluctuate 100 per cent. according to the demand of the season.

Servants are engaged by the month, and should be procured through residents. The stranger should be cautious not to engage them without a proper recommendation. *Cooks* or *grooms* receive from 30s. to 40s. per month in Constantinople, and from 40s. to 50s. per month *for travelling*. The cooks are generally Greeks or Armenians ; the best grooms are Turks.

Conveyances : N.B.—In paying bridge-tolls, tram, boat, and railway fares, the Mejidieh is worth P. 19 (silver); in paying horse and carriage hire it is worth P. 20 (silver).

Horses (*at, Begir, Haivan*) stand for hire at the hotels, at both ends of the *outer* bridge, at the Stambûl end of the *inner* bridge, at the landings of Topkhâneh, Dolmabâghcheh, Bâghcheh Kapusi, and near the outer doors of some of the principal mosques. Riding is a convenient way of getting about the narrow, dirty, and sometimes steep streets ; but the street hacks are being gradually superseded by carriages. In the city the rider is generally accompanied by a lad, *surúji*, who runs after the horse and holds it when the rider dismounts ; the lad expects a small "tip." *Note :* - Start, *haide* ; quick, *chapuk* ; slow, *yavásh* ; stop, *dur* ; make way, *destúr* or *Vardeh. Approximate prices:* P. 3 to 5 for a "course"; P. 5 to 10 per hour. For *long excursions* it is usual to get a better class of horse from a *livery stable* through an hotel-keeper or dragoman. The charges are for half a day, P. 40 to 50 ; for a day, P. 60 to 80. As there is no fixed tariff it is well to make a bargain beforehand. Bridge-toll, P. 1¾.

Carriages (*Araba*): Good two-horsed carriages, open and closed, stand for hire in *Pera*, at Taksim, the Grand Hotel, Galata Serai, and at the head of the Pera-Galata rly. ; in *Galata*, near the inner bridge, and near the foot of the Pera-Galata rly. ; at *Top-khâneh, Dolmabâghcheh*, and *Beshiktash* ; and in *Stambûl*, at the end of the outer bridge, near St. Sophia, near the Mosque of Sultan Bayezid, and at Ak Serai. The following is the *tarif* authorised by the Municipality, but usage alone fixes the rates, and it is well to make a bargain beforehand. For a "short course," not exceeding 20 min., P. 5, after sunset, P. 2¾–5 extra; for a "long course," not exceeding 40 min., P. 10, after sunset, P. 5–10 extra; per hour, P. 15 for the first two hours, and P. 10 for subsequent hours; for a day, P. 80. Hirers pay the bridge-tolls, P. 5–6. Complaints should be addressed to the Municipality. *Superior carriages* may be obtained from livery stables at P. 50–60 the half day, and P. 100–110 the day ; driver, P. 10–20 extra.

Sedan Chairs are much used in winter for going to dinner parties, &c., P. 20, including return.

Tramways (*Tramweh*): There are three lines, one in Stambûl, and two in Pera and Galata. (1.) From the Stambûl end of the outer bridge to the Serai, S. Sophia, Hippodrome, Burnt Column, Mosque of Sultan Bayezid, Laleli Jami', and Ak Serai, where the line divides into two branches— one proceeding to Top Kapusi in the Land Walls, the other, parallel to the shores of the Sea of Marmara, through the Vlanga Bostan, and Psamatia Quarters, to the close vicinity of Yedi Kuleh (the Seven Towers). Passengers to Yedi Kuleh dismount before reaching the Ak Serai fountain, and change cars by walking from A to B (see map). (2.) From Azab Kapu, at the Galata end of the inner bridge, along the Grande Rue of Galata and Top-khâneh, to Funduklu, Dolmabâghcheh, Beshiktash, and Orta-keui on the Bosporus. (3.) From the foot of "Step Street," Galata, near the outer bridge, to the Petits Champs, Galata Serai, Grand Hotel, Taksim, Pankaldi, and Chichli. The *carriages* (1st and 2nd class) are divided into two compartments, one of which is reserved for ladies. *Fares*, P. 1–2¾, according to distance. From Galata to Orta-keui, P. 1¾ ; Galata to Chichli, P. 2¾ ; Bridge to Yedi Kuleh, P. 2¾.

The **Underground**, or **Funicular Railway**, between Pera and Galata runs through a tunnel from a station near the Mosque of the "Dancing" Dervishes to a station near the outer bridge. Trains run from each end every 3 min. ; time 1¾ min.

Fares, 1st class, P. ⅛; 2nd, P. ⅛. Tickets at the booking office.

Railways: (1.) *Oriental Company. Station* in Stambûl at *Sirkeji Iskelesi*, two trains daily to and from Adrianople. *Waggon - lit* trains with dining saloon leave every Mond. and Thurs. for Vienna and Paris. Several *local trains* daily to Kûm-Kapu, Yeni-Kapu, Dañd Pasha, Psamatia, Yedi Kuleh, Makri-keui, San Stefano, and Kuchuk Chekmejeh (the first five within the walls). *Time tables* (European time) in the daily papers, and in an *Indicateur* (P. 1) to be obtained at the stations. (2.) *Asiatic line.* Haidar Pasha to Ismid, Eski-shehr, and Angora; two trains daily to and from Ismid, and one train to and from Eski-shehr. Travellers proceeding to Angora pass the night at Eski-shehr. One train daily between Eski-shehr and Angora both ways. Several *local trains* daily to Kizil Toprak, Eren-keui, Maltepeh, Kartal, and Pendik. There is also a *branch line* to Fanar-bâghcheh, on which frequent trains run on Sundays and holydays. *Steamers* (P. 1-1⅛) run, in connection with the trains, from the Galata end of the outer bridge to Haidar Pasha. *Time tables* (Turkish time) in the daily papers.

Boats, manned by Greeks or Italians, can be obtained at the principal landing-places. There is no tarif; the usual rate to or from a ship is P. 10; or if there are several passengers, P. 5 each. For excursions on the Bosporus, or along the sea walls of Stambûl, it is well to make an arrangement with the boatmen before starting. The boatmen patronised by the large hotels charge 2 fr., or its equivalent in piastres, for landing or embarking each passenger with his luggage.

Kaïks are always to be found at the landing-stages. There is no tarif; usage alone fixes the rates, which vary with the number of oars. The ordinary rates

for a kaïk with one pair of oars are: P. 3 to cross the Golden Horn; P. 5 to go on board a ship; P. 10 if the kaïk waits and brings its fare back. When engaged for the day, or for an excursion on the Bosporus, or Golden Horn, a bargain should be made with the boatman, *kaïkji*, before starting. The *kaïkjis* are Greek or Turks, of whom many come from the inland towns of Asia Minor. Ladies who are nervous should not enter kaïks.

Steamers: I. Local. *The Bosporus and Skutari.* The steam navigation of the Bosporus is a monopoly in the hands of the *Shirket-i-Hairieh Company*, which has a fleet of about 35 steamers—many of them large, comfortable, and fast boats. These steamers *start* from a landing-stage near the Stambûl end of the outer bridge, and make frequent voyages each way daily between the bridge and the villages on the Bosporus. Steamers plying along the *European* shore carry a *green* flag at the masthead; those along the *Asiatic* shore a *red* flag; and those following a *zigzag* course from shore to shore carry a *green and red* flag. The names of the stations at which each steamer stops are written in Latin and Turkish characters, on a board placed on the bridge; European stations in black, Asiatic in red. The stations on the *European side* are: Kabatash, Beshiktash, Orta-keui, Kuru Cheshmeh, Arnaut-keui, Bebek, Rumili Hissar, Boyaji-keui, Emirghian, Stenia, Yeni-keui, Therapia, Kirech Burnu, Buyukdereh, Mezar Burnu, Yeni Mahalle, and Rumili Kavak. On the *Asiatic side*: Skutari, Kuzgunjik, Beylerbey, Chengel Keui, Vani-keui, Kandili, Anadoli Hissar, Kanlijeh, Rifät Pasha, Pashabâghcheh, Beïkos, and Anadoli Kavak. All steamers plying on the European side go to Yeni Mahalleh, and one at least each day to Rumili Kavak; the steamers on the Asiatic side run to Beïkos and thence to Therapia, Buyukdereh, and

Anadoli Kavak. Numerous steamers, stopping at Kabatash, Beshiktash, Orta-keui, and Kurucheshmeh, run from the bridge to Arnaut-keui.

The steamers sail by *Turkish time,* and the *time tables,* which are published in "La Turquie" and other leading papers, are therefore frequently altered. The *first steamer* leaves each end in the summer season about 6 A.M., Frank time, and in winter shortly after sunrise. The *fares* vary according to the distance; from the bridge to Rumili Kavak is P. 5⅛; stern and upper deck are 1st class, *mevki;* fore deck is 2nd class. Tickets are taken at the landing-place before embarking.

N.B.—The voyage from the bridge to Buyukdereh takes from 1⅛ to 2 hrs., so that the *tour of the Bosporus* can be made in half a day, but it is better to allow a whole day, and several days may be pleasantly passed at Therapia or Buyukdereh. A *good position* should be secured, on the upper deck, for the view. The *time tables* should be consulted before starting, as the steamers do not always stop at every station. *Wraps* should be taken in April and May.

To Skutari, in addition to the steamers running up the Asiatic side, there is a *direct line,* boats at least once an hour, from a landing-stage near the centre of the outer bridge. There is also a *steam ferry* that runs several times a day from Sirkeji Iskelesi (S.), and Kabatash to Skutari with carriages, horses, goods, &c.

(2.) The *Golden Horn Company* run small steamers up the Golden Horn, every 15 min., from the Galata end of the Outer Bridge to Eyûb; and during the spring to Kara-agatch near the Sweet Waters of Europe. The steamers stop at Yemish Iskelesi, Jub-Ali, Aya Kapu, Phanar, Balat, Tersâne, Haskeui, Aivan Serai, Kaliji Oghlu, Defterdar Iskelesi, and Eyûb. *Fares,* from station to station, P. ⅛; for each additional station, P. ⅛.

Time, from the bridge to Eyûb, 1 hr.

(3.) The steamers of the *Mahsúse Company* run from the Galata end of the Outer Bridge:—a. Several times daily to Princes' Islands, stopping at Kadi Keui, Proti, Antigone, Khalki, Prinkipo, Maltepeh, Kartal, and Pendik. The three last places, on the coast of Asia Minor, can be more easily reached by the Haidar Pasha-Ismid Railway. *Fares*, to Prinkipo, 1st, P. 4, 2nd, P. 2½; Pendik, 1st, P. 5, 2nd, P. 3½. *Time*, to Prinkipo, 2 hrs. b. To **Haidar Pasha** and **Kadi Keui** several times daily. *Fares*, 1st, P. 1½, 2nd, P. 1. c. To **Skutari** every half hour, P. 1½ and P. ½.

N.B.—For hours of sailing consult the *time tables*; Turkish time, in the newspapers.

II. **Mediterranean and Coasting** :—A. *Messageries Maritimes*. Every Thurs. i. Alternately for Syra and Marseilles. ii. And Smyrna, Syra, and Marseilles. iii. Fortn. Thurs. for Smyrna, Mersina, Alexandretta, Lattakia, Tripoli, Cyprus, Beirût, Jaffa, Port Said, and Alexandria. iv. Fortn. Thurs. for Dedeagatch, Porto Lagos, Kavalla, Salonika, and Syra. v. Fortn. Sat. to Samsûn, Kerassund, Trebizond, and Batûm. vi. Fortn. Tues. to Kustenjeh, Sulina, and Galatz, in summer only. vii. Fortn. Tues. to Odessa.—B. *Austro-Hungarian Lloyd*. i. Every Mond. to Piræus, Patras, Corfu, Brindisi, and Trieste. ii. Every Tues. and Sat. to Varna. iii. Every Sat. to Odessa. iv. Every Sat. to Kustenjeh, Sulina, Tultja, Galatz, and Braila (summer only). v. Every Sat. to Ineboli, Samsûn, Kerassund, Trebizond, and Batûm. vi. Fortn. Thurs. to Gallipoli, Tenedos, Mytilene, Smyrna, Chio, Rhodes. Limassol or Larnaca, Beirût, Haifa, Jaffa, and Egypt. viii. Fortn. Thurs. to Gallipoli, Dedeagatch, Porto Lagos, Kavalla, Orfano, Salonika, Volo, Syra, Piræus, and Trieste. viii. Fortn. Thurs. as in vi. to Smyrna, and thence to Chio, Samos,

Candia, Retimo, Canea, Ionian Islands, and Trieste. —C. *Navigazione Generale Italiana*. i. Every Wed. to Piræus, Corfu, Brindisi, Bari, Ancona, Venice, and Trieste. ii. Every Mond. alternately to Smyrna, Chio, Piræus, Sicilian ports, Naples, Genoa, and Marseilles. iii. And to Salonika, Piræus, and same ports. iv. Every Thurs. to Odessa. v. Every Tues. to Sulina, Galatz, and Braila —D. **Russian Company**. i. Every Mon. and Thurs. to Odessa. ii. Every Wed. to Sevastopol. iii. Every Fri. to Ineboli, Sinope, Samsûn, Ordu, Kerassund, Trebizond, and Batûm. iv. Every Tues. alternately to Smyrna, Chio, and Alexandria. v. And to Syra and Alexandria. vi. Every Sat. to Smyrna, Chio, Mersina, Alexandretta, Lattakia, Tripoli, Beirut, Jaffa, Port Said, and Alexandria. —E. *Fraissinet et Cie*. i. Every Sat. to Dedeagatch, Salonika, Volo, Piræus, Naples, Genoa, and Marseilles. ii. Every Tues. to Rodosto, Mytilene, Smyrna, Syra, Genoa, and Marseilles. iii. Every Tues. to Kustenjeh, Sulina, Galatz, and Braila.—F. *Egyptian Mail Steamers (Khedivieh)*. Every Wed. to Mytilene, Smyrna, Piræus, and Alexandria.— G. *Panhellenic Company*. i. Fortn. Thurs. to Samsûn, Kerassund, Trebizond, and Batûm. ii. Fortn. Mond. to Piræus and Trieste.—H. *N. Paquet et Cie*. i. Once a fortnight to Smyrna and Marseilles. ii. Once a fortnight to Samsûn, Batûm, and Poti.— I. *Courtji et Cie*. i. Every Tues. to Gallipoli, Tenedos, Molivo, Mytilene, Smyrna, Chio, Andros, Syra, Canea, Retimo, and Candia. ii. Fortn. Wed. to Gallipoli, Mt. Athos, Salonika, and Volo. iii. Every Fri. to Ineboli, Sinope, Samsûn, Ordu, Kerassund, and Trebizond. iv. Every Mond. to Burgas, Varna, Sulina, Tultja, Galatz, and Braila. —J. *Mahsúse Company*. i. Fortn. Wed. Gallipoli, Mytilene, Smyrna, Chio, Rhodes, Adalia, Selefkeh, Mersina, Alexandretta, Tripoli, Beirût. Saida, and Jaffa. ii. Every Tues. alternately to

Gallipoli, Mytilene, Smyrna, Chio, Syra, Candia, Retimo, Canea, Derni, Benghazi, Tripoli, and Malta. iii. And as in ii. to Syra, Canea, Retimo, and Candia. iv. Every Fri. alternately to Gallipoli, Dedeagatch, Porto Lagos, Kavalla, and Salonika. v. And to Gallipoli, Lemnos, and Salonika. vi. Fortn. Wed. to Gallipoli, Tenedos, Molivo, Edremid, Aivali, Mytilene, Dikili, Smyrna, Cheshmeh, and Chio. vii. Every Thurs. to Eregli, Ineboli, Sinope, Samsûn, Unieh, Ordu, Kerassund, Tireboli, Trebizond, and Rizeh. viii. Every Tues., Thurs., and Sat. to Yalova, Darija, Karamursal, Eregli, Gonja, Kadikli, Deirmendereh, Seyban, and Ismid. ix. Every Wed. and Sat. to Perama and Panderma. x. Every Tues., Fri., and Sun. to Mudania and Geumlek. xi. Every Mond. and Thurs. to Kara Bogha, Rodosto, Ganos, Khoja, Merefte, and Sharkeui. xii. Every Thurs. and Mond. to Merefte as in xi., and thence to Kutali, Marmara, Pasha Limân, and Erdek. xiii. Every Tues. and Sat. to Epivatos, Silivri, Eregli, and Rodosto. x.v. Every Wed. to Eregli and Bartin.—K. *Dutch Company*. Twice a month to Smyrna, Salonika, Piræus, Malta (occasionally), and Amsterdam.

All steamers stop at the Dardanelles (Chanak) approaching and leaving Constantinople. For hours of sailing, consult the itineraries of the several Companies.

Embassies : British ; in Pera in winter, Therapia in summer. *Ambassador*, Rt. Hon. Sir Philip Currie, G.C.B. ; *1st Secretary*, Hon. Michael H. Herbert. *Mil. Attaché*, Col. Chermside, C.B., C.M.G. United States; in Pera, *Minister*, Hon. A. Terrel. Austria, France, Germany, Italy, Persia, and Russia have embassies; Belgium, Greece, Holland, Roumania, Servia, Spain, Sweden, and Norway have Legations at Constantinople. **Consulates : British ;** in Galata. *Acting Judge*, C. J. Tarring, Esq. ; *Acting*

Consul-General, W. H. Wrench, Esq., C.M.G. Attached to the Consulate are a Supreme Court, Prison, and Seaman's Hospital. Uni'ed States; in Pera, Grande Rue; *Consul-General*, Mr. Short.

Passports, Tezkerehs: *Passports* are necessary, and should be *visés* before leaving Constantinople for a foreign country; and to obtain a travelling tezkereh. The fees are:—

British Consulate . 2s. 0d.
American ,, Gold P. 25
German ,, ,, 16.25
Russian ,, ,, 10.
Belgium ,, 5 frs.
Bulgarian ,, 2 ,,
French ,, 5 ,,
Greek ,, 5 ,,
Italian ,, 5 ,,
Roumanian ,, 5 ,,

To obtain a *Yol Tez' ereh*, or *travelling pass/ort* for the interior of Turkey, the traveller must present his passport, personally or by deputy, at the *Consulate*. The Tezkereh order is then delivered on payment of a fee of 2s.; on presentation of this order at the Tezk'reh Office, in the Ministry of Police (S.), or at the Custom House (G.), the Tezk'reh is delivered without further question for a small fee. (Tezkereh, gold P. 5; *visa*, gold P. 2.) The dragoman of the hotel may be entrusted with these simple formaliti's. The *Yol Tezkereh* must be *visé* in each Vilâyet (p. [6]).

Churches: *Church of England.* British Embassy Chapel in *Pera*, or in *Therapia* (S. Mary's Church) during the summer months, when the chapel in Pera is closed. Holy Comm. 1st Sun. in month after morning service; 2nd, 3rd, and 4th Sun. 8.30 A.M.; services, 10.30 A.M. and 5 P.M. *Rev. H. K. Anketell.* —Christ Church (Memorial Church) in *Pera*; Holy Comm. 1st and 3rd Sun. in month 8.30 A.M.; 2nd and 4th at noon. Festivals 8.30 A.M.; Greater Festivals 8.30 A.M. and noon; services 11 A.M. Sun. and Fri., all Holy Days, Wed. in Lent, and every day in Holy Week. *Rev. Canon Curtis, M.A.*—All

Saints, *Kadi Keui*. *Rev. G. Paterson, M.A.*—*Evangelical Union Church*. Chapel of Dutch Legation in *Pera*; services in English every Sun. 11 A.M. and 4 P.M. *Rev. F. W. Anderson.*— *Established Church of Scotland* in *Haskeui*; service Sun. 11 A.M. *Rev. D. B. Spence.*—*Evangelical Union Church* in *Bebek*. Service at Robert College, *Rumili Hissar*, at 10.45 A.M., by the *Professors*; and at the American College for Girls, *Skutari*, at 11 A.M.—*Lutheran Church.*—German Embassy Chapel in *Pera*, Rue Ainali Cheshmeh.—*Roman Catholic Church.*- Cathedral Ch. of S. Esprit, 107, Grande Rue de Pankaldi; Ch. of S. Antoine, 377, Grande Rue, Pera; Ch. of S. Marie, 429, Grande Rue, Pera.

Banks: The *Imperial Ottoman Bank*, Rue Voïvoda (G.), gives letters of credit, payable in the principal towns, and has agencies or sub-agencies at Adalia, Adana, Aïdin, Denizli, Konia, Manisa, Mûghla, Nazli, Sivas, and Smyrna, in A. Minor; and at Larnaca, Limassol, and Nicosia, in Cyprus. *Crédit Lyonnais*, near the Outer Bridge (G.); *Société Ottoman de Change et de Valeurs*, R. Voïvoda (G.); *Crédit Générale Ottoman*, R. Voïvoda (G.); *Asarian Bros.*, 22, Pershenbe Bazár (G.).

Money Changers, *Sarrâfs.* Money changing plays an important part in the daily life of Constantinople. Public offices, local steamers, tramways, bridges, &c., give no charge; the obligation to provide change is thrown upon the payer or buyer, and he has to purchase it in the market. Sarrâfs will be found in most of the principal streets of Pera and Galata ready to sell small money. In changing a Mejidieh about 5 p. c. is lost, and in changing a quarter Mej. another 5 p. c. The rates of exchange, which are constantly fluctuating, are published in the newspapers and posted in the Clubs; but travellers not initiated in the mysteries of the Turkish money

market should get their change through the porter of the hotel, or their dragoman. There is much false money in circulation, and sarrâfs are not always honest; therefore accept no foreign coin, no Turkish coin on which the characters on ob. and rev. are not legible, no copper coin, and not more than P. 5 in *metalliks*. When large sums are required in silver or *metallik*, for a journey, recourse should be had to a Bank. *Money*, see p. [9].

Post Offices: **Imperial Ottoman Post.** Chief Office, *Stambûl*, near Yeni Jami'. Branches, Ak Serai (S.); *Galata*, Khasta - khâneh Khân; *Skutari*; *Beshiktash*. Letter-boxes in Pera, Galata, and some of the hotels. *Rates.* To foreign countries according to the international tariff, an ordinary letter of 15 *grammes*, or ¼ oz., P. 1. **Inland post:** To coast towns served by steamers and railway stations, 10 gr., P. ¼; to towns in the interior, 10 gr., P. 2. **British P.O.** Office, *Galata*; Branch, Whittall Khân, near Omer Effendi's (S.). Letter of 15 gr. or ¼ oz., P. 1. Postage on newspapers and books, ¼d. (0 par.s), for every 2 oz. or 60 grammes. No book must exceed 4 lbs., 1814 grammes. Samples, 2¼ paras for the first 2 oz., and 10 paras for every succeeding 2 oz. up to 12 oz. Malis are despatched daily for the U. Kingdom, the continent of Europe, and the U. S. of America. Also to Smyrna, Beirût, Cyprus, and Alexandria by every steamer leaving. Correspondence for India, &c., is sent *viâ* Alexandria. A British postage stamp will prepay a letter to any part of Europe. Money and Postal Orders issued. Parcel Post *viâ* Liverpool and Marseilles.

Austrian P. O. Office, Rue Kara Mustafa (G.). Branches, 438, Grande Rue (P.), Yeni Kamondo Khân (S.). **French P.O.** Office, Rue Voïvoda (G.). Branches, Passage Oriental (P.); Yeni Kamondo Khân (S.). **German P. O.** Office, Rue Voïvoda (G.); Passage Hazzopulo (P.); Havuzlu Khân (S.). Letter-boxes in P. and at Tunnel Station, (G.). Russian P. O. Office, Kirech Kapu (G.). Branch, Rue Baghcheh Kapu (S.).

The postal arrangements of the above offices can be ascertained by inquiry at the hotels, and are given in the *Levant Herald Almanac*. There is no postal delivery at Constantinople; letters must be called for at the P. O.'s at which they are expected to arrive. There is no town service; letters for town are sent by messengers.

Telegraphs: Local Offices, *Pera*, 181, Gde Rue; *Galata*, Khasta-khâneh Khân; *Stambûl*, 23, Rue S'oûk Cheshmeh (General Office), the Seraskerat, and Yeni Jami'; *Kadi Keui*; *Yenikeui*; *Therapia*; *Buyukdereh*. For every telegram of 20 words between these stations P. 2½; and for every 10 or fraction of 10 words above 20, half the rate is charged in addition. The charge to Prinkipo. Halki, Haidar Pasha, Pendik, and stations on the line of railway to Ismid is P. 5 for a telegram of 20 words. For rates to the interior of Turkey and to Foreign States, see p. [7]. N.B.—In payments the Mejidieh is worth P. 19.

British Indian Telegraph Agency, 4, Manukoglu Khân, Galata. *Eastern Telegraph Company*, 181, Gde. Rue, Pera.

Dragomans, *Ciceroni*, or *Valets de place*, should always be obtained through the landlord of the hotel at which the traveller is staying. If the traveller be not at an hotel, he should ask the Consulate to recommend a man. Greeks and Armenians, most of whom belong to the *Société des Courriers d'Orient*, have a monopoly of the hotels; the Jews tout in the streets. Dragomans are indispensable, whether for sight seeing or purchasing, if the traveller do not know the language. From long habit they know all the objects of interest, but they are ignorant of the meaning and importance of what they show, and their

explanations are worse than useless. With a smattering of many languages, they know none thoroughly, and, being unable to appreciate Western modes of thought, they often misunderstand what is said to them, and give answers which they think will please their employers, or save themselves trouble. They are often wanting in truth, and have all the defects of servants who, believing themselves to be indispensable, prey on the weakness or good nature of their masters. In *making purchases* it is well to remember that the dragoman receives a commission on the price paid, and that, though he may pretend to bargain, it is his interest to have as high a price as possible. The *Hotel Dragomans* charge from 5-10 francs per diem.

Police, *Zabtieh* or *Zaptieh*. The Ministry of Police, *Zabtieh Nazareti*, is in Stambûl, near the Hippodrome, and here are the Chief Police Station (S.) and the office at which travelling *tezkerehs* are issued. The *Prison* and *Hospital* of the Police Force are in the At Meidân. The other *chief stations* are Galata Serai (P.), with secondary stations at Voivoda, foot of Step Street (G.), Takslim (P.), Haskeui, and Beshiktash; and Skutari, with a secondary station at Kadi Keui. Minor stations, *Kulluk*, are established at several places in the city. The police are all Moslems; the *gendarmes* (Guardhouse Zaptichs) wear a blue uniform with red facings; the *police*, a black uniform with purple and green facings; the police *commissare*, a long frock coat and sword with a white cross-belt.

Dervishes: *Whirling*, or *Dancing Dervishes*, every Tuesday and Friday, after the midday prayer, at the Tekkeh in the *Tunnel Square* (P.), and, near *Top Kapu*, outside the walls (S.). Admission free; a few piastres given to the doorkeeper on leaving. *Howling Dervishes*, every Thursday at *Skutari*, and

every Sunday at *Kassim Pasha*, after midday prayer. Places are set apart for visitors. Admission free; a few piastres given to the doorkeeper on leaving.

Palaces: No permission is necessary to visit the palaces of *Beyler Bey* and *Sweet Waters*, but a present is made to the servants. Permission to visit the Selamlik, or official apartments, at *Dolmabaghcheh Palace*, the *Imperial Stables*, and the *Treasury*, in the Old Seraglio, can only be obtained from the Grand Master of the Ceremonies, through the Embassy, or through personal friends in the Sultan's suite.

Mosques: No special permission is required to visit the mosques; but it is usual to give the caretaker, *Kâim*, a fee of P. 5-10 per head. Moslems of the better class always wear overshoes, which are removed on entering a mosque. Europeans who do not adopt this custom must take slippers with them to draw over their boots, or hire them at the mosque door. Moslems never take off their fezzes or turbans, but it is usual for Europeans to remove their hats as a mark of respect. Mosques should not be visited at prayer time or on Fridays. It is advisable to take a dragoman when visiting the mosques.

Museums: *M. of Antiquities*, Chinili Kiosk in the old Seraglio Gardens (S.). Open 11-4 daily, except Fridays. Admission, P. 5, *M. of Ancient Costumes*, or of the Janissaries, in the At Meidân (S.), open daily till dusk. Admission, P. 3. There is a small collection of Greek antiquities in the possession of the Hellenic Literary Society "Syllogos."

Directory, &c.: *Annuaire Oriental du Commerce*, 23 fr., gives addresses in Constantinople and the large provincial towns, with other information. *Levant Herald Almanac*, P. 10, gives postal and telegraph rates, and useful notes on Consular Staff, Turkish time, &c.

Barristers: *Clifton*, G. H., 14, R. Médressé (G.)

Pears, H. E., 2, R. de la Banque (G.); *Pedrelli, V.*, 11, Kévork Bey Khân (G.).

Baths : *Bains du Luxembourg*, 15, R. Sakiz Aghatch (P.), P. 10–15. *Turkish Baths*, Galata Serai Hammami (P.), Mahmûd Pasha Hammami (S.), P. 6–8. *Saltwater Baths.* The bathing on the Bosporus, at Prinkipo and S. Stefano, is excellent, and it is very good at Kadi Keui and Moda Burnu. There are baths at the Outer Bridge and at Salibazâr, but the water is not very clear. *N.B.*—Money, watches, and articles of value should not be taken to any of the baths.

Bazâr : The best shops in the Stambûl Bazâr are— *Sadoullah & Co.*, "Faraway Moses," whose shop is decorated in Turkish style, and who do a large business especially with Americans. Their carpets, which are made for them in Smyrna and in the interior, are beautiful, and their modern embroideries and woven stuffs are very good. They deliver goods free to England, and make arrangements with Americans. *Sadyk Effendi* is best for old embroideries. *Hajji Osman Bey, Abraham Eskanazi, Elia, Antoine, Suleiman Effendi*, and *Hajji Baba*. Mr. *George Baker*, 500, Grande Rue (P.), has also an excellent selection of modern and old Turkish embroideries, and there is less trouble in bargaining, &c., with him. He makes special arrangements for shipping goods.

Birdstuffer : *Consoli*, 63, R. Kabristan (P.).

Booksellers : *Lorentz and Keil*, to H.I.M. the Sultan. All books on the East; Murray's Handbooks; photographs; water-colours by Preziosi, 457, Gde. Rue (P.); *Weisz*, books and maps, 483, Gde. Rue (P.); *Macgil*, 5, Tunnel Passage (P.); *Turkish* and *Persian* books in the Stambûl Bazâr, Sahaflar Street.

Brasseries, conducted on the German system. *Viennoise (Janni)*, 396, Ge. Rue (P.). *Suisse*, 380, Ge. Rue (P.). *Vogl*, 15, R. Voi-

vode (G.). *Rly. Station, Refreshment Room* (S.).

British Institutions : The *Brit. Literary and Mechanics Institute*, in the Francis Memorial Building, near the Galata Tower. The *Sailors' Home*, near the Institute. The *Brit. Seamen's Hospital*, adjoining the British Consular buildings. The *Rest* for British sailors, R. Voivoda (G.). The *English High School for Girls*, 353, Gde. Rue (P.), founded by Lady Stratford Canning. *Somerville House* in which the Governess Home and other philanthropic agencies are accommodated. Rue Ensis (P.), near Tunnel.

Butcher : *Prieur*, 470, Gde. Rue (P.).

Cafés Chantants : *Concordia, Eldorado*, and *Palais de Cristal*, all in the Grande Rue (P.). In summer there is an open-air theatre in the garden of the Concordia.

Chemists : *Canzuch Frères (Pharmacie Britannique)*, 156, Gde. Rue (P.); *Zanni*, 84, Gde. Rue (P.); *della Sudda*, 169, Gde. Rue (P.).

Clubs : *Cercle d'Orient*, Gde. Rue (P.). Very good and comfortable; excellent cooking. *Club de Constantinople (commerciale et maritime)*; good. There is a branch at the Tunnel Station, Galata, for breakfast. In these two clubs strangers must be introduced by a member. The German Society *Teutonia* combines a club with a theatre, in which, during winter, concerts and performances are given.

Coal Merchants : *A. A. Hill*, agent for Glamorgan Coal Co., Kara Mustafa Sokak, near the end of the Outer Bridge (G.); *Gilchrist, Walker, & Co.*, Halagian Khân (G.).

Confectioners : *Lebon and Bourdon*, 434, Gde. Rue (P.). **Turkish Sweetmeats :** *Haji Bekir Agha*, 16, R. Baghcheh Kapusi (S.); *Ahmed Hussein*, 54, Dîvân Yolu (S.).

Cook's Tourist Office, 170, Gde. Rue (P.).

Dressmaker : *De Melville*.

European Articles : *G. Baker*, 241 and 500, Gde.

Rue (travelling outfit, Oriental goods, linendraper); *Bon Marché*, 354, Gde. Rue (French goods, toilet articles, &c.); *Paluka*, German Bazâr, 388, Gde. Rue (bronzes, artistic and toilet articles); *Streater & Co.*, Tunnel Square (linendrapers and millinery); *Minasian*, American Magazine, 13, Jami' Kapusi (G.); *Mir & Cottereau*, 140, Gde. Rue (millinery, hosiery, artistic objects, &c.); *Haydn & Co.*, 187 and 479, Gde. Rue (linendrapers); *Burness*, 21 and 23, Rue Beuyûk Hendek (G.) (ironmonger); *A. Kun*, 399, Gde. Rue (millinery, hosiery, &c.).

Fairs, at which all kind of produce is sold, are held on *Monday* at Yeni Jami' and Chichek Bazâr (S.); *Tuesday*, Defterdar Yokushu, Top-khâneh, and Sbeh Zadeh Bashi (S.); *Wednesday*, S. Sophia and Sultan Muhammad (S.); *Thursday*, Pershenbe Bazâr (G.) and Jub-Ali (S.); *Friday*, Kassim Pasha, Eyûb, and Skutari; *Saturday*, Beshiktash; *Sunday*, Yeni Shehr (P.).

Forwarding Agents : Globe Express Agency, *A. Laughton*, agent for Wheatley & Co., M'Craken & Co., and for Morris of New York, 25, Pershenbe Bazâr (G.). *G. Baker* and *Sadullah & Co.* forward goods bought at their shops.

Gunsmith : *Chedan*, 492, Gde. Rue (P.).

Hairdressers : *Kritich*, Passage Oriental (P.); *Isidore* (for ladies), 433, Gde. Rue (P.); *Petchoff*, 474, Gde. Rue (P.). Charge, 1 franc.

Hatter : *Baldasar*, 424, Gde. Rue (P.).

Jewellers : *Saury & Co.*, 422, Gde. Rue (P.); *Vartan*, 395, Gde. Rue (P.).

Livery Stables : *Marco*, 164, Gde. Rue ; *Noios*, 8, Gde. Rue (P.).

Musical Instruments : *Comendinger*, 179, Gde. Rue (P.).

Newspapers : The most important are : English and French, the *Levant Herald and Eastern Express*, daily and weekly edition, founded in 1856; *Moniteur Oriental*. French, *Stambûl*,

La Turquie. **Armenian,** *Arevelk,* daily, *Jeridei Shar-kiyeh,* daily, *Anedaper,* weekly. **Greek,** *Neologos, Byzantis, Konstantinupolis.* **Turkish,** *Tarik, Terjuman Hakikat, Saadet,* all daily, and *Osmanli* (Turk. and Fr.). There are also a Persian and two Jewish papers.

Optician : *Verdoux,* 482, Gde. Rue (P.).

Orient Express Office : For sleeping berths, 152, Gde. Rue (P.).

Oriental Carpets, Curiosities, Embroideries, &c. : *O. Baker,* 500, Grande Rue (P.), near Tunnel entrance; *Sadoullah & Co.,* Tarakjilar Khân (S.), *Sadyk, Elia, Hajji Osman Bey, Abraham Eskanazi,* and others in the Grand Bazâr Stambûl (p. 27). Japanese and Chinese articles, *Tallers & Co.,* near the Tunnel entrance (P.).

Photographers : *Abdullah Frères,* 452, Gde. Rue (P.); *Sebah and Joailler,* 439, Gde. Rue (P.); *Berggren,* 414, Gde. Rue (P.).

Physicians and Surgeons : *Dr. Patterson,* 3, R. Medresse (G.); *Dr. Sarell* (Surgeon), 11, R. Serkis (P.); *Dr. Mordtmann,* 3, R. Kartal (P.); *Dr. Mahé,* 243, Gde. Rue (P.); *Dr. Mühlig,* 94, R. Kombaraji (P.); *Dr. Lardy* (Surgeon), Tepe Bashi (P.); *Dr. Delacour,* 16, Gde. Rue (P.); *Dr. Kambouroglou,* 14, R. Agha Hamam (P.). **Oculist and Aurist:** *Dr. van Millingen,* Passage Oriental (P.). **Dentists:** *M. Dorigny,* 17, R. Asmali Mesjid (P.); *M. van der Heyde,* 194, Gde. Rue (P.) **American Dentists:** *Drs. Ledyard and Faber,* 473, Gde. Rue (P.).

For cases of serious illness the *German Hospital* is recommended; the nurses are German Sisters (Kaiserswerth Deaconesses). There is also a *French Hospital,* 22, Gde. Rue (P.), with "Sisters of Charity" as nurses. Private rooms on payment.

The **Porters,** *Hammâl,* most of whom are Armenians from the interior of A. Minor, form a corporation, and are divided into sections, each of which takes a Quarter of the city. They stand for hire at the street corners, and carry very heavy weights. The charge or a porter from Galata to Pera is P. 4–5.

Professors : Travellers wishing to study Turkish, Arabic, Greek, or Armenian should ask at the Embassy for the names of the Professors employed by the Student Interpreters.

Public Gardens: *Petits Champs.* Admission, P. 1. Band afternoon and evening in summer. Restaurant and Theatre. *Taksim,* or *Grands Champs.* Admission, P. 1. Band Sundays. A favourite Sunday afternoon promenade.

Reading Room : The *Ottoman,* founded in 1867. Divân Yolu opposite the tomb of Reshid Pasha (S.).

Restaurants and Cafés: *Restaurant Lebon (C. de St. Petersbourg),* 434, Ge. Rue (P.). Good French cooking. *Rest.* and *Café du Luxembourg,* 130, Ge. Rue (P.); good. *Rest.* and *Café* in *Municipal Gardens,* Petits Champs (P.). *Rest.* and *Café del Genio,* 32, Place Kara-keui (G.), near end of Outer Bridge. *Rest. Gambetta,* 14, R. Voïvode (G.), near Tunnel; fair Italian cooking. *Rest. Tokatlian,* 29, R. Mûhafasajilar, near the Bazâr (S.); fair. *Café,* Muncpl. Gardens, Taksim.

There are many Greek and Turkish eating-houses in Stambûl, but none of them are good. *Turkish Cafés* are numerous in all Quarters of the city ; a cup of coffee is Par. 20, a glass of raki or mastic, Par. 20, and a nargbileh, Par. 20.

Shoeblacks, *Boyaji;* at the street corners, the Tunnel, and Galata Serai.

Shoemakers : *Burguy,* 495, Gde. Rue (P.); *Heral,* for ladies, 9, Passage Hazzopoulo (P.).

Stationer: *Bailly,* 374, Gde. Rue (P.).

Tailors : *Botter & Co.,* 252, Gde. Rue (P.); *Mir and Cotterau,* 140, Gde. Rue (P.).

Theatres : *Théatre Français,* 176, Gde. Rue (P.); *T. Municipal des Petits Champs,* in the Municipal Gardens, R. Mezarlik (P.). Prices, P. 5–25. *T. Verdi,* 134, Gde. Rue (P.); Greek plays. *T. Osmaniyeh,* in Gedik Pasha Quarter (S.); Operettas and comedies in Turkish, translated from the French. Open in winter and Ramazân. During Ramazân the *Kara-gyuz,* a kind of marionette entertainment, is much patronised by Turks.

Tobacco (*tütun*); **Cigars :** *Angelides,* 323, Gde. Rue (P.) for *foreign cigars; Régie Headquarters,* Rue Pershenbe Bazâr (G); *Régie Depôts,* 158, Gde. Rue (P.), and Rue Sirkeji (S.), for cigarettes and best Turkish tobacco. *Cigarettes,* 50–120 fr. per 1000; *tobacco,* 30–60 fr. per kilogramme.

Tumbaki: Persian merchants in Misr Charshi (S.) and Yeni Charshi (Topkhâneh).

Watchmakers : *Bauer,* 22, R. Kara-keui (G.); *Meyer,* 35, R. Yeni Jami' (G.).

Wines, Spirits, &c. : *Economic Coop. Stores,* near I. O. Bank (G.); *Baker and Silleh,* Rue Voivoda Khân (G.); *Thompson,* 209, Gde. Rue (P.); *Stevenson,* 19, Rue Mertevani (G.).

SEVEN TOWERS, 39, **4**, **8**, **18**, **25**, **26**, **29**, **33**, **64**, **84**.
SHAH MELIK LIMAN, **134**.
SHAHR EUYUK, **119**.
SHAR DÁGH MOUNTAIN, [18].

SHAR-KEUI, **115**.
  Mahsûse Steamer three times a week to and from Constantinople.
Shah-zadeh Mosque, 63, **4**, **18**, **22**, **25**, **52**, **64**, **72**, **83**.
SHEHÍDLAR, **94**.
Sheikh Murad Mesjidi, 57.
Sheitan Akindisi, The, 92, **93**, **88**.
Sheitan Kemeri, The, **98**.
Shemsi Pasha Jami', 107.
SHILEH, **88**.
SID-EL-BAHR, **137**.
SIDON, 70.
SIGEAN PROMONTORY, **137**.
SIGEUM, **145**, **146**.

SILIVRI, _Selymbria_, 114, **2**, **85**, **101**.
  Kaza of Chatalja.
  Mahsûre Steamer twice a week to and from Constantinople.
Silivri Kapusi, 34, 53.
SIMOIS RIVER, **139**.
Sinan Pasha Mosque, 129.
Sinan Pasha Mesjidi, **57**.
SINASLI KUYUK, **86**.
SIRKEJI ISKELESI, 25, **26**, **86**, 107.
SKOMBRE KEUI, **99**.
SKUTARI, 107, **2**, **5**, **6**, **8**, **11**, **12**, **14**, **15**, **17**, **19**, **22**, **31**, **77**, **78**, **84**, **87**, **93**, **102**, **106**.
Skutari Cemetery, 109, **83**.
Slave Markets, 76.
SMYRNA, [1], [2], **145**.
SORGUN DEREH, **118**.
SO' UK CHESHMEH FOUNTAIN, **74**.
SO' UK CHESHMEH KAPUSI, **24**, **43**, 66, 67, 69.
Sport, 85.
Staff College, 78.
STAMBÛL, 58, **4**, **6**, **8**, **9**, **11**, **13**, **14**, **15**, **17**, **19**, **21**, **25**, **71**, **73**, **74**, **76**, **77**, **79**, **84**, **86**, **89**, **91**, **98**.
STAMBÛL BOGHASI, **87**.
STENIA, **94**, **95**, **86**.
STENIA HARBOUR, **96**.
STRUMA RIVER, [18].
Studius, Monastery of, **53**, 25, **31**, **52**.
SUBLIME PORT, 76, 18, 66.
SUDLUJE, 14, **17**, **21**, **103**.

Suleiman I., Türbeh of, **61**.
Suleimaniyeh Mosque, 59, **4**, **11**, **18**.
Sultan Abdul Mejid, Türbeh of, **22**.
Sultan Ahmed Fountain, **11**.
Sultan Ahmed Mosque, 11, **18**, **24**, **39**.
Sultan Bayezid, 6.
Sultan Bayezid Mosque, 11, **18**, **74**.
Sultan Mahmûd II., Tomb of, 11, **18**.
Sultan Muhammad, 6.
SULTAN CHIFTLIK, **109**.
SULTANIEH, **104**.
SULTANIYEH KALESI, **137**.
Sultan Muhammad II., Mosque of, 62, **23**, **28**, **52**.
SULTAN OSMAN HÂWUSI, **99**.
Sultan Selim, Mosque of, 11, **18**, **23**, **28**.
Sultan Suleiman, Mosque of, **4**, **11**, **18**.
Sultan Valideh Jami', 16.
Sultans, List of, [16].
SÓLU KULEH, **35**.
Sulu Monastir, 53.
Sureh-Emineh, Procession of, 13.
Sururi Mosque, 20.
Su-terazi, The, 73, **98**.
SWEET WATERS, 85, **12**, **8**, **9**, **11**, **14**, **17**, **25**, **69**, **71**, **74**, **99**, **105**.
SYKI, **120**.
SYMPLEGADES, **101**.
SYRIA, [2], [18], [19].
SYRIAN MOUNTAINS, [19].

T.

Tahmis Bazâr, 75.
TAKSIM, 17, **18**, **77**, **89**.
TAKSIM GARDENS, 19, **85**, **89**.
Taksim, The, 37, **73**, **97**, **99**.
TARSUS, [2].
TASHLANJIK BURNU, **101**.
Taûk Bazâr, 24, **42**.
Taurus, Forum of, 43, **64**.
TAURUS MOUNT, [18], [19].
TAVLAJIK CHIFTLIK, **104**.

TAVSHANJIK, **116**.
  Station: Haidar Pasha.—Ismid Rly.
Taxes, [26].
TEKFÛR SERAI, 36, **18**, **23**, **32**, **35**, **37**, **86**.
Tekkehs of Dervishes, 79.

Telegraphs, [7].
TENEDOS, **140**, **145**.
Tersâne, The (Arsenal), **20**, 17.
Teskereh, [6].
Theatres, 82.
Theodosius, Cistern of, **72**.
Theodosius, Column of, **42**, **69**.
Theodosius, Forum of, 24, **25**, **43**.
Theodosius I., Palace of, 64.
Theodosius II., Walls of, 32, **37**, **86**.

THERAPIA, **95**, **85**, **86**, **92**, **98**, **102**.
  Hotels: _Summer Palace Hotel_, good but expensive. _H. d'Angleterre_, better known as _H. Petala_, good and comfortable; _H. Costi_, or _New Hotel_; 16 fr. per diem.
  Horses and _kaiks_ for hire. Constantinople prices.

  Lodgings by agreement.
  Telegraph Station:
  Communication with Constantinople and Bosporus ports by steamers of _Shirket-i-Hairieh Co._ several times a day.
  Carriage - road to Pera, about an hour's drive.
THERAPIA HARBOUR, **96**.
Thermæ Constantinianæ, 25.
THRACE, [18].
THRACIAN BOSPORUS, **1**.
THROSMOS, THE, **145**.
Thunderbolt, Mosque of the, 124.
THYATIRA, [1].
TIH, DESERT OF THE, [19].
Titles, [33].
TOKAT DEREH VALLEY, **104**.
TOP-KHÂNEH, 19, **8**, **9**, **10**, **14**, **15**, **17**, **18**, **76**, **77**, **88**, **89**, **93**.
Top-Khâneh Arsenal, 19, **89**.
Top-Khâneh Barracks, 17.
Top-Khâneh Fountain, 19, 17, **74**.
Top-Khâneh Mosque, 17.
Top Kapusi, 35, **26**, **29**.
Toklu Dede Jami', 28.
Trade, [24].
Transfiguration, Monastery of the, 112.
Treasury, 12.
TREBIZOND, [2].

TRIESTE, [3].
  H. B. M. Consul: John G. Haggard, Esq.
  Hotels: _H. de Ville_; _H. Delorme_; _Aguila Nero_.

LONDON: PRINTED BY WILLIAM CLOWES AND SONS, LIMITED, STAMFORD STREET AND CHARING CROSS.

MURRAY'S HANDBOOK

ADVERTISER,

1895-1896.

CONTAINING

USEFUL INFORMATION FOR TRAVELLERS,

RAILWAY

AND

STEAMBOAT COMPANIES,

HOTELS,

AND

MISCELLANEOUS ADVERTISEMENTS.

ENGELBERG.

THE VALLEY OF ENGELBERG (3200 ft. high), near Lucerne.
Season 15th May—30th September.

KURHAUZ AND HOTEL SONNENBERG.

THE property of Mr. H. HUG. Summer stay unrivalled by its grand Alpine scenery. Clear bracing air, equable temperature. Recommended by the highest medical authorities. The HOTEL SONNENBERG, in the finest and healthiest situation facing the Titlis and the Glaciers, is one of the most comfortable and best managed hotels in Switzerland. Lawn Tennis Ground. Excellent and central place for sketching, botanising, and the most varied and interesting excursions. The ascent of the Titlis is best made from here. Shady Woods. Vapour and Shower Baths. Waterspring 5° R.; 200 Rooms; Pension from £2 6s. a week upwards. Because of its so sheltered situation specially adapted for a stay in *May* and *June*. Resident English Physician. English Divine Service.

ENGELBERG, SWITZERLAND.

KURHAUS HÔTEL ET PENSION TITLIS.

THIS First-Class Hotel, in the best situation of the valley, in the middle of an extensive garden, has been much enlarged and improved. 200 Beds. Lofty Dining Saloon. Large Saloon de Réunion, with Verandah. Smoking-Room. Reading-Room. Billiards, Salle de Musique. Lift. Electric Lighting in all Rooms. Baths in the Hotel. Lawn Tennis Ground. Good attendance, with Moderate Charges.

English Chapel in the garden of the Hotel.

ED. CATTANI, *Proprietor.*

VALAIS—EVOLENA—SUISSE.

GRAND HOTEL D'EVOLÈNE.

Most beautifully situated. With view of the Dent Blanche, the Dent d'Herens, and the Glaciers, 800 metres above the village. Built with the latest comforts. Grand Rooms. Reading Room. Billiards. Verandah. Gardens. Numerous walks. Same Proprietors as the Hotel du Mont Collon at Arolla—tickets exchanged. Excellent Cooking. Pension. Evolène is 5 hours from Sion.—Carriage Road.—Travellers are asked to engage their carriages at the Hotel. Prices much reduced in June, commencement of July and September. Open from June 1st to October 15th.   J. ANSIVUL, Proprietor.

EXETER, DEVONSHIRE.

POPLE'S NEW LONDON HOTEL.

PATRONISED BY H.R.H. THE PRINCE OF WALES.

ADJOINING Northernhay Park and near the Cathedral. Large covered Continental Courtyard.

Table d'Hôte. Night Porter. Hotel Omnibuses and Cabs.

POSTING ESTABLISHMENT.

Also Proprietor of the Globe Hotel, Newton Abbot, Devon.

FLORENCE.

HOTEL HELVETIA,
STROZZI SQUARE.

Built expressly for a Hotel. *Full South.* Opposite the Strozzi Palace Bath Rooms. Ladies Drawing Room. Reading and Billiard Rooms. Large Suite of Apartments. Best English Sanitation. Pension from 8 francs. Steam Heating Throughout. Hydraulic Lift.

INNSBRUCK.

Thirty-one hours from London, via Arlberg, to Innsbruck. Through tickets and luggage registered through. Twenty-three hours from Paris.

INTERLAKEN.

D

E

Milton Keynes UK
Ingram Content Group UK Ltd.
UKHW022345220124
436511UK00005B/201

9 781020 522796